Politics of Practical Reasoning

Politics of Practical Reasoning

Integrating Action, Discourse and Argument

Edited by
Ricca Edmondson and
Karlheinz Hülser

LEXINGTON BOOKS
Lanham • Boulder • New York • Toronto • Plymouth, UK

Published by Lexington Books
A wholly owned subsidiary of The Rowman & Littlefield Publishing Group, Inc.
4501 Forbes Boulevard, Suite 200, Lanham, Maryland 20706
www.rowman.com

10 Thornbury Road, Plymouth PL6 7PP, United Kingdom

Copyright © 2012 by Lexington Books

British Library Cataloguing in Publication Information Available

Library of Congress Cataloging-in-Publication Data

Politics of practical reasoning : integrating action, discourse, and argument / edited by
  Ricca Edmondson and Karlheinz Hülser.
    p. cm.
  Includes index.
  ISBN 978-0-7391-7226-1 (cloth : alk. paper) — ISBN 978-0-7391-7227-8 (electronic)
  1. Practical reason. I. Edmondson, Ricca. II. Hülser, Karlheinz.
BC177.P58 2012
128'.4—dc23   2012018320

∞™ The paper used in this publication meets the minimum requirements of American National Standard for Information Sciences—Permanence of Paper for Printed Library Materials, ANSI/NISO Z39.48-1992.

Printed in the United States of America

For Markus H. Woerner

Contents

Preface   ix

Introduction: Integrated Practical Reasoning   1
Ricca Edmondson and Karlheinz Hülser

PART 1: FUNDAMENTAL STRUCTURES OF PRACTICAL REASONING

1   Aristotle's Political Anthropology   17
Fran O'Rourke

2   Pragmatics and the Idea of the Illocutionary in Stoic Language Theory   39
Karlheinz Hülser

3   *Utrum gratitudo sit virtus moralis vel passio animae*, or: Gratitude—An Aristotelian Virtue or an Emotion?   65
Thomas Nisters

4   Seeing Ourselves as Others See Us: The Place of Reason in Adam Smith's Theory of Moral Sentiments   79
Gerard Casey

5   Reasons to Act and Practical Reasoning   95
Thomas Gil

PART 2: DEVELOPING CONVINCING ARGUMENTS

6   Practical Reasoning in Place: Tracing "Wise" Inferences in Everyday Life   111
Ricca Edmondson

7   Toulmin's Rhetorical Logic   131
         Frank Canavan

8   Reason, Production, and Rival Visions of Working Life   147
         Keith Breen

9   Reasoning About Disability in the Light of Advances in
         Technology   171
         Richard Hull

10   Principles in Practice: Reasoning with Principles in
         Biomedical Ethics   185
         Heike Felzmann

PART 3: ENGAGEMENT FOR THE PRACTICAL UNITY OF LIFE

11   The Theory of Double Truth Revisited   205
         Karsten Harries

12   Philosophia sine qua non: John Rawls's
         Transcendental-Political Reflections   227
         Sebastian Lalla

13   Skeptical Wisdom: Descartes, Pascal and the
         Challenge of Pyrrhonism   245
         Felix Ó Murchadha

14   Art as "Organizer" of Life: The Case of Jackson Pollock   267
         Elizabeth Langhorne

Afterword: Signs, Bodies, Artworks   291
         Terry Eagleton

Index of Names   297

Index of Subjects   301

About the Contributors   305

Preface

Practical reasoning, manifestly, is a central theme in contemporary philosophical debate. It is an activity carried out by and among people in the context of human interaction, mostly in situations marked by uncertainty but decisive for human life-courses, and developing over time. This collection represents a conversation between authors addressing this common topic from subject areas that interrogate human agency from different viewpoints: applied ethics, aesthetics or metaphysics, rhetoric and argumentation theory. Their methodological approaches include analytical philosophy, phenomenology and analytical Thomism. This diversity is designed to allow the capture of features of practical reasoning that are otherwise easily occluded. The complementarity of these contributions is strengthened too by the fact that they develop approaches within which practical reasoning has been interrogated during the career of a specific philosopher, Markus H. Woerner. His work stresses the need for an unblinkered exploration of factors in verbal communication that can give us grounds for being convinced by each other, particularly in connection with human affairs.

The first section of this book thus highlights implications of the fact that practical reasoning is immersed in life and geared to action, interpersonal and in the end political. It explores the multifaceted nature of political reasoning in the work of Aristotle, with his stress on the conjoined and relational aspects of human action. It continues to the radically pragmatic dimensions of language interrogated in the insights of the Stoics: they are related to features of language which Woerner also explored, in the first monograph in German to reflect on J. L. Austin's work on performatives and illocutionary acts. This section of the book treats Thomas Aquinas as another ally in this tradition; his stringent conception of reasoning would not have supposed it entirely divorced from other human capacities such as emotion or habits of character.

It explores the work of Adam Smith, influenced by Aristotle and the Stoics, who expressly returned to the concept of reasoning as involving sympathy and imagination, and concludes by examining contemporary research about reasoning and the version of naturalism it supports.

The second part of the book focuses on practical reasoning in social and political life, analyzing how argumentation proceeds in detail in cases that cannot rest on certainty, and interrogating the influence of particular conceptions of practical reasoning on public life. This section responds to Woerner's work on argument and rhetoric, reflected not only in his analyses of Aristotelian rhetoric but also in his contemporary work on the most constructive forms of rhetoric, wise arguing. It underlines the political implications of this approach to reasoning, for example, showing how different forms of organization of work are based on different conceptions of practical reasoning, how public policy on disability is influenced by different argumentation styles, or how attempts to apply ethical principles in public life cannot be conducted without the types of case responsiveness and practical wisdom in which Woerner is particularly interested.

The last section begins by addressing themes central to his work: on the one hand, religious and other sources of meaning, and on the other hand science—interrogating their compatibility in a lived life. It deals too with philosophical responses to overall uncertainty, before going on to a field crucial to Woerner's work on reasoning as an integrative set of creative and imaginative human responses to the world: aesthetics. Thus it approaches the ways in which works of art may be regarded as cases of practical reasoning, and in which artistic production as a practice is a (political) form of reasoning.

In this way, this book follows a narrative that explores the ways in which reasoning about human affairs is enlivened by its embeddedness in action; this narrative is deepened by the friendship of its authors with its dedicatee.

We wish to acknowledge the support for this book given by its publisher, Lexington, and our editor, Jana Hodges-Kluck, as well as by the Grant-in-aid-of-Publications Fund of the National University of Ireland, Galway, and by its Social Sciences Research Centre.

The cover shows an etching by Francisco José de Goya y Lucientes (1746–1828), no. 43 in his 1799 collection *Caprichios*, entitled "El sueño de la razón produce monstruos/Sleep of Reason Produces Monsters." This image is reproduced by kind permission of the Brooklyn Museum, 200 Eastern Parkway, Brooklyn, NY. The five works by Jackson Pollock rendered in c. 14 on pp. 270–283 are reproduced by kind permission of the respective copyright owners listed on p. 290.

Ricca Edmondson is grateful to the Institute of Philosophy at the University of Potsdam (in particular Professor Hans-Peter Krüger), for allowing her the opportunity to complete much of the work involved in this collection. She would also like to thank Professor Marja-Liisa Kakkuri-Knuuttila of the Aalto University School of Economics, Helsinki, and the late Professor Richard Harvey Brown of the University of Maryland for their constant encouragement and their passion for understanding the nature of practical reasoning. Karlheinz Hülser would like to thank Professor Mauro Nasti De Vincentis of the University of Salerno in Italy, whose symposium in the autumn of 2000 provided him with his first opportunity to discuss his ideas on pragmatics in the context of Stoic logic. Both editors would like to recall the services to philosophy of Professor John Cleary of Boston College and the National University of Ireland, Maynooth, who wished to contribute to this book but was prevented by his untimely death.

R. E. and K. H.

Introduction

Integrated Practical Reasoning

Ricca Edmondson and Karlheinz Hülser

In everyday language as well as in some academic conventions, practical reasoning is often understood in the context of differentiations: in opposition to theory and theoretical argument, to mere speaking, to productive reasoning and production, to scientific argument, technology and statistics, to the world as such. All these distinctions can be useful for pragmatic purposes connected with what reasoning is used for on particular occasions: an argument about technology will look very different from one about, say, history. But this diversity masks a more fundamental unity of practical reasoning and human practice, a unity that demands an integrated understanding of what we are doing when we take decisions and make choices about the world in which we move.

This collection explores this integrative concept of practical reasoning, considering it first and foremost as a characteristically human *activity*. It examines multiple implications of seeing reasoning about human affairs as a process of engaged interaction with the world and other people. Thus it asks what follows from stressing that reasoning is performed by and between people, in particular practical circumstances, predicaments and environments that are shared in multifaceted ways, yet may be heavily contested. On this approach, practical reasoning is not simply a cognitive process, distinct from other human activities and in need of reconnection with them. Nor is it a defective or subordinate form of thought, but on the contrary at the center of human activity itself: embedded in acting in the world, in relationship with other people and their interwoven forms of reason, emotion and character. The contributions to this collection exhibit the appeal and the challenges of treating practical reasoning as integrating interpersonal, political sets of capacities, closely entwined with virtues and practices, and inseparable from communication and action.

Practical reasoning is the commonest form of reasoning there is. It is also the most complex, embracing not only explicit reasoning about what I, you, we or they ought to do or practicably can do, but also the whole realm of implicit reasoning built into directed activity itself and the social and political contexts in which it is carried out. Thus, the field of practical reasoning is not focused narrowly on what precisely constitutes "a reason." It embraces reasoning as a process, characteristically an interactive one with discursive causes and effects, incorporating assumptions and implications about who the reasoners involved are, how they should be envisaged, and what capacities they possess.

Problems about what individuals can and should do are not altogether separable from questions about what can and should be done by larger groups and societies; social and political deliberations are central forms of practical reasoning. Key among the capacities they involve are those concerned with communication and argument, forms of action with conspicuous consequences whose real-life modes of functioning can tell us much about appropriate criteria for assessing them.

The impacts of this integrative position can be understood against the background of powerful efforts during the last century to reconcretize our understanding of reasoning. In different ways, phenomenological, Wittgensteinian and Austinian approaches to philosophy all urged views of reasoning which located it within an understanding of everyday action. Parallel emphases were achieved by the link underscored between interpretation, tradition and reasoning by Gadamer, by the stress placed on the concept of communicative and emancipatory action by Habermas, or on praxis as highlighting deliberation within communities by MacIntyre. But much longer traditions featuring responses to practical reasoning *as practical* derive from classical Greece, including among others aspects of the work of Aristotle or the Stoics. Medieval theologians and philosophers such as Aquinas confront these issues, as do thinkers of the Scottish Enlightenment and as does Kant. In sum, for over two and a half thousand years, informal, emotional, characterological, aesthetic, social and political aspects of thought have been explored as potential constituents of reasoning as well as influences on it, and demand engagement today.

Human beings in their daily lives, singly and together, deliberate and act in ways that try to embody reasonable inferences in which a variety of emotional and evaluative processes and effects of virtue or character are intertwined: when weighing the advice of psychologists, when deciding how to act in political dilemmas, when trying to understand how something can seem good grounds for action to someone from another culture. Exploring what is done in the course of such activities allows us to interrogate the multivalency of the term "reasonable" and to identify, and critique, some of its implications. This does not present reasoning as less rational than might have been expected, but it exposes new challenges to the sorts of justification it needs. The problems examined in this collection—what it means to respond to arguments about meaningful work or disability, or how to communicate in terms of habitual or traditional aspects of everyday inferences, for instance— are not susceptible to exclusively "cognitive," technical solutions; this does not mean abandoning them to unreason. It may mean situating reasoning in close relationship to other activities central to engagement with the human condition: acknowledging, and evaluating, its intrinsically hybrid nature (see Dunne 1992).

Practical reasoning itself responds in complex ways to problems with roots in disparate sources. It therefore seems inevitable that attempts to understand what processes are involved in it demand contributions from a wide variety of sources. In this collection we aim at cooperation between different theoretical approaches, trying to make perspicuous the conventions of particular intel- lectual practices in order to make their fundamental rationales intelligible to others. The contributors to this volume show that it is possible for seemingly diverse approaches to converse with each other, even over historical time, beginning with accounts from ancient Greece but not omitting a Kantian interest in principles and their application, or a Heideggerian concern with reasoning as embedded in conditions of living itself. In this way we are able to do justice to features of practical reasoning that may be overlooked from within the confines of individual traditions. At the least, to understand prac- tical reasoning contributions are needed from ancient philosophy, with its special understanding of the rootedness of practical reasoning in public life; the theory of rhetoric and argumentation, which analyzes the details of how practical reasoning is carried out; phenomenology, which can take account of the meaning of practical reasoning in terms of human lives and lifetimes; analytical philosophy, especially ethics and political philosophy; and not least aesthetics, with its focus on the creativity and commitment that are featured in the other approaches too, but often not adequately explored by them in their relation to reasoning.

Because each of the chapters of this volume is founded in a concern for what human reasoning can be expected to involve, and what justifying it can be expected to achieve, they address each other in relevant and intel- ligible ways. This collection thus takes seriously the contention (endorsed by contemporary writers such as Martha Nussbaum or Seyla Benhabib) that engaging with different views of the world expands our own comprehension of what human reasoning involves. Because it entails engaging with the po- tentials of human lives in a range of possible contexts, exploring it also means exploring more about the human condition.

This is because the way in which we regard reasoning is inseparable from how we regard people and what they do in everyday and public life. If we model our ideal of reasoning in terms of "technocratic," bureaucratic rationality, we give priority to standardized forms of judgment based on aspects of human life that are seen as quantifiable and replicable, where differences in interpreting language can be minimized—pursuing what Bishop Sprat saw as the "primitive purity and shortness" in which speakers "delivered so many things almost in an equal number of words" (1667/1966, II. xx: 2). This form of reasoning is central in operations dealing primarily with matter insofar as it is unaffected by human activity, though here too procedures and criteria are far from undisputed (see, e.g., Rehbock 1995). If this model is transposed to human affairs it quickly assumes managerial form, in which people are treated as if they themselves were material objects. Not only this, but if forms of reasoning rooted in human life are pushed to one side, criteria that should operate there remain insufficiently discussed—adding to the mistaken impression that discourse in the human realm is somehow immune to meticulous assessment.

By exploring the idea of an integrated practical reasoning, this collection takes further steps toward tracing just what is involved in reasoning: not just cognition, emotion, or virtue, but also practices, including imaginative practices: as Adam Smith pointed out, we have to imagine each other's situations to interact with each other at all. Hence the cover illustration: if we deaden our image of reasoning, allowing it to drop into an overcognitivized slumber and denuding it of all that gives it life, we produce monsters which are easily allied with nightmarish states of society. This book, in contrast, investigates what follows from treating reasoning as human and alive.

DEBATING PRACTICAL REASONING

This collection begins, therefore, by interrogating the ways in which reasoning is bound up with the interrelated lives that human beings lead in their public, political and everyday worlds. Thus its first section underlines the grounding of practical reason in what came in the twentieth century to be termed "the life-world," showing how this preoccupation was explored in different ways from Antiquity onward. Aristotle concludes the *Nicomachean Ethics* by announcing his treatise on politics, indispensable for completing his "philosophy of human affairs": human beings attain happiness and fulfillment only within political communities, whose point is to aim at the highest possible human good through political partnership.

Fran O'Rourke's chapter explores Aristotle's emphasis on this connection and his description of the human being as a person living and thriving in the community of the polis. In what sense may the polis be described as natural? How can its primacy be reconciled with the fact that citizens are somehow independent, with autonomous activities and their own purposes? The chapter distinguishes different types of "naturalness" in Aristotle's account, discussing connections between the origins of the polis and humans' dependence on cooperation for survival, then identifying benefits of citizenship justified by Aristotle's account of human nature: the basic ends at which humans aim and the role of language in relation to them. The deepest explanation for the existence of both family and polis is shared participation in our social nature—grounded, through the capacity to reason using language, on a community of values. Humans' communicative and communal dispositions are thus simultaneous: a matter not just of pragmatic interdependence but of friendship and mutual satisfaction. Without trying (anachronistically) to restore Aristotle's notion of a Greek polis for the present, O'Rourke shows that the relationship between individuals and the polis in Aristotle's thought nonetheless lays the basis for situating practical reasoning within political communities—in a way that stresses that "autonomy," as a facet of human flourishing, does not entail an image of solitary individuals responsible only for themselves, but can only be achieved together.

Karlheinz Hülser's chapter goes on to interrogate the Stoics' appreciation of the pragmatics of language and the constitution of what we do in speaking. Stoic language theory flourished during the third and second centuries B.C.; Hülser's work on surviving fragments of this precise and illuminating work shows that it reveals a puzzle. On the one hand, the Stoics show that a potentially limitless number of speech acts can be made, but on the other they provide an extremely constricted list of basic speech acts (usually between ten and fifteen). Hülser's solution to this apparent contradiction allows him to develop the treatment of the illocutionary act with which Austin inaugurated modern speech-act theory in the 1950s and 1960s. He demonstrates that it is precisely the precision of the Stoics' work that in the end threatens the bounds of philosophical semantics itself. Asking what we do in saying brings us, in the end, to questions of fiction and pretending, the real and the unreal, elements addressed again later in the collection. For the Stoics it was fundamental that human existence, society and practical reasoning are both bound together and communicated via the pragmatic dimension of language.

Since these chapters have underlined the significance of ways in which practical reasoning encompasses features such as virtue and emotion, in the next contribution Thomas Nisters tackles some intricacies relevant to analyzing how such components interact. Aiming to heighten precision by dissecting a particular case, he explores gratitude as an example of a "moral sentiment," reproducing the strict lines of scholastic analysis followed by

Thomas Aquinas. Nisters considers seven arguments supporting the view that gratitude is an emotion rather than a virtue, and then examines counter-positions. He argues that gratitude is composed of a complex combination of emotions which characteristically give rise to particular speech acts and other actions; but in a subsidiary sense it is a virtue too, exercised with regard to the same emotions, utterances and deeds, and opposed by characteristic vices. This complex account is tested by reviewing the gamut of arguments and counterarguments presented earlier in the chapter—accounting afresh for what initially appeared conclusive claims and (an important subtext) exhibiting the rigor of scholastic argument.

Gerard Casey's chapter on moral reasoning in the work of Adam Smith responds to such an approach. It begins by examining Smith's view of "sympathy," then exposes "genuinely ethical dimensions" in his exposition of "propriety," connecting it with Smith's account of the impartial spectator, general moral rules, and the way in which reasoning operates in his ethical system. It functions, not to ground our moral notions, but "to overcome the human inclination to self-centredness" in applying them; reason and feeling work in concord. Practical reasoning is at the center of our humanity; the reasoning involved in guiding action is not some sort of "soft" or "personal" derivation from reasoning, but reasoning *tout court*. Thus, in making a feeling or sentiment such as sympathy foundational to his ethical analysis, Smith does not collide with ethical theories where reason plays a central role. On the contrary, what he rejects is an austere ultra-rationalism that would make reason a stand-alone "source" of ethical judgment. Instead, his complex theory of morality permits reason to play a significant role embedded within human beings' moral lives.

Last in this section, Thomas Gil turns to the contemporary consideration of characteristics of reasons, situating it among treatments by writers such as Raz, Kenny or von Wright. When asked why we have done what we have done, we refer to heterogeneous phenomena: needs, interests, desires, aims, decisions, norms, promises and orders, among many others. In reasoning processes aimed at justifying how we should act in certain specific situations, we use practical reasons in a specific way: *as arguments*. Gil describes some of the phenomena we take as reasons to act, dissecting how the relevant language functions. Although knowing other people's reasons helps us to understand what they do, *having* reasons to act is not always identical with the *activity* of reasoning. While "having reasons" describes a way of being situated in the world, practical reasoning is a deliberative activity carried out within communicative contexts in which we are related to the world, each other and our own lives. This underlines the reasonableness of "moderate" naturalism: both our reasons and our reasoning activities are intrinsically connected with real processes going on in the world.

While the first five chapters have located practical reasoning as central to questions about what human beings are and what they do in their public and personal lives, the next part of the book focuses on how communication and argument in practical reasoning work in detail, over a range of personal, public and political predicaments. They show too that patterns of practical reasoning are—consciously or otherwise—bound up with underlying ideas about the good life for human beings.

Ricca Edmondson's chapter also focuses on reasoning processes connected with human affairs, aiming to show how personal aspects of argumentation can heighten rather than detract from its reasonableness, which allows us to develop criteria for understanding positive forms of reasoning rather than concentrating only on avoiding fallacy. She too uses instruments derived from Aristotle's and Cicero's accounts of rhetoric to illuminate inferential processes used in everyday practical reasoning. This chapter explores parts played in reasoning by sociopolitical and ethical components such as "character," as well as the taken-for-granted assumptions which arguers actively bring into play by selecting particular "topoi" to bestow reasonableness on their arguments. Edmondson asks exactly how these features can interlock with each other in reasonable ways: how, for example, activities involved both in taking character into account and in exhibiting it can be reasonable aspects of argument, or how "pathos" need not simply involve impacts on hearers but can transform speakers' positions too. She argues that interrogating practices involved in informal reasoning can cast light on discursive standards; when these elements are exercised well, excellent or even "wise" arguing is involved. But since reasoning in daily life is so often suppressed, allusive, and fragmented, we need to make special efforts to trace the partly shared habits, assumptions and prescriptions which arguers draw on to take argumentative steps, using ethnographic methods to reconstruct cases of real-life reasoning. Aristotle himself makes formidable concessions to the sociality of reasoning; his own account of topoi can be seen as partially ethnographic, for instance. Edmondson argues that this approach allows us to explore a type of wise reasoning that is processual and culturally situated, a social interaction rather than the possession of a single speaker. The chapter thus begins to address problems in the interdisciplinary and intercultural analysis of reasoning.

The next chapter also develops questions highlighted earlier in Gil's chapter: what is actually involved in making inferences in practical dilemmas, when logical conclusiveness is unavailable? Frank Canavan turns to Stephen Toulmin's efforts to reconstruct how arguments are actually carried out, in real-life situations in which conclusions may be important and pressing, but cannot be established with certainty: the types of argument in public life central to Aristotle's *Rhetoric*. In *The Uses of Argument* (1958) Toulmin exposed common structures of arguments, seeing them as setting out claims made, data on which claims were based, warrants for moving from data to claims, backing for warrants, conditions of rebuttal, and qualifiers denoting strengths of connection between these elements. Canavan situates Toulmin's efforts alongside others both at the time—in work on rhetoric and on implicature—and subsequently. Philosophical reactions to Toulmin's work have highlighted questions about fallacy, acceptability and its connections to the demands of concrete situations, the imports of different argumentative layouts, and the "pragma-dialectical" view of argumentation as involving moves and procedures aimed at solving differences of opinion (van Eemeren and Grootendorst 2004). Canavan concludes by stressing Toulmin's desire to formulate criteria for arguments used by "reflective practitioners," combining "informed intellect, the human imagination and a well-cultivated desire to know."

Next, Keith Breen's chapter turns to the way in which particular forms of life are underlain by corresponding conceptions of what practical reasoning is. Thus it both shows and challenges what happens if we shape crucial aspects of social and political life around "technocratic" reasoning. It deals with the concept of "meaningful work," stressing the closeness of this term to Alasdair MacIntyre's idea of "practice." Then it examines ongoing threats to this ethical conception of work, arguing that they are based on a false dichotomy between efficiency and meaningfulness that rests on an impoverished account of practical reason. "Decent work" might be expected to involve proper remuneration for effort expended, freedom from social degradation or embarrassment, and "meaningful" activities for workers. This comes close to what MacIntyre intends by "practice," which he derives from a modified Aristotelian conception of practical reason. In late modernity, this ethical conception of work has been challenged by alternative conceptions focusing on "external" goods such as productivity, efficiency, and profitability. This chapter argues that a Taylorist conception of workplace organization and the notion of practical reason underpinning it are inherently hostile to meaningful modes of work, but still dominate within many industries. Breen contends instead that experiments in industrial design during the 1970s and 1980s show not only that alternative forms of workplace organization are normatively preferable to Taylorism, but also that they can be just as efficient in terms of productivity and quality control. Meaningful work and efficiency need not be rivals, but can operate according to a "phronetic" understanding of productive reason. Yet failing to ensure their compatibility in modern workplaces results in an underskilled, dispensable, socially vulnerable "reserve army of labor." This should not be attributed primarily to technological imperatives or limitations, but rather to an impoverished conception of practical reason.

These three chapters have indicated that the conduct of practical reasoning is oriented to ways of envisaging a constructive, productive form of life for human beings, which makes it inherently political. This is clear too in the subsequent two chapters in the section. First, Richard Hull discusses reasoning with regard to the domain of disability: what disability is, why it matters and to whom, and how to respond to a range of issues to which it is pivotal— with highly political implications for questions of freedom and the individual. Early, "biomedical" efforts to understand disability attempted to be clear-cut and unambiguous; instead, they arbitrarily imposed a flow of reasoning whose effects were ethically and politically as well as analytically flawed, occluding the effects of social interaction on what disability is. Yet the "social" approach, stressing impacts ranging from the consequences of building styles to fundamental expectations of human beings, both leaves out essential aspects of disability and ascribes too much power to social habit. Thus Hull suggests that much contemporary reasoning in this field is (in Aristotelian terms) either excessive or deficient. Rather than endorsing entirely "social" models, therefore, he draws on recent work by Jonathan Glover, building on a hybrid approach to disability and encouraging a more nuanced approach to issues raised by advances in new technologies. The types of reasoning we engage in here are central to life in contemporary societies, not least because we are all likely to spend some portions of our lives as disabled. But, in conclusion, Hull urges us to think very seriously about the impact that more permissive approaches to disability might have on the lives of future children.

Heike Felzmann also deals with reflections addressing how to reason and behave in pressing circumstances, in this case the influential attempt by Beauchamp and Childress to design a textbook for use in the biomedical professions to guide practitioners' decision processes. An almost universal characteristic of the codes now common in a range of professions is a statement of core ethical principles. In medical ethics as elsewhere, the "principle-based approach" has been by far the most influential one taught. Does this imply that ethical reasoning in professional practice can be understood as a "top-down" reasoning process, "applying" principles to the practice area in a relatively straightforward fashion that can be interpreted similarly by everyone? In over three decades since the first appearance of Beauchamp and Childress's book, its authors have struggled with the need to clarify both the theoretical and practical implications of their work. They acknowledged early that their principles—respect for autonomy, nonmaleficence, beneficence, and justice—demanded more complex treatment in order to connect with practice. This detail was broached in terms, for example, of "specification," making norms fit contexts by detailing further subsets of norms, attempting to clarify "what, where, when, why, how, by what means, by whom, or to whom the action is to be, is not to be, or may be done," or how the action in question is to be described or at what it should aim. Yet it remains unclear how to accommodate competing interpretations in such cases. "Balancing" involves finding reasons that support beliefs about which norms should operate. But Felzmann shows that as specification and balancing are pursued further, differences between principlism and other ethical approaches such as casuistry begin to fade away. Beauchamp and Childress draw too on ideas associated with virtue ethics, in particular the Aristotelian conception of *phronesis*: practical wisdom. The point for Felzmann is that not only principles but both responses to cases and "virtues of perception and reasoning" play significant parts in judging complex issues. She concludes that, while principles are among the most easily identifiable aspects of a reasoning process, much of the moral work is done by elements other than principles.

The following section deals with practical reasoning and living a human life itself, under the title "Engagement for the Practical Unity of Life." We turn to the ways in which people reason about how life as such can or should be lived, and connections between practical reasoning, truth and art. This takes account of the continuously renewed efforts needed to defend the unity of practical reasoning. Without constant concern for integrating boundary areas, reasoning can descend into sleep and dreaming, haunted by monstrous conceptions of what reasoning might be. This section therefore interrogates aspects of the ways humans reason as embodied beings, including their uses of the imagination and art—returning reasoning, as Eagleton points out, to politics again.

Karsten Harries begins by pointing out the long-standing nature of preoccupation with the supposed bifurcation between scientific and nonscientific apprehensions of the world. His chapter takes as its point of departure the Church's condemnation in 1277 of views influenced by the medieval Arab scholar Ibn Rushd (known in the West as Averroes), notably the views of Siger of Brabant. Siger was responding to the fact that received natural science at the time, based on Averroes's interpretation of Aristotle, was incompatible with central articles of Christian faith, notably with respect to God's creation of the world, divine and human freedom, and a personal afterlife. The theory of double truth (whether or not Siger actually really held it) contends that there is one sort of truth for science, and another for one's personal beliefs. Harries underlines a modern version of the double-truth theory, one envisaging our moral views as both true and false at the same time. If the world described by physics *is* the world, for only physics can describe what is real, then other beliefs, such as that in free will, that we are selves that exist until we die, or that we should embrace religious tolerance, must be "inescapable framework illusions"—even while we may feel compelled to live by them. Such a double theory, Harries argues, is psychologically unacceptable. Drawing on Kant's antinomies and Heidegger's attempt to think the ways in which human beings experience the reality of the real, he shows that the understanding of reality presupposed in the double-truth theory must be rejected in order for us to take our practical reasoning seriously.

Sebastian Lalla's chapter then interrogates the work of John Rawls, inquiring why it is that Rawls's arguments have had no perceptible impact on what they address—the degree of justice in the world. Lalla argues that in fact Rawls's "theory of justice" is not properly understood as a continuation of liberal contract theories but is, rather, a statement of idealist metaphysics. It is metaphysical in the sense of beginning from conditions of the possibility of just societies that are consciously counterfactual. Lalla offers the concept of "transcendental politics" as a tool showing how philosophy can demonstrate its value when *not* intervening in the practical sphere. For Lalla, in contradistinction to other authors in this collection, this is the only approach possible for modern political philosophy, which should not necessarily be expected to have practical consequences. Thus this chapter remains skeptical toward the practical aspects of life, but has the underlying aim of turning theory into "praxis" as a genuine form of itself.

Taking a different approach to the juxtapositions examined by Lalla, Felix Ó Murchadha grapples with what Kant or Heidegger viewed as "the scandal of philosophy": the strict distinction posited between the thinking self and the world of meaning within which human beings act. Other chapters in this collection have referred to widespread acknowledgment in the ancient world that certainty cannot be attained in human affairs; Ó Murchadha recurs to the position taken by the Pyrrhonists from about 100 B.C. onward, in particular by Sextus Empiricus in the second and third centuries AD: we should suspend judgment on all that we cannot know for certain. For such Pyrrhonists, the realization that we live in an irreducible aporia, "in the space *between* claims to know," led to a serene state of living without beliefs. In early modernity, in contrast, skepticism became an exercise in limiting reason for the sake of faith. "Skeptical wisdom" became merely a way of living without the guarantees of reason, while trusting God. Ó Murchadha shows how the Ancient skeptics' serenity becomes an imitation of divine will in Descartes, and a wager beyond reason in Pascal. Both were preoccupied with the loss of "world," in the sense of a prefiguring, ordered cosmos; famously, Pascal felt "terrified" by "the eternal silence of these infinite spaces." Both were caught up in a process in which the search for objectivity, paradoxically, ended by elevating human subjectivity itself as "the arbiter of reasonableness." But Ó Murchadha tries in closing to suggest that a phenomenological reappropriation of skepticism (in Husserl and Heidegger), reinterpreting "world" from subjectivity, can reopen a dialogue with ancient Pyrrhonism in a manner true to the original goal of skepticism: serene wisdom.

Elizabeth Langhorne now goes on to consider the practice of art—here, painting—as a boundary case of practical reasoning. Aesthetic cognitivists, interested in relations between epistemic and aesthetic value in works of art, explore among other things the types of reasoning in which recipients of art engage (see, for example, Gaut 2007). Langhorne, however, examines the life and work of Jackson Pollock "as a vehicle for discovering how to live," first symbolically and then through the process of painting itself. Langhorne argues too that struggling with Pollock's art, and the light it casts on the human condition, can make the viewer wiser—an approach to practical reasoning through a unique form of practice. She surveys an array of approaches to practical reasoning which many regard as having failed, or at least as unresolved: life as organized by religion or by reason, or by the existential individual. Kant saw "wisdom" as organizing human life, in parallel to the organization of knowledge by science; but, since it remains far from clear how we should interpret this, Langhorne takes recourse to Schiller's suggestion that wisdom needs art. Throughout his life, the American painter Jackson Pollock understood the making of art as a vehicle for discovering how to live, at first through visual thinking with symbolic images, then later through the very process of painting his mature, abstract, poured canvases. Confronting personal and public crises, he discovered how, in the face of death, to aspire toward an erotic opening, whether to woman, nature, or simply to paint. The specificity of the forms and rhythms in his mature work makes them powerful conveyors of mood. Responding to its moods, the viewer encounters Pollock's struggle between an existential desire for unbound freedom and a longing for totalization and homecoming. Pollock's art is not so much a communication of specific insights as a way of making the person who struggles with his art more wise, by revealing to us something about the meaning of the human condition in an age that has experienced the death of God.

Terry Eagleton concludes the section by referring to a second "scandal" of modern philosophy, the inability of Enlightenment rationality to take account of the bodiliness of human thought. Efforts at repairing this omission led to the beginning of aesthetics, stressing that in art the "sensuously specific" enjoys a "subtle interplay of freedom and relatedness" in which autonomy derives from "the context created for it by the others," "a cooperative commonwealth in miniature." From Plato to postmodernism, therefore, "Aesthetics is an allegory of the political from start to finish." The work of art is thus a work of practical reason, albeit in a sense "purposeless": "like virtue," it is most effective when true to the laws of its own formation. In the phenomenology of Heidegger and Merleau-Ponty, Eagleton argues, the human body is thought of as a form of practice in this way: activities engaged in as ends in themselves are those we think of as most precious, "human flourishing" "at its most valuable and vigorous." This too is political; for art and human praxis to flourish, for "self-realizing energies" to "become an end and delight in themselves," political transformation is needed to oppose the "commodifying, instrumentalist reason of industrial capitalism." Art and human bodiliness are also linked by their "peculiar interweaving of meaning and materiality" in which signs are simultaneously autonomous and allusive. "Practice is the life of the body in the sense that meaning is the life of a sign." Human bodies are "suffused with sense"; thus it is, for Eagleton, in both bodily experience and art that practical reasoning "is most tangibly illustrated."

The integrated approach to practical reasoning explored in this book is placed in opposition to the imagined split between intuitive, inductive reasoning and evidence-based rationality portrayed in C. P. Snow's "two cultures." It is not a matter of warmth and vagueness on the one hand, versus exactitude but chill on the other. The model of thinking underlying this contrast is fundamentally mistaken. Our point is rather that all argumentation concerning human affairs is inextricably in the midst of life; dialogue concerning human questions has been recognized as a form of action since ancient times (Hülser 2005). The implications this has extend to argumentation in the human sciences (Edmondson 1984) as well as, for example, in politics or ethics (Woerner 1990). Exactitude and impartiality must be achieved wherever they are appropriate, and evidence assessed, within the confines of dialogue which cannot but be committed, however little its stylistic conventions may customarily reveal this fact. The contributions in this book stress that faulty conceptions of reasoning not only lead to failed understandings of practical and political arguing, they are used to justify forms of life there are strong reasons to reject. This makes it crucial to explore and expose the potential reasonableness of practical reasoning itself.

REFERENCES

Dunne, Joseph. 1992. *Back to the Rough Ground: "Phronesis" and "Techne" in Modern Philosophy and in Aristotle.* Notre Dame: University of Notre Dame Press.

Edmondson, Ricca. 1984. *Rhetoric in Sociology.* London: Macmillan.

Gaut, Berys. 2007. *Art, Emotion and Ethics.* Oxford: Oxford University Press.

Hülser, Karlheinz. 2005. *Platon für Anfänger: Der Staat.* Munich: dtv.

Rehbock, Theda. 1995. *Goethe und die 'Rettung der Phänomene': Philosophische Kritik des naturwissenschaftlichen Weltbilds am Beispiel der Farbenlehre.* Konstanz: Verlag am Hockgraben.

Snow, Charles P. 2000/1959. *The Two Cultures.* Ed. and introd. by Stefan Collini. London: Cambridge University Press.

Sprat, Thomas. 1667/1966. *The History of the Royal Society of London: For the Improving of Natural Knowledge.* Repr. of the 1667 edition, ed. by Jackson I. Cope. St. Louis: Washington University Press.

Toulmin, Stephen E. 1958. *The Uses of Argument.* Cambridge: Cambridge University Press.

Van Eemeren, Frans H., and Grootendorst, Robert. 2004. *A Systematic Theory of Argumentation: The Pragma-Dialectic Approach.* Cambridge: Cambridge University Press.

Woerner, Markus H. 1990. *Das Ethische in der Rhetorik des Aristoteles.* Freiburg/ Br.: Alber Verlag.

Part One

FUNDAMENTAL STRUCTURES OF PRACTICAL REASONING

Chapter One

Aristotle's Political Anthropology

Fran O'Rourke

Aristotle concludes the *Nicomachean Ethics* by announcing his treatise on politics. Only thus, he explains, will his "philosophy of human affairs" be complete (NE X 9, 1181b12–15).[1] The transition from the *Ethics* to the *Politics* is natural and essential, since human beings attain happiness and fulfillment only within the political community. The *Politics* opens with the assertion that the city or political community aims at the supreme human good (Pol. I 1, 1252a1–7). While all partnerships aim at some good, political partnership is paramount. Aristotle confirms this priority by describing the human being as a political animal. In this chapter I consider a number of interrelated questions arising from this description.[2] Is the term "political" proper to humans, and only predicated metaphorically of animals? Or does Aristotle's definition refer to an elementary zoological characteristic common to members of gregarious species that collaborate in common tasks? In what sense may the polis be described as natural if it does not conform to Aristotle's definition of what it is to be a nature (φύσις)? How may the primacy of the polis be reconciled with the fact that the citizen is somehow independent, with autonomous activities and a separate purpose? The answers to these questions underline the status of practical political reasoning in human life and society.

While Aristotle emphasises the citizen's autonomy, his exploration of what a human being is and can do makes clear that autonomy can only be actuated as this person acts and communicates within a series of nested relationships. It is a political and shared, not an individual, form of autonomy. "Politics" encompasses guiding and enacting the relevant relationships and the decisions to which they give rise. Thus, investigating in what sense politics is both paramount and "natural" to human beings helps us to understand the place among them of reasoned communication about public life.

17

THE ORIGIN OF THE POLIS

At the start of the *Politics* Aristotle sets out to establish that humans are by nature political animals, and the polis accordingly a natural entity. He offers what are apparently two distinct explanations. The first is a detailed description and empirical narrative of the genesis of the polis: how it arose, and the evident purpose it exists to serve. The second is a compacted theoretical explanation of humans as political animals, based on the possession of *logos*, roughly translated as communicative reason (see below). Later I shall consider the relationship between these two arguments. For the moment let us note that in the first he seems at pains to emphasize that the polis exists by nature (κατὰ φύσιν, φύσει); the second argument is itself a reflection on human nature.[3]

Aristotle suggests that the best way to investigate things is to see how they have grown (φυόμενα) from the beginning.[4] He explains that the first natural human association is the family or household: "a union of those who cannot exist without each other" (Pol. I 2, 1252a26–27). This is the union of male and female, which exists for the continuance of the human race, motivated by the desire—common to all living things—to leave behind another of the same kind. It also incorporates the relationship of master and slave, grounded in their shared need for security; the one who envisages the means of defense is a natural ruler, the one who provides these is a natural subject. Aristotle defines the family as, in Jowett's translation, "the association established by nature for the supply of men's everyday wants" (Pol. I 2, 1252b12–14).

Aristotle goes on to explain that families in turn combine to form a village, an association aiming at something more than the supply of daily needs (Pol. I 2, 1252b15–16). Finally, when several villages coalesce into a self-sufficient community, they constitute a polis. Aristotle notes (in the same translation): "A polis only begins to exist when it has attained a population sufficient for a good life in the political community" (Pol. VII 4, 1326b7–9). There is a graded hierarchy in the goals of family, village, and polis, responding incrementally to the citizen's needs, from daily necessities to the fulfillment of the good life. Aristotle emphasizes that all three associations—family, village, polis—come about in accordance with nature (κατὰ φύσιν). The polis is natural because it derives from the family and village, which grow out of the citizen's essential and immediate dependence on human cooperation.

In his ethical works Aristotle adds valuable remarks on the social or political role of the family. In the *Nicomachean Ethics* he remarks that the love of husband and wife exists by nature (κατὰ φύσιν), "for human beings naturally tend to form couples more than to form cities, to the extent that the household is prior to the city, and more necessary" (NE VIII 12, 1162a16–19; Irwin's translation). He also points out that "human beings cohabit not only for the sake of begetting children but also to provide the needs of life" (NE VIII 12, 1162a20–22). More important from our point of view is his emphasis in the *Eudemian Ethics* on the foundational character of the family: "In the household are first found the origins and springs of friendship, of political organization and of justice" (EE VII 10, 1242a40–b2; Rackham's translation).

While the family exists for the sake of everyday needs, and the village for nonessential goods, Aristotle makes a significant distinction between the *genesis* and continued *existence* of the polis: it *came into being* for the sake of life, but *exists* for the sake of the good life (Pol. I 2, 1252b27–30). Once in existence, it offers its citizens an enhanced mode of life. It provides added benefits not envisaged in advance. These correspond, presumably, to the pre-eminent, outstandingly human capacities of individual citizens. The city came into being so that men might be *able* to live, but continues to exist so that they may live *well*. As Rowe remarks (see Pol. III 9, 1280b38–39), Aristotle

> does not want to claim that all, or indeed perhaps *any,* actual cities in fact "exist for the sake of the good life." We have to live and survive, but what we live *for* is the realisation of our potential as human beings, which is impossible outside a political community. (Rowe 2000, 408)

Aristotle repeatedly affirms that "the polis was formed not for the sake of life only but rather for the good life."[5]

In his first argument that the polis exists by nature, Aristotle has so far referred to the collective combination of families and villages, both of which result from nature (Pol. I 2, 1252b30–31). To emphasize the point he changes perspective from the material, compositional, origin of the polis to its purpose as the goal, end or telos of the family and village. The most important principle in any reality is its end and purpose; finality defines and determines the nature of each substance (Pol. I 2, 1252b32–1253a1). The polis has a clear and indispensable goal, the self-sufficiency of its citizens. Aristotle is thus able to carry his genetic explanation to its ultimate conclusion and identify the purpose for which the polis exists. "The object for which a thing exists, its end, is a chief good; and self-sufficiency (αὐτάρκεια) is an end, and a chief good. From these things therefore it is clear that the polis is a natural growth, and that man is by nature a political animal" (Pol. I 2, 1253a1–3). One of the strengths of Aristotle's method is his reliance upon observation, and the most obvious reason for the polis is the human dependence upon cooperation. No individual is self-sufficient, but attains adequacy in collaboration with others. Aristotle reinforces the point by noting that whoever is either incapable of, or has no need of, partnership, must be either an animal or a god (Pol. I 2, 1253a4; also a26–9). He illustrates the fate of the individual deprived of city life by referring to the "clanless, lawless, hearthless" man reviled by Homer.[6] Sophocles conveys the same plight in Philoctetes' lament that as ἄπολις he is a living corpse.[7] Self-sufficiency is a requisite for happiness, but the self-sufficiency of the citizen ultimately depends upon the self-sufficiency of the polis (NE I 7, 1097b7–11), for

> it is felt that the final good must be a thing self-sufficient in itself. The term self-sufficient, however, we employ with reference not to oneself alone, living a life of isolation, but also to one's parents and children and wife, and one's friends and fellow citizens in general, since man is by nature a social being.

Aristotle first establishes through observation the *fact* that humans are political beings.

In his second argument he proceeds to examine the *reason* for their political nature. The answer appears obvious: "Why man is a political animal in a greater measure than any bee or gregarious animal is clear. For nature, as we declare, does nothing without purpose; and man alone of the animals possesses speech" (Pol. I 2, 1253a7–10). While other animals have voice (φωνή), which allows them to communicate pain and pleasure, they are restricted to the domain of the senses. Human beings experience deeper levels of value within reality:

> Speech is designed to indicate the beneficial and the harmful, and thus also what is right and wrong; for it is special to man as distinct from the other animals that he alone has any sense of good and bad, of right and wrong and other moral qualities: it is association in these things that makes a family and a polis. (Pol. I 2, 1253a10–18)

This short passage has raised two fundamental questions. What is the exact meaning and scope of the term "political"? What is the context of Aristotle's definition: is it biological, rational, or metaphysical?[8]

"POLITICAL ANIMALS": LITERAL OR METAPHORICAL?

There are two interpretations of the meaning and scope of "political" as understood by Aristotle in his definition. According to one, the concept refers properly and primarily to humans as animals that live in political partnership and community—the only ones capable of doing so since, uniquely endowed with *logos*, they alone share with their fellow humans the common and universal values upon which society is based. According to this interpretation, the term "political" is used for those gregarious animals that collaborate in a common task (bees, ants, and so on) in a secondary, derived, metaphorical sense. Such creatures are not properly "political" but, resembling humans in the performance of a common project, merit the transferred application of the term on the basis of this similarity. This interpretation appeals to the etymological roots of the word, and Aristotle's penchant for analogy and metaphor.

According to the second interpretation, the use of the term "political" in respect to animals is not metaphorical, but proper and intrinsic; its meaning is not confined to human society, but refers equally to every animal group engaged in communal activity. This interpretation appears confirmed by Aristotle's definition of political animals at the start of *History of Animals* as "those which have some one common task" (κοινὸν ἔργον) (HA I 1, 488a7–8); Aristotle lists humans, bees, wasps, ants, and cranes.[9] The word has an extensive—rather than extended—meaning, covering many and diverse degrees of sociality. Thus, when Aristotle says that humans are "more" political than bees or other gregarious animals (Pol. I 2, 1253a9), he is referring to a superior grade along a continuum.

In *History of Animals* VIII Aristotle distinguishes two ways in which qualities may be common to animals and humans. Some are common "more or less," others by analogy. Examples of characteristics that can be found in varying degrees are tameness/wildness, gentleness/roughness, courage/cowardice, fear and boldness. While admitting of gradation, such qualities (we may add uncontroversially) are understood intrinsically and properly and thus univocally. By contrast art, wisdom, and comprehension are proper to man, while "certain animals possess another natural capability of a similar sort" (HA VIII 1, 588a29–31). Had Aristotle placed "political" in one or other of these two categories, the present discussion would never have arisen; but tantalizingly he did not. I will argue that the qualification "political" in its intrinsic sense is unique to humanity, but that it is recognized analogically, according to varying degrees, in select animal groups.

Whatever about Aristotle's supposed metaphorical use of the word *polites*, there was undeniably in ancient Greek an extension beyond the original meaning of the word. As Miller points out, "The word '*polis*' originally referred to a high stronghold or citadel to which the Greeks of the dark ages repaired when their villages were under attack" (1997, 3; cf. Sakellariou 1989, 155ff.). Πολίτης, *polites*, originally meant the watchman on the citadel, and was later generalized as "citizen." Significantly the word contrasts with ἰδιώτης (*idiotes*), referring to the private city-dweller who took no part in the affairs of his community.

The case for a literal interpretation of "political," when affirmed of animals, would be strengthened if the intention of Aristotle's definition were shown to be biological, rather than rational or metaphysical. Because Aristotle invokes the principle "Nature does nothing in vain" ("the basic proposition

of his zoology"), Kullmann (1991, 99) takes Aristotle to mean that man is
political by nature, "insofar as he is a biological being" (cf. Kullmann 1998,
334). He suggests that "the reference to bees and herd animals makes clear
[that] man is indeed understood as a biological species," explaining that

> The political is a characteristic which necessarily results from the special
> biological nature of man. In this connection, Aristotle proceeds as if it is self-
> evident that this concept is not coextensive with the concept of man, but has a
> wider scope. It is only when compared with certain other animals that men are
> political to an especially high degree. . . . It also follows from the description of
> man as *zoon* that "political" above all describes a biological condition of a group
> of animals. (Kullmann 1991, 100–1)

This, Kullmann argues, is also the meaning of Aristotle's assertion that "man
is a political animal in a greater measure than any bee or gregarious animal"
(Pol. 1 2, 1253a7–8). A different interpretation is defended by Richard Bodéüs, who argues that with this remark Aristotle does not intend "that the
human species possesses a political character more marked than every other
species of the same genus, but that the human species, rather than any species of bee or gregarious animal, possesses this character" (Bodéüs 1985, 66;
cf. Kullmann 1998, 339 n. 70). Before stating my reasons for adopting this
reading too, I will examine in closer detail the case for a broader, literal and
biological, reading.

If I understand Kullmann correctly, he maintains that for Aristotle the
concept "political," while initially deriving from humans' political character
understood as a *biological* function, is recognized as applicable—properly
and with equal validity—to all gregarious animals sharing a common task
(Kullmann 1998, 354). From the fact that Aristotle invokes the "statement
from his writings on natural science" that Nature does nothing in vain,
Kullmann deduces that Aristotle is here proposing a biological description
of humanity. This conclusion, I suggest, is not entirely obvious. While it is
true that Aristotle employs the principle with great frequency in his biological writings, his commitment to its validity is not confined to these. Perhaps
it was necessary to affirm it more frequently as a programmatic maxim with
regard to the lower level of physical minutiae, than in the domain of human
experience where purposiveness is more apparent. Aristotle's confidence in
the beneficence of nature extends throughout the living world, human and
subhuman, confirming his overall teleological concept of the universe and
humanity (Verbeke 1983, 76). The principle is cited twice in *De Anima* III
(9, 432b21–2 and 12, 434a31), which culminates in a discussion of the human soul. Aristotle notes that since the goal of politics is human excellence
and happiness, the student of politics should study the activities of the soul

(NE I 13, 1102a24–26). The soul, ψυχή (*psyche*), is a synonym for the φύσις (*physis*) or nature of living things—the principle of all their activities, from digestion to contemplation. In the *Nicomachean Ethics* Aristotle asks rhetorically if we could suppose that, while the carpenter and the shoemaker have definite functions—as do also the eye, hand and foot—human beings themselves should have none (NE I 7, 1097b28–30).

Aristotle's conviction that nature does nothing in vain extends to the highest desires of human nature. From the fact that we always act for the sake of a goal, he concludes there must be a final end which satisfies our tendencies: otherwise the process would go on infinitely, so that the desire would be vacuous and futile (NE I 2, 1094a21). When he declares that all people by nature (φύσει) desire to know, this does not mean that metaphysical reflection has its roots in human biology. A person's nature is his or her ψυχή, soul, which, as well as defining their biology, opens them through the intellectual capacity of *nous* or reasoning to the totality of the real (De an. III 8, 431b21), which they are drawn through wonder to explore. Aristotle is convinced that humans' desire for truth and knowledge is not in vain. In the *Rhetoric* (I 1, 1355a15–17) he states that "men have a sufficient natural instinct (πεφύκασιν) for what is true, and usually do arrive at the truth." Humans have likewise a natural propensity for what is good and noble; it is upon the shared experience of these that political partnership is established (Bonitz 1961, 836a34ff., 837a18ff.). Kullmann suggests that the "strong biological elements" of Aristotle's thought are not confined to the *Politics*; he points to Aristotle's repeated appeal to natural human impulses across a wide area of human activity in philosophy, morality and creativity in the *Metaphysics*, *Ethics* and *Poetics* (Kullmann 1998, 341). I propose that rather than characterize these activities as biological, it is Aristotle's intent to understand their nature as embracing not only humans' biological aspect, but also their metaphysical nature, since these are inseparable.

Kullmann refers to a distinction between *physis* understood in the general sense of *universitas rerum*, and as referring to the nature of a particular thing (1998, 339). Thus when Aristotle declares "Nature does nothing in vain," he would not be referring to individual natural things in the world, but to the overall economy of nature. However, for Aristotle the realist, nature has no existence apart from particular things that grow. His commitment is not to a universal Platonic law in light of which the world is interpreted; it is a profound insight, based upon his empirical observations as biologist, but also on his observation of human affairs and aspirations.

A biological interpretation of humans' political nature might suggest that it is their biological instinct to congregate, as a bird builds its nest and a spider weaves its web. While there is doubtless a biological foundation to humans' social character, the *ground* for their political engagement is, within an

Aristotelian framework, primarily rational with a metaphysical foundation. Language, as it were the tangible epiphenomenon of reason, an expression of rationality and vehicle of conceptualization, is the requisite medium of community, allowing us to articulate our thoughts and values, first for ourselves and second to fellow humans.

At the logical level it is correct to read Aristotle as offering through his definition a class description, setting humans apart from other animals; in this sense the definition is biological. His purpose, however, is to give the profound reason why humans are by nature political. It is true that humans constitute a distinct biological species, something which cannot be said, for example, of the gods. That does not mean that their essence is entirely biological. Humans are essentially biological, yet their essence or φύσις is not exclusively biological, but eminently rational and intellectual. Admittedly one might take the definition as referring to human beings in an exemplary or normative sense: they are "natural to a higher degree than other animals" (Inc. An. IV 4, 706a19–20; translation Farquharson; see also 706b10). For Aristotle human beings are the most natural animal: they most perfectly embody what it is to be an animal.

I suggest that the essential meaning of "political" is the distinctively human meaning. It is then applied by derivation and metaphorically—analogously and in a weaker sense—to ants and bees and other such beings.[10] We cannot say that bees live in *poleis*; we may observe parallel similarities between their collective life and mode of organization, and the manner in which humans dwell in cities, and thus validly apply the term "political" to nonintelligent creatures. Aristotle's definition indicates that it is part of man's nature to live in cities. The etymological connection between *politikon* and *polis* is clear. According to Cooper (1999, 357), Aristotle "means that human nature demands that, in general and as a normal thing, human beings live in cities of some sort: cities (*poleis*) themselves or citizens (*politai*) are explicitly mentioned . . . the etymological connection between *politikon* and *polis* is plainly in the forefront of Aristotle's mind." As R. G. Mulgan notes (1974, 439), since the word πολιτικά, *politika*, as used by Aristotle in *History of Animals,* cannot mean "belonging to the πόλις," most translators of this work resort to the word "social"—which simply implies a common group activity without specifying anything further either about the activity or the group. "But this obscures the fact that Aristotle is taking a word with a clear, literal sense, 'belonging to the πόλις,' and giving it a wider, metaphorical extension, meaning roughly speaking, 'belonging to a πόλις-like association.'"

According to Depew,

The worst mistake one can make about "political animal" is to think that this phrase picks out the defining essence of humankind, and to hold that in consequence Aristotle must be speaking metaphorically when he says that animals other than humans are political. (Depew 1995, 162)

Depew is correct in his criticism of Heidegger, Arendt (1958, 27), and others for locating the "defining essence of humankind" in man's political nature (cf. Kullmann 1998, 342–43). Although the phrase ζῷον λόγον ἔχον, *a living being that has reason,* was coined by later commentators, it approximates more satisfactorily to what one would expect an Aristotelian definition to be. Depew's criticism will not apply if we seek to derive humans' political nature, at least in part, from their rational nature.

The phrase "political animal" does not express the "defining essence of humankind." We may, however, legitimately conclude that their political nature inevitably ensues from humans' nature as material, biological, dependent animals, endowed not only with rationality, but with the intellectual power that provides them with an openness to their fellow humans, and the recognition of a common task. Conscious of this shared condition, and the obligation to make their way in the world, they recognize that their situation is one of shared solidarity, not solitary isolation. Human beings are by essence political animals since participation in life of the city is indispensable for the realisation of their well-being and happiness, the optimal attainment of human excellence and maximal exercise of virtue. While the term "political animal" does not define the essence of human nature, it indicates a uniquely human property (*Wesenseigenschaft*: Kullmann 1998, 351), as does—though clearly more significant than—laughter. In that sense the terms "human" and "political animal" are interchangeable.

Aristotle recognizes that in their natural state, compared with most animals, humans are physically weak (PA IV 10, 687a23–26; though his point is that manual dexterity and intelligence more than compensate). They are least well equipped for survival as regards food, shelter, and defense. They have the longest period of total dependence after birth, hence the prolonged need for family for survival. Of all animals they are the most dependent upon others of their species; this need is greatest for their mental development—the most obvious example being language—and this dependence is lifelong. Aristotle stresses the importance of language for humans' social nature and the formation of the polis. While *logos* refers primarily to the rational character of humans, it is the ground of language. To reason, deliberate, and articulate our thoughts we need language, which we can only learn in a community. Offering the deepest explanation for the existence of the polis and of the family, Aristotle does not refer to the practical needs of survival, but to shared participation or communication (κοινωνία) in such universals as good and bad, right and wrong. According to Aristotle, humans are political beings because they are by nature social, and this social nature is grounded through rationality upon a community of metaphysical values. We may speculate as to the order of priority between humans' rationality and their social character. It seems to me that humans' communicative and communal dispositions are essentially simultaneous. Aristotle appears to allot primacy to humans' rational character when he remarks that "just as statesmanship does not create human beings but having received them from nature makes use of them" (Pol. I 10, 1258a21–3).

In the *Nicomachean Ethics*, Aristotle provides a valuable insight into the personal motivation for society, in which he emphasizes the rational and metaphysical dimension:

> It is the consciousness of oneself as good that makes existence desirable, and such consciousness is pleasant in itself. Therefore a man ought also to share his friend's consciousness of his existence, and this is attained by their living together and by conversing and communicating their thoughts to each other (ἐν τῷ συζῆν καὶ κοινωνεῖν λόγων καὶ διανοίας); for this is the meaning of living together as applied to human beings, it does not mean merely feeding in the same place, as it does when applied to cattle. (NE IX 9, 1170b8–14)

In the *Politics* also he notes the importance of friendship for political partnership. All societies are the work of friendship, for it is friendship to choose to live together (Pol. III 5, 1280b38–39; IV 9, 1295b24). In the *Nicomachean Ethics* he goes so far as to declare:

> Friendship appears to be the bond of the polis; and lawgivers seem to set more store by it than they do by justice, for to promote concord, which seems akin to friendship, is their chief aim, while faction, which is enmity, is what they are most anxious to banish. And if men are friends, there is no need of justice between them; whereas merely to be just is not enough—a feeling of friendship also is necessary. Indeed the highest form of justice seems to have an element of friendly feeling in it. (NE VIII 1, 1155a22–28)

Dependence is therefore not the only reason for political partnership. Aristotle notes that even if a person were equipped with all the goods he desired, he would not wish to live alone: "Surely it is absurd to make the blessed man a solitary; for no one would choose to possess all good things on condition of being alone, since man is a political creature and one whose nature is to live with others" (NE IX 9, 1169b16–22; Ross's translation, modified).

In *Politics* IV we find an interesting variation on Aristotle's statement that man is by nature a political animal. He presents the paradoxical thesis that humans seek society not only when the necessities of life have been provided, but also when they cannot be provided. In the first condition, the aim of society (συζῆν) is the good life (τοῦ ζῆν καλῶς); in the second, political partnership (πολιτικὴν κοινωνίαν) is sought for the sake of mere life itself (τὸ ζῆν αὐτὸ μόνον). Bare life—living at subsistence level—must contain some element of value, provided it is not excessively burdened by hardship. He seems to imply that there is a sweetness and satisfaction simply in the fact of being alive, and that one of the delights is the fellowship of being that all people share together. The text is best cited in full:

> Man is by nature a political animal; and so even when men have no need of assistance from each other they none the less desire to live together. At the same time they are also brought together by common interest, so far as each achieves a share of the good life. The good life then is the chief aim of society, both collectively for all its members and individually; but they also come together and maintain the political partnership for the sake of life merely, for doubtless there is some element of value contained even in the mere state of being alive, provided that there is not too great an excess on the side of the hardships of life, and it is clear that the mass of mankind cling to life at the cost of enduring much suffering, which shows that life contains some measure of well-being and of sweetness in its essential nature. (Pol. III 6, 1278b19–30)

The point of this passage seems to be that political life is essentially sought without regard for the necessities of life. Not only do humans seek society when replete with the requirements of life; when deprived of the minimum necessities we also benefit from society, even when no physical gain is to be had.

Jean-Louis Labarrière suggests (2001, 108) that there is no intrinsic link between the two reasons given at *Politics* I 2 for man's social nature. According to Aristotle's first argument, man is destined to live in the city through a natural law governing the union of male and female; it is not a matter of agreement or convention. He subsequently argues that man is *more* political than other social animals,[11] since he not only has voice (φωνή) but also λόγος, intellect or reason, which permits him to apprehend good and bad, justice and injustice. However, it is precisely partnership in goodness and justice, as highlighted by the second argument, that makes possible the household and polis described in the first argument; animals do not form families or cities. There is no logical entailment between the first and second arguments. There is more importantly a material connection: humans enter into family partnerships for the same reason they enter political society—for the sake of the good life; both presuppose a community of goodness and justice (see Pol. I 2, 1253a16–18). There is an intrinsic and fundamental link between man's naturally social nature and the fact that he is endowed with *logos*.

For Aristotle the polis results inevitably from the kind of beings that we are. It is not the coincidental or arbitrary result of human compact or agreement, but has its origin in the essential and universal nature of human beings as such. It arises spontaneously wherever humans are found. We may thus reject the interpretation that the Greek citizen historically *became* a political animal during the apogee of the Greek polis.[12] At the other extreme we may reject the view that to be human in ancient Greek society was automatically to be a politically active citizen (cf. Gigon 1973, 13). Humans' sociality defines their place within the natural cosmic hierarchy, midway between beast and divinity. Brutes are unable to enter society: they lack the requisite openness to share common projects, ideals and values. The gods, on the other hand, entirely sufficient in themselves, have no need of association.[13] Human beings' situation between the two is precarious: "perfected, man is the best of animals; separated from law and justice he is the worst" (Pol. I 2, 1253a32–33; Jowett's translation).

Applying the categories of Aristotle's metaphysics, we are obliged to seek the origin and explanation for the polis in its constituents, in other words, in individual citizens. Neither the family, village, nor city contains within itself the principle of individuality or identity that defines *physis*. The polis is natural in a derived sense, having grown gradually—organically, as it were—from lesser associations, which it embraces and organizes into a structural unity. The polis is an outgrowth of the nature of individual citizens, as they establish ever wider spheres of relationship for their survival and fulfillment. The polis is a product of nature, having developed from the first forms of human association. It has grown accumulatively out of the family, clan and village; empirically it is the most advanced form of community, and humans are plainly dependent on it. The metaphysical ground of the polis is the need and capacity of its citizens: the conjunction of their reciprocal dependence and support.

We should not seek to diminish the strong biological elements in Aristotle's political anthropology, which, as Kullmann points out (1998, 341), are not confined to the *Politics*. If human beings were disembodied souls, they would not be political. Aquinas notoriously theorized that each angel might be considered a complete and distinct species, without need of others of its kind: it has no need for society (although as pure spirit it can communicate perfectly). Given that humans are in nature biological *and* rational/intellectual, their political nature is together determined by both essential aspects—in various combinations and at diverse levels. Kullmann writes (1998, 349): "The political polis is for Aristotle neither a purely rational construction in a Hegelian sense, nor merely a community of bees. It has something of both." While I entirely agree with this assertion, it seems to me that Kullmann introduces too sharp a separation between alternative biological and rational interpretations of humans' political nature as understood by Aristotle. I do not share the view of those who maintain that ζῷον as used by Aristotle in the political context has no biological connotation, because of their reluctance to rank human beings among the animals.[14] I merely question Kullmann's opposing assertion (1998, 338) that the context for Aristotle's definition in the *Politics* is first and foremost biological.

THE POLIS AS NATURAL

Aristotle repeatedly affirms that the polis exists "by nature" (Pol. I 2, 1252b30). It is "one of those things that exist by nature," "one of the things that are constituted according to nature" (ibid., 1253a2; VII 8, 1328a22). He likens the polis to an animal or living being (Pol. IV 4, 1291a24). Understandably there is considerable debate regarding the meaning of these assertions, since the polis is obviously not an individual natural substance. *Physis* (Φύσις) is the paradigm for *ousia* (οὐσία)—a living entity with an intrinsic principle of identity, growth and activity, and is also the exemplar of *eidos* (εἶδος), which profoundly determines the individual in its entirety as it unfolds from within. The polis is not φύσις in that sense, since it does not have a single principle of autonomous growth, but is composed of a multitude of individual substances.

Referring to the goal and purpose of the polis Aristotle declares: "That which each thing is when its growth is completed we speak of as being the nature (φύσις) of each thing, for instance of a man, a horse, a household" (Pol. I 1, 1252b32–1253a1). This statement is problematic, since the assumption could be that the polis, like the household, has its own *physis* or nature. But this is impossible, since neither may be counted among those things that "have within themselves a principle of movement and rest" (Pol. I 2, 1252b32–1253a1). While the polis has its origin in nature and provides for its citizens' natural development, it does not possess an immanent organic formal principle that governs its constituent material elements, directing them dynamically toward their telos. The polis certainly has a defining εἶδος, which may perhaps be understood after the manner of a work of art; it is more natural, however, than an artefact, since it emerges spontaneously as the result of intrinsic natural tendencies within its members. It would seem that Aristotle is speaking loosely when in *Politics* I he refers to the polis as φύσις. That the polis may not be viewed *simpliciter* as a natural entity is obvious from his analogy with the craft of the weaver or the shipwright who needs a suitable working material: "So also the statesman and the lawgiver ought to be furnished with their proper material in a suitable condition" (Pol. VII 4, 1326a3–5; see Keyt 1987, 55). One of the merits of Aristotle's naturalist explanation for the polis is that, though he was aware of the view that citizenship was a matter of choice and convention, he is using a richer concept than, say, Hobbes's view of the State as contravening man's natural condition (cf. Miller 1997, 29, 31).

Aristotle was familiar with the view that the law is nothing more than a covenant (συνθήκη), in Lycophron's view a surety of men's just claims on one another, but that it is not intended to make the citizens good and just. For Aristotle, good government must be concerned with political virtue and vice (περὶ δ' ἀρετῆς καὶ κακίας πολιτικῆς) (see Pol. III 9, 1280b5). He recognizes the practical difficulties involved, which sometimes lead to the belief that justice and goodness are conventions without real existence in the nature of things (NE I 3, 1094b14–16; Miller [1997, 37] refers here to Aristotle's "political naturalism"). Aristotle distinguishes: "Political justice (τὸ πολιτικὸν δίκαιον) is of two kinds, one natural, the other conventional. A rule of justice is natural that has the same validity everywhere, and does not depend on our accepting it or not" (NE V 7, 1134b18–20). He sees a parallel between the immutable laws of natural justice that have the same force everywhere, and those of the physical world: fire burns in the same manner in Greece as in Persia (ibid., b25–27). He is aware that rules of justice (natural and conventional) vary according to circumstances, but affirms that some of these are nonetheless laws of nature (ibid., b29–30).

CITIZEN AND SOCIETY

One of the charges made on occasion against Aristotle is that of totalitarianism. This is understandable in light of his assertion:

> We ought not to think that any of the citizens belongs to himself, but that all belong to the polis, for each is a part of the polis, and it is natural for the superintendence of the several parts to have regard to the superintendence of the whole. (Pol. VIII 1, 1337a27–30)

A variation is found in his statement: "the whole must necessarily be prior to the part" (Pol. I 2, 1253a20). Having asserted the importance of the family as providing the basic necessities of life, he states that "the polis is prior in nature to the household and to each of us individually" (ibid., a18–20). His analogy with a living organism illustrates not only the primacy of the polis in relation to its citizens, but also its natural character. Citizens are likened to the organs of the polis, fulfilling a subordinate role, which cannot function or survive apart from the body. When the body ceases to exist, one speaks ambiguously of its hands or feet, as of those of a sculpture. "All things are defined by their function and capacity, so that when they are no longer such as to perform their function they must not be said to be the same things, but to bear their names in an equivocal sense." Aristotle concludes: "It is clear therefore that the polis is also prior by nature to the individual; for if each individual when separate is not self-sufficient, he must be related to the whole polis as other parts are to their whole" (ibid., a20–27).[15]

We have seen why the polis may not be described as an individual natural substance; however, on the basis of similarity in certain respects between the natural organism and the polis we speak figuratively of the "body politic." The weakness of Aristotle's position is inherent in the metaphor. Insofar as the polis lacks a single animating principle as far as the most essential—life itself—is concerned, it resembles the statue or the deceased body (see PA I 1, 640b33–35; 641a17–21; cf. Gen. An. II 1, 734b24–25). The parallel between the body politic and a living organism may not be taken as implying that the members of the community resemble those of the physiological body whose purpose is entirely absorbed in subservience. Nor is there a hierarchic command structure between higher and lower members, since the polis is a community of equals and freemen (Pol. III 4, 1277b7–8).[16] The analogy of the polis as a living body is limited, and in the final analysis breaks down at the limit. Miller points out (1997, 30): "Certain terms such as 'nature,' 'prior,' and 'political' may be used in an imprecise manner." At most one may accept the analogy in respect to secondary activities that are exclusively social.

Aristotle has, needless to say, a nuanced view of the relation between the polis and its citizens. Newman (1950, II 230) emphasizes that he is less totalitarian than Plato: "the individual counts for more with him, and is less lost and swallowed up in the State." The polis is a multiplicity of citizens (Pol. III 1, 1274b41, II 2, 1261a18; cf. Sakellariou 1989, 229–232), not an undistinguished mass or artificial aggregate. It is a unity and a whole. It is a unity of individuals, each more unified than either family or polis (Pol. II 2, 1261a20–21). It is a whole composed of individuals, each an intrinsic and integral whole; the citizen is a ὅλον or integral unit, the polis a σύνολον or ensemble. The city is an accidental whole: not a chance multitude of people, but rather one that aims at self-sufficiency of life (Pol. VII 8, 1328b16–17). Although a unity and a whole, the polis is not simple or single, but differentiated from within and composed of dissimilars. "Not only does a city consist of a multitude of human beings, it consists of human beings differing in kind. A collection of persons all alike does not constitute a polis" (Pol. II 2, 1261a22–24, a29–30). Since they share a common goal he can say without contradiction that the city is a community of similar people whose purpose is the best life possible (Pol. VII 8, 1328a35–37). The polis is a partnership, with a continuity of community in spite of a continually changing membership. Aristotle reverses Heraclitus' image: the river remains the same though streams flow in and streams flow out. The principle of identity of the polis is its constitution (Pol. III 3, 1276a34–b1; see Newman 1950, II 41–44).

Aristotle's emphasis upon the status of citizens at the start of Book III seems to contradict the primacy of the polis which had been stressed in Book I. Simpson remarks (1998, 134): "It is tempting to claim that there are signs here of confusion and contradiction in Aristotle's text." While some commentators have suggested this, I believe that Simpson resolves the problem satisfactorily by pointing out that instead of confusion it is rather a difference of emphasis. "For the city, one may say, is prior [to the individual] as the whole to the parts that it perfects, but the citizens are prior [to the city] as the parts to the whole that they define. Individuals as individuals thus exist for the city (since it perfects them) but the city subsists in the individuals as citizens (since it *is* them)."

The city is a diversity ordered together as one; its unity is that of purpose, the good life of its members. It needs a unity of control, according to a minimum and maximum limitation of space suitable for efficient self-sufficiency; it differs from a nation, which is a society amorphously related by race and spatially dispersed. The aims of the polis go beyond defense and prosperity, so it is more than a trade alliance:

> All those who are concerned with good government take civic virtue and vice into their purview. Thus it is also clear that a polis truly so called, and not merely in name, must pay attention to virtue; for otherwise the community becomes merely an alliance, differing only in locality from the other alliances, those of alliances that live apart. (Pol. III 9, 1280b5–10; Rackham's translation, amended)

A city exists not for security or commerce, which though necessary are not sufficient. The polis is a "partnership of families and clans in living well" for the perfect and independent life (see ibid., b29–35). This constitutes the happy and noble life (τὸ ζῆν εὐδαιμόνως καὶ καλῶς); political society exists for noble actions and not merely for life in common (ibid., 1280b38–1281a4).

Aristotle warns against excessive unification of the polis: "It is certain that both the household and the polis must somehow be a unit, but not entirely" (Pol. II 5, 1263b31–32). Individual citizens retain their independence and autonomy: "The city is a partnership of free men" (Pol. III 4, 1279a21). Its unity is one of purpose: "The polis is a plurality, which should be united and made into a community by education" (Pol. II 5, 1263b36–37). The poet Simonides proclaims: "The polis teaches the man" (fr. 95; see Edmonds 1958, 337), and it is in the context of education that Aristotle argues that no citizen belongs to himself alone, but that all belong to the polis: "Inasmuch as the end for the whole polis is one, it is manifest that education also must necessarily be one and the same for all and that the superintendence of this must be public, and not on private lines" (Pol. VIII 1, 1337a21–27). The education of citizens is best achieved collectively; the good of each coincides with the good for all, but is only possible if citizens submit to a common regime. The polis exists for the sake of the individual citizen. It does not possess an end in itself, apart from its members; its only importance is that citizens depend upon it for their development, and ultimately their happiness. They retain their identity and differences. The unity of the family and the polis resembles a musical harmony which will be destroyed if reduced to unison, or a poetic rhythm that is lost if reduced to a single beat (Pol. II 5, 1263b31–35).

The question of the primacy of the polis occurs at the start of the *Nicomachean Ethics* (see NE I 1/2, 1094a1–b6), where Aristotle argues that Politics is primary among the sciences. The reason given is extrinsic: he asks which science deals with man's ultimate end or supreme good—that for the sake of which he desires everything else. Politics, he argues, is the master science for two reasons: first, it regulates the study of all other sciences in the polis, prescribing those which must be studied, by whom, and to what level; second, politics exploits all lesser arts or powers; even the most noble (ἐντιμοτάτας) are subordinate to it: military strategy, economics and rhetoric. His reasoning is that since politics employs all the other sciences and practical arts, legislating what citizens should and should not do, it embraces the goals of the other sciences and has as its end human beings' comprehensive good (see Woerner 1999). He affirms:

> The good of man must be the end of the science of Politics. For even though the good is the same for the individual and for the polis, nevertheless, the good of the polis is manifestly a greater and more perfect good, both to attain and to preserve. To secure the good only of one person is better than nothing; but to secure the good of a nation or a polis is a nobler and more divine achievement (κάλλιον δὲ καὶ θειότερον).

Politics is concerned, he remarks, with the noble and the just (τὰ δὲ καλὰ καὶ τὰ δίκαια) (NE I 2/3, 1094b6–15).[17]

There should be no conflict between the citizen and the polis. On the contrary, Aristotle suggests that personal happiness cannot exist without politics (NE VI 8, 1142a9–10). The happiness of the polis coincides with the happiness of each individual citizen (Pol. VII 2, 1324a5–8). The good constitution pursues alike the interest of the polis and the common welfare of citizens (Pol. III 13, 1283b40–42). We may assume Aristotle is stating his own view when he remarks: "If anybody accepts the individual as happy on account of his virtue, he will also say that the polis which is better morally is the happier" (Pol. VII 2, 1324a12–13). Again: "It is evident that that form of government is best in which every man, whoever he is, can act best and live happily" (Pol. VII 2, 1324a23–25, Jowett's translation). In the perfect polis, the virtue of the good man and that of the good citizen are necessarily the same (Pol. III 18, 1288a38–39). The collective virtue of the polis derives from the virtue of its citizens: "For even if it be possible for the citizens to be virtuous collectively without being so individually, the latter is preferable, since for each individual to be virtuous entails as a consequence the collective virtue of all" (Pol. VII 13, 1332a32–38). In harming himself or committing suicide, he remarks, the citizen commits an injustice to the polis (see NE V 11, 1138a4–14).

This argument for the primacy of politics (and the status it accords to political reasoning) seems contradicted when shortly afterward Aristotle distinguishes three possible modes of life: pleasure, politics, and contemplation (NE I 5, 1095b16–19). In the final book of the *Nicomachean Ethics* he confirms that the highest human happiness consists primarily in θεωρία, theory; the intellect is our highest capacity, and deals with the highest realities (see NE X 7, 1177a12–b4). We may ask how we should span the divide between man as active and contemplative. We find a hint in a cryptic remark in the *History of Animals* where, having distinguished between gregarious and solitary animals, he notes that man partakes of both characters. Man is the only animal that "dualizes" between solitary and social existence (HA I 1, 487b34–488a7; see Clark 1983, 98; Cooper 1999, 359f.). He exercises certain activities that can only be done individually; in contemplation he exercises his truest self, and most closely resembles divine reality (cf. Kullmann 1998, 360). Θεωρία (theory) is not a group activity, although Aristotle suggests that in the company of others we can engage in it for longer periods:

> A solitary man has a hard life, for it is not easy to keep up continuous activity by oneself; it is easier to do so with the aid of and in relation to other people. The good man's activity therefore, which is pleasant in itself, will be more continuous if practised with friends. (NE IX 9, 1170a5–6)

The polis is prior in that it provides the means necessary for the citizen to exercise precisely this kind of independent activity and attain full perfection as an individual. The priority of the polis is that of a necessary condition, without which humans could neither survive nor prosper.

The polis relates to the kinds of beings we are in a dual sense. It is the highest historical instantiation of human beings' dependence on relationships in family, clan and village for their survival and fulfillment; they depend on it entirely if they are to achieve their highest development. The essential point of its continuance lies in this conjunction of citizens' needs with their abilities: their dependence on each other and their capacities to afford each other support. The sense in which the polis is primary to the citizen takes a nuanced view of individuals. It depends on them and their participation, but they need the city in a sense so profound that they could not be themselves without it. Our social and political nature is grounded in our dependence on each other: *logos*, the capacity to reason and communicate, can only be acquired in a community. The deepest aspect of our dependence on family and polis is thus our shared participative communication in standards of good and bad, right and wrong. Politics and political reasoning are in this sense supreme: not only do they make use of all others, their aim is human beings' comprehensive good in the form of life fundamental to them.

NOTES

1. While page and line numbers follow the standard Bekker text, chapter numbers are cited according to the revised Oxford translation, ed. Jonathan Barnes. When citing translations from Aristotle I have substituted "polis" for "state."

2. While I use the terms "description" and "definition" interchangeably here, Aristotle should not be taken as offering a strict definition (see below).

3. Referring to Pol. I 2, 1252b27–1253a38, Alasdair MacIntyre remarks (1988, 96–97): "This is a passage whose importance for the interpretation of everything that Aristotle wrote about human life cannot be underrated, and it is peculiarly crucial for understanding his claims about justice, practical reasoning, and their relationship."

4. Pol. I 2, 1252a24–5. Aristotle adopts a different approach at PA I 1, 640a10–640b4.

5. Otherwise, he states, "a collection of slaves or of lower animals would be a polis, but as it is, it is not a polis, because slaves and animals have no share in well-being or in purposive life" (Pol. III 9, 1280a31–34).

6. *Iliad* IX 63; see Pol. I 2, 1253a5, trans. Rackham.

7. Sophocles, *Philoctetes*, 1018; see Roberts 1989, 200 (n. 20).

8. Cf. Finley (1991, 24): "In the *Politics* Aristotle defined man as a *zōon politikon*, and what that meant is comprehensible only in the light of his metaphysics."

9. Aristotle refers to the social behavior of cranes, which emigrate from the steppes of Scythia to the source of the Nile in the marshes of Egypt. As well as a leader, signalers patrol the flock for cohesion; at night, the leader keeps watch and cries an alert in the event of danger. See HA VIII 12, 597a3–6; IX 10, 614b18–26. Plato had already noted the "political" character of bees, wasps and ants (*Phaedo* 82b5–8).

10. Kullmann correctly states: "Aristoteles war überzeugt, daß die Sozialstrukturen bestimmter Tiere mit denen der Menschen Ähnlichkeiten haben" (1998, 338). The question, however, is whether such similarities point to a political capacity in the full sense of the term: whether "political" is affirmed of other animals literally or figuratively.

11. At HA VIII 1, 589a1–2, Aristotle uses the term "more political" as a comparative term among nonhuman animals. He notes that while some animals terminate

contact with their offspring after birth or first nourishment and have no further association with them, "those that have more understanding and possess some memory continue their association, and have a more political (πολικώτερον) relationship with their offspring" (trans. Balme, modified).

12. The view of B. H. Bengston, as discussed by Kullmann 1991, 94 (fn. 2). Despite its common usage, the term "city-state" is unsatisfactory. It is itself a literal translation of the German *Stadtstaat*, used first in 1765 by Herder to translate *polis*. *Stadtstaat* distinguished a city that was also a state in the German empire from the *Stadt* or city-settlement. The acceptance of the English equivalent was largely due to the classical scholar William Warde Fowler; see Sakellariou 1989, 19–20.

13. Pol. I 2, 1253a27–29. In Alasdair MacIntyre's phrase (1988, 98), "Separated from the polis, what could have been a human being becomes instead a wild animal."

14. This view takes support from Aristotle's reference to God as the "best eternal living being," ζῷον ἀΐδιον ἄριστον: Met. XII 7, 1072b29.

15. Aristotle convincingly employs the analogy to illustrate the strength of democracy in the collective wisdom of its citizens: "Where there are many, each individual, it may be argued, has some portion of virtue and wisdom, and when they have come together, just as the multitude becomes a single man with many feet and many hands and many senses, so also it becomes one personality as regards the moral and intellectual faculties. This is why the general public is a better judge of the works of music and those of the poets, because different men can judge a different part of the performance, and all of them all of it" (Pol. III 11, 1281b4–10; see also b34–38).

16. Höffe (2001, 23, 25) points out that Aristotle already had the recently revived concept of subsidiarity: higher organs of society support the independence of its inferiors.

17. Cf. Pol. I 2, 1253a15–18, where Aristotle says that it is partnership in goodness and justice that makes the household and polis. The *Politics* also opens with the declaration that the city or political community aims at the supreme human good (Pol. I 1, 1252a1–7). In the *Nicomachean Ethics* Aristotle compares the ad hoc and sectional partnerships that arise among humans: "But all these associations seem to be subordinate to the association of the Polis, which aims not at a temporary advantage but at one covering the whole of life. . . . All these associations then appear to be parts of the association of the Polis" (NE VIII 9, 1160a20–23, 28–30). A different perspective is offered at NE VI 7, 1141a20–22, a33–b1: "It is absurd to think that Political Science or Prudence is the loftiest kind of knowledge, inasmuch as man is not the highest thing in the world. . . . It may be argued that man is superior to the other animals, but this makes no difference: since there exist other things far more divine in their nature than man."

REFERENCES

Arendt, Hannah. 1958. *The Human Condition.* Chicago: University of Chicago Press.
Aristotle. 1963. *De Anima.* Trans. by J. A. Smith. Oxford: Clarendon Press. (First publ. 1931.)

———. 2002. *Historia Animalium.* Ed. and trans. by David M. Balme. Cambridge: Cambridge Press.

———. 1965. *De Partibus Animalium.* Trans. by William Ogle. Oxford: Oxford University Press. (First publ. 1912.)

———. 1965. *De Generatione Animalium.* Trans. by Arthur Platt. Oxford: Oxford University Press. (First publ. 1912.)

———. 1998. *Nicomachean Ethics.* Trans. by W. D. Ross. Oxford: Oxford University Press.

———. 1966. *Politica.* Trans. by Benjamin Jowett. Oxford: Clarendon Press. (First publ. 1921.)

———. 1946. *Rhetorica.* Trans. by W. Rhys Roberts. Oxford: Clarendon Press.

Bien, Günther. 1973. *Die Grundlegung der politischen Philosophie bei Aristoteles.* Freiburg, Munich: Alber.

Bodéüs, Richard. 1985. "L'animal politique et l'animal économique." In *Aristotelica: Mélanges offerts à M. De Corte,* ed. by A. Motte and Ch. Rutten, 65–81. Brussels: Éditions Ousia / Liege: Presses Universitaires.

Bonitz, Hermann. 1961. *Index Aristotelicus.* Darmstadt: Wissenschaftliche Buchgesellschaft. Repr. of the 1870 edition.

Clark, Stephen R. L. 1983. *Aristotle's Man: Speculations upon Aristotelian Anthropology.* Oxford: Clarendon Press. (1st ed. 1975.)

Cooper, John M. 1999. *Reason and Emotion: Essays on Ancient Moral Psychology and Ethical Theory.* Princeton: Princeton University Press.

Depew, David J. 1995. "Humans and Other Political Animals in Aristotle's *History of Animals.*" *Phronesis* 40 (2): 156–181.

Edmonds, John M., ed. 1958. *Lyra Graeca.* Vol. 2: *Stesichorus, Ibycus, Anacreon, and Simonides.* London: Heinemann.

Finley, Moses I. 1991. *Politics in the Ancient World.* Cambridge: Cambridge University Press. (1st ed. 1983.)

Höffe, Otfried. 2001. "Aristoteles' Politische Anthropologie." In *Aristoteles: Politik,* ed. by Otfried Höffe, 21–35. Berlin: Akademie Verlag.

Gigon, Olof. 1973. *Aristoteles: Politik.* Munich: Deutscher Taschenbuch Verlag.

Keyt, David. 1987. "Three Fundamental Theorems in Aristotle's Politics." *Phronesis* 32 (1): 54–79.

Kullmann, Wolfgang. 1991. "Man as a Political Animal in Aristotle." In *A Companion to Aristotle's Politics,* ed. by David Keyt and Fred D. Miller Jr., 94–117. Oxford: Blackwell's.

———. 1998. *Aristoteles und die moderne Wissenschaft.* Stuttgart: Steiner.

Labarrière, Jean–Louis. 2001. "Aristote penseur de la différence entre l'homme et l'animal." *Anthropozoologica* 33–34: 105–112.

Lennox, James G. 2001. "Nature Does Nothing in Vain . . . " In *Aristotle's Philosophy of Biology: Studies in the Origins of Life Science,* by James G. Lennox, 205–223. Cambridge: Cambridge University Press.

MacIntyre, Alasdair. 1988. *Whose Justice? Which Rationality?* Notre Dame: University of Notre Dame Press.

Miller, Fred D., Jr. 1997. *Nature, Justice, and Rights in Aristotle's Politics*. Oxford: Clarendon Press.

Mulgan, Richard G. 1974. "Aristotle's Doctrine That Man Is a Political Animal." *Hermes* 120: 438–45.

Newman, William L. 1950. *The Politics of Aristotle* (of 1887), ed. with an introd., two prefatory essays and notes critical and explanatory. Vol. I–III. Oxford: Clarendon Press.

Ritter, Joachim. 1969. *Metaphysik und Politik*. Frankfurt: Suhrkamp.

Roberts, Jean. 1989. "Political Animals in the *Nicomachean Ethics*." *Phronesis* 34: 185–204.

Rowe, Christopher J. 2000. "Aristotle For and Against Democracy." In *Political Equality and Justice in Aristotle and the Problems of Contemporary Society,* ed. by Demetrios N. Koutras, 408–416. Athens: To Lykeion.

Sakellariou, Michael B. 1989. *The Polis-State: Definition and Origin*. Athens/Paris: National Hellenic Research Foundation/De Boccard.

Simpson, Peter L. Phillips. 1998. *A Philosophical Commentary on the Politics of Aristotle*. Chapel Hill: University of North Carolina Press.

Verbeke, Gerard. 1983. *Moral Education in Aristotle*. Washington: Catholic University of America Press.

Woerner, Markus. 1999. "Elements of an Aristotelian Theory of Political Discourse." In *Aristotle's Political Philosophy and Its Influence,* ed. by Demetrios N. Koutras, 56–73. Athens: To Lykeion.

Chapter Two

Pragmatics and the Idea of the Illocutionary in Stoic Language Theory

Karlheinz Hülser

In his William James Lectures, published in 1962 under the title *How to Do Things with Words,* J. L. Austin drew universal attention to linguistic doing, and thus inaugurated modern speech-act theory. He must have been quite aware of breaking new ground, for he chose a very considerate method of making his audience acquainted with his ideas. Nevertheless, he hesitated to claim complete novelty for his views, declaring at the start:

> The phenomenon to be discussed is very widespread and obvious, and it cannot fail to have been already noticed, at least here and there, by others. Yet I have not found attention paid to it specifically. (Austin 1976, 1)

The phenomenon had indeed been observed already, and very much earlier: it had been reflected upon in antiquity. The Stoics in particular discussed it in more than merely superficial terms. That Austin did not notice this, is quite understandable. Stoic language theory flourished during the third and second centuries B.C. That was a long time ago, and only a very few fragments of these Stoic considerations survive. In Austin's time, these sources were so difficult to access as well as so sporadically commented upon that it would have been a miracle if he had come across the relevant documents.[1] In the meantime it has become easier to access these texts. To investigate them in the present context is all the more appropriate, since Markus H. Woerner showed in *Performative und sprachliches Handeln* (1978) how fruitful it can be systematically to discuss milestone contributions to speech-act theory very carefully—in his case the contributions by J. L. Austin. Those by the Stoics, milestones too, though less developed, form the subject of the present chapter.

Such an enterprise presupposes that in Stoicism the phenomenon of linguistic doing actually was at least a theme. That this was really the case shows best in the Stoic theory of lekta, right at the center of the Stoic philosophy of language. The term *lekta* itself is a plural term; the singular is *lekton*. Literally translated it stands for "what is" or "can be said." As Diogenes Laertius points out in his systematic survey of Stoic dialectics, the Stoics declared the lekton to be "what subsists in accordance with a rational presentation,"[2] and they subdivided lekta into complete lekta and incomplete ones.

While only predicates are named as instances of incomplete lekta, in the case of the complete lekta Diogenes submits a striking list. He enumerates "propositions, syllogisms, interrogations, and inquiries," and somewhat later lists further types: the command, the adjurative, the optative, the address, and others. Moreover he explicates the various complete lekta (also alluded to as "things") by describing them as well as by giving examples. The command, for instance, is said to be "a thing of such a kind that by saying it we command it, e.g., 'Go thou to the waters of Inachus!'" Roughly half the complete lekta on the list are described in this way, among them the proposition and the address (DL 7, 62f. 65–68 = FDS 696, 874): the schematics of their description itself suggests that linguistic doing belonged to the scope of the theory of lekta. Certain types of complete lekta and the doing of certain things are interrelated in a way that is relevant to speech-act theory.

Stimulated by these observations, in the sources for Stoic dialectics we discover more material that is interesting for speech-act theory. Sextus Empiricus reports quite similarly on the definition of the lekta and on their division (AM 8, 69ff. = FDS 876). Diogenes Laertius adds that the Stoics declared all propositions, without any exception, to be either true or false, but that all the other complete lekta are neither true nor false (DL 7, 65–68 = FDS 874; also SE, AM 8, 11f. = FDS 67). And some sources clearly show that the Stoics made further theoretical use of speech acts. For instance, they differentiated both some of the lekta and the so-called moods of the verb by referring to the *use* of linguistic units.[3]

Although this material has been investigated from various points of view, for example, in comprehensive studies by G. Nuchelmans (1973) and D. Schenkeveld (1984), some crucial questions remain unanswered. One of them is how many complete lekta the Stoics differentiated, and from what point of view. Of course, compared to similar Aristotelian or Peripatetic differentiations of various forms of speech, the Stoics' list seems to be rather extensive, and Schenkeveld offers explanations for the list's increase until it standardly included about a dozen items (1984, 322–324). But there the syllogisms are ignored, though they are called complete lekta too, and hence tend to confuse the boundaries reconstructed for the Stoic list. Another crucial question is why the Stoics wished to extend the scope of dialectics so that it included speech acts.

In the present chapter I shall argue, first, that Stoic semantics embraces a fundamental pragmatic component. As a rule, to say something is to do something that exceeds mere uttering (cf. Austin 1976, 92–96; Woerner 1978, 90f. 97). In this very general and basic sense, speech acts were central to the Stoics' philosophy of language and were accounted for in their concept of the lekton. Thus far, the theory of lekta covers a potentially limitless number of speech acts.

Second, if this is correct, the list of complete lekta handed down to us reveals a puzzle. While it seemed too long to Ammonius and to other commentators on Aristotle (cf. FDS 897ff.), it now appears to be surprisingly short, since it cannot be intended to reduce the vast diversity of speech acts to a dozen or so types of acts. Hence, the list is a selection that is not governed only by the idea that speaking is doing; it must have been determined by additional aspects too.

Third, to bridge the gap from the limitless pragmatic aspect of the theory of lekta to the relatively short standard list of complete lekta, we shall attempt to apply the idea of the illocutionary and show to what degree it explains the Stoic list. The quasi-propositions, unexplained so far, require a different approach, in part reminding us of Austin's performatives.

Finally, we shall see that there are further challenges in Stoic speech-act theory, concerning interpretation as well as concerning the concept of the illocutionary.

1. STOIC DIALECTICS AND THE SPEECH-ACT VIEW

The Stoics, then, tried to account for linguistic doing in the most general and basic sense, pointed out above. Several instances of direct evidence in the sources demonstrate this thesis, and do so in three ways. The first group of instances shows that linguistic doing belongs to the scope of Stoic dialectics from the beginning, the second that linguistic doing plays a crucial role in the explication of the lekta, whereas the third consists of corroborations that the diagnosis presented so far is underpinned by a number of significant detailed observations.

Linguistic Doing and Stoic Dialectics

Following a suggestion coming from the academy of Xenocrates, the Stoics divided philosophy from the very first into three parts: logic, ethics and physics. But they transcended Xenocrates's ideas by establishing logic as that part of philosophy that embraced all studies concerning the form of speech and scientific or educated procedure (cf. Hirzel 1879, 62–76). Logic in this Stoic sense was subdivided into rhetoric and dialectics, sometimes additionally into the doctrine of recognition and that of definition. "Dialectics" in turn was coined predominantly by Chrysippus (281/77–208/04 B.C.); according to him it deals with the "signifying" on the one hand, and with the "signified," "things," or the "lekta" on the other hand. The latter are subclassified into complete and incomplete lekta, and within the context of the complete lekta we find the perspicuous results of the speech-act considerations mentioned above.[4]

To discuss those in the context of "logic" or dialectics was new and not self-evident move. What Protagoras and other sophists contributed to the topic were at best preliminary observations.[5] Aristotle was the first to draw relevant distinctions. Specifying the subject of his *De interpretatione* he explicated a λόγος/*logos*/speech as a texture of words, and differentiated several species of it. Every *logos*, he said, points something out or has a meaning; yet not every *logos* is an assertive one and true or false; the prayer, for instance, "is a sentence, but is neither true nor false." The succeeding inquiry would concern solely the assertive *logos*; all other types of sentences might be dismissed, since their discussion "belongs rather to the study of rhetoric or of poetry."[6] But even there Aristotle reflected on them only briefly, without systematic inquiry and without troubling about an homogeneous terminology.[7]

With his immediate successors, little changed. We have no indicators that the Peripatetics studied the nonassertive types of speech in greater detail or that they made significant contributions to any connected topics, either speech-act theory or the doctrine of the moods of the verb. Only at about 500 A.D. do we learn from Ammonius Hermeiou's commentaries on Aristotle that the Peripatetics usually acknowledged five "types of speech" (εἴδη λόγου/*eidē logou*).[8] They might already have done so some time before Ammonius. But how long before? It is quite improbable that this tradition will reach back to the second century A.D. At any rate, in Alexander of Aphrodisias' commentaries on Aristotle nothing of this kind can be found; far from it: in connection with the definition of the syllogism his argument points in almost the opposite direction (cf. Schenkeveld 1984, 297–299).

Thus it was a very unusual step to include in the field of dialectics not only propositions and syllogisms but also all the other complete lekta, and to expose in some detail nonstatemental forms of speaking as well as speech acts. Obviously this happened with intent. In Stoicism it belonged to the themes foreseen in the logical part of philosophy from the outset. Posidonius at the latest actually reformulated the definition of dialectics in this sense. He explicitly included in its field those things that cannot be true or false. According to him dialectics is "the science dealing with that which is true, which is false, and which is neither true nor false."[9]

Linguistic Doing and the Lekta

According to Chrysippus, dialectics deals with the "signifying" on the one hand and with the "signified" on the other, with linguistic means of expression on the one hand and with the expression of content, the "said" or the "lekta" on the other. To explain this distinction, the Stoics refer, Sextus tells us, to the situation of a foreigner who does not speak the language of his guest country, and to a layperson amidst a group of experts. Both foreigner and layperson realize *that* the others are speaking, but are unable to understand *what* is said (SE, AM 8, 12 = FDS 67; 1, 155 = FDS 514). According to this explanation, the Stoics resort to the general human competence of language and speaking in order to make the distinction between the signifying and the signified, between speech and lekton. This general competence includes the faculty of identifying language as such even if the content remains cryptic. In everyday life we meet many cases in point, and everybody is familiar with them. What remains from language in these cases is the Stoic "signifying." What is missing, however, is the "signified" or lekton. It comprises not only the semantic meaning of an utterance but in addition, and fundamentally, also the purpose of it, as the example of the layperson and the experts conclusively shows. What he or she fails to understand is not just what the others are talking about but also what their interaction is doing or achieving. To this extent, lekta are conceptualized on the basis of linguistic pragmatics.

However, linguistic acting is not only involved in the concept of lekta, it is crucial for their differentiation as well. Diogenes explains the division of lekta into complete and incomplete ones as follows: "Incomplete are those the enunciation of which is unfinished, as e.g., 'writes'; for we inquire 'Who?' Complete on the other hand are those lekta the enunciation of which is finished, as e.g. 'Socrates writes'" (DL 7, 63 = FDS 696; trans. Hicks). Certainly, one would have wished for a more extensive explanation with respect to the shift from the level of lekta to the level of utterances, as well as to the distinguishing mark "finished/unfinished." But so far it is clear at least that a person who merely utters "writes" at best provokes questions; as long as nothing and nobody is pointed out who is referred to as writing, the speaker is not really doing anything that would exceed the utterance. This happens only with a complete lekton, in other words, if by one's utterance one makes a statement, puts a question, formulates a wish, or does anything else.

Finally, the aspect of linguistic acting is even embraced by the further differentiation of the complete lekta. I have already mentioned the scheme the Stoics often used in order to characterize the individual complete lekta, which involves the interrelation of complete lekta and linguistic action. In addition I would like particularly to point out the proposition and the address.

The proposition (*axiōma*) should be mentioned since Chrysippus defined it as "a complete lekton capable of being asserted as far as this depends upon [the assertable lekton] itself" (DL 7, 65 = FDS 874; Gellius, NA XVI, 8, 4 = FDS 877). Because of its final clause this definition is notoriously difficult to understand. According to Bobzien it means that propositions (*axiōmata*) are complete lekta which are capable of being asserted only for their own sake, that is (among other things), only for the purpose of being asserted, without additional actions and without any indication of subsequent actions as is the case with questions, commands and the like (1986, 12f.; 1999, 93f.; 2003, 85–87). The address on the other hand is a significant special case, for instance the address "Most glorious son of Atreus, Agamemnon, lord of men."[10] This does not include a predicate, nor an incomplete lekton. Yet it is in itself a complete lekton, apparently since it is appropriately usable in order to attract Agamemnon's attention. Here too, what is to be achieved by the utterance is important for the meaning of the formulation.

Further Corroborations

Linguistic acting belonged to the scope of the logical part of philosophy from the outset, and it was also of some importance for the subdivision of dialectics and of the lekta. Correspondingly the Stoic dialecticians turned their attention to the nonasserting lekta at an early stage. In the case of Chrysippus the list of his writings proves that he not only composed many books on the various types of propositions, but also wrote a number of works on commands, on yes/no-questions, inquiries, and answers respectively, and one book on explanatory lekta (DL 7, 191, 196 = FDS 194). Comparable titles by other Stoics are unknown, but occasionally they joined in the discussion. This can safely be attested for Cleanthes, one of the representatives of the pre-chrysippean Stoa; he commented on the oath (cf. FDS 905). In the second century B.C., Diogenes the Babylonian and Antipater of Tarsus wrote their handbooks, respectively *On voice* and *On linguistic expression and what is said* (DL 7, 55, 57 = FDS 197f.). Schenkeveld assumes that at least Antipater commented on questions concerning speech act theory, when discussing the adverb (1984, 342f.). Posidonius (ca. 135–51/50 B.C.) not only had an opinion on the definition of dialectics, but also enlarged the list of the complete lekta by differentiating the *hypothesis* and the *ekthesis*—certainly "in order to clarify the difference between their functions" (Schenkeveld 1984, 323).

Furthermore we should note here that the Stoics rudimentarily differentiated the so-called moods of the verb. In doing so they considered the various grammatical forms or predicates according to their typical uses. For instance, the predicate ὀργίζεσθε/*orgizesthe*, being primarily incomplete, was considered, according to its employment, a command predicate ("Be angry!") or a declarative predicate in the indicative mood ("You are angry").[11]

Next, discussing Stoic ideas Plutarch not only makes use of but also stresses the fact that in our utterances we are regularly doing something that exceeds the uttering itself. Indeed his remark also clarifies the fact that there are conventions for the more detailed specification of what we do in and by an utterance; the Stoics seem to have been well aware of this. For, according to Plutarch, they said

> that those who pronounce a prohibition say one thing, prohibit another, and prescribe a third: for example, he who says "Do not steal" says just this, "Do not steal," but he prohibits stealing and prescribes not stealing. . . . Furthermore, they say that the physician's prescription to his pupil to cut and cauterize is given with ellipsis of the phrase "in due time and measure" and the musician's to play the lyre and sing with ellipsis of the phrase "in tune and in time"; that is why the pupils who have performed inartistically and poorly are chastised, for "correctly" was implied in the prescription and they performed incorrectly.[12]

Finally, there have survived from Chrysippus various passages of book III of his *Logical investigations*. There he discusses some topics specific for propositions, but also considers other complete lekta.[13] For instance he is interested in requests like "Go for a walk, since it is day!" "Go for a walk, otherwise sit down!" "Do either this or that!" and he realizes that these commands can be extended at will ("Do this, if not, then do that, if not, then do that, . . . then do that"). These examples are taken from everyday life; people giving such orders are indeed doing something and acting somehow. That utterances of this kind are appropriate to perform effective speech acts is clear in advance, and in col. XII, 19f. Chrysippus explicitly refers to the common usage of language. The scheme of these commands, however, allows modification only within rather narrow limits and must not be interpreted arbitrarily. For, as Chrysippus observes, formations like "This man is going for a walk, if not, then he is sitting," linguistically end up spinning their wheels, as it were; they are fruitless. In this statement, practicability in everyday life is considered to be a preferential criterion of sense. Furthermore Chrysippus considers that it would be altogether impossible to adjust a formation like "to go for a walk, if not, to sit" such that it could be used as a unitary command (PHerc 307 = FDS 698: col. XII; Marrone 1997, 94f.). This may or (under certain circumstances) may not be the case; the decisive point is whether there are conventions according to which a person speaking in this manner is doing something; and this aspect is included in the completeness of the lekta.

Apart from this, dialectical discourse proceeds by means of yes/no questions. In Aristotle a premise (πρότασις/*protasis*) therefore is strictly speaking an answered yes/no question. Moreover each proposition can be transformed into a yes/no question which in turn can be reformulated as an inquiry: "It is day," / "Is it day?" / "Is it day or is it not?." At least with regard to propositions and yes/no questions it is appropriate not just to study the various complete lekta separately but to be mindful of how far they are systematically connected with one another. Up to a certain degree this holds true for propositions and commands or other complete lekta too, as far as there are comparable possibilities for transformation. Chrysippus apparently paid attention to those interrelations. This is revealed by the column from his *Logical investigations* just mentioned as well as by the following one.

Furthermore, with regard to speech-act theory it will be convenient to take into account that the Stoics also called the "signified" or the "lekton" a πρᾶγμα/*pragma*, which term in its etymology points directly to action. This clue was followed by Nuchelmans.

2. ON THE INTERPRETATIONS BY NUCHELMANS AND SCHENKEVELD

Nuchelmans's Reconstruction

Gabriel Nuchelmans appears to have been the first to study Stoic speech-act theory in more detail and to discuss, among the propositions, the other complete lekta too (1973, 45–87, esp. 62–67). First, he asked what might have enticed the Stoics not only to turn their attention to propositions but to extend it to all speech acts or indeed to all lekta. Second, he wondered why the lekta were additionally qualified as signified or meanings (σημαινόμενα/ *sēmainomena*), as intended things (πράγματα/*pragmata*) and as incorporeal (ἀσώματα/*asōmata*).

As to the first point, he states that in dialectical discourse, question and answer are closely interrelated. In the yes/no questions and in the corresponding propositions the "thing" would be precisely the same

> and also everything that complements the *pragma*. The only difference is that in the one case the complex is used to express a question, which cannot be true or false, and that in the other case it is used to express a true or false assertion. . . . Once yes-or-no questions and assertions had become the object of a special branch of study, it was only natural to pay some attention to other complete *lekta* as well, if only to contrast them with the two privileged ones. (1973, 62f.)

With regard to his second question Nuchelmans starts from certain predicates and propositions, and produces a multilevel answer. Initially he reconstructs the interlinkage of the four terms for simple predications by means of verbs expressing an activity or an undergoing. In the framework of these propositions the Stoic doctrine of cause and effect offers itself to explicate the connection. Zeno of Citium, the founder of the Stoa, had already considered a cause (αἴτιον/*aition*) to be what was, as a consequence of Stoic influence, later widely seen in the same way: as a thing through the activity of which an effect is produced. According to Stoic analysis this "cause thing" is corporeal; the effect, however, is incorporeal. Represented linguistically, the former comes out as a noun and the latter as a verb signifying an activity or an undergoing. What is said by it, the associated lekton, its meaning, is therefore an incorporeal predicate; moreover it is a πρᾶγμα/*pragma*, in other words, etymologically: an activity or an undergoing. Even the later Greek grammarians kept up this basic meaning for *pragma*, which no doubt had some relevance too for the Stoics themselves when they divided the predicates into active and passive ones (ὀρθὰ/*ortha* vs. ὕπτια/*hyptia*).

The conceptual interrelation determined by this reconstruction has yet to be modified if propositions including other types of predicates are formed, or if propositions are logically interconnected. Moreover this conceptual interrelation is overstrained as soon as not only propositions are concerned but other complete lekta too. In all these cases it has to be argued anew why what is said should be incorporeal and a *pragma*.

In the case of the complete lekta, Nuchelmans allows himself to be guided by the Stoic pattern of explanation described above in the introduction: "There is a *pragma* which is said and there is a certain kind of speech act which determines the specific character of the *pragma* said." Referring to a number of sources, Nuchelmans works out in more detail "that the *pragma* or *lekton* was at least primarily the asomatic action or passion signified by the verb." Apparently Nuchelmans is thinking of verbs like "to assert," "to ask," "to wish" or "to beg," perhaps also of verbs like "to warn" or "to baptize," in short of verbs which characterize a speech act and may count as cases of linguistic acting in the sense of the Stoic paradigm of definition. In the performance of a speech act of this kind, something is said that possibly could be said in the performance of a different speech act too. It was the *pragma* or *lekton* said—"viewed in abstraction from the different speech acts in which it can play a role" (1973, 64). Accordingly the definition of a complete lekton would have been formed originally from such a *pragma* or *lekton* "as action or passion which is said" as the generic element, and from a reference to the speech act as the specific difference. "In general the principle of division was difference of speech activity. Formal differences, of mood for instance, play only a secondary role" (1973, 65).

Although the propositions and the other complete lekta are approximated so far, there still remain the many cases where the verbs neither signify an action nor a passion nor a speech act. Nuchelmans therefore assumes that there were gradual modifications in the use of the terms ἀσώματον/*asōmaton* and πρᾶγμα/*pragma*. In the case of *pragma* the commitment to an action or passion would have been abandoned, and one would have used the word quite generally to signify "a thing thought," "something that is merely thought" (1973, 67); in the case of *asōmaton* the meaning and use would have been modified so that the word does not primarily refer to an effect but rather to something inaccessible to the senses. Through this shift to a more general meaning the four terms could be considered interconnected without taking the earlier restrictions into account. At this point, however, the interconnectedness of the four terms loses its impact. It now appears only in a special case, that is, only if the sentence thematizes a cause/effect relation or a speech act. In this case the aspects pointed out on the basic level of the reconstruction occur as merely *additional* points of view, not as fundamental. Seen from this vantage point, a form of address, for instance, like "Most honoured son of Atreus, lord of the warriors, Agamemnon" (DL 7. 67 = FDS 874), would have to be read as "a *pragma* of such a kind that if a person says it he will address somebody";

> this must . . . mean that it is a thought which a person expresses in the speech act of addressing somebody, or that it is that which a person means when he addresses somebody in these words. All the examples of complete lekta can be read in this way. (Nuchelmans 1973, 67)

Why We Should Study Not Only Propositions but All Complete Lekta

As to the question what caused the Stoics' interest in lekta different from the propositional ones, Dirk Schenkeveld agreed with Nuchelmans at least in part: "Nuchelmans . . . is right in seeing the starting-point of the Stoic doctrine of complete *lekta* in the study of yes-or-no questions and the answers that are given to them." But with regard to the associated amplification of attention to all of the complete lekta, Schenkeveld was hesitant: "One wonders how natural this process, in fact, is" (Schenkeveld 1984, 319). He looked for different ways to explain the enlargement of the list of dialectical topics, yet without discovering much:

> A specific reason cannot be detected; we can only surmise that a great interest in language, together with an endeavour to cover the whole field of philosophy in one consistent system, led the Stoics to research into these kinds too. (1984, 324)

With respect to our earlier observations this is not surprising. If indeed linguistic acting was within the focus of Stoic dialectics from the beginning, there need hardly have been a specific reason to amplify the horizon gradually. If questions really formed the starting point, then this was not because they too occurred in dialectical discourse (since this had already been the case in the Academy and with Aristotle), but most likely because the Stoics looked at them with an amplified theoretical interest. It is an intriguing question whether the sophisms, a central theme of dialectics from ancient times onward, served as a kind of bridge here.

On the Understanding of Pragma

Nuchelmans rightly insists on understanding the systematic interrelation between the terms σημαινόμενον/*sēmainomenon*, λεκτόν/*lekton*, πρᾶγμα/*pragma* and ἀσώματον/*asōmaton*. In the following paragraphs I shall argue that his solution to the problem is not entirely convincing; an alternative suggestion, however, can only be hinted at here. One should try to read the interrelation as a result of language and its inherent sense of action. Based on this assumption, the incorporeal nature of the "signified" and of "what is said" ought to be understandable. As for the intended "thing," it would be sufficient to reckon with a rather unspecific meaning of the term, provided that no difficulty was caused by the original sense of the word "*pragma*," if indeed it is really connected.

The first critical issue concerns Nuchelmans's interpretation of *pragma*; it is precarious because it postulates that the Stoics were aware of the original sense of *pragma* but draws its evidence mainly from later grammatical documents. Even if the Stoics occasionally connotated the word's etymologically obvious relation to actions it is questionable whether this already constituted the basic or leading sense of the word for them. In the remains of Chrysippus's *Logika Zētēmata* the word "*pragma*" is used in six places.[14] In two of those six places there is much too little context preserved to allow any relevant interpretation (col. X, 2; XI, 33). A third place, also without a suitable larger context, just hints at a difference between *pragmata* and *sēmainomena*: καὶ κατὰ τὰ πράγματα καὶ κατὰ τὰ σημαινόμενα ("both according to the things and according to the signified") (col. XIV, 32–34). In col. VIII, 19 πρᾶγμα is either interchangeable with λεκτόν or it is used somewhat less specifically than the latter word. In col. IX, 13 Chrysippus applies πρᾶγμα to what actors say and signify just as if they were swearing or commanding something or seriously performing any other normal speech act. Finally, in col. XII, 18 Chrysippus uses πρᾶγμα to signify something that, though it formally corresponds to a proposition, does not reveal anything and is inappropriate for use as a normal speech act, which was considered above to be linguistically spinning its wheels and fruitless. In view of this Chrysippean usage, especially in view of the last two examples, it is rather unconvincing to justify the fact that complete lekta are seen as *pragmata* by going back to the etymologically basic meaning of this word and by connecting it to particular predicates.

Toward the Internal Relation between Pragma/lekton and Linguistic Doing

Another critical issue already underlined by Schenkeveld is more crucial. If *pragma* has only the meaning of "something that is merely thought," as suggested by Nuchelmans, then the sense of addressing somebody, of asking a question, of commanding something and so on does not belong to the thing thought, but depends on its utterance, and this is contrary to the entire Stoic theory of the signifying and of the signified. Hence, we need "a closer link between 'a thing thought' and the action/passion of the various speech acts," closer than the one involved in Nuchelmans's interpretation (Schenkeveld 1984, 313); and Schenkeveld argues "that, as far as the non-axiomatic *lekta* are concerned, we have to explain the erotematic etc. *pragma* as containing the idea of Question etc." (1984, 314). More elaborately put, and more precisely with respect to formal notation, this means

> that in the cases of examples without a verb form the *pragma* itself contains not only the "thing thought" . . . , but also the thought of addressing, or, in other cases, that of swearing an oath etc. This means that the correlate of the physical sign Ἀτρείδη . . . Ἀγάμεμνον in the asomatic realm is the *pragma* "ADDRESS (Atreus' son)," or to put it into another notational scheme, "Atreus' son being addressed." (1984, 313f.)

According to Schenkeveld this assumption also explains why, as was already observed by the Stoics,[15] one and the same linguistic form can be used to perform various speech acts and why for instance sentences in the indicative mood may often be applied for more than just one purpose in communication.

Schenkeveld's criticism of Nuchelmans is justified. As is argued more closely in the next section, the speech act may by no means be external to what is said. In Schenkeveld's own interpretation this is, indeed, excluded. Nevertheless, his proposal is not unproblematic either, for there are cases where the utterance does not contain any verb, for example the case of the address. By assuming that in these cases there is to be inserted a predicate according to the intended speech act on the level of meaning, Schenkeveld presumes that in all other cases the insertion of such a predicate is not possible or not necessary. To judge from Schenkeveld's formulations this applies even to cases like "It is day," where we have a predicate, though it is one that does not determine any speech act.

This assumption is astonishing—in view of the question as well as the sources and also in comparison with Nuchelmans. Nuchelmans provided for differentiations and assumed with regard to only a rather few verbs that they signified speech acts and had a paradigmatic status for the Stoics; with regard to other verbs he sought a different interpretation and reckoned with a modified meaning of πρᾶγμα/*pragma*. With respect to the sources, Schenkeveld's assumption is surprising, since the sources in question elucidate all of the nonassertoric lekta, including using examples. The verbs included in the various examples signify things of many kinds, but no speech acts; in all these cases the specification which linguistic action is or can be performed by means of the respective lekta does not belong to the meaning of the verb. Why Schenkeveld's suggestion is inappropriate in view of the question at stake here is almost self-evident. His proposal only takes into account whether or not a lekton includes a predicate, but it does not differentiate between various types of predicates; particularly it does not require that the intended linguistic action is explicated in or described by the predicate. This brings us to our next topic.

3. THE STOIC LIST OF COMPLETE LEKTA AND ITS DIFFICULTIES

How Many Items, and Which Ones?

When Ammonius discussed the five types of speech differentiated according to the Peripatetic tradition, he additionally reported on a Stoic list with ten entries, which however he saw as unnecessarily long and easily reducible to the Peripatetic list.[16] We read the same in some further sources, probably influenced by Ammonius (cf. FDS 899f.). These accounts transform the (ten or more) complete lekta of the Stoics into correspondingly many modes of speech, apparently presupposing that there was nothing more than a terminological problem to deal with, and they also argue that on the level of linguistic expression there was no convincing explanation for the Stoic distinctions (see also FDS 681ff.). The Stoics might have been ready to accept the second step, provided they had accepted the first beforehand. But certainly they did not do so, since if they had, they would have seen the signified as signifying, the lekta as logos (speech), and would have surrendered one of their key distinctions. Hence Ammonius and his followers misunderstood them, and this misunderstanding makes us realize once more that the Stoic interest in speech-act theory is primarily concerned with the meanings of linguistic utterances; linguistic expression as well as possible grammatical differentiations align themselves with this.[17]

When read with the appropriate corrections, these sources indicate that the Stoics would have differentiated ten complete lekta. This number would be characteristic for their school; and we are told too which lekta they had in mind. Yet the apparent incongruences cannot be overlooked. The complete lekta are listed also by a number of other sources apart from Ammonius; Schenkeveld in his tabular overview juxtaposes nine texts.[18] Only two of them have identical lists; all the others show particular variations. Furthermore, we do not find only ten or eleven different complete lekta but about fifteen, depending how we count. Ammonius himself mentions only a single type of question, or rather he ignores the inquiry (πύσμα/*pysma*), which appears in all the other sources. It might therefore seem tempting to differentiate this unique lekton so that yes/no questions and inquiries are counted as different types of complete lekta; but if we do so the allegedly characteristic number of ten complete lekta is exceeded. Despite this, in Diogenes Laertius's report the ekthesis is missing, though it appears in Ammonius's and two further lists. If we follow Egli's suggestion and add the ekthesis to Diogenes Laertius's list, then this list matches the one by Ammonius;[19] but then Diogenes Laertius's list too surpasses the number ten.

In order to account for these difficulties, Schenkeveld argued that precisely those ten types of lekta definitely mentioned by Diogenes formed the original Stoic standard list and that this original list was later enlarged by means of sub-distinctions; in several cases the Stoic logicians specified subtypes for various complete lekta but subsequently counted some of them as independent (1984, 309–311). This interpretation still raises further questions. Matters to be pondered include, for instance, the tradition of the number of ten complete lekta and the reduction of the Stoic list from eleven to ten items. The tradition of the number requires reflections, if the number of ten was really exceeded at the latest with Poseidonius, who in turn was mentioned several times by Diogenes Laertius as his source of information. And the reduction of the Stoic list needs attention, since it must have been conducted by Ammonius or one of his forerunners, in order to reestablish ten instead of eleven entries in the Stoic list of complete lekta.[20] Yet whether and how all this can be clarified must be discussed elsewhere.

But yet another oddity remains. According to the passage preceding the list in Diogenes Laertius, syllogisms were also counted as complete lekta (DL 7, 63 = FDS 696); thus the number of ten complete lekta is already exceeded. Schenkeveld's table does not take the syllogism into consideration at all, although this item is of the highest systematic interest, since its inclusion entitles us to classify the argument and the sophism as complete lekta, too. Furthermore, it reminds us of Plutarch's text, quoted in section 1 above, which opens up even more possibilities for enlarging the list.[21] But, above all, this passage reminds us that according to our earlier argumentation it is essential for complete lekta to be usable for the performance of linguistic actions. In view of this essential requirement it is difficult to see why there should be only 10 or 15 or even only 50 types of complete lekta. How did the Stoics justify not so much the length but the *restriction* of their list?

The List, and the Scheme for the Definition of the Various Complete Lekta

The same question arises with respect to the scheme often used by the Stoics in order to characterize the individual complete lekta, which has already been mentioned here at a number of points. The scheme appears as follows:

A lekton of the	command	type is	a thing such that by saying it we	command
	address		(dto.)	address
	question		(dto.)	ask
	proposition		(dto.)	assert
	etc.			

The general form therefore is:

(1)   A lekton of the   X type is   a thing such that by saying it we are x-ing.

According to its syntax this formula is a single principal clause containing several subordinate clauses. If we transform it such that it consists of two self-dependent though equivalent formulations, we have:

(2)   *A* is a lekton of the X type   iff   by saying *A* we are x-ing.

To elucidate this we need to add that the universalizing step toward formulation (1) is unproblematic; what is perhaps worth discussion is the range of what can be substituted for X. The conversion from (1) to (2) predominantly means eliminating the saying of a "thing" which is referred to in the second part of the clause; instead one and the same letter representing a certain lekton appears twice. Through this alteration the desired two formulations result; both are self-dependent and equivalent.

The way from the "thing" to the "letter" is to be understood as follows. To call something a lekton of the X type according to (1) requires that it is a thing of such a kind that by saying it we are x-ing; i.e., it must be a) a thing which we say and b) more specifically a thing of a particular type. Expressed in the terms of Stoic dialectics it must be a lekton or something signified

respectively, and not something signifying either a linguistic sign or an utterance. Accordingly in formula (2) "*A*" represents a lekton of this kind and
may be substituted by convenient examples, for instance, by the examples
offered in the sources. Thus, "It is day," is a lekton of the proposition type
iff (= if and only if) by saying "It is day," we make an assertion and say
something that is true or false.

Varying the examples slightly, the flexibility of the scheme becomes
clearer:

To say: "We are going" is—according to the circumstances—a statement
or an announcement or a threat or something else of this kind :iff: by saying
"We are going," a person states or announces something or threatens or does
something else of this kind.

Or: to say "There is a draft." is an assertion :iff: by saying "There is a
draft." a person performs an assertion. And to say "There is a draft." is a demand :iff: by saying "There is a draft." a person demands something, while
to say "There is a draft." is a command to close the window :iff: by saying
"There is a draft." a person gives the command to close the window.

Or: To say "Mumbo-jumbo" is an example for a nonsense word :iff: by
saying "Mumbo-jumbo" a person gives an example for a nonsense word.
And to say "Mumbo-jumbo" is an affront :iff: by saying "Mumbo-jumbo" a
person classifies someone else's utterance as nonsense and thus affronts him.

To return to our sources on Stoic dialectics, we can state in addition that
the scheme for the definition of complete lekta, even if not used in all cases,
might be applicable all the same. Diogenes Laertius abstains from it, for instance in the case of inquiries.[22] Expanding the bounds of the items on the list
of complete lekta, we may note that the scheme also brilliantly fits those cases
cited by Origenes and Plutarch.[23] In particular the physician's order to his pu-
pil to cut and to cauterize, and the musician's instruction to his student to play
the lyre and sing, fall under the scheme. These briefings are to be interpreted
according to the rules of the respective art and circumstances—given that
they are to be understood in the sense of demands; and they pass for carried
out correctly only if they are performed at an adequately high level, that is, at
the right time or through well-played music, and so on.

Obviously the Stoic pattern for the explanation of complete lekta presupposes that a component of linguistic pragmatics is included in the lekta. If
we utter something we normally thereby do something that exceeds the utterance, quite in the sense of modern speech-act theory. It is worth stressing
that it is the formulation in the second part of the scheme by which the action-
character of normal speaking is both pointed out and utilized for the explication of the complete lekta concerned; it is the formulation that by saying *A*

we are x-ing. Whether or not the word "*pragma*" occurs in the definition of a complete lekton is as unimportant with regard of the pragmatic character of the lekton as is the question whether or not *A* itself includes a more specific signification of the x-ing as asserting, questioning, ordering or the like.[24] The scheme does not require any syntactic or semantic correspondence between the formulation used for the lekton on the one hand and the action which is performed by it on the other hand; it only calls for conventions ruling the connection of the two. And since it does not require any such correspondence the scheme is qualified to represent each and every action (or at least incalculably various ones) which are performed by means of language.[25]

At any rate the scheme is so comprehensive as again to raise the question why the Stoics confine their list of complete lekta so sharply. Why do they regularly accept only about a dozen types instead of many more? Is it possible to reduce linguistic acting to so few basic forms, or is there a different point of view that allows the justification of such a massive restriction?

4. TWO VIEWPOINTS FOR SPECIFYING COMPLETE LEKTA

In various respects the Stoics' concept of the complete lekton also took linguistic doing into consideration; it allowed them to direct attention to innumerable kinds of speech acts. In contrast to this, the list of complete lekta handed down to us is rather clearly laid out; it comprises 10 to 15 entries at most, shows little variation, and because of its longevity is certainly not a random collection. How, then, to bridge the gap from a limitless multitude of speech acts to the standard list?

It would be quite implausible to argue that the list should represent *all* imaginable speech acts or cover all fundamental types of complete lekta. To justify such a claim would be impossible and would contradict some sources. For instance, Plutarch's text, quoted in section 1 above, shows that the Stoics knew how to describe many speech acts in several ways, and that they looked on prohibitions and rules as *different* speech acts; such considerations undermine any view of the list as exhaustive. Furthermore, in his *Logical Investigations* Chrysippus raises the question what *actors* do; for on stage, what take place are not doings in the general sense even though the performance is constituted almost entirely by ordinary speech acts. The sense of action in our utterances is abrogated by a theatrical framing, and Chrysippus knew that this would not be the only occasion on which the standard sense of action is or could be damaged.[26] For this reason, too, the list of the complete lekta cannot embrace *all* complete speech acts; for it surely does not capture any speech act that threatens to damage the particularities of the speech acts listed. This leaves us with the possibility that the list contained a selection following a specific viewpoint.

More precisely, at least two such viewpoints are to be expected, one covering the great majority of the complete lekta listed, among them the propositions, while the other opposes the quasi-propositions precisely to this group. As to the first point, the idea of the illocutionary offers itself, the thesis to demonstrate next will be that the Stoics were in fact led by this idea when establishing their list of the complete lekta.

The Idea of the Illocutionary and the List of Complete Lekta

The concept of the illocutionary varies in various respects and requires clarifications that are not unanimously accepted in contemporary philosophy of language (cf. Woerner 1978, 90ff.). Thus, before testing whether it helps us to understand the Stoic list, it will be adequate to outline the basic idea of the term. When discussing linguistic doing, Austin differentiated between various linguistic acts, even partial acts, and conceived of the so-called locutionary act, in which we express a sentence in a certain language with sense and reference, such as "The cat is on the mat." This act was then separated from the illocutionary as well as the perlocutionary act. The illocutionary act exceeds the locutionary insofar as the performance of the latter usually means that additional action takes place, for instance, pronouncing a warning, whereas the perlocutionary act refers to the results of the locutionary act, for instance, provoking attention, causing anxiety or belief (cf. Austin 1976, 94ff.; Woerner 1978, 91f.).

To clarify these differentiations further, a very important point is the fact that illocutionary acts can be performed in two different ways, whereas perlocutionary acts cannot. Performing an illocutionary act means being able to *name* what one does and simultaneously perform the act itself in the first person present tense indicative. Moreover, when performing the illocutionary speech act in its explicit linguistic form, one can inversely *reduce* that form and continue to perform the act as well. If, for instance, I want to state that it is snowing I can do so by saying either "It is snowing," or "I assert that it is snowing." Or else, if I want to state an order I can say "I order you to go" or simply "Go!" Accordingly we can apply for any speech act X:

X ε illocutionary   ::IFF::
                     if a person says "y" this person is x-ing
                     :iff: if the person says "I am x-ing: y", he/she is x-ing

The right-hand side of this formula expresses the condition of being expand-
able when read from left to right or from the second to the third line respectively, and the condition of being reducible when read the other way round.
If both of these conditions are fulfilled, then the speech act is illocutionary.
Admittedly, this concept of the illocutionary requires further improvement.
But it is sound enough for checking whether it is useful for the interpretation
of the Stoic list of complete lekta.

In order to represent the idea of the illocutionary in the framework of the
Stoic scheme for the definition of complete lekta, we have to demand that
the lekton used for x-ing can be enriched by an element naming this very
doing and still be used to perform it. In more technical terms and adapted to
the formulations in the preceding section, if "X:thing" or "$X:A$" respectively
symbolizes the enriched lekton, we may express the restriction as follows:

A complete lekton fulfilling the formulae (1) and (2) respectively is illocutionary IFF
it also fulfills the formulae (3) and (4) respectively:
  (3)   A lekton of the X type is a X: thing such that by saying it we are x-ing.
  (4)   X: A is a lekton of the X type   iff   by saying X: A we are x-ing.

This more special version of the Stoic scheme is not necessitated by the
original one, but it is reasonable insofar as illocutionary speech acts seem to
be most convincing instances of the scheme, and appropriate to show how it
works. In this weaker sense, first, the Stoics were indeed guided by the idea
of the illocutionary.

A stronger sense appears from the Stoic list of complete lekta, except the
quasi-propositions: illocutionary speech acts constituted the formal object
of the list. This assumption suggests itself not only because of the factually
listed complete lekta but also because the condition of expansion and reduction characteristic for all illocutionary speech acts fits extremely well with
the famous formalism of the Stoic logicians. Once it is discovered that there
are lekta with the particularity that someone who by saying "y" is precisely at
that moment x-ing when he, if he says "I am x-ing: y" is x-ing at that very moment—as soon as this is discovered, Stoic formalism can connect to speech
acts; thus, it is highly reasonable to focus attention on speech acts with this
characteristic.

With respect to predications this is clear from the start, and the Stoics were
obviously aware of that. We can say "It is day," or else "I assert that it is day";
in both cases the assertion is the same. As to the *Stoic* view on this matter, I
want to offer three pieces of evidence. First, the Stoics call the propositions
axiomata. In doing so they deviate from Aristotle's terminology, follow
the dialecticians around Diodorus Cronus, and justify their signification by

pointing to the verb ἀξιοῦσθαι/*axiousthai*; "for when saying 'It is day,' one seems to accept (the fact) that it is day" (DL 7, 65 = FDS 874). This peculiarity hence justifies expanding or reducing the proposition if required. Second, there is a remark by Epictetus that is mainly concerned with hypothetical assumptions and distinguishes these from propositions. Here it is also almost explicitly stated that the same is asserted by "I assert it is day" as it is by "It is day"; the expanded form of a proposition and the reduced one are considered equivalent (Diss. I, 25, 11–13 = FDS 907). Third, if we have a syllogistic argument and substitute an equivalent proposition for one of the premises or the conclusion, particularly either the corresponding expanded form of the premise or conclusion, or a proposition which is equivalent thereto according to the formula "p iff 'p' ε true," then the Stoics declare that the original syllogism turns into a sub-syllogism. They claim that it becomes something different, though not differing with regard to validity. Galen did not appreciate this subtlety of Stoic syllogistics. But in order to underline the equivalence, he strongly set out the illocutionary conditions within propositions and made clear that it was a common view which could not have been unknown to the Stoics: "He who says, 'It is true that it is day,' says the same as he who says, 'It is day'" (Galen, Inst. Log. 17, 4 = FDS 1094).

With commands, requests, and the three species of questions (yes/no questions, inquiries, timid suggestions), it also goes almost without saying that it is reckoned as equivalent whether a person explicitly adds what he/she is doing or whether he/she does not make such a supplement or eliminates it. In any case, the respective speech acts are ruled by clear conventions, and they come about successfully. The same holds true for the adjurative, the hypothesis and the ekthesis, except that there may be a tendency to prefer the expanded linguistic form to the reduced one, even though using the latter would still be possible. As to evidence from the Stoa, in the case of the hypothetical assumption all that is required follows from the passage in Epictetus just mentioned (FDS 907; cf. also 1121). In the case of questions, particularly yes/no questions, it follows from the material on the *metapiptontes logoi* (fallacies due to a change in the meaning of terms), since these arguments precisely utilize the equivalences under discussion (FDS 1121, 1200). Moreover we should again point out the passage from the *Logika Zētēmata* where Chrysippus refers to actors in order to make a comparison; "They say the things and signify (them), although they neither do swear nor do command nor do pray nor do ask nor do inquire."[27] Actors make the same utterances as other people in everyday life but do not thereby perform all the speech acts usually performed by making them; on the stage the lekta change and lose their usual power.

Even the address falls into the group of lekta meeting the definition of illocutionary speech acts outlined above. The purpose of an address is to attract a person's attention, and that is typically reached by addressing him/her with his/her name or title, though nothing prevents us from additionally making the speech act explicit, for instance, by saying: "Mr. President, I address myself to you . . . " By such means we perform the same speech act as by the reduced form; we do nothing different, neither more nor less.

Finally, the same holds true for syllogisms, ranged by Diogenes Laertius among the complete lekta. By implication it is possible and would bring no diversion in content to precede a syllogism with the explicit indication: "I draw the following conclusion: . . . " Hence, the logical conclusion itself is an illocutionary speech act, too. The same criterion is also applicable to telling a tale; and many other speech acts could be considered illocutionary speech acts according to this criterion. It is very unlikely that the Stoics would have opposed such an expansion of their list of complete lekta, as long as the syllogism counts as a complete lekton.

Apart from the quasi-proposition, then, all the complete lekta on the Stoics' list are illocutionary in the sense of the above definition. To this extent this list of complete lekta is indeed governed by the idea of the illocutionary.

Quasi-propositions

Concerning the quasi-proposition Diogenes Laertius reports that, though it "has a propositional enunciation" (or "the enunciation of a judgement," according to R. D. Hicks's translation),[28] it falls outside the class of propositions (or "judgements proper") and does so "in consequence of the intensified tone or emotion of one of its parts." The examples given by Diogenes are: "Yea, fair indeed the Parthenon!" and "How like Priam's sons the cowherd is!" (DL 7, 67 = FDS 874; trans. Hicks). These examples are to be found in other sources as well; and further sources give further instances, among them quotations from poets: "How Fate gives itself airs towards human life," and "It is good to honour parents and to respect the laws."[29]

Quasi-propositions, therefore, not only fall outside the class of propositions, but also cannot be counted as illocutionary speech acts. Examples include expressing admiration, nurturing suspicion, breaking a secret, advising a rule of wisdom, and other things; if they were explicitly added to what is said, such as, "I am suspicious how much the cowherd resembles Priam's sons," the expanded speech certainly would not perform the same action as the reductive one. Diogenes' description of the quasi-proposition leads to the same result. An illocutionary speech act would have to perform exactly the same action, be it with the expanded or the reduced lekton. But for quasi-propositions that cannot be guaranteed; on the contrary, it fails as a rule. If the pathos or another inserted particle disrupts the meaning of an utterance and turns it into a quasi-proposition, this fact will certainly have a different effect with respect to the expanded form of the utterance, which will no longer correspond to the meaning of the whole utterance.

To delimit quasi-propositions more precisely, the first question is how to classify those complete lekta that do not have "a propositional enunciation" but the linguistic form of, say, a question or a request, yet fall outside the category of questions or commands. According to the fragments of the *Logika Zētēmata* Chrysippus also dealt with these borderline cases, analyzing the consequences if orders are connected with "or," and arguing that this might lead to linguistic idling, and furthermore he reflected upon what actors say. Therefore, it is appropriate not to classify these complete lekta as quasi-propositions, but to take Diogenes' precondition of adopting "a propositional enunciation" as constitutive for quasi-propositions. As a consequence this class refers to declarative sentences insofar as they are being used for non-propositional purposes. It includes only those complete lekta which fall out of the class of *propositions*, and is not, as Schenkeveld wrote (1984, 319), just a kind of receptacle for *all* complete lekta which cannot be allocated to *any* other class.

The second question refers to the reasons why something might not belong to the class of propositions. Once again we should mention actors on stage; furthermore there are social conventions using particular statements to perform rituals; sometimes, linguistic conventions remove the propositional character from a pretended statement, turning it away from the class of propositions, as we find in Chrysippus' analysis of the liar antinomy. In all these cases the complete lekta fall outside the class of propositions for other reasons than those named by Diogenes, and at least in some cases (actors, social conventions!) it seems adequate to call them quasi-propositions. Thus, the scope of this lekton remains worth considering.

What of Further Challenges in Stoic Speech-Act Theory?

The foregoing reflections confirm that the Stoics' list of complete lekta focuses on illocutionary speech acts in the sense that, among the almost limitless range of complete lekta with respect to speech acts, they particularly consider those that are illocutionary according to our working definition. Furthermore, the list reflects the fact that a considerable number of complete lekta, though performed by declarative sentences, are not illocutionary but serve various other purposes. In both of these respects further considerations are desirable.

As stated earlier, our working definition of the illocutionary still needs further development. It requires testing against objections, and some specification with regard to Austin's work. Correspondingly, we might ask whether the definition is satisfactory with regard to the Stoics, or if they have something up their sleeves that might challenge the concept of the illocutionary. On this the surviving fragments on Stoic dialectics seem to offer at least two hints worth following. As Schenkeveld has pointed out, according to Diogenes Laertius *propositions* are *asserted*, according to Seneca *asserting* is considered *a move of the mind*, and according to Theon the Stoics supposed that there were also *other moves of the mind*, bringing about *other complete lekta*.[30] The question follows in what terms the Stoics discussed these *other moves of the mind*. Moreover, the Stoics were engaged in contemporary discussions on ambiguity (cf. FDS 632ff.). Perhaps they did use their analyses on these topics to delimit the illocutionary from other complete lekta in a more precise way!

Regarding quasi-propositions the crucial question is whether the Stoics found ways to describe these lekta in greater detail or even to sub-classify them. To explore this, we might think on the one hand of Austin's performatives. On the other hand one recalls Chrysippus' question what actors do, as well as his thesis that each word has several meanings (Gellius, NA XI, 12, 1 = FDS 636). Combined with Plutarch's account of the Stoic description of commands, these sources challenge future analysis, and they might help us detect Stoic ideas about institutionally organized speech acts.

NOTES

1. In the 1950s only Hans v. Arnim's collection *Stoicorum Veterum Fragmenta* was available (Leipzig, 1903–1924).

2. DL 7, 63 = FDS 696: τὸ κατὰ φαντασίαν λογικὴν ὑφιστάμενον.

3. Cf. for instance FDS 698 and 897ff., and in particular 909ff. as far as the moods of the verb are concerned.

4. As to the Stoic division and subdivision of philosophy, see the "systematic" overview given by Diogenes Laertius: DL 7, 39ff., as far as dialectics is concerned = FDS 1, 33, 255, 476, 536, 594, 621, 696, 874, 914, 1036, 1207, and 87. There were, of course, a number of variants described in the introduction to *FDS*, vol. 1, p. LXXVIII–XC.

5. Cf. DL 9, 54, and the comment by Fehling 1976.

6. Aristotle, De int. 4, 16b33–17a7; quotes 17a4 and 5f., trans. Edghill.

7. Aristotle, Poet. 19, 1456b8ff.; 20, 1457a18ff. A brief examination of these passages is in Schenkeveld 1984, 292f.

8. Ammonius, In Arist. de int. 2, 9ff.; 5, 6ff.; 64, 28ff.; In Arist. Anal. pr. II 3–5; 26, 31–33.

9. DL 7, 62 = FDS 63, 696; see also DL 7, 42 = FDS 33 and SE, AM 11, 187 = FDS 61.

10. DL 7, 67 = FDS 874. The example comes from the *Iliad* (2.434 and various other locations).

11. Cf. FDS 910–913; the example in FDS 913 (from Origenes). More on the Stoic moods of the verb in Schenkeveld 1984, 331–345.

12. Plutarch, De Stoic. repugn. 11, 1037D–E = FDS 909; trans. Cherniss.

13. Papyrus Herculanensis 307 = FDS 698: esp. col. X–XIII; a new edition of the passage in Marrone 1997, 93–96.

14. According to the index of words in Marrone's edition (1997, 99).

15. See above on ὀργίζεσθε/*orgizesthe* and similar cases.

16. See FDS 897f.: Ammonius, In Arist. De interpr. 2, 9–3, 6; In Arist. Anal. pr. 2, 3–5, 26, 31–33.

17. With exceptional conspicuousness this is said by Dionysius of Halikarnassus, De comp. verb. 8, 32, 7–13, and Aelius Theon, Progymnasmata 4, 13–21, 87 (= FDS 900a, 900b). Cf. also Schenkeveld 1984, 332f.

18. See Schenkeveld 1984, 302–308, esp. 304. Cf. also the testimonies put together in FDS 875–876a and 897ff.

19. FDS 874 gives the text according to Egli 1981. M. Marcovich in his new edition of Diogenes Laertius's *Vitae philosophorum* (1999) did not accept Egli's conjecture (supplementation of καὶ ἐκθετικὸν/*kai ekthetikon* in DL 7, 66). Schenkeveld (1984, 323) supposed that only Posidonius separated the *ekthesis* from the *hypothesis* because of their different functions in mathematics.

20. As to the questions to Schenkeveld, cf. also my remarks in *FDS* on the text no. 897 (p. 1117).

21. As a consequence one could mention the interdiction separately, in addition to the command. But one could also add that some speech acts were very complex, and this ought to be kept in mind when interpeting the Stoic list.

22. DL 7, 66 = FDS 874, but cf. SE, AM 8, 71 = FDS 876.

23. For the respective sources, see above, section 1.

24. The action aspect of normal speaking is documented, therefore, also by those sources which do not use the word πρᾶγμα in this context, particularly by Sextus Empiricus who apart from Diogenes Laertius is one of the principal witnesses with regard to the list of complete lekta; where the scheme has the term πρᾶγμα/*pragma* Sextus always speaks of a λεκτόν/*lekton*: AM 8, 69–77 = FDS 876.

25. Schenkeveld seems to have overlooked the great variety in the relationship of linguistic expressions and speech acts and (on the grounds of the metalinguistic way of expression in the definitions of complete lekta) to have erroneously assumed instead that the metalinguistic means for the description of speech acts always need to appear in the utterances used to perform the speech acts. Nuchelmans apparently noticed this independence of utterance and speech act; when he spoke about the few cases which for the Stoics offered the possibility of transferring their cause/ effect analysis to speech acts he was obviously thinking of those cases where the linguistic means for the description of speech acts form an element of the speech acts themselves, for instance of cases like "I assert that . . .", against these basic cases he distinguished all those cases in which the type of speech act is not explicitly signified.

26. In connection with the text by Plutarch, I mentioned certain other passages of the *Logical Investigations*; there Chrysippus comments how orders can degenerate into linguistic idling. Moreover, one could highlight the liar antinomy here; according to Chrysippus it disrupts the involved propositions of their assertoric character; cf. FDS 1210ff. as well as Rüstow 1910, 39ff., and in more recent times Cavini 1993, esp. 103ff., also Castagnoli 2007, esp. 55–59.

27. PHerc 307: col. IX, 12–17 = Marrone 1997, 92 (FDS 698).

28. DL 7, 67 = FDS 874: τὴν ἐκφορὰν ἔχον ἀξιωματικήν .../*tēn ekphoran echon axiōmatikēn*.

29. "How Fate . . ." is a verse by Menander (fr. 788 Körte = 855 Kock). Schenkeveld 1984, 306f. provides a table showing the various locations where the verses appear.

30. DL 7, 65 = FDS 874.; Seneca, Ep. 117, 13 = FDS 892; Theon, Progymn. 62, 13ff. = FDS 876a. See Schenkeveld 1984, 314, 332f.

REFERENCES

von Arnim, Hans, ed. 1964. *Stoicorum Veterum Fragmenta*, vols. I–IV (IV: Indices by Maximilian Adler, 1924). Leipzig: Teubner 1903–1905, 1924. Repr. Stuttgart: Teubner.

Austin, John L. 1976. *How To Do Things With Words: The William James Lectures Delivered at Harvard University in 1955.* 1962, 2nd ed. by J. O. Urmson and M. Sbisà. London/Oxford/New York: Oxford University Press.

Bobzien, Susanne. 1986. *Die stoische Modallogik.* Würzburg: Königshausen & Neumann.

———. 2003. "Logic." In *The Cambridge Companion to The Stoics*, ed. by B. Inwood, 85–123. Cambridge: Cambridge University Press.

Castagnoli, Luca. 2007. "'Everything is true,' 'everything is false': Self-refutation arguments from Democritus to Augustine." *Antiquorum Philosophia* 1: 11–74.

Cavini, Walter. 1993. "Chrysippus on Speaking Truly and the Liar." In *Dialektiker und Stoiker: Zur Logik der Stoa und ihrer Vorläufer*, ed. by Klaus Döring and Theodor Ebert, 85–109. Stuttgart: Franz Steiner.

Egli, Urs. 1981. *Das Dioklesfragment bei Diogenes Laertius.* Konstanz: Universität Konstanz. (Publications by the SFB 99 Linguistik vol. 55.)

FDS: see Hülser 1988/1989.

Fehling, Detlev. 1976. "Protagoras und die ὀρθοέπεια." In: *Sophistik,* ed. by Carl Joachim Classen, 341–347. Darmstadt: Wissenschaftliche Buchgesellschaft. (Reprint of: D. Fehling. 1965. "Zwei Untersuchungen zur griechischen Sprachphilosophie." *Rheinisches Museum* 108: 212–217.)

Frede, Michael. 1974. *Die stoische Logik.* Göttingen: Vandenhoeck & Ruprecht.

Hirzel, Rudolf. 1879. "De logica Stoicorum." In: *Satura philologa: Hermanno Sauppio obtulit amicorum conlegarum decas,* 61–78. Berlin: Weidmann.

Hülser, Karlheinz, ed. 1988/1989. *Die Fragmente zur Dialektik der Stoiker: Neue Sammlung der Texte mit deutscher Übersetzung und Kommentaren.* 4 vols. Stuttgart: frommann-holzboog.

Marcovich, Miroslav, ed. 1999/2002. *Diogenis Laertii Vitae Philosophorum.* Vol. I: Libri I–X, Vol. II: Excerpta Byzantina et Indices, Stuttgart: Teubner 1999; vol. III: Indices, confecit Hans Gärtner, München/Leipzig: K. G. Saur 2002.

Marrone, Livia, ed. 1997. "Le *Questioni Logiche* di Crisippo (*PHerc. 307*)." *Cronache Ercolanesi* 27: 83–100.

Nuchelmans, Gabriel. 1973. *Theories of the Proposition: Ancient and medieval conceptions of the bearers of truth and falsity.* Amsterdam/London: North-Holland Publishing Company.

Rüstow, Alexander. 1910. *Der Lügner: Theorie, Geschichte und Auflösung.* Leipzig: Teubner.

Schenkeveld, Dirk M. 1984. "Stoic and Peripatetic Kinds of Speech Act and the Distinction of Grammatical Moods." *Mnemosyne* 37: 291–353.

SVF: see v. Arnim 1964.

Woerner, Markus H. 1978. *Performative und sprachliches Handeln: Ein Beitrag zu J. L. Austins Theorie der Sprechakte.* Hamburg: Buske.

Chapter Three

Utrum gratitudo sit virtus moralis vel passio animae, or: Gratitude— An Aristotelian Virtue or an Emotion?

Thomas Nisters

This chapter aims at answering the question whether gratitude is a moral virtue or an emotion, and it does so by using the form taken by scholastic authors in approximately the thirteenth century. On the one hand it considers seven arguments supporting the thesis that gratitude is not an Aristotelian virtue but an emotion. This may at first appear to form an overwhelming case. We go on, however, to consider two counterarguments. Rather than abandoning the debate at this impasse—is gratitude an emotion or is it a virtue?—we then introduce considerations which show that gratitude is in fact composed of a complex combination of emotions which characteristically give rise to certain speech acts and even actions; moreover in a subsidiary sense it is a virtue too, a virtue exercised precisely with regard to the same emotions, utterances and deeds. Virtues of course are normally opposed by vices, and it extends our understanding of gratitude to examine the various vices which are opposed to it. The resulting, much more complex comprehension of what gratitude entails is then tested in terms of a review of the entire gamut of arguments and counterarguments presented at the beginning of this chapter. In each case, we are able to account anew for what appeared to be conclusive claims.

It seems that gratitude is not a virtue but an emotion. For:

Argument 1

Nouns denoting an emotion can function as a direct object of the verb "to feel." The sign X in the phrase
(1) Peter feels X
can be replaced by a noun denoting an emotion:
(2) Peter feels angry/sad/envious.

But the sign X in (1) cannot possibly be replaced by a noun denoting a virtue:
(3) *Peter feels generous/courageous.
However, the sign X in (1) can be replaced by the noun "grateful":
(4) Peter feels grateful (toward Paul).
Therefore, gratitude is an emotion and not a virtue.

Argument 2

The sign X in the phrase
(5) I am X
can be replaced by nouns denoting an emotion. It is perfectly acceptable to
form sentences in the first person singular, such as
(6) I am angry/sad.
Equally, a phrase in the first person singular with a verb denoting the speaker's emotional state is acceptable, for example:
(7) I pity/envy/love him.
But sentences in the first person singular characterizing the speaker as virtuous are acceptable to a far lesser degree.
If Peter says
(8) I am generous/courageous
eyebrows will presumably be raised. To characterize oneself as virtuous is
slightly indecent since it is considered to border on praising oneself. What
is more, to characterize oneself in terms of one's moral qualities is highly
problematic owing to epistemic considerations—in that I am everything else
but an impartial judge when it comes to my virtues and vices.
Yet, to say in the first person singular
(9) I am very/extremely grateful.
will pass with no objection.
Therefore, gratitude is an emotion and not a virtue.

Argument 3

According to Aristotle every emotion can be cast in a triadic structure, as in
the following:
(10) Q feels emotion E toward R because of C.
Q denotes the person who feels the emotion, in other words, the subject of
the emotion. R, technically speaking, denotes the object of the emotion. C
denotes the cause of the emotion E, showing what has given rise to it (cf.
Aristotle, Rhet. II 1, 1378a22ff.). For example:
(11) Peter (Q) is afraid (emotion E) of the dog (R) because it is frothing at
the mouth (C).
(12) George (Q) envies (emotion E) John (R) because John has been promoted.

(13) Sarah (Q) hates Bill (R) because Bill is notoriously unfaithful (C).
Virtues, unlike emotions, do not fit smoothly into this triadic structure (10).
Yet gratitude displays precisely the triadic structure which is typical of emotions:
(14) Q is grateful to R because of C.
Therefore, gratitude is an emotion and not a virtue.

Argument 4

Emotions are actually bound up with pleasure or pain (cf. Aristotle, Rhet. II
1, 1378a20–22). Saying
(15) Mary is angry/afraid/full of pity/envious/gleeful
implies
(16) Mary is pained by a slight.
(17) Mary is pained by the expectation of an imminent evil.
(18) Mary is pained at the sight of some undeserved evil befalling Martha.
(19) Mary is pained by Martha's gorgeous hair.
(20) Mary is pleased because the stylist has spoiled Martha's hairdo.
In contrast to emotions, however, virtues are only potentially or conditionally
bound up with pleasure or pain. The generous person does not permanently
feel pleasure or pain. He or she is only disposed to feel pain or pleasure under
particular circumstances, for example, in giving alms to those in need, as opposed to a sordid miser who suffers when losing money.
But gratitude by definition implies pleasure. Gratitude without the beneficiary's delight in accepting turns out to be a contradiction in terms. Hence,
pleasure is a necessary ingredient of gratitude.
Therefore, gratitude is an emotion and not a virtue.

Argument 5

An emotion has one and only one opposite. Love is opposed to hatred, hope
to despair, fear to confidence, shame to pride. A virtue, instead, has two opposites (cf. Aristotle, NE II 7, 1107a32ff.): courage is opposed to cowardice
and rashness; liberality is opposed to prodigality and meanness.
But gratitude has one and only one opposite, namely, ingratitude.
Therefore, gratitude is an emotion and not a virtue.

Argument 6

Emotions are by their very nature rather ephemeral. Virtues, being habituated states of character, are more stable and longer lasting (Aristotle, Cat. 8,
8b27–28). But gratitude more often than not wanes only too soon. Therefore,
gratitude is an emotion and not a virtue.

Argument 7

Emotions are also called passions of the soul. This wording bears witness to the fact that emotions are rather passive phenomena. Somebody's emotion is stirred up or aroused without the person being active or contributing to its arousal. We cannot help feeling pity, anger, or sorrow, or at least we cannot suppress or divert these emotions without long training.

The virtues are rather active dispositions. They are active *ex ante* or *in statu nascendi*, in that they are acquired by deciding and acting constantly in a specific manner; they are active *ex post*, in that they enable or dispose us to decide and to act in exactly that manner (Aristotle, NE II 2, 1104a27–29).

But gratitude is rather passive, being brought about by the benefactor's benefaction.

Therefore, gratitude is an emotion and not a virtue.

On the other hand, gratitude can be argued to be a virtue rather than an emotion on the basis of two counterarguments.

Counterargument I

Emotions are ethically neutral (cf. Aristotle, NE II 5, 1105b28ff.). To feel an emotion is, as such, neither positive nor negative. We neither praise nor blame people just for their being afraid, sad or confident. But virtues are positive in terms of moral evaluation. It is praiseworthy to be generous or courageous. However, gratitude is far from being neutral in this sense. It is thought to be the beneficiary's moral duty to feel and to behave grateful toward his or her benefactor. A beneficiary neglecting that duty is rightly criticized.

Therefore, gratitude is a virtue and not an emotion.

Counterargument II

A virtue presupposes a specific intention. To carry out certain types of action without having the right intention does not meet the standards of virtue. Giving alms to the poor, for instance, with a view to impress others or with the intention to persuade a possible creditor that you are credit-worthy falls short of what generosity as a virtue requires. Not to desert for fear of punishment or being downgraded is not courage in the strict sense.

But the same goes for gratitude. To utter words of gratitude and to offer tokens of gratitude only because one is fishing for further benefactions is not grateful in the proper sense. Gratitude, in other words, presupposes a specific intention.

Therefore, gratitude is a virtue and not an emotion.

The following answer might help to reconcile the contradiction between these two groups of arguments.

Answer

Primarily, gratitude is a complex emotion. As an emotion it is composed of two other, more simple or basic emotions. These emotions in turn induce actions typical for gratitude. First, gratitude entails the beneficiary's being pleased by the benefaction bestowed on him or her by the benefactor. Gratitude is or gratitude implies a pleasure of a kind. Second, gratitude is, roughly speaking, the beneficiary's counterbenevolence, answering the benefactor's original or initial act of benevolence. The beneficiary's counterbenevolence prompts the beneficiary—third—to thank the benefactor by speaking words of gratitude and possibly, even (fourth) to carry out a counterbenefaction.

We can therefore say that gratitude in the original and basic sense is a two-fold emotion, consisting of (a) pleasure and (b) counterbenevolence, prompting (c) speech acts and (d) actions proper.

But gratitude in a secondary sense is a virtue referring to the emotions (a) and (b) and to the actions (c) and (d). Gratitude as a virtue disposes or enables us to feel gratitude and to feel the tendency to act accordingly if and only if we are supposed to feel thus.

Let us, for brevity's sake, call gratitude as an emotion gratitude E and gratitude as a virtue gratitude V.

Just as in the case of other virtues, there are two vices which are opposed both to gratitude V and to one another.

The first vice is a defect, falling short of what one should feel or do. The second vice errs on the side of excess, overdoing things.

The first, deficient, vice is called ingratitude. Ingratitude disposes us not to feel gratitude E and not to feel the tendency to act accordingly, although we are supposed to do so. The ungrateful person does not do what he or she is obliged to do.

The second excessive vice has no name at present. Let us call it hyper-gratitude. Hyper-gratitude disposes us to feel gratitude E and to feel the tendency to act accordingly although there is no good reason to expect us to do so. The hyper-grateful person does what he or she is not obliged to do.

Ingratitude, or hypo-gratitude, as it might be called, has three degrees (cf. St. Thomas Aquinas, STh II/II, 107, 2c, 3c).

(1) The ungrateful of the first degree does feel gratitude up to a point but not enough. He or she does not feel it long enough or not intensely enough. He or she expresses it too late or with a telling lack of cordiality. The counter-benefaction is desperately out of tune with the initial benefaction, undervaluing it shamelessly.

(2) The ungrateful of the second degree utterly abstains from gratitude E. He or she accordingly holds his tongue in response to what the benefactor does, and does not even dream of answering the initial benefaction with some counterbenefaction.

(3) The ungrateful of the third degree goes as far as to render evil for good. He or she is pained by the benefaction; nourishes malevolence toward his or her benefactor; runs down the benefactor and the benefaction; in the worst case he or she does not stop short of actually harming the benefactor.

Ceteris paribus, the third degree is ethically the most negative form of ingratitude, and is followed by the second and the first degrees.

Hyper-gratitude has two degrees.

(1) The hyper-grateful of the first degree feels gratitude E when he or she should not feel it at all. Hyper-gratitude of the first degree can take different forms:

(1.1) The hyper-grateful of the first degree might feel gratitude E, although no benefaction at all has actually occurred. Here, a pseudo-benefaction may erroneously be taken to be a real benefaction. For example, the pseudo-benefaction might be an action to which the pseudo-benefactor is legally bound; or it can be an action springing from sheer egoism; or the pseudo-benefaction was carried out by mistake.

(1.2) The hyper-grateful of the first degree might feel gratitude E in a case where there is a benefaction, but he or she is not the addressee of the benefaction. The hyper-grateful person here falsely believes that he or she is the intended object of what has been done.

(1.3) The hyper-grateful of the first degree might, even if he or she is in fact the intended addressee of a benefaction, still mistake a nonbenefactor for the genuine benefactor. Here, gratitude E is misaddressed.

(2) The hyper-grateful of the second degree feels gratitude E when he or she should feel it. But he or she feels it more than he or she should. The hyper-grateful of the second degree is delighted at receiving the benefaction more than he or she should be. He or she too often or too enthusiastically expresses his or her gratitude, probably embarrassing the benefactor or even making him- or herself a nuisance. The hyper-grateful of the second degree responds to the received, initial benefaction by tactlessly surpassing it.

However, we may chide the hyper-grateful of the second degree only mildly, echoing what Aristotle says about the spendthrift (NE IV 1, 1121a25ff.): He is felt to be not really bad in character, but foolish rather than evil or ignoble.

As a corollary it might be worth adding that ingratitude at times coincides with hyper-gratitude. To mistake, for example, a pseudo-benefactor for the real benefactor makes the beneficiary ungrateful toward the latter and hyper-grateful toward the former.

In line with this general answer the problems raised by the arguments can be solved.

Solution to Argument 1

Gratitude as an emotion (gratitude E) can replace the sign X in the phrase
(1) Peter feels X.
The sentence
(4) Peter feels gratitude (toward Paul)
is perfectly acceptable.

But gratitude as a virtue (gratitude V) is an inappropriate object of the verb "to feel." Peter cannot *feel* that he is disposed to feel gratitude E and that he is disposed to feel the tendency to speak and act according to gratitude E, if and only if Peter should feel it.

Solution to Argument 2

There is, in crude terms, an asymmetry to the effect that person Q is entitled to utter a sentence in the first person singular with an predicative adjective denoting an emotion, such as
(6) I am angry.
But Q's uttering a sentence in the first person singular with a predicative adjective denoting a moral quality, such as
(8) I am generous
sounds somewhat odd.

In the third person singular each is possible. There is nothing wrong with (a) Paul's characterizing Peter as sad (an emotion) and there is nothing wrong with (b) Paul's characterizing Peter as generous (a moral quality).

Hence, a sentence in the third person singular with a predicative adjective denoting a moral quality, such as
(22) Peter is generous
is just as adequate as a sentence in the third person singular with a predicative adjective denoting an emotion, such as
(23) Peter is sad.

Thus, sentences expressing a person's own gratitude E, that is, gratitude as an emotion, are flawless. But sentences in the first person singular *expressis verbis* characterizing the speaker as a grateful person (gratitude V) are either (i) not intended to be understood *sensu stricto* or (ii) simply to be dismissed as a faux pas, betraying the speaker's lack of grasp of appropriate conventions. An interpretation which is (i) not *sensu stricto* might be that the speaker is making a promise in disguise: "Come on, you can do me that favor. I won't forget about it and I'll reward you!"

In other words: the principle that a sentence in the first person singular characterizing the speaker as virtuous is questionable holds good. But this principle combined with the perfect acceptability of sentences like

(9) I am very/extremely grateful

does not necessarily entail the conclusion that gratitude is only an emotion and in no sense a moral quality. It is certainly possible that the semantics of "grateful" in first-person singular sentences are restricted to gratitude E or that these sentences are by convention meant and understood not verbatim but, for example, as indirect promises to recompense the benefactor for the benefaction.

Solution to Argument 3

The triadic structure

(14) Q is grateful to R because of C,

bears witness to the fact that gratitude E is indeed an emotion. What is more, this structure might be of some help to tell apart ingratitude, hyper-gratitude and gratitude V. Gratitude V has been defined as a virtue disposing us to feel gratitude E and to feel the tendency to speak and act accordingly if and only if we are supposed to feel it. On the other hand, ingratitude is a vice disposing us not to feel gratitude E when we *are* supposed to feel it. Hyper-gratitude is a vice disposing us to feel gratitude E when we are *not* supposed to feel it. Structure (14) helps to answer the question: when are we supposed to feel gratitude E and when are we not supposed to feel gratitude E? I suggest that the answer is: we are supposed to feel gratitude E, if and only if a particular set of constraints on Q, R and C are met.

For example:

- C must be an action or an omission not harming Q, but it must benefit Q.
- R must do or omit C on purpose and with a view to benefiting Q.
- R is not legally obliged to do C.

If these and many other constraints are met and Q fails to be grateful E, Q is ungrateful.

Conversely: If not all these constraints are met and Q nevertheless is grateful E, Q is hyper-grateful.

For example: R supports her poor old father Q only because she is legally bound to support him. In fact, she is sick and tired of him. But the old man wrongly assumes that his daughter R performs her care out of charity and filial affection. Q is hyper-grateful.

Solution to Argument 4

Virtue in general enables us to feel pleasure or pain if we are supposed to do so, and not to feel pleasure and pain if we are not supposed to do so (cf. Aristotle, NE II 3, 1104b3ff.). With vice, it is the other way about. The following table gives an overview of the possible cases.

	Q feels pleasure.	Q feels pain.	Q feels neither pain nor pleasure.
Q is supposed to feel pleasure.	(i) Virtue	(ii) Vice	(iii) Vice
Q is supposed to feel pain.	(iv) Vice	(v) Virtue	(vi) Vice
Q is supposed to feel neither pleasure nor pain.	(vii) Vice	(viii) Vice	(ix) Virtue

Gratitude E implies at least three forms of pleasure: (a) the pleasure of receiving the benefaction and (b) the pleasure provided by (b1) thanking the benefactor and (b2) by rewarding the benefactor's benefaction.

Hence, gratitude V, ingratitude, or hyper-gratitude engender pleasure, pain, or the absence of pleasure and pain, with reference to (a) receiving, (b1) thanking and (b2) rewarding. That is, sometimes with reference to (a), (b1) and (b2), but sometimes with reference only to one or two of the three forms of pleasure and pain, which are integral parts of gratitude. For example:

Case (i) applied to gratitude V means feeling (a), (b1) and (b2) when you are supposed to do so.

Case (ii) and case (iii) are forms of ingratitude. Case (ii) means being actually pained at (a) receiving, (b1) thanking or (b2) rewarding, let alone being pleased.

Case (iii) means the absence of pleasure and pain, which is a rather inactive form of ingratitude.

The grateful, conversely, is pained because of being unable to, or being prevented from uttering words of gratitude or rewarding the benefaction, which might well happen; for example, if the beneficiary is destitute or the benefactor is dead or unknown to the beneficiary (case (v)). Case (iv) is met by the ungrateful, who feels secret delight at being thus prevented from thanking and from rewarding. Case (vi) is similar to case (iv): here we have a milder form of ingratitude. The beneficiary is not actually pleased because of being unable to thank or to reward; but he or she is not pained, as he or she should be. The hyper-grateful (case (vii)) is pleased at receiving, thanking or rewarding when he or she should not be pleased, because there is no justification for these emotions. Accordingly the hyper-grateful is pained without being supposed to be (case (viii)) when unable to reward or to thank, although no one expects him or her to do so. The grateful, last but not least, is neither pleased nor pained as long as there is no reason to be so (case (ix)). Even his not being grateful E is an expression of his being grateful V, in that he does react adequately.

Solution to Argument 5

Gratitude E is a conjunction of pleasure and counterbenevolence. The simple negation of gratitude E means the absence of pleasure or the absence of counterbenevolence. The simple negation of gratitude E takes three forms.

(1) Pleasure is absent, but counterbenevolence is present.
(2) Pleasure is present, but counterbenevolence is absent.
(3) Pleasure is absent and counterbenevolence is absent.

Now, pleasure and counterbenevolence each have two opposites. Opposed to pleasure are (a) pain and (b) neither pain nor pleasure. (a) Pain is opposed as a contrary to pleasure; (b) the absence of pain and pleasure is opposed as a contradictory to pleasure.

By the same token, (a) malevolence is opposed to benevolence as a contrary; (b) the absence of malevolence and benevolence is opposed to benevolence rather as a contradictory.

Hence, form (1), (2) and (3) have sub-forms, specifying those opposites to gratitude E which are at least theoretically possible.

(1.1) R is pained, but feels counterbenevolence.
(1.2) R is neither pained nor pleased, but feels counterbenevolence.
(2.1) R is pleased, but feels malevolence.
(2.2) R is pleased, but feels neither countermalevolence nor counterbenevolence.
(3.1) R is pained and feels malevolence.
(3.2) R is neither pained nor pleased and feels malevolence.
(3.3) R is pained, but feels neither counterbenevolence nor malevolence.
(3.4) R is neither pained nor pleased nor does R feel malevolence nor counterbenevolence.

Each sub-form again has three varieties, in that pain or pleasure can be felt at receiving the benefaction, in thanking or in rewarding.

It is highly questionable whether forms (1.1), (1.2), (3.2) and (3.3) in fact ever occur. But the other forms are endemic in our social life; examples include the following:

The greedy miser gladly accepts being invited to the splendid dinner, but in his or her heart of hearts he hates and envies his or her benefactor (2.1).

The callous glutton at the same dinner wolfs down one delicacy after the other casting not a single thankful glance toward his or her benefactor (2.2).

The arrogant is pained because accepting help comes as a debasing experience to him or her. But at times even the arrogant cannot avoid falling back on the help of others. Thus, the arrogant is pained and hates the benefactor (3.1).

Those who are inattentive, hence indifferently taking what they can get without bothering about the source, are neither pained nor pleased at taking nor is there any sympathy or antipathy toward the benefactor (3.4).

It has to be remarked that form (3.4) is logically opposed to gratitude E, but that form (3. 4) is not an emotion due to the complete lack of pain and pleasure involved. The forms implying malevolence or counterbenevolence are emotions, in that they imply pain or pleasure.

To cut a long story short: Gratitude E has at least eight opposites, of which seven are emotions. Four of these eight opposites are rather common.

Solution to Argument 6

The beneficiary's gratitude E waning too fast, although he or she could properly be expected to harbor it for a long time, is a sign of the beneficiary's lack of gratitude V.

Solution to Argument 7

Virtues and vices dispose us to be active and to be passive as we should. Hence, gratitude V disposes us to be moved by others' behavior, to feel grateful E, if we are supposed to do so; and gratitude V prevents us from being moved by others' behavior to feel grateful E, if we are not supposed to be. In addition, gratitude V regulates our actively thanking and rewarding in tune with what we are expected to do.

Solution to Counterargument I

Gratitude E is a reaction on an emotional plane to what others have done. This reaction is morally neutral as long as we do not know what others have done. It is not neutral as soon as we know what others have done. To be more specific:

If gratitude E is the reaction to a benefaction, it is praiseworthy.

If gratitude E is a reaction to a malefaction or to something which is neither a benefaction nor a malefaction, it is blameworthy or at least not praiseworthy.

Solution to Counterargument II

Fighting is not automatically courageous; giving alms to the poor is not automatically generous. The mere act is not enough; virtue has to meet further criteria (cf. Aristotle, NE II 4, 1105a28–33):

(1) The agent has to act with knowledge, that is, he or she must not be ignorant.
(2) The action must result from a considered decision.
(3) The decision has to be made with a view to an adequate objective, that is with an appropriate intention.
(4) The action must spring from a firm and unchangeable trait of character.

Gratitude V has to meet these criteria just as much as any other full-blown virtue must.

Ad (1) A benefaction rewarded in ignorance does not meet the standards of gratitude V. For example: Q helps R in distress. R does not realize Q's help. Later R gives Q a present, thinking this present to be an initial benefaction.

Ad (2) Thanking and rewarding a benefaction on the spur of an overwhelming emotion without considering or really appreciating the relevant circumstances is not grateful V in the strict sense of the word.

Ad (3) To behave as though you were grateful but with the wrong intention is far from grateful V. A pseudo-grateful beneficiary who is just fishing for further benefactions from the benefactor or from those observing his seemingly grateful demeanor is not grateful V. Or a pseudo-grateful beneficiary who wants to get rid of the burden and obligation of gratitude as soon as possible, who just wants to pay off his benefactor, is anything but grateful V.

Ad (4) Words and acts of gratitude V must spring from a firm and unchanging disposition—forming a second nature, as it were. Hence, if the beneficiary behaves like the grateful this would do, but behaving thus out of duty, controlling the urge to behave otherwise, is not grateful V.

ACKNOWLEDGMENT

Without the invaluable support of Almut Baumgarten (MA), Dr. Dirk Fonfara and David Nisters (MA) the manuscript would not have the shape it has.

REFERENCES

Aquinas, Thomas. 1265–1274/1963–1981. *Summa Theologiae*. Trans. by Dominican Fathers. London: Blackfriars.

Aristotle. 1980. *Nicomachean Ethics*. Trans. by David Ross. Oxford: Oxford University Press.

———. 1946. *Rhetorica*. Trans. by W. Rhys Roberts. Oxford: Clarendon Press.

Chapter Four

Seeing Ourselves as Others See Us

The Place of Reason in Adam Smith's Theory of Moral Sentiments

Gerard Casey

O wad some Pow'r the giftie gie us
To see oursels as ithers see us!
It wad frae monie a blunder free us,
An' foolish notion[1]

At first glance, the ethical writings of Adam Smith would seem a most unlikely place in which to find reason recognized as a significant factor in ethical reflection. As a contributor to the Scottish Enlightenment, a student of Francis Hutcheson and a friend of David Hume, Smith should, it seems, if he is to be faithful to his heritage, demonstrate an anti-rationalist bias in ethical matters. That such appears to be the case is supported by the very title of his seminal work in ethics, *A Theory of Moral Sentiments*,[2] and is apparently reinforced when one starts to read through the work and discovers that notions such as sympathy are central to his analysis.[3] In making a feeling or sentiment such as sympathy foundational to his ethical analysis Smith appears to set himself on a collision course with those ethical theories in which reason plays a central role. I shall claim, contrary to appearances, that reason has an important part to play in Smith's final account of ethics; that what Smith rejects when he appears to reject reason, is a kind of austere ultrarationalism (à la Cudworth, Plato, or the Stoics) that would make reason the original independent source of our ethical judgments; and that, in the end, Smith does not reject reason but rather develops a complex theory of morality which permits reason to play a significant role in man's moral life. The chapter that follows begins with an account of Smith's treatment of sympathy, traces the emergence of a genuinely ethical dimension in Smith's thought with the notion of propriety and its further strengthening and refinement with the introduction of the idea of the impartial spectator. It then goes on to consider the emergence of general moral rules and the place of reason in Smith's ethical system. When Smith explicates the way in which we reason about how we should conduct ourselves as human beings, he makes clear not only how the operations of feeling and of reason support each other but how reasoning itself can be a moral capacity.

SMITH THE SENTIMENTALIST

Smith's analysis in TMS begins squarely with human psychology. Part I, Section I, Chapter I, is entitled "Of Sympathy" and in it Smith gives an account of the native and untutored human disposition to experience feelings of a certain kind whenever we witness others in certain situations. Smith combines this psychological account with a robust denial, a denial that echoes similar denials on the part of Hume and Butler, that human beings are ineluctably selfish (TMS I. i. 1. 1). We can and do desire the happiness of others, not merely as means to our own happiness (though if it increases our own happiness so much the better) but for its own sake. The sympathy[4] which we feel when we witness others in distress is engendered not by some mysterious causal connection to their feelings but by an imaginative conception of what we should feel if we were in that other's situation (TMS I. i. 1. 2).

There may well be a disparity between what another actually feels in a given situation and what we should feel were we to be in that situation. Our sympathy, then, is not necessarily an identification with what the other actually feels but an imaginative projection of what we should feel were we to be in that situation. That Smith's sympathy is clearly counterfactual can be seen in the case of the sympathy we feel for one who has lost the use of reason. A person in this position obviously cannot be rationally distressed; nevertheless, the spectator feels sympathy for him "from the consideration of what he himself would feel if he was reduced to the same unhappy situation, and, *what perhaps is impossible*, was at the same time able to regard it with his present reason and judgment" (TMS I. i. 1. 11; emphasis added).

PROPRIETY—FROM PSYCHOLOGY TO ETHICS

The starting point of TMS is a kind of psychology but very early in Part I Smith moves from psychology to ethics. While it is a brute psychological fact that we experience feelings in any given situation, and a brute psychological fact that spectators experience sympathy through an imaginative projection of themselves into the patient's place, the question can and does arise as to whether the relationship between the feelings aroused and the situation that arouses them is appropriate. This, for Smith, is where the concept of propriety enters into the picture and it is at this point that we see Smith begin to shift away from the first-person psychological perspective to a third-person ethical perspective.

Initially, Smith suggests that the standard of the appropriateness of the patient's feelings in any given situation is whether or not they correspond to the feelings of the spectator. Where there is concord between the feelings of the spectator and the feelings of the patient, there is approval; where such concord is lacking, the spectator disapproves of the patient's feelings. But it turns out that Smith is talking not so much about actual feelings (after all, the spectator may be out of sorts, depressed or unusually elated) but about what the spectator judges that the appropriate feelings *should* be.

Smith imagines himself encountering a man whose father has just died. The bereaved man naturally experiences grief and we, the spectators, approve of his grieving. But Smith notes that we may not in fact feel any particular pain or discomfort ourselves—perhaps we do not know the man or his father. He remarks:

> We have learned, however, from experience, that such a misfortune naturally excites such a degree of sorrow, and we know that *if* we took time to consider his situation, fully and in all its parts, we *should*, without doubt, most sincerely sympathize with him. It is upon the consciousness of this *conditional* sympathy, that our approbation of his sorrow is founded, even in those cases in which that *sympathy does not actually take place*; and the *general rules* derived from our preceding experience of what our sentiments *would* commonly correspond with, correct upon this, as upon many other occasions, the impropriety of our present emotions. (TMS I. i. 3. 4; emphasis added)

The conditionality in this passage expressed by "if," "should," "conditional," "not actually," and "would" is noteworthy. It is not what we in fact *do* feel but what we judge on the basis of general experience we *should* feel that is the basis of the judgment of propriety. The determination of propriety is the result of a judgment, not a mere feeling, and in making that judgment, we have moved from the factual to the normative.

For Smith, the existence of human society requires that sympathy operates in the human heart immediately and without calculation. However, it is not all one-way traffic from the spectator to the patient. Just as the spectator tries to imagine the appropriate feelings of the patient, so too, the patient tries to bring his feelings into line with what he imagines the spectator would judge to be appropriate (TMS I. i. 4. 7, 8). This produces a tendency toward a kind of equilibrium or, to use Smith's favorite musical metaphor, a concord. Smith claims that what he calls the soft, gentle and amiable virtues—condescension, indulgent humanity—are founded upon the efforts of the spectator while the great, awful (i.e., awesome) and respectable virtues—self-denial, self-government, self-control and propriety—are founded upon the moderating efforts of the patient (TMS I. i. 5. 1).

A society cannot subsist unless it has laws and unless those laws are generally observed. But the reason we generally act in accordance with justice is not that we have nicely calculated that by so doing society in general will flourish. On the contrary, our resentment of injustice, whether on our own behalf or on behalf of others, is instinctive and particular. "All men, even the most stupid and unthinking, abhor fraud, perfidy, and injustice, and delight to see them punished. But few men have reflected upon the necessity of justice to the existence of society, how obvious soever that necessity may appear to be" (TMS II. ii. 3. 9). We are constructed so as to have a natural sympathy with others and they with us, to judge the propriety of another's conduct inasmuch as he entertains the feelings that we consider appropriate, and to judge the propriety of our own conduct inasmuch as it stands to be approved by the spectation of others.

CONSCIENCE AND THE IMPARTIAL SPECTATOR— THE EMERGENCE OF REASON

But[5] however spontaneous and natural the process of sympathetic projection may be, would not a system of morality based upon such a foundation be irreducibly subjective and boundlessly variable? Even taking into account the counterfactual element that was noted above, how can we be sure that the consensus of judgments of approbation would in fact target actions that are truly praiseworthy? Enter the Impartial Spectator (who actually appears for the first time in TMS I. i. 5. 4). "But though man has, in this manner, been rendered the immediate judge of mankind, he has been rendered so only in the first instance; and an appeal lies from his sentence to a much higher tribunal, to the tribunal of their own consciences . . ." (TMS III. 2. 32). Sympathetic approbation, then, provides, as it were, only a decision of a court of first instance whose decisions are susceptible to judicial review by a higher court, the court of conscience, and the judge sitting in this court is "the supposed impartial and well-informed spectator . . . the man within the breast, the great judge and arbiter of their conduct" (TMS III. 2. 32).

Continuing with his judicial metaphor, Smith contrasts the function of what he describes as two tribunals within the human person; one external, the other internal. The external tribunal relates to the desire for actual praise and the avoidance of actual blame; the internal tribunal relates to the desire to be worthy of praise and to an aversion to being worthy of blame. One can be praised or blamed without in fact deserving either; and one can be praiseworthy or blameworthy without actually being praised or blamed. One tribunal is purely psychological; the other, ethical.[6] The impartial spectator which we have seen described as "the man within the breast, the great judge and arbiter" is a little later described as "this demigod within the breast." The task of this demigod is to provide a critical perspective from which one can imaginatively enter into the feelings of another person (or, in the limiting case, oneself), the point of such imaginative projection being to lend a degree of objectivity to a process prone to subjective distortion.

Smith moves even further away from the psychological and subjective elements in his account when he comes to develop his notion of conscience. In a passage that is reminiscent of Butler and anticipative of Newman, Smith asks us to conduct the following thought experiment. "Let us suppose that the great empire of China, with all its myriads of inhabitants, was suddenly swallowed up by an earthquake, and let us consider how a man of humanity in Europe, who had no sort of connection with that part of the world, would be affected upon receiving intelligence of this dreadful calamity" (TMS III. 3. 4).

Pause here for a moment before reading on and conduct the thought experiment that Smith suggests. Call to mind some recent disaster from far away—an earthquake in Haiti or Chile, a tsunami somewhere in Asia—and try to remember what you said, what you thought and what you did. In what way, if any, did the news of this disaster affect your daily routine or your mundane enjoyments? Now, come back to Smith's account:

> [The man of humanity] would, I imagine, first of all, express very strongly his sorrow for the misfortune of that unhappy people, he would make many melancholy reflections upon the precariousness of human life, and the vanity of all the labours of man, which could thus be annihilated in a moment. . . . And when all this fine philosophy was over, when all these humane sentiments had been once fairly expressed, he would pursue his business or his pleasure, take his repose or his diversion, with the same ease and tranquillity, as if no such accident had happened. (TMS III. 3. 4)

Callous as it may seem, I suggest that Smith is absolutely correct in his supposition. How could it be otherwise? Were we to be overset by bad news from anywhere affecting anybody we should spend our days in a permanent state of sorrow and distress—but in fact, we can eat our dinners while watching reports of death and destruction on television.[7] Contrast our apparent callous unconcern regarding the faraway disaster with the emotional turmoil brought on by some event, insignificant in the grand scheme of things, which upsets the even tenor of our way. Smith remarks somewhat cynically that if a man were to be told that he would lose his little finger tomorrow "he would not sleep to-night; but, provided he never saw them, he will snore with the most profound security over the ruin of a hundred millions of his brethren . . . " (TMS III. 3. 4; cf. also II. ii. 2. 2 and 3. 4).

Given this disparity in our reactions to the outlandish outrage on the one hand, and the cozy catastrophe on the other, how should we act if presented with a choice between the two? Smith wonders if a man of humanity would "be willing to sacrifice the lives of a hundred millions of his brethren, provided he had never seen them . . . to prevent . . . this paltry misfortune to himself?" (TMS III. 3. 4). You might expect Smith to answer this question in the affirmative but he doesn't. But why does Smith think this, given our natural inclination to prefer ourselves and our interests to those of others? It cannot be because of "that feeble spark of benevolence which Nature has lighted up in the human heart" that we are capable or resisting our selfish urges (TMS III. 3. 4). The emotional impulses of sympathy and benevolence are far too weak to overcome our natural disinclination to favor others over ourselves. Similarly weak is our love of neighbor. What in fact allows us to transcend our self-centeredness is "a stronger power, a more forcible motive, which exerts itself upon such occasions. It is reason, principle, conscience, the inhabitant of the breast, the man within, the great judge and arbiter of our conduct" (TMS III. 3. 4; emphasis added).

Let us be quite clear about what Smith is saying here. Reason is a stronger force than either sympathy or benevolence. It is reason rather than sympathy or benevolence that brings home to us that as moral beings we are simply one among others, *unus inter pares*, and in no rationally defensible way can we be considered to be more important than any other moral being. If I am the center of the universe to myself, so too is every other person the center of his universe. It is reason that "whenever we are about to act so as to affect the happiness of others, calls to us . . . that we are but one of the multitude, in no respect better than any other in it; and that when we prefer ourselves so shamefully and so blindly to others, we become the proper objects of resentment, abhorrence, and execration" (TMS III. 3. 4).

Smith's idea of the emergence of a distinctly moral perspective from a sub-moral context is paralleled in the thinking of a philosopher who is geographically, linguistically and culturally remote from him. The Confucianism tradition recognizes four spheres of ethical significance, nested one within the other: the natural, the consequential, the moral and the transcendent.

The natural sphere is the realm of instincts, of unreflective desires and habits, of raw emotions. Here, we operate spontaneously, not according to calculation. Developmentally, it is the way we begin when we are babies. As a baby, I am the center of the universe. I want what I want and I want it now. In so far as I recognize other people, they exist only to serve me. While most of us develop beyond this sphere as we mature morally, we never abandon it completely and, in times of stress, we can easily revert to it.

The consequentialist sphere is characterized by a conscious and calculated maximizing of self-interest. At this stage, we have learned to refrain from acting upon our instinctive, spontaneous desires, all the better to achieve them in the long run. Other people, though no longer ignored, are still regarded primarily as means toward the attainment of our goals; now, however, we have learned to dissemble our self-centered goals so as to manipulate others into helping us to achieve what we desire. What is objectionable here is not using others as means to ends—it is difficult to see how we could live if we did not do this; think of our relation to bus drivers, waiters, and the like— what is objectionable is using others *solely* as means to ends so that they are fundamentally unrecognized as ends in themselves.

For Confucius, as for Smith, the real breakthrough in moral development comes when we finally realize that other people are not simply helpful or obstructive items in our environment, not simply means to the realization of our own particular purposes, but are ends in themselves, persons just like us, with their own needs, desires and interests, their own hopes and fears, sorrows and joys, centers of their own moral universes. This insight and its realization in practice is, for Smith, the achievement of reason, principle and conscience.

THE EMERGENCE OF GENERAL RULES AND THE PLACE OF REASONS

Smith's[8] ideal man is the man of constancy, firmness, wisdom and justice who is ever aware of the judgment of the impartial spectator. In an anticipation of a typically Kantian theme, Smith believes that the ideal man does not merely conform to the sentiments of the impartial spectator, he actually adopts them (TMS III. 3. 25). From our continual observations of the conduct of others, we come to form certain general rules[9] about what is fit and proper to be done. Smith believes that these general rules of morality "are ultimately founded upon experience of what, in particular instances, our moral faculties, our natural sense of merit and propriety, approve, or disapprove of" (TMS III. 4. 8). It is important for Smith that we remember that approval and disapproval come first and then the rules emerge rather than the other way around. "We do not originally approve or condemn particular actions; because, upon examination, they appear to be agreeable or inconsistent with a certain general rule. The general rule, on the contrary, is formed, by finding from experience, that all actions of a certain kind, or circumstanced in a certain manner, are approved or disapproved of" (TMS III. 4. 8).

These general rules emerge from our social practices of approbation and disapprobation as those are exercised in particular cases. Moreover, these rules emerge from practice without conscious advertence. "Our continual observations upon the conduct of others, *insensibly* lead us to form to ourselves certain general rules concerning what is fit and proper either to be done or be avoided" (TMS III. 4. 6; emphasis added). The rules are not *constructed* upon some scheme or plan but are rather *discovered* in our practices and are then applied reflexively to practice. In moral development, both individual and social, this application of rules to practice is secondary and derivative. Smith is rejecting any theory which makes morality, *in the first instance*, a direct intuition of the general nature of the good, whether in Hutcheson's moral sense (see TMS III.4. 5) or in the form of some kind of rational intuitionism. Smith accepts that once general rules have been formed we do in fact appeal to them in our judgment on particular cases: "[The general rules] are upon these occasions commonly cited as the ultimate foundations of what is just and unjust in human conduct" (TMS III. 4. 11). It is this very practice of appealing to general rules that leads us to think, erroneously, that the rules come first, to suppose that "the original judgments of mankind with regard to right and wrong, were formed like the decisions of a court of judicatory,[10] by considering first the general rule, and then, secondly, whether the particular action under consideration fell properly within its comprehension" (TMS III. 4. 11). The derivation of the general rules does not detract from reason's role in ethics.[11] We saw above that Smith believes that only reason has the power to accomplish what neither benevolence nor sympathy can accomplish, namely, the ability to overcome the human inclination to self-centeredness.

Smith does in fact reject a certain rationalist conception of ethics but, I believe, the target of his criticism is, for the most part, certain specific classical or contemporary forms of exaggerated rationalism. According to Smith, the ethical doctrine that we have a rational intuitive faculty that enables us to distinguish right from wrong resulted from attempts to confute the horrid doctrine of Thomas Hobbes. "In order to confute so odious a doctrine, it was necessary to prove, that antecedent to all law or positive institution, the mind was naturally endowed with a faculty, by which it distinguished in certain actions and affections, the qualities of right, laudable, and virtuous, and in others those of wrong, blamable, and vicious" (TMS VIII. iii. 2. 3). Because the mind was held to exercise this capacity in an a priori fashion, our notions of right and wrong must then emerge from reason operating in the same manner in which it makes intellectual judgments: "Since the mind, therefore, had a

notion of those distinctions antecedent to all law, it seemed necessarily to follow, that it derived this notion from reason, which pointed out the difference
between right and wrong, in the same manner in which it did that between
truth and falsehood" (TMS VII. iii. 2. 5).

Now comes a remarkable set of paragraphs that, it seems to me, contains
the essence of Smith's thinking on the originative sources of ethics and the
place of reason in ethics (TMS VII. iii. 2. 6–9). In these paragraphs, Smith
begins by remarking "that virtue consists in conformity to reason, is true *in
some respects*, and this faculty may very justly be considered as, *in some
sense,* the source and principle of approbation and disapprobation, and of all
solid judgments concerning right and wrong" (TMS VII. iii. 2. 6; emphasis
added). Smith, then, is willing to allow reason some place in the ethical
scheme of things. What place, precisely? Just what is it that reason contributes to the process? Reason discovers the general rules of justice; reason
forms our ideas of what is prudent, decent, generous and noble[12] (TMS VII.
iii. 2. 6). How does reason do all this? Initially, at least, by a process of induction from experience, induction, as Smith rightfully remarks, being one of the
operations of reason. "We observe in a great variety of particular cases what
pleases or displeases our moral faculties, what these approve or disapprove
of, and, by induction from this experience, we establish those general rules.
But induction is always regarded as one of the operations of reason" (TMS
VII. iii. 2. 6). The general maxims of morality thus derived via induction
from experience act to regulate most of our moral judgments, what Smith
terms "our most solid judgments . . . with regard to right and wrong," which,
if they were dependent upon sentiment and feeling, would be multiple and
various. In this way, then, "virtue may very properly be said to consist in a
conformity to reason, and so far this faculty may be considered as the source
and principle of approbation and disapprobation" (TMS VII. iii. 2. 6).

Given Smith's reputation as a sentimentalist, this seems to be an extraordinary position for him to hold. Why, then, given these passages, is Smith
commonly taken to be a rationalist in his ethics? It is clear that he has some
deep-rooted objection or other to reason's role in ethics but whatever that
might be it is clear that it is not a blanket rejection. What exactly is it in the
rationalist approach to ethics that Smith is objecting to? It turns out to be
connected with the *point of origin* of the process. Smith is willing to grant
that reason is the source of our general moral rules and of the judgments we
make in accord with them but he contends that "it is altogether absurd and
unintelligible to suppose that the *first* perceptions of right and wrong can be
derived from reason, even in those particular cases upon the experience of
which the general rules are formed" (TMS VII. iii. 2. 7; emphasis added).
These first perceptions are not, as it were, deductions from general principles

but the matrix in which and out of which our moral notions develop. "These first perceptions, as well as all other experiments upon which any general rules are founded, cannot be the object of reason, but of immediate sense and feeling" (TMS VII. iii. 2. 7). Smith adverts once again to the role of induction in the formation of moral rules[13] but denies that reason can, ab initio, ground our moral notions: "But reason cannot render any particular object either agreeable or disagreeable to the mind for its own sake" (TMS VII. iii. 2. 7).

This passage contains a description of the operation of reason that seems to reduce reason's function to the purely instrumental: "Reason may show that this object is the *means* of obtaining some other which is naturally either pleasing or displeasing, and in this manner may render it either agreeable or disagreeable *for the sake of something else*" (TMS VII. iii. 2. 7; emphasis added) but, I would argue, this reduction is more apparent than real. What Smith is keen to controvert is the ultrarationalist thesis that reason *alone* is the *original* source of moral judgment, not, as we have seen him aver, that reason discovers the general rules of justice and forms our ideas of what is prudent, decent, generous and noble. On the contrary, the roots of morality lie in our immediate emotional engagement: "nothing can be agreeable or disagreeable for its own sake, which is not rendered such by immediate sense and feeling" (TMS VII. iii. 2. 7).

Smith's use of the term "perception" in this passage ("the first perceptions of right and wrong") is revealing. These original perceptions are not purely rational, which is not to say that they are irrational or anti-rational, merely that they are a-rational or pre-rational.[14] It is from these perceptions, however, that reason, through a process of induction, arrives at the general moral rules that Smith admits provide the means by which we moderate and regulate our moral life.

As a way of seeing what Smith is about in these passages it might be useful to consider the account of the generation of concepts given by St. Thomas Aquinas. Aquinas believes that all our knowledge has its roots in our contact with the world through our senses. The original sensory matrix is transformed in time into a perceptual matrix which is prolonged in us beyond the point of actual contact with the world by means of what have come to be called the interior senses—memory, imagination, the cogitative sense and the common sense. Latent in these sensory/perceptual matrices are concepts, the primary purpose of which is, after their abstraction, their reapplication to the matrices from which they emerged. Human beings then have no unmediated conceptual knowledge of the world around them. All their knowledge, however conceptually refined it may become, has its roots in sensation and perception. In a similar way, then, Smith appears to claim that our moral knowledge, that knowledge embodied in principles and rules, is inductively derived from a pre-rational experience of human social life to which it is then reapplied.

While it may well be true that the principles and rules are derived ultimately from experience, Smith admits that, once derived, they can and do themselves become norms of judgment. Clearly, in saying that "reason cannot render any particular object either agreeable or disagreeable to the mind for its own sake" and that "nothing can be agreeable or disagreeable for its own sake, which is not rendered such by immediate sense and feeling" (TMS VII. iii. 2. 7), Smith is denying something to reason. But that something is not any and every role in the process of moral judgment. It might be worth reminding ourselves again that Smith believes that reason, not benevolence or sympathy, is the power by which the human inclination toward self-centeredness can be overcome. What Smith *is* denying is that we have a primary, rational, intuitive experience-independent insight into matters of right and wrong.

CONCLUSION

I have argued in this chapter that Smith's theory of moral sentiments opposes an ultrarationalist conception of ethics but is consistent with the modified rationalistic theories of some classical and medieval authors. So, for example, Aristotle's ethical theory is constructed upon the basis of the proper training of emotional responses and the habituation of actions, both of which are pre-rational (*not* anti-rational) in their beginnings. Likewise, Thomas Aquinas gives us a sophisticated treatment of the structure of human action which links it firmly to the emotional and affective dimension of human existence.

By grounding his moral theory on the pre-rational sentiment of sympathy, Smith ensures its motivational force is not compromised. But sentiment, while a starting point and thus a necessary condition of morality, is not sufficient and so Smith refines and develops the rational element in his account via the notions of propriety and the impartial spectator and from those ideas to the notion of general moral rules. In making clear the way in which we reason about how we should conduct ourselves as human beings, Smith shows not only how the operations of feeling and of reason support each other but how reasoning itself can be a moral capacity.

Smith's naturalistic approach is capable of being generalized and extended outside the context of ethics; he himself seems to be aware of this when he says that "The rules of justice may be compared to the rules of grammar" (TMS III. 6. 11). If morality is taken to be the reflective appropriation of the norms embedded in the practices of human sociability, grammar would be the reflective appropriation of the socially embedded practice of language speaking, and logic the reflective appropriation of the socially embedded practice of argumentation. Seeing this approach applied to the normative elements of language, law and logic—a task well beyond the scope of this chapter—could well make Smith's approach to ethics appear less singular and all the more persuasive.

NOTES

1. From Robert Burns: "To a Louse: On Seeing One on a Lady's Bonnet at Church" (1786). In an interview in *The Scotsman* (14 January 2009) Robert Crawford remarks that "Burns read Adam Smith's *Theory of Moral Sentiments*, published in 1759, and he knows it well because he refers to it several times." The notorious passage from "To a Louse" is "just a straight versification of something in Adam Smith." Compare Adam Smith, *The Theory of Moral Sentiments* (hereafter TMS) III. 4. 6: "This self-deceit, this fatal weakness of mankind, is the source of half the disorders of human life. If we saw ourselves in the light in which others see us, or in which they would see us if they knew all, a reformation would generally be unavoidable. We could not otherwise endure the sight."

2. *The Theory of Moral Sentiments*/TMS is divided into seven parts, these parts being indicated by large Roman numerals. The parts in turn are subdivided into sections (small Roman numerals), chapters (Arabic numerals) and paragraphs (Arabic numerals). So I. iii. 3. 8 signifies: Part One, Section 3, Chapter 3, Paragraph 8. Parts III, IV and V have no sections.

3. According to the writers of the "General Introduction" to the Glasgow edition of Smith's *Wealth of Nations,* Smith offers an account of the origin of the rules of morality "which places him in the anti-rationalist tradition of Hutcheson and Hume" (see Smith 1976a, 16).

4. Smith's account of sympathy allows it to range over others' joys as well as sorrows—sympathy is thus any kind of fellow-feeling (TMS I. i. 1. 5). Today, we should probably describe Smith's sympathy as "empathy."

5. For "conscience" see Otteson 2002, 66–84.

6. A comical portrayal of the agony of receiving praise which is not one's due can be seen in Preston Sturges's film *Hail the Conquering Hero.* The inappropriately heroically named antihero, Woodrow Lafayette Pershing Truesmith, desires nothing more than to follow in the footsteps of his Marine-hero father. He dreams of returning to his home town to a hero's welcome; unfortunately, he is rejected for service on medical grounds. Befriended by a group of Marines under the command of the redoubtable Sergeant Heppelfinger, he ends up getting the hero's welcome he has always imagined but under false pretenses. The praise of those from whom he most desires praise when he knows he has done nothing to deserve such praise makes his hero's welcome turn to dust and ashes.

7. Smith remarks caustically on the "whining and melancholy moralists, who are perpetually reproaching us with our happiness, while so many of our brethren are in

misery." A mind so tender of the undoubted if unknown sufferings of others as to be incapable of repose could, Smith says, "serve no other purpose than to render miserable the person who possessed it" (TMS III. 3. 9).

8. For the whole section, see Otteson 2000.

9. "Without this sacred regard to general rules, there is no man whose conduct can be much depended upon. It is this which constitutes the most essential difference between a man of principle and honour and a worthless fellow" (TMS III. 5. 2).

10. His comment on the law is apt in that while, once the common law is up and running, the courts are concerned with the application of existing rules to novel circumstances; however, in the first place, the rules were formed from particular judgments about particular cases and, in fact, are constantly emended in the light of particulars.

11. Smith describes the lawlike nature of these rules in a passage whose prose is a startling shade of purple: "All general rules are commonly denominated laws. . . . But those general rules which our moral faculties observe in approving or condemning whatever sentiment or action is subjected to their examination, may much more justly be denominated such. They have a much greater resemblance to what are properly called laws, those general rules which the sovereign lays down to direct the conduct of his subjects. Like them they are rules to direct the free actions of men: they are prescribed most surely by a lawful superior, and are attended too with the sanction of rewards and punishments. Those vicegerents of God within us, never fail to punish the violation of them, by the torments of inward shame, and self-condemnation; and on the contrary, always reward obedience with tranquillity of mind, with contentment, and self-satisfaction" (TMS III. 5. 6).

12. In her paper "Adam Smith's Reconstruction of Practical Reason," Maria Carrasco challenges the conventional interpretation that sentiments are the foundations of Smith's theory of morals, arguing that his system can be seen as a theory of practical reasoning. Why do many, if not most, commentators think that reason has little or no place in Smith's system? According to Carrasco, largely for historical and contextual reasons. Hutcheson, Hume and Smith all aimed to refute the egoistic theories of Hobbes and Mandeville, and so "discarding medieval theological systems and the implausible (for them) rationalistic theories of some of their modern predecessors (the Cambridge Platonists), sentiments were the natural alternative for these three philosophers" (Carrasco 2004, 83). There, however, the similarity between our three philosophers ends. While Hutcheson and Hume proposed "two different sentimentalist accounts of ethics," Carrasco believes that Smith constructed a system of practical reasoning "mainly through the introduction of the supposed impartial spectator" (ibid.). She argues that "when Smith rejects reason as the foundation of morality, he only rejects theoretical reason, leaving practical reason untouched" and that when he talks of "sentiments" "he means something much more elaborate than simple emotions" (ibid., 84).

13. "It is by finding in a vast variety of instances that one tenor of conduct constantly pleases in a certain manner, and that another as constantly displeases the mind, that we form the general rules of morality" (TMS VII. iii. 2. 7).

14. "The man, however, who deviates from goodness is not blamed, whether he do so in the direction of the more or of the less, but only the man who deviates more

widely; for he does not fail to be noticed. But up to what point and to what extent a man must deviate before he becomes blameworthy it is not easy to determine by reasoning, any more than anything else that is perceived by the senses; such things depend on particular facts, and *the decision rests with perception*" (Aristotle, NE II 9, 1109b18–23, trans. by David Ross; emphasis added).

REFERENCES

Aristotle. 1980. *Nicomachean Ethics*. Trans. by David Ross. Oxford: Oxford University Press.

Bonar, J. 1926. "*The Theory of Moral Sentiments* by Adam Smith, 1759." *Journal of Philosophical Studies* 1 (3): 333–53.

Carrasco, Maria A. 2004. "Adam Smith's Reconstruction of Practical Reason." *The Review of Metaphysics* 58 (1): 81–116.

———. 2008. "Adam Smith on Morality, Justice and the Political Constitution of Liberty." *The Journal of Scottish Philosophy* 6 (2): 135–56.

Coker, Edward W. 1990. "Adam Smith's Concept of the Social System." *Journal of Business Ethics* 9 (2): 139–42.

Darwall, Stephen. 1999. "Sympathetic Liberalism: Recent Work on Adam Smith." *Philosophy and Public Affairs* 28 (2): 139–64.

Dun Uyl, Douglas J., and Charles L. Griswold, Jr. 1996. "Adam Smith on Friendship and Love." *Review of Metaphysics* 9 (3): 609–37.

Hetherington, Norris S. 1983. "Isaac Newton's Influence on Adam Smith's Natural Laws in Economics." *Journal of the History of Ideas* 44 (3): 497–505.

Locke, John. 1959. *An Essay concerning Human Understanding*. Vol. 2. New York: Dover Publications.

Macfie, A. L. 1959. "Adam Smith's Moral Sentiments as Foundation for His Wealth of Nations." *Oxford Economic Papers* New Series 11 (3): 209–28.

Paul, Ellen F. 1977. "Adam Smith: A Reappraisal." *Journal of Libertarian Studies* 1 (4): 289–306.

Otteson, James R. 2000. "Adam Smith on the Emergence of Morals: A Reply to Eugene Heath." *British Journal for the History of Philosophy* 8 (3): 545–51.

———. 2002. *Adam Smith's Marketplace of Life*. Cambridge: Cambridge University Press.

Raynor, David S. 1984. "Hume's Abstract of Adam Smith's *Theory of Moral Sentiments*." *Journal of the History of Philosophy* 22 (1): 51–79.

Schertz, Matthew V. 2007. "Empathy as Intersubjectivity: Resolving Hume and Smith's Divide." *Studies in Philosophy and Education* 26 (2): 165–78.

Sen, Amartya. 2009. "Adam Smith and the Contemporary World." *Erasmus Journal for Philosophy and Economics* 3 (1): 50–67.

Smith, Adam. 1976a. *An Inquiry into the Nature and Causes of the Wealth of Nations*. Volume 1. General eds. R. H. Campbell and A. S. Skinner; textual ed. W. B. Todd. Oxford: Clarendon Press.

———. 1976b. *The Theory of Moral Sentiments.* Ed. by D. D. Raphael and A. L. Macfie. Oxford: Oxford University Press.

———. 2002. *The Theory of Moral Sentiments.* Ed. by Knut Haakonssen. Cambridge: Cambridge University Press.

Witztum, Amos. 2005. "Property Rights and the Right to the Fruits of One's Labor: A Note on Adam Smith's Jurisprudence." *Economics and Philosophy* 22 (1): 279–89.

Chapter Five

Reasons to Act and Practical Reasoning

Thomas Gil

When asked why we have done what we have done, we normally refer to different and heterogeneous kinds of phenomena that have the function of explaining what we did. We mention needs and interests, desires, aims and decisions, norms, promises and orders, to name but a few of the phenomena we consider to be reasons for what we do. In reasoning processes aimed at justifying how we should act in certain specific situations, we use the practical reasons we have to behave in a specific way *as arguments*. In this contribution I attempt to describe, in a first section, some of the phenomena which can become reasons to act for us. Then, in a second section, I try to show how we use our reasons to act as arguments in our reasoning activity about what we should do, or what we should abstain from doing.

This is intended to be a specific way of presenting practical reasons and practical reasoning. It is not intended to reconstruct, using a complicated two-phase-model, what would be a single process of justifying our doings and omissions; rather it stresses that having reasons to act is not always identical with reasoning activity about our practical reasons. In addition, there is a further advantage this way of reconstructing the nature and functioning of practical reasons may have. If we proceed in this way, the reasonableness of a certain moderate naturalism concerning our reasons and reasoning activities may become manifest.

HAVING REASONS

Human beings have needs and interests. Like animals and plants, human beings have different needs. They need food to go on existing, they need air to breathe, and they need a certain temperature to survive. Without nourishment, oxygen, and a certain bodily temperature, they are not able to go on living. Their lives depend on such basic things for their physical continuity. In addition to this, human beings are interested in getting good food, in eating it in the company of other pleasant human beings, in breathing uncontaminated air, and in wearing nice clothes, or in living in comfortable houses. Because they have needs and interests, human beings have reasons to act in certain ways, so that they can have food, get air, and maintain their bodily temperature.

Needs and interests are reasons to act. There are different sorts of needs and interests. Talking about needs and interests is talking about the motivational structure of human life. Concerning needs, we cannot concentrate exclusively on physiological needs such as hunger and thirst. There are many other needs with a physiological basis, but which cannot be understood in only physiological terms: needs like safety needs (security, stability, protection, freedom from fear and anxiety), and the need for an orderly, predictable, lawful, and organized environment. Some of these further needs are of a psychological nature. Others are culturally acquired and recognized needs, like the need for secure jobs (with tenure and social protection), the now-instinctive desire for a savings account, and for insurances of various kinds (for example those concerning medical, dental, unemployment, disability, old age). Certain needs are of a very complex nature, like the need for social and emotional recognition, love and aesthetic needs, the need to belong to some social class or group, the need to be esteemed, or the need for happiness and self-actualization. Many of these needs could also be understood in terms of basic interests human persons have.

All these needs and fundamental interests motivate and activate individuals. They move them to act in different ways, and are for them, therefore, real reasons to act, guiding principles of action. Of course, not all the reasons to act that human beings actually have are needs and interests. Nevertheless, needs and interests are powerful reasons to act for human individuals. Apart from needs and interests, beliefs, desires, and decisions can also be reasons for action. A person's belief that it will rain is a reason for that person to take an umbrella before leaving the house. A person's firm belief that it is morally right to keep promises can be the reason why that person keeps his or her promises. The person's desire to please her friends can be the reason why that person gives a party. And her decision to go to London is the reason why she goes to the travel agency (or goes online) to buy a ticket to reach the English capital.

Desires, like needs and interests, are powerful reasons to act. When we want to have something, we have a reason to act in such a way that we get the thing we want. If we want to go to the pictures, we have a reason to leave our house and walk or drive to the cinema in which the film we are interested in is going to be shown. If we want to spend a holiday on a sunny island far away from the town in which we live, we have a reason to book a hotel on that island, and we have a further reason to book a flight that will bring us to the island. Desires are reasons for action, reasons that motivate us to act in specific ways. They guide our doings and actions.

Every desire, whatever its object, is a reason to act for the person who has it. Of course, this does not imply that the person will actually act according to his or her desire. He or she could have other reasons, stronger reasons not to act in such a way. In this case, the desire is a reason to act that is overridden by stronger or more important reasons. Desires are, consequently, not the only reasons we have. Occasionally, we have reasons to act that are independent of our desires. Imagine the author of a good book we have read with enthusiasm is in town in a bookshop reading parts of his book in public, or giving a lecture about the difficult art of writing. We always had wanted to meet him personally to see how he speaks, how he develops his thoughts, how he argues. Thus, we have a *reason* to go to the bookshop to the public lecture on writing he is delivering there. But it may be that we do not actually *want* to go out: what we *want* to do is to slouch around at home. This example shows that there being good reason for a certain person's doing such-and-such a thing is independent of his or her wanting to do it. Not all reasons to act are desires. Frequently, we have reasons to act that do not coincide with the desires we have. In fact, they may be in opposition to them or in conflict with them.

There are other cases that can better illustrate this independence of certain reasons to act from our desires. Suppose someone would enjoy a certain activity more than any other she could do at the time, but she has not thought about that activity as a possibility for her at the present moment. If this were so, there would be a reason for her doing it. It follows from this, that there can be a reason for someone's doing something even though she does not want to do it, for it may not have crossed her mind to do it. And if it has not crossed her mind, she cannot want to do it.

Desires are reasons for action. Interests are reasons for action too. But there are more reasons for action than desires and interests. The fact that we enjoy doing something is a strong reason for us to do it. The fact that something is in our interest is a strong reason for doing it too. But, and this is the point at which the whole matter gets complicated, there are present and future desires, present and future interests, and there are present and future desires and interests of others which may become reasons for us to act in certain ways. An action may be in my present interest because I would enjoy it, because it would give me immediate satisfaction, or relieve me from an unpleasant feeling, or cure a certain pain I feel. Another action may be in my future interest because it will lead to a considerable annual income, or to a happy retirement, or to the acquisition of something valuable that I will enjoy in future times. Present interests are not identical with future interests. The same happens with desires. My present desires, strong reasons to act for me, are not identical with future desires I may have. So I may have different reasons to act, depending upon which desires or interests I prefer now, either my present desires and interests, or future desires and interests I may have, and that I am able to anticipate at the present moment.

Taking into consideration present and future desires and interests of others makes the story even more complicated. For some authors, this is the beginning of moral reasoning, as they identify the taking into consideration of others' rational desires and interests with morality. Moral reasons would then be the reasons I have to do something because others have a legitimate claim that I must take into consideration when I act. Others, who have their own desires and interests, expect from me that I do certain things, and they do so on a rational basis, with a moral legitimation. Therefore, the reasons that I have to act are not all of them based on my own desires and interests. Some of them may derive from the desires and interests of others, from their legitimate expectations concerning my own actions.

Our reasons to act may also be the decisions we have taken to perform an action. Decisions can, therefore, also be reasons for action. Four features characterize decisions: 1) To decide is to form an intention at a certain time, an intention that had not existed before that specific point of time. 2) Decisions are normally reached as a result of deliberations. In the normal case, someone decides to do something when he or she forms the intention to do it after a process of deliberation whether to do it or not. The process of deliberation comes about in order to examine if the action to be performed is a suitable means to solve a certain practical problem with which the agent is confronted. This does not mean that sometimes, in exceptional cases, decisions to perform an action are not taken without having first considered the reasons for it. Standard cases are, however, those of intentions formed on the basis of deliberation. 3) Decisions are taken some time before the action. Occasionally, we speak of a decision that is immediately carried out. But normally one decides to perform an action some time in the future. 4) Decisions are reasons to act. A decision is, for the agent, always a reason for performing the act he or she decided to perform and for neglecting further reasons and arguments. To make a decision is to put an end to deliberation, and to reach a conclusion as to what one ought to do. To decide what to do is to rule out the competing claims of other possible reasons. In this respect decisions have a certain similarity with promises. Promises are designed to increase trust and predictability in interpersonal relations. Decisions are designed to enable people to settle matters in their own minds and put an end to deliberation, something that also contributes to increasing trust and predictability in interpersonal relations, when others know how the person who is going to act has decided to proceed. The analogy between decisions and promises is a close one, as can be seen by comparing both with oaths and vows. Decisions, like promises, are reasons for performing certain acts, namely the acts decided upon.

Functionally seen, which means according to the role they factually play in certain concrete practical contexts of action, there are different sorts of reasons. These include prima facie reasons, overridden and conclusive reasons, operative and auxiliary reasons, primary and derivative reasons, prudential, moral, mandatory and exclusionary reasons, and first-order and second-order reasons (Raz 1990, 33ff.).

Sometimes, we have reasons to act in ways that contradict each other. The single reasons we have to do this or that are reasons that have not been critically examined. These single reasons are called prima facie reasons, or reasons not yet examined and critically analyzed: reasons we would accept if they did not conflict with each other, recommending incompatible actions to perform. When we have examined conflicting reasons in a process of deliberation after which we are able to arrive at a conclusion, we obtain conclusive reasons, the reasons we accept after critical examination that will guide our practical conduct. The other reasons involved in the critical examination become the "overridden" reasons we decide not to take into consideration anymore.

When conflicting reasons bear on a problem or a decision situation, we determine what ought to be done by assessing the relative strength or weight of the conflicting reasons. In the presence of conflicting, mutually incompatible reasons we think the agents should act on the balance of reasons. Conflicting reasons, we take it, are to be resolved by the relative weight or strength of each reason singly, which determines which of the reasons will override the others and will thus become the "operative" reasons that will determine our course of action. Once we have critically selected which reason is the operative reason, the reason that states the valid goal to be attained, we can discover that we have other reasons, "auxiliary" reasons, necessary or suitable to realize our goal. Expressed in a formalized language: 1) "G" is my interest; 2) "that p" is sufficient for "G"; 3) doing "A" will bring about (or is likely to bring about) "that p"; it follows that relative to 1), 2), 3) I ought to do A. Here 1) states an operative reason; 2) and 3) state auxiliary reasons. While 1) is a complete reason, the operative reason, 2) and 3) are by themselves not reasons for any action. They are able to act as reasons only due to 1), which is to say that they are auxiliary reasons of the operative reason. We could also call them "derivative" reasons of the "primary" reason on which they are dependent and without which they would not be reasons at all.

"Auxiliary" reasons play a variety of roles in practical reasoning. For instance, some auxiliary reasons can be interpreted as identifying reasons, for their function is to identify the concrete acts or actions for which there is a reason. Consider the case: I want to help someone. Lending him a certain amount of money will help him. Therefore, I have a reason (an auxiliary reason) to lend him the money. The operative reason is my intention to help him. Lending him the money is the act recommended by an auxiliary reason, namely the reason I have to give him some money since I want to help him.

There is another possibility for determining the meaning of the adjectives "primary" and "derivative" when applied to reasons. "Primary" could be called the reasons I have on the basis of my own needs, interests, and spontaneous desires. The "derivative" reasons would be the reasons I have, independently of my primary reasons, because of the primary reasons other people have. Such a distinction can be identified with the distinction made by some authors between "prudential" and "moral" reasons. "Prudential" reasons are internal reasons that motivate me to act in a specific way. "Moral" reasons are external reasons, the reasons I have or should have because of the legitimate expectations of others.

"Moral" reasons are often abstract, theoretical reasons. They represent then what I should do, what I ought to do, even if I do not internally want to do it. "Moral" reasons are confronted in many situations that involve some motivational problem. They are the right reasons, the rational reasons that should guide our conduct, but they do not actually guide our conduct, because we factually want something else, namely what we should not want in such circumstances.

Why should individuals who have their own internal reasons, in other words their own needs, desires, interests, and motives, act according to reasons that do not really motivate them, or move them to act? This is the main problem every exclusively normativistic ethical theory generates. In addition to this, normativistic ethical theories are not able to understand ethical formations, communities, and constellations in which different sorts of norms are valid, that have evolved in a long contingent history of practical trials and errors. These norms are generally rational and functional for the moral survival of the communities whose norms they are. From the perspective of the human individuals involved, members of the communities concerned, such norms can be conceived as "exclusionary" reasons or "second-order" reasons not to do what they otherwise would tend to do. They are "exclusionary" or "second-order" reasons that do not necessarily have exclusively restrictive characters, as they generate positive results for the particular communities and their individual members. As regulations of acts and actions, collective, social norms can guarantee the coexistence of free and autonomous individuals. Social and collective norms have a prescriptive, "mandatory" nature. They prescribe what to do in a certain situation. As rules and normative prescriptions they can be affirmed in statements of the form "X ought to (should or must) do A, B and C." As rules and norms, they change the reasons people have. They are themselves reasons for action in the communities in which they are recognized as rules and norms. Some of them may be of a fairly trivial nature, for instance the rules of etiquette. But all of them exclude some conflicting reasons, this being the main difference between them (the mandatory rules and prescriptive norms) and the ordinary first-order reasons. Having mandatory rules and prescriptive norms is for the communities and groups in which they are valid like having decided in advance what to do in conflict cases, rules and norms being exclusionary reasons for not acting on conflicting reasons.

"Exclusionary" reasons are second-order reasons to refrain from acting for some other first-order reason. Conflicts between first-order and second-order reasons are resolved not by the relative strength of the competing reasons but by a general principle of practical reasoning which determines that exclusionary reasons, when in conflict with first-order reasons, always prevail. In a relatively formalized language: If p is a reason for a person X to do the act A in a specific situation S and q is an exclusionary reason for person X not to act on the reason p, then the two reasons p and q are not strictly conflicting reasons (first-order reasons); q as exclusionary reason is not a reason for doing not-A in S. It is a reason for not doing A in S for the reason p.

Orders to be obeyed are mandatory or exclusionary reasons. They are to be obeyed even if no harm will come from disobeying them. That is precisely what it means to be subordinate to receiving orders. It means that it is not for the subordinate to decide what is best. The subordinate may see that, on the balance of reasoning, one course of action would be right and yet be justified in not following it. Orders are reasons for doing what one has been ordered regardless of the balance of reasons. It is not for those who receive orders to judge the merits of the case, this being the responsibility of the commanding agent, the one who gives the order. Orders are second-order reasons for the ones who receive them not to act on the merits of the case. It is not for them, according to the logic of orders, to act on a complete assessment of the pros and cons relevant in the respective action situation.

Promises, like orders, are also second-order reasons to act in a certain way. The film *The Promise*, based on the novel by F. Dürrenmatt and starring Jack Nicholson in the role of a retired inspector who had promised before retiring to find a murderer, illustrates this practical logic of promises. Even if the retired inspector had many first-order reasons to abandon the case, he had just one strong second-order reason not to leave the case: his own promise. And precisely this second-order reason is the one that prevails.

Second-order reasons are any reasons to act for a reason or to refrain from acting for a reason. Exclusionary reasons are second-order reasons to refrain from action for some reason.

Reasons agents have guide them in their concrete actions. They are the causes of their actions. They can be prima facie or conclusive reasons, operative or auxiliary reasons, primary or derivative reasons, prudential or moral reasons, mandatory and exclusionary reasons, first-order or second-order reasons. Reasons are action-guiding principles. For the social scientist and philosopher who wants to understand human beings, reasons are a powerful instrument for explaining human action, to understand why individuals do what they do and behave the way they do. Reasons have, then, a double function: a guiding function for individual agents and an explanatory function for anyone who wants to understand and conceptually grasp human behavior, since they allow us to say why individual agents do what they do.

USING REASONS AS ARGUMENTS

Reasons are referred to when we want to explain how and why people do what they do. The observer of human behavior refers to the reasons people have when they do things. He or she rightly assumes that nothing happens without a reason, and makes an effort concerning the concrete case to be explained to find out what is the reason that prevailed in that specific case. For example, we say in appropriate circumstances that a man married a certain woman for her money, and that people should marry for love, and not for money or for the political influence of a woman's family, and therefore, we go on to say, that man married for the wrong reason so that we conclude he behaved badly. In the end, we recommend other men not to act like this, but instead to marry for love.

Using reasons in our concrete thinking processes we start arguing for this or that, maintaining cases. Arguing for a certain view, or for a certain way of behaving, we use reasons that we employ as arguments to show or prove that something is better or worse than something else, that something should be done, or that something should not be done. The reasons we use as arguments are the premises of our practical inferences through which we arrive at certain conclusions. The reasons we use as arguments, that is, the reasons that function as premises in our practical inferences, are our desires, our interests, our beliefs, our convictions, our duties. They set out the facts of the case and the possibilities open to us. The conclusions we obtain in our practical inferences are certain actions or plans of action. Consider the following piece of practical reasoning G. H. von Wright proposes: I want to attain the end E (make this hut habitable). Unless I do action A (heat the hut) I shall not attain E. Therefore I heat the hut, which means I do A. The action A accomplished by the agent is explained by placing it in the "teleological" perspective of the agent's aiming at some end and his epistemic attitude to the requirements of the situation. The action performed by the agent is an intentional action through which certain means are used to attain something, namely the agent's goal. Explaining the behavior of the agent in this way, we transform it through the application of our teleological interpretation scheme into an intentional action. We see a person go through some movements, the significance of which we at first do not understand. We have a strong hunch that he evidently intends to do something in behaving like this. So we assume that he wants to do something (we infer it!), and the agent's behavior becomes completely understandable, intelligible, or explicable. Explaining the agent's behavior, we practically infer in the same way the acting subject had inferred what to do before he started to do what he has done. The agent's practical inference leads up to or ends in action. Its conclusion is an action.

Generally, as in the examples above, the first premise mentions an end of action and the second premise some means to this end. The practical conclusion results from the premises, consisting in using the means to secure the end. Aristotle often illustrates practical inferences with examples in which the first premise mentions something generic that is good or ought to be done, for instance, that dry food suits every human being, or that sweet things ought to be tasted. The second premise mentions some particular thing falling under the generic label, for instance, that this particular dish is dry, or sweet. The conclusion is then that the person who argues in this way has to eat the dish. The practical inference in all these cases is the transition (not always necessarily conscious) from belief in the premises to acceptance of the putative conclusion. Valid practical inferences are, accordingly, ordered sets of statements, the last of which is a practical conclusion adequately supported by the others. All practical inferences are characterized by having an appropriate practical conclusion, the premises of the valid practical inference stating a reason.

Frequently the premises are quite general. They are not specific. They do not contain all the details that would make the conclusion clear-cut, unequivocal, and definite. Therefore the premises do not determine, logically, exactly what we are to do in every possible circumstance. They lack nomological precision or determination. Practical reasoning leads then to conclusive statements that recommend or would recommend doing something, the performance of an action, that action not being completely entailed or made inevitable by the premises. Practical reasoning proceeds from premises that indicate that a certain action has certain desirability characteristics. But it is an "open" piece of reasoning, not necessarily forcing the agent to perform the recommended action. The agent could, after such an open sequence of practical reasoning, go on failing to desire the action despite the action's desirability as demonstrated by the reasoning. The reasons used as premises or arguments do not, consequently, render the action inevitable. They do not logically determine the desirable action. In sentences that use the simple "ought" (not the moral "ought") we express this openness and nondeterminateness, as when we say that someone ought to do something, meaning that there is a reason, or that there are many reasons for that person to do it, but not meaning that he or she must do it, and will certainly do it. "The train ought to be here in ten minutes," may be the conclusion of a practical inference: an open conclusion that does not imply that the train will certainly be here in ten minutes. Corresponding to this open use of the conclusive inferential "ought" are different senses of "must" and "may." There is, for example, a weak "must" of expectation, as when we say "The train must have arrived by now," which does not mean that it is certain that it has arrived by now. And there is a "may" or "might" of expectation, as when we say "The train may arrive in a few minutes," or "The train might have arrived on time," expressions which are open and which do not articulate faits accomplis.

When there are conflicting reasons that we use as arguments, openness prevails till we are able to estimate or appreciate which reasons are the strongest ones. If a person has conflicting aims that are not compatible or exclude each other, it is not at all clear which is going to be the conclusive action at the end of his inferences until we know the aim or the goal finally preferred. Reasons and the arguments they become when we argue using them have, indeed, a dimension of strength. Some reasons and arguments are stronger or weightier than others, able to override the weaker ones. The relative strength of a reason and of an argument can, therefore, be explained in terms of the power to override other reasons. We could distinguish conclusive and absolute reasons and arguments, a conclusive reason being the one that leads to a specific action. A conclusive argument is the one that I favor and whose conclusions I factually acknowledge. Using one of Raz's examples, the fact that my son has been injured is a reason for me to drive him to the hospital exceeding the permitted speed limit. If I had to argue in court, I would transform such a reason into the appropriate argument. But it is possible that, if a pedestrian suddenly steps into the road, my conclusive reason will be overridden. My reason to drive fast, faster than the legal speed limit, is conclusive, but not absolute, something which would be reflected in my reasoning in court where I would need to mark the difference between conclusive and absolute arguments.

In practical reasoning or in the process of argumentation we use reasons we have to do or not to do something as arguments. Practical reasoning activities or pieces of argumentation are, for the linguist, conversational interactions. Philosophers concentrate on the strength and power of the arguments put forward in such a conversational interaction. Reasons are used as arguments in reasoning contexts. It is sensible, therefore, to take a more detailed look at the structure of the reason sentences we build and use in the practical contexts of argumentation. Reason sentences contain, logically speaking, reason operators, expressed in the canonical form: R(f). Every reason-giving statement, regardless of whether or not it is standardly made, can be transformed into a sentence of the canonical form "R(f)p, x": The fact that p is a reason for agent x to f. Such sentences are true only if both p is the case, and if it is a reason for x to f. In sentences like "The fact that it is raining is a reason for a person who does not want to get wet to take an umbrella," the part of the sentence "the fact that it is raining" refers to the rain as a state of the world, easily verifiable. Such a fact or state of the world is actually a reason for a specific agent (who does not want to get wet and catch a cold) for doing something, namely "taking his umbrella." Other possible reason sentences are: "There is a reason for X to f"; "X has a reason to f"; "X believes that p is a reason for Y to f"; "X's reason for f-ing was p." Sentences of the form "There is a reason for X to f" are equivalent to "There is a fact p such that R(f)p, x." Sentences like "X has a reason to f" are less clear. Sometimes they are equivalent to the type of sentences falling under "There is a reason for X to f." On other occasions they are used to assert that there is a reason for X to f and that X knows it. Sentences of the form "X believes that p is a reason for Y to f" carry with them a certain degree of ambiguity. "X's reason for f-ing was p" can be used to assert several things. A detailed examination of this type of sentences would be too complex and of too little relevance for my main concern here.

Reason sentences, the sentences used in practical reasoning activities in which specific reasons are mentioned whose purpose is to make possible a transition to the conclusive sentence, are, normally, clearly structured. They contain statements of the facts that are reasons for the performance of a certain action by a certain agent. The statements of the facts are the premises of the argument whose conclusion is that there is a reason for the agent to perform the action or that he ought to do it. Statements of the form "P is a reason for X to f" correspond to the inference of which "p" is the premise and "There is a reason for X to f" the conclusion. The "phrastic" part of the inference contains the descriptive content of the reasoning. The "tropic" part of the inference marks a mood which in practical inferences is normally an imperative mood, proposing or affirming something that is to be done or that ought to be done. In theoretical inferences, the "tropic" is an assertoric mood, a proposition that is theoretically asserted, proposed or affirmed. In practical inferences we have as conclusions actions to be performed, plans to be realized, directives to be followed, commands to be obeyed, projects to be taken care of, or simply acts to be done. Anthony Kenny uses the concept of "fiats" to refer to these actions, plans, directives, commands, projects, and acts which constitute the conclusive part of practical inferences. Kenny's "fiats" are the tropic of practical inferences, the result of the series of sentences that make them up.

In practical reasoning, as in theoretical reasoning, we pass from certain sentences to other sentences according to certain rules. Kenny stresses the fact that this passing or transition always happens according to a logic of "satisfactoriness," so that, similarly to the truth-preserving rules of theoretical or assertoric inferences, there are satisfactoriness-preserving rules in practical inferences (Kenny 1978, 68). The idea of satisfactoriness is a relative idea. Something, a fiat, is satisfactory only in relation to a given set of wishes, wants, desires, or goals, and never in absolute terms. In reasoning about what to do, we get from certain premises to actions, plans, directives, commands, projects, and acts that will satisfy or could satisfy our desires and interests.

Practical reasoning is always context-dependent. It has a context in which it is performed. And in this context there are different collective beliefs and representations that regulate what is possible to affirm or to deny. Beliefs and representations that form the mental structure of the reasoning context are shared beliefs and representations of individuals existentially involved in that context. They regulate the emergence and the administration of sense. They play a fundamental role, namely they form the cognitive basis of the practical inferences performed in the context, guiding them, and demarcating fields of assertive possibilities and meaningful alternatives.

As in the case of legal reasoning, different practical inferences are institutionalized in the sense that certain field-dependent procedures and techniques of putting forward and defending a claim are provided for, according to which concrete reasoning operations are performed. Practical reasoning can be conceived of as a game; to use Wilfrid Sellars's terminology, they make up "the game of giving and asking for reasons." And like all games, practical reasoning is a rule-governed activity. It is a practice, the practice of giving and of accepting or refusing reasons. It is a critical, evaluative practice, performed socially as an interaction between human agents who have socially learned to argue.

Reasons are actually given and accepted in reasoning practices which Sellars, among many others, conceives of as a rule-governed game. This, however, cannot mean that reasons are always discourse-dependent. Derek Parfit and Maria Alvarez propose an "objective view" of reasons according to which reasons are given by facts. Because there are certain facts, they argue, that count in favor of our having some attitude, or our acting in some way, we have reasons to believe or to do something, namely, what the facts are reasons for. It is precisely such an objective view (or some slightly modified version of it) that I find worth defending against all the idealistic approaches (such as, for instance, R. Brandom's pragmatic inferentialism or C. Korsgaard's Kantian constructivism) that concentrate exclusively upon our reasoning activities to determine what reasons are all about.

Having reasons is being specifically situated in a world, responding to different sorts of facts and phenomena. Practical reasoning, on the other hand, is the deliberative inferential activity of using reasons as arguments in communicative contexts in which we are related in complex ways to the world, to other human beings, and to our own experiences and lives.

REFERENCES

Alvarez, Maria. 2010. *Kinds of Reasons: An Essay in the Philosophy of Action.* Oxford: Oxford University Press.

Brandom, Robert B. 2000. *Articulating Reasons: An Introduction to Inferentialism.* Cambridge, Mass.: Harvard University Press.

———. 2008. *Between Saying and Doing: Towards an Analytic Pragmatism.* Oxford: Oxford University Press.

Dretske, Fred. 1988. *Explaining Behavior: Reasons in a World of Causes.* Cambridge, Mass.: MIT Press.

Gil, Thomas. 2011. *On Reasons.* Hannover: Wehrhahn Verlag.

Kenny, Anthony. 1978. *Freewill and Responsibility.* London: Routledge.

Korsgaard, Christine M. 1996. *The Sources of Normativity.* Cambridge: Cambridge University Press.

Parfit, Derek. 2011. *On What Matters.* Vol. 1. Oxford: Oxford University Press.

Raz, Joseph, ed. 1978. *Practical Reasoning.* Oxford: Oxford University Press.

———. 1990. *Practical Reasons and Norms.* Princeton: Princeton University Press. (1st ed. 1975.)

Sellars, Wilfrid. 1997. *Empiricism and the Philosophy of Mind.* Cambridge, Mass.: Harvard University Press.

Von Wright, Georg Henrik. 1963. "Practical Inference." *Philosophical Review* 72: 159–79.

White, Alan R. 1975. *Modal Thinking.* Oxford: Basil Blackwell.

Part Two

DEVELOPING CONVINCING ARGUMENTS

Chapter Six

Practical Reasoning in Place

Tracing "Wise" Inferences in Everyday Life

Ricca Edmondson

This chapter begins by exploring Aristotle's account of rhetorical discourse, which traces how people argue and infer in practice, in public situations which demand deliberation about what stance to take or what to do. Such circumstances tend to be pressing, often urgent; they are characterized by incomplete, often insufficient knowledge of relevant facts and how to assess them. They constantly develop and change, and pose dilemmas to which neither expert nor everyday opinion can offer easy, straightforward responses with clear expected effects. Aristotle's account of how these predicaments can be dealt with offers a model which preserves the common intuition that deduction and induction lie at the heart of reasoning, but does so in a way that expands the notion of reasoning itself.

This expanded notion not only recognizes emotional, interpersonal and sociopolitical components as potential elements in "reasoning," it does so in a way that both justifies and sets limits for the kind of practice involved. In other words, the explication of how reasoning works in Aristotle's *Rhetoric* suggests criteria for its execution. This account also undermines many aspects of the contrast sometimes drawn between reasoning specifically directed at action and other types of deliberation: it is not that reasoning would be clear-cut if not contaminated by the need to act, but that reasoning about human affairs is itself inextricable from the uncertain and the social. For Aristotle, this circumstance does not rule out the possibility of good argument. For this reason I argue here for the appeal of his account of rhetorical reasoning, suggesting too that it can be expanded to offer criteria for a constructive interpretation of excellent or "wise" forms of reasoning. At the same time, it conveys a challenge to some currently conventional forms of disciplinarity. The methods involved in understanding how people argue, as well as in constructing criteria for deliberation, take seriously the philosophical implications of ethnographic material that can tell us more about how arguing works.

What Searle (2001) rightly disdains as the "classical model" of practical reasoning in the twentieth century includes the view that human actions are caused by beliefs and desires, which are not themselves subject to rational appraisal—so the sole place for rationality in practical reasoning is its use in devising means to these a-rationally-chosen ends. The *Rhetoric*'s alternative is a close examination of how people do in fact reason about human affairs, using this same examination to lay bare what can be acceptable about that reasoning and what standards to use in criticizing it. This is not a quasi-empirical report on what deliberators merely happen to do, but interrogates in what ways normal practice is capable of striving at excellence. Reasoning as a practice, when pursued as well as the circumstances allow, provides participants with reasons (they can adopt) for acting. Aristotle does not look down on public reasoners who are genuinely attempting to offer the best arguments they can; he tries to make constructive sense of what they are doing. Concentrating on political deliberation, forensic deliberation, and epideictic speeches designed to endorse public virtue, he describes how people do and must argue, in order to discern the best available means of doing so.

The motivation for this approach does not rest on a benign tolerance of vague, inexact argumentative habits. It precisely confronts "the world" and the place of reasonable human beings within it. First, we are obliged to deliberate in cases, for instance in medicine, which intrinsically involve uncertainty, thus where perfect syllogisms cannot be constructed (cf. Ar., Rhet. I 1, 1355b10ff.). We still need as high standards for argument as possible. Political debate is at least as uncertain, but this does not make it a second-rate form of argument. Insofar as human beings are first and foremost members of political communities, whose capacities for reason are central to their participation in these communities and hence to their humanity itself (see O'Rourke in this volume), debate about what should be undertaken in the polis is not intrinsically deficient, but in principle noble (Ar., Rhet. I 1, 1354b24). Ideally it helps to map out how to be human, though Aristotle did not endorse its public pedagogic power to the extent of contemporaries such as Isocrates. But both envisaged rhetoric as an interactive process allowing participants in debate to arrive at convictions which are sufficiently well founded to ground reasonably justified decisions which either lead to justified action, or support criteria which can be relied on in order to live well (Edmondson 1984, 2007; Woerner 1990). The central use of discourse of this kind is to deliberate, in a given predicament, about what is a good thing to do, or better than the alternatives, or best of all. It is a distortion of public political discourse to use it to ends contrary to this—which is not to say that it never happens (Ar., Rhet. I 1, 1354a25). Hence it is a key task to discover and understand the aspects of discourse which cannot begin from perfect premises but must still be used: most human decisions have this sort of contingent character (ibid., I 2, 1357a25). These aspects of discourse need to be refined so that they enhance the reasonableness of debate rather than detract from it. Aristotle's method therefore involves starting from what reasoning about human affairs *can* do, rather than distorting it to fit some Procrustean bed of his own devising.

This stance sets Aristotle apart from logicians who assume that human reasoning would make better sense if it were not so human: if it were divested of social, emotional or political elements, for instance, or were more similar to what "science" is taken to be. His investigation is not guided by a search for purity of argument, but has other excellences in mind. He is aware that sometimes people offer fallacious inferences or try to deceive each other. At the start of the *Rhetoric* he points out that these phenomena in the last analysis undermine the principles of communication: they are in the end self-defeating, considered not as strategies intended to reach given immediate ends but regarded *as* pieces of communication (ibid., I 1, 1354a24–5). This by no means entails that since deception involves extra-cognitive ends, everything that is noncognitive should be abstracted from good arguing. (Such an inference would in fact commit the fallacy of the undistributed major: "All deception involves noncognitive ends; no good arguments are deceitful; therefore, no good arguments involve noncognitive ends.") In practice, none of Aristotle's major argumentative components (ethos, pathos and logos) can function properly if used deceptively or if they are systematically skewed— by distortions arising from the exercise of power, for example. Hence his account simultaneously analyzes what happens in debate and offers the potential for its critique.

"LOGOS"-BASED ELEMENTS OF REASONING

Far from assuming that cognition, in a pared-down sense of the term, is the only source of good reasoning, Aristotle examines public deliberative habits to discover elements that may be noncognitive in themselves, but are open to cognitive processes: they may not only contribute to debate but even enhance it. It is, in other words, possible to trace *reasoned* uses of extra-cognitive phenomena. This nondogmatic method implies that we can learn from what people actually do in good or acceptable real-world instances, in order to construct an intelligible account of what reasoning might properly involve. This does not detract from the fact that reasoning, pivotal to a citizen's contribution to the polis, centrally relates to *logos*; but it offers us a modulated picture of what acting according to logos involves.

Thus this approach to representing what goes on in reasoning when people debate political decisions does not start by assuming that it involves an intrinsically deficient derivation of formal logic\ Aristotle sees human beings as arguing in ways which *relate*, often by complex paths, to deduction or induction, but he expects the formal standards for using these logical patterns as they stand to be unattainable in the types of situation in which deliberation is most salient (ibid., I 2, 1357a22–29). We seldom have access to true, well-confirmed empirical generalizations to act as major premises, for example, when we are dealing with contingent matters. Aristotle turns instead to the question of what *other* processes can be employed to make arguments work. He parallels the notion of deduction with the enthymeme, and induction with the paradigm; we shall concentrate here on the former, in which the support which personal and interpersonal features can give to reasoning is particularly clearly displayed.

The enthymeme is often described as a syllogism in which either the major or the minor premise, or even the conclusion, is taken for granted and left unspoken; this is not Aristotle's account, though he does refer to it (ibid., I 2, 1357a16–21; II 22, 1395b25–30). An interpretation which restricted his account of the enthymeme in this way would in fact render incoherent his analytical explication of its uses in arguing. For Aristotle, the enthymeme is a rhetorical syllogism inferring from what is (held to be) likely to be the case, or valid, or from something that can be taken to be a sign of some other state of affairs (ibid., I 2, 1357a32ff.)—whether or not the entire inferential process is made explicit. This crucially depends on the communicative needs of the situation in question, which is key to the specificity of this account. What details enthymemes contract or omit, or what support for their claims they expand in long speeches, indeed the general modality of their expression, depends on the *communicative* demands of the argument in question (see section below).

"Enthymemes" are used much more often in everyday life than pure deductions from confirmed generalizations can possibly be. They infer either from what is, or seems to be, or can reasonably be taken to be, generally (but contingently) the case. But how do we know what it is reasonable to suppose here? Aristotle makes a remarkable concession to the sociality of knowledge: we cannot know everything firsthand, but need to go by "reputable opinions" on what is the case. Reputable opinions, *endoxa*, are what "appears" or can sensibly be taken to be valid, "for everyone, either most people or for the wisest" (in the broad sense of the most experienced or knowledgeable), "and among these either all or most of them, or those who are the best-known or reputed to be the best" (Ar., Top. I 1, 100b21–23). Here Aristotle offers an account of how we deal with complex problems in which sociological accuracy and reasoning precisely overlap. If you are ill with various symptoms, you tend to rely on what everyone would say is the matter with you; if there is no general agreement, you consider what most people think, or those with the best reputation for judgment—doctors recommended by your neighbors, or with wide acclaim in the field. If they do not all agree, you go by what most of them say, or the ones who are said to be expert at interpreting the symptoms in the case. If this sifting of opinion happens in medicine, which attempts to proceed as factually as possible, then *ex hypothesi* it is even more necessary in social or economic affairs, where certain knowledge is harder to acquire.

Enthymemes from signs may infer from necessary or "infallible" signs (for instance, a high temperature is a necessary sign of fever), but more often we are obliged to fall back on fallible signs. How we interpret them in particular cases is already a matter of judgment: enthymemes do not characteristically infer as automatically as strict deductions would. It is part of the realism of this approach that it specifically allows for the fact that various types of inference differ in terms of their stringency (Woerner 1982; Burnyeat 1994). This does not entail that they are not all reasonable; it shows that the degree of reasonableness attainable in a particular predicament must be estimated in relation to what the circumstances allow. This gives added force to Aristotle's remark that

> the educated person will seek exactness so far in each subject as the nature of the thing admits, it being plainly much the same absurdity to put up with a mathematician who tries to persuade instead of proving, and to demand strict demonstrative reasoning of a rhetorician. (NE I 1, 1094b23–27)

We need not read this as meaning merely that human affairs in general cannot be debated with arithmetical precision. It stresses that the stringency of each particular argument will differ according to the type of reasoning its circumstances permit.

A source of confusion in relation to the enthymeme is Aristotle's use of the term "topos," sometimes translated as "commonplace" (or "line of argument" in Rhys Roberts's (1954) translation). The Ramist use of "topos" to mean "theme" is now frequent in literary studies, but Aristotle uses it to refer to meta-assumptions which are seldom actually stated but which function to *legitimate* a piece of reasoning. Topoi are *not* essentially major premises. Rather, they have a bridging function: tending to remain unstated, they *permit the movement* from premises to conclusion (Woerner 1995). We do not take the trouble to enunciate the general topos, "If what is less likely is the case or is valid, then what is more likely will be the case or valid." But it makes immediate sense to argue, "If even the Gods are deficient in knowledge, then certainly men will be." The meta-communicative pattern supporting this is termed by Aristotle the topos "from the more or less," an abbreviation of the more technical description, "If a predicate which is more probably affirmable of a thing does not belong to it, then neither does it belong to another thing of which it is less probably affirmable" (Ar., Rhet. II 23, 1397bff). This is a general topos because it is applicable to any subject area at all: "If it is not even raining in Ireland, how can it be raining in Italy?" The issue in real discourse is to connect states of affairs that are generally believed to be the case, or valid, so as to produce a convincing conclusion that provides relevant information—not just for the speaker but, more importantly, for the hearer too. This makes everyday conversation creative in a way that formal logic is not, for it cannot go beyond its own premises. When we apply the bridge of a topos to a real-life situation, it does have the effect of showing the hearer something new.

In order to form part of such a store of potential legitimations, topoi must have overall acceptability, in a sense. Special topoi operate like general ones, as meta-communicative rules, but apply to special areas, particularly to human action (Woerner 1990, 168ff.). It is reasonably accepted as true, say, that it is not good to expend energy in a fruitless enterprise. *If* we can show that a given enterprise is foolish, it follows reasonably that it would be good to abandon it. It is also true that if one has invested a great deal of effort to achieve progress in a sensible project, it would be foolish to give up just at the last moment. The issue is to produce an argument showing why a particular action falls under one of these rubrics rather than the other. We can then infer what to do: whether to stop or to go on. The question *which applies* is precisely one of experience and judgment. Hence, early rhetoricians in the Roman tradition speak of "seeking" commonplaces: if we have a certain number of considerations at hand, the task is to discern under which general sense-making pattern they can reasonably be thought to fall (Edmondson 1984; Perelman and Olbrechts-Tyteca 1958). Reasoning is not a question of applying a standard template which will supply an automatic chute from facts to their implications: we need to *judge* which to apply in a given case, taking its circumstances and its setting into account.

This explains what is sometimes misinterpreted as the contradictory nature of topoi. It is not that they contradict each other: they are designed for application to different cases, according to judgment. Even a topos which apparently cannot be contradicted, such as "Recommend people to do what will have good consequences and dissuade them from what has bad consequences," or "Do first things first," still demands deliberation, because we need to argue about what does have good consequences in this case, or what count as first things on this occasion. These topoi are relatively empty of content, but this is their virtue: their function is not to give new information, but to make inference possible by identifying deliberative movements which are acceptable as *reasonable*. If the legitimating assumption supporting an enthymeme has been chosen judiciously, then even though logical conclusiveness is ruled out, it can sensibly be accepted as convincing by hearers. Topoi thus introduce into our understanding of deliberation a category of expectations about what is and is not reasonable, one which lies *between* the world of facts and values and the world of logic. They are not quite substantive, but they direct us how to connect matters that are discussed in substantive arguments.

Aristotle's account here fuses what is generally accepted as reasonable with what *is* reasonable (a point to which we return in the last section of the chapter). This engages with the desire of writers such as Lawson (2004, 28–29, 44) to argue that "human reasoning" is "hard-wired" to follow a "hypothetico-predictive" pattern even in everyday cases; he stresses that when we find that the barbecue is no longer lit we test the inference that it has run out of gas, and so on. Lawson's view is allied to the "Hempel-Oppenheim model" (Hempel 1965) which takes a "deductive-nomological" approach to explanation, seen as sharing its logical structure with prediction. Laws, or at any rate "law-like" generalizations, must be amassed, and "the sentences constituting the explanans must be true"; then a sound deduction follows in which the explanandum is a logical consequence of the explanans (Hempel 1965, 248). Considerable argument was precipitated by this approach when it was broached from the 1940s onward, featuring apparently conclusive suggestions that none of these major conditions is likely to be satisfiable in most real historical and political cases. It is hard to imagine any reconstruction of Lawson's barbecue example that did not fall foul of the objections in the Hempel-Oppenheim literature. Aristotle might point out that the man with the barbecue is guided entirely by probabilities and signs, even if, after the fact, he frames them in quasi-syllogistic style. His own account preserves the centrality of deduction and induction to deliberation, but points out that they are buttressed by general notions of how the world works, without which they could scarcely get under way, still less make sense to recipients. It indicates too that the role of experience in deploying these probabilities and signs inevitably introduces further elements into argumentation.

Since arguing with the use of logos depends on a speaker's judgment, its acceptance must depend partly on recipients' assessment of his discernment (or hers, in today's terms). This discernment cannot standardly derive from applying rules, laws, or other recipes for thought, since the cases about which people argue are precisely cases in which such recipes do not uncontroversially apply. Speakers are obliged to base their reasoning at least in part on experience and knowledge about human behavior. However, one of the defining features of other people's experience is that, while they can perform judgments on its basis, they cannot normally exhibit this knowledge in its entirety. It therefore belongs to my assessment of your argument whether I judge, based on what you say, that you possess the relevant experience and other capacities to argue effectively in this case. Since I need to be equipped with the probabilities and signs that help me to make this assessment, it follows that it is part of your argument to provide the indications in question; when you have done so, I need to react appropriately. These components of arguing are drawn together in the phenomena "ethos" and "pathos."

ETHOS, PATHOS, AND THE SEEDS OF CRITIQUE

Aristotle's account of deliberation is specifically designed to respond to the fact that reasoning about human affairs is inevitably rooted in the judgment and experience of those arguing. Since this is so, it is *reasonable* that real-life speakers should convey, as they argue, something of their fitness to support their positions: this is part of what hearers need to be able to estimate in order to respond to the argument. Thus, the 2011 television debates among presidential candidates in Ireland focused less on "issues," such as candidates' opinions on economic justice, than their moral qualifications: whether they had shown doubtful integrity in public office or abused financial power. Audiences seemed most interested in speakers' *characters*, taken as a guide to their likely future performances. This is the area covered by the Aristotelian notion of ethos. The notion of pathos deals with the ways listeners are affected by an argument and what they themselves contribute to it.

The ethos of the speaker, as it is communicated in the argument, itself reflects the communicative triad of speaker, hearer, and theme. It is often—perhaps standardly—the case that an audience is listening to someone precisely because *the speaker* possesses sufficient knowledge, circumstances or skill enabling him or her to address the problem in a particular way. The members of the audience will not have an identical set of skills and knowledge, or they would not need to listen to the speech, and will seldom have the time or opportunity to attempt to duplicate them. They must decide whether they can—reasonably—*trust* the speaker. Not least because he (or she) knows things and has skills which they do not, their estimate of the speaker's trustworthiness can be decisive in reaching conviction about a position. Aristotle's account of ethos (Ar., Rhet. I 2, 1356a22f.; I 9; II 12) permits further analysis of the interlocking phenomena which this involves; at the same time, it justifies their presence and, by extension, excludes items which lack this justification.

According to Aristotle, it is *reasonable* to trust the argument of someone whose character one judges to be good (the central aspect of ethos, most strongly related to the person of the speaker as it is shown in the speech), who shows intellectual and other forms of mastery of the topic in hand (these are more logos-related aspects of ethos), and who is well disposed to the audience (the more pathos-related aspects of ethos) (Edmondson et al. 2009). Being of good character is relevant to reasoning because it indicates that the speaker need not be expected to try to deceive the audience, deliberately or otherwise. It is relevant to the standard of an argument if the speaker is just or unjust, generous or mean, modest or conceited; these are features of a person such that if the negative side of the pair is exhibited, the speaker's arguments are in danger of becoming skewed. The logos-related part of ethos refers to the efforts made by the speaker actively to seek excellent arguments, and in doing so to exercise informed, considered and circumspect judgment. Then, in terms of the most audience- or pathos-related aspects of an audience, it is the relationship to the audience which is crucial: is the speaker indifferent to its particular concerns? Does he or she take trouble to understand their needs in the case and construct arguments that meet them? Such components allow an estimate of trustworthiness in deliberation, and can reasonably be allowed to reinforce the strength of the argument. In practice, showing excellent ethos may be the most effective means of persuasion someone possesses (Ar., Rhet. I 2, 1356a13).

Thus, to be reasonable and convincing in deliberation, and to be recognized as such, a speaker must be able not only to find good arguments in some abstract sense, but to express them in a way that embeds them in their human and public setting and activates them there. This is a rounded interpersonal process, and on Aristotle's account it is one whose components can be assessed both intellectually and ethically. They can also be evaluated in terms of their impacts on hearers. Taking "pathos" into account involves successfully assessing where the argument's *hearers* stand: what their needs, feelings and beliefs involve and how the argument can address them, dismantling unnecessary barriers to assent or to appreciating the force of an argument. Hearers in an inappropriate frame of mind judge a case differently from the way they might otherwise do (ibid., II 1, 1377b30–1378a9). If, therefore, they are assisted by communicative phenomena falling under pathos to relinquish inappropriate intellectual practices, viewpoints or prejudices, then partly emotional interaction again augments the argumentative process. Moreover, arguments about public, politically significant states of affairs involve issues—such as war, peace, legislation, the economy (ibid., I 4)—in which it is unreasonable to remain wholly emotionally disengaged. Here it would be admissible to construct an enthymeme legitimated by a topos actually centered on an emotion, if it were applied reasonably. Take, for example, "We should feel aversion to proposals which undermine the carefully worked out standards of our state." The topos strengthens the links between premises and conclusion: not only does the option in question undermine important principles, it is reasonable to dislike it for that reason. The inferential force of the argument is enhanced by appropriate feelings which arise in the course of and on account of it.

Emotions here are not envisaged as merely private "feelings." To feel anger about genuinely undeserved injustice to someone, for example, is more reasonable than to feel indifference. In ordinary public life, emotions do motivate us to make and change judgments, to decide what to do; moreover, these emotions are partly based on beliefs and assumptions that we see as justifying them. The fact that it is possible to influence emotions by using argument shows that they are capable of being reasonable; to believe otherwise would be to claim that a well-constructed society must condemn all feeling as irrational and suppress it. (This is not to suggest that in standard circumstances emotions are *sufficient* reasons for action.) The emotions involved in pathos are also structured according to the triad of theme, speaker and addressee (Edmondson et al. 2009). They are effective as means to *reasonable conviction* when they can be considered properly productive parts of the enthymematic or paradigmatic argument concerned. At the same time, we can see that it is the audience's position and needs that determines much of what is said and how it is said. Reasonable discourse is fundamentally audience-directed: "It is the hearer that is the speech's end and object" (Ar., Rhet. I 3, 1358b1). In addition, the audience participates actively in co-constructing the reasonableness of the argument. Arguer and listeners cooperate in evolving their stances in mutual interaction, intertwining elements of ethos, pathos and logos in a joint rhetorical process.

The active, and in the best cases adventurous, nature of this co-construction becomes clear when we consider what the speaker has to do in the course of adjusting the argument to the hearer. If the speaker wants to convince another person of something on the basis of genuine insight rather than manipulation, and adjusts his or her position in order to make it accessible to the hearer, then s/he does not know what is going to arise from this process or exactly what s/he might perceive or feel given the new point of view: this makes genuine rhetorical communication a risk for speaker as well as hearer.[1]

This interwoven structure is composed not simply of fortuitous emotional or communicative elements characteristic of human beings, but of those that are capable of augmenting reasonableness. They are those able to drive home conviction in a human sense. If an argument, in addition to striking hearers as intelligible and plausible, is not structured so that their feelings and attitudes are coherent with it, they are less likely to be able to "take it on board" (Edmondson 1984). If they feel assured in all the three respects of ethos, pathos and logos that an argument is convincing, then it is reasonable for them to feel convinced (and to take any appropriate action). They will have been able to test the argument in terms which include the speaker's honesty, familiarity with relevant knowledge, and efforts on their behalf; if the speaker fails to take the trouble to understand hearers' positions and find appropriate arguments to meet them, this is an appropriate basis for distrust. All these non-"cognitive" aspects of Aristotle's account of deliberation are assembled on intelligible grounds connected with the process of reasoning at hand.

Hence, they generate criteria for identifying extraneous or harmful elements in deliberation. As far as the first is concerned, Aristotle sees elements apart from the argument itself which might affect such judgments, for example reputation, as external to this immediate analysis: they are used to support an argument rather than forming part of it (Ar., Rhet. I 2). The reputation someone has before s/he comes to the debate is not a product of the argumentative process itself; if it is introduced, this is a matter for scrutiny of its own. As far as internal conditions are concerned, Aristotle is aware that arguers may be insufficiently intelligent for the subject-matter at hand, disingenuous and of bad character, or badly disposed to their audiences; these failings matter because of their effects on arguments. In addition, they distort every human aspect of the speaker's relation with hearers, and with this the whole phenomenon of *logos*, as the reasoned participation of citizens deliberating together in a polis. Suppose a debate shows regular skewing in which, say, the interests of the audience are systematically ignored or misrepresented. These are internal deficiencies; but their systematic nature might encourage us to seek an external cause, for example the impact of power interests. Conversely, Aristotle's account can in principle be developed—though he does not explicitly do so—to support an exploration of particularly positive forms of deliberation: what might be termed "wise" reasoning.

WISE REASONING AND WISE ACTION

Traditionally, wise reasoning is needed when people are confronted by just the predicaments on which the *Rhetoric* focuses: in which decisions or actions are needed where knowledge is constantly changing but insufficient, and where both expert and everyday expectations are insufficient to provide clear direction. Not only problems such as whether to go to war, but everyday problems such as how to bring up children or what career to choose, lack recipe-like solutions, and demand responses combining cognitive, emotional, social, political, and moral capacities. Aristotle's own analysis of rhetoric is not overtly linked with wisdom, perhaps partly owing to his contrast between practical and contemplative wisdom, but the *Rhetoric*'s account does suggest criteria for excellent forms of reasoning.

Aristotle's celebrated depiction of the "practically" wise person also stresses the capacity to produce excellent argument. It highlights the possession of "an understanding which enables him to deliberate well in relation to the goods (and evils) conducive to (or disrupting) a good life" (Ar., Rhet. I 9, 1366b20ff.; cf. Rorty 1966, 2011).[2] This person has a temperament which generates *feelings and reactions* which permit good *judgment*. For example, he (or she) is not inclined to be either too reckless or too sensible of danger, and is hopeful where appropriate, without abandoning the capacity to discern what should reasonably cause alarm (ibid. II 14, 1390a29ff.). There are good grounds in terms of reasoning for stressing such qualities, since, Aristotle believes, persons of such character are more likely than others to be capable of judging according to the truth (ibid., 1390a32). They are qualities which specifically enhance deliberation, since they work against sweeping judgments, exaggerated impetuosity or misplaced pessimism. The person who behaves wisely examines cases on their merits, and other people also, neither trusting everyone too much nor mistrusting others on principle. We can see how such characteristics operate in terms of the account of rhetoric Aristotle gives. He adds another element too, embedding practical wisdom in its social and temporal context. The practically wise person has the capacity to assess aims and goals in terms of lifetimes, those of individuals or of society. Moreover, human beings themselves, in Aristotle's view, are prone to misjudgments characteristic of particular life-stages—often behaving too precipitously when young and too cautiously, even bitterly, when older. It is wise to be able to resist these errors, balancing virtue of character with a capacity to work out what is or is not practicable. Reasoning of this sort is not abstract, but situated within concrete, common or individual, life-courses. Much more can be said about it than there is room for here. It is performed in place, in the thick of the dilemmas which affect human beings, and is carried out with the help of capacities which specifically enhance dealing with them.

Even if we confine inquiries to the Western tradition rather than including Eastern versions, there are many traditions of wisdom to be found, including that regarding wisdom as a rarely encountered property of rarely endowed persons (Curnow 1999). This venerable version of wisdom, compatible with much that Plato says about wisdom in the *Republic*, focuses on wisdom as a gift of the few. Aristotle's own work on ethics, by contrast, has been interpreted as focusing on what the wise deliberating agent should do in his or her own moral dilemmas (Kekes 1995). Partly from at least partial allegiance to the Platonic conception, leading him to connect *sophia* with contemplation, and possibly too from distaste for some Sophists' overblown offers to mold the characters of the young, Aristotle remains distant from an explicitly interactive, communicative and pedagogic treatment of wisdom as such. However, his frequent quotations suggest admiration for Isocrates, who does specifically associate rhetoric, philosophy, and the pursuit of both virtue and wisdom. It is important to stress, too, that neither Aristotle's account of rhetorical reasoning nor his exposition of ethics examines individuals' deliberations about their own personal decisions. The word "I" does not occur in his writings. The dilemmas he explores are public ones, developed interpersonally in dynamic processes of debate; just as "logos" is associated with political life in the community. (Maxwell's (2007) account of wisdom aptly focuses on public decisions about what ought to be done, but discusses their content rather than their form.) It therefore seems in principle possible to associate excellent or wise forms of rhetorical deliberation (in Aristotle's sense) with a "wisdom" that involves interaction and change, a process in which several people typically participate.

The consequences of this approach throw further light on what "practical reasoning" involves. First, since an Aristotelian account of rhetorical deliberation encourages us to expect (at least one version of) wisdom to be interpersonal, it draws attention to processual aspects of what people do and say in connection with wise reasoning. Second, it throws light on aspects of "practical reasoning" that relate to action. The fact that we can fruitfully apply an Aristotelian analysis to reasoning which is not designed specifically to result in decision to act, but to understand sociopolitical dilemmas, suggests that a dogmatic association of "practical reasoning" with action is inappropriate. The account of practical reasoning offered in the *Rhetoric* seems to present it as reasoning about human affairs in general—which often straightforwardly involves action, but may not: as in the case of many of Aristotle's examples, particularly in connection with epideictic speeches. On the other hand, when we apply rhetorical analysis to contemporary reasoning about human affairs—in sociological texts, for example—we find that they contain more action than might have been expected, in a different sense. Readers are constantly asked to take stances on theories of society, or to agree to see particular issues as salient: theoretical inquiry is also action-related. Third, when we bring these points together and examine processual instances of "wise" reasoning, then even if they *are* putatively concerned with what to do, they often give reasons for *not* acting rather than for doing so. The notion of action itself requires complex disentanglement, rather than simply being contrasted with theoretical forms of thought.

First, the processual account of wisdom which stems, by extension, from the *Rhetoric* allows us to understand what is wise about some otherwise opaque cases of "wise" reasoning, exposing deliberative interactions that we might otherwise overlook and indicating more about what this rhetorical version of "wisdom" means. For example, uses of proverbs have perennially been accounted wise; just as perennially, they have been dismissed as hackneyed and trite, and from a contemporary viewpoint it is hard to see what is special about them. We can discover more by using the notions of ethos and pathos to analyze what goes on among people who can use them preeminently well. In the West of Ireland, when proverbs are used convincingly, by people with high ethos, their distinguishing mark seems to be their capacity to put recipients in a new position from which to regard predicaments. Aristotle mentions proverbs' graphic power and their ability to surprise (Rhet. III 11, 1411b22ff.). People who can select an appropriate proverb at the right time, understanding their interlocutor's problem and concerned enough for his or her capacities to choose a saying which will have the appropriate impact, can trigger a process using pathos to remarkable effect (Edmondson 2011; 2012). Thus, someone who is behaving inflexibly in a dispute might be brought up by a wry remark—"Ní thuigeann an sách an seang" or "The well-fed can't understand the thin." The brevity of such an interjection would respond to the *hearer's* communicative need for surprise, if delivered by a trustworthy interlocutor; it might be more effective than lecturing interference. Speaking appropriately like this might enable a sudden transition from one deliberative perspective to another. The "logos" part of the speaker's contribution is almost completely implicit, but could in principle be reconstructed in argumentative terms. This spoken contribution is not made in terms of deliberation about what the *speaker* should do, or, in the first instance, about what action to take at all.

This interchange is embedded in a human situation, one in which augmented wisdom is required; this is reached as the result of *interaction*, carried out among at least two people and based on a *process* embedded in the predicament concerned. It is not abstract in the sense of being a discussion purely "in principle," but nor does it advise specifically what to do. In addition, attention to the interaction between ethos, pathos and logos explicates the sense in which wisdom, as a characteristic of an action or policy, may be associated with the *manner* in which deliberation or interaction evolves. It is reasonable to reason in a way that will allow participants to respond on all the human levels it engages. The rationale for seeking an appropriate manner of deliberating is also fundamentally connected with logos. Hence this interpretation of discursive wisdom has implications in terms of the social interaction promoted in situations where wisdom is sought. This is not an exclusively modern point; the *vita mixta* of twelfth-century friars, adjured to come down from their "high horses" and preach on a level with their listeners, living as vulnerably as they did, was intended to enhance speakers' trustworthiness. What is more modern is seeking systemic or society-wide conditions that might be sought for appropriate public deliberation.

The suggestion that practical reasoning is characterized by the sort of human situation it deals with finds some reflection in Aristotle's remark that epideictic speech (centered on bestowing praise or blame on someone) is *connected* with action, rather than directly urging to it. We praise people publicly for what they have done, and this may imply that we think listeners should act similarly in similar circumstances; epideictic speech is engaged in against the background of concern for society and what conduct should be undertaken within it, but does not say so directly (cf. Ar., Rhet. I 9, 1367a26ff.). So some reasoning classed as rhetorical certainly does not immediately urge to action. Conversely, reasoning in the field of human social and political affairs may not urge to action though it does make use of rhetorical argument. Sociological arguments rely heavily on rhetorical moves and relationships, without characteristically directing to action (Edmondson 1984). Their contents, however, involve more movement than one might expect; getting readers to accept that certain sorts of predicament are important, or certain approaches needed to comprehend them, can depend on provoking action of a sort: getting readers to *move* from their stances and *adopt* new ones. Especially in contrast to the ethereal sphere of contemplation Aristotle associates with *sophia*, debating human affairs takes place within an arena in which action in some sense figures: but not necessarily in the immediate sense sometimes imputed to practical reasoning. It is not the element of action as such that causes problems in "practical reasoning," but the multiple interactions in social and political realms with which it deals.

Assembling these points makes clearer how cases accepted as associated with wisdom are not necessarily instances of advice with regard to action. Donald Schön (whose views on "the learning society" refer explicitly to Athens), remarks in relation to "reflective practitioners" that "situations of practice are not problems to be solved but problematic situations characterized by uncertainty, disorder, and indeterminacy" (1983, 15–16). Here the type of progress aimed at does not envisage conclusions, nor necessarily any action as such. This position is echoed in the comments of a psychotherapist interviewed by this author in November 2010:

> If I ever talked to anyone and they ended up thinking I'd been wise and been helpful, it would be because I had asked them questions. Being wise I think is based on asking a series of questions. . . . The questions I ask aren't looking for right answers, they're to help people explore their dilemmas. It's for when issues and dilemmas are complex or ethically problematic.

In relation to the question "where wisdom resides, if it belongs to an individual," the speaker concludes,

> Like everything, it's an interaction, it's something that develops in a relationship. What I say allows her to speak in a particular way, to ask her certain things, but the way she responds allows me to speak too.

Examples could be multiplied, from contemporary "learning communities" under development to comments on Hebrew and other forms of reasoning in theological contexts (Edmondson 2009; 2012; Edmondson and Pearce 2007). Wisdom of this discursive type impacts on situations where people need stances making a difference to engagement with their surroundings, rather than direction toward specific actions. This model has the potential to make explicit some reasoning processes implied rather than detailed in psychological models of wisdom (Sternberg 1998; Baltes and Staudinger 2000; Ardelt 2004). However, a rhetorical-discursive interpretation of wisdom stresses that individuals need not feel isolated where wisdom is required; to the extent that wise discernment is a joint process, it can be supported by appropriate social arrangements.

REASONING AND INTERDISCIPLINARITY

A difficult, but significant, feature of Aristotle's *Rhetoric* arises from the fact that its largest portions are made up of pages of apparent truisms: what can be expected about people's attitudes at various stages of their lives, why they may be supposed to have committed crimes, what frames of mind can be anticipated to make people calm or angry. At first sight it seems hard to understand the function of these items in the text. They become explicable when interpreted as a semi-empirical collection of connectors that Aristotle considered to be accepted, and by and large acceptable, as capable of conferring reasonableness in arguments in the society around him—if used aptly. They are crucial to his method, for they populate the category mentioned above, the intermediate category between logic and "the world."

Philosophers cannot work out from first principles what human beings take to be reasonable connectors between steps in an argument; these steps must be observed, not constructed. This does not entail that they must be endorsed wholesale; but it is their *application* that must be criticized in particular cases, for in themselves they are components for potential reasoning, not active claims. The need to observe these connectors gives a new meaning to Austin's term, "philosophical fieldwork" (1956–1957, 25), bestowing on it more radical interdisciplinary implications than Austin himself may have intended.

First, since many aspects of practical reasoning in daily life are, as examples here have illustrated, suppressed, allusive, ambiguous and fragmented, tracing steps in cases of reasoning is not straightforward. Reconstructing partly shared habits, assumptions and prescriptions which arguers draw on to make themselves mutually intelligible requires skills which are ethnographic as well as philosophical. Aristotle's work also draws attention to the influence of processes and relationships in deliberative communication; this alerts us to the fact that definable "concepts" are not the only sources of meaning in discourse. To understand the purport of real-life deliberation, we must be able to interpret what is going on at deep argumentative levels.

The type of ethnography this demands needs to be performed using philosophical conceptualizations of argumentative interaction which make visible what sorts of interaction are taking place. Otherwise, observers' own habitual expectations of argument will be imposed on what deliberators are doing, producing flattened and distorted accounts of their interchanges. First, observers may not understand what remarks and actions are "for": they may not realize that a given remark is intended to provoke effects in terms of pathos rather than to make a substantive claim, for example, interpreting it more literally than its deliberative function warrants. Second, they may not appreciate how certain effects are achieved in local settings. In the West of Ireland, for example, speakers characteristically convey "ethos" reticently and wryly: very differently from the style in, say, New York. Without an understanding of local communicative practices at this level, deliberative interaction cannot be reconstructed accurately.

Aristotle himself was aware that people argue differently in Athens and Sparta, say (Rhet. I 8). It seems consistent with his position to suggest that he may have envisaged a preference in Sparta for certain sets of topoi, rather than imagining Spartans to use topoi unknown in Athens altogether. Perhaps in Sparta the topos urging interlocutors not to give up easily is more often applied than elsewhere, for instance. Different frequencies and constellations of such topoi can add up to profound cultural differences—in effect, local cultures of reasoning. Their existence does not mean users are necessarily behaving in a fundamentally unintelligible manner, rather that our judgments about when to apply a given topos might differ from theirs. In fact Aristotle generally expected human beings to reason in a way which would tend to produce the truth in the end ("*Temporis filia veritas*": "Truth is the daughter of time"). He did not expect people to deliberate in ways which would be finally unintelligible to each other—though it is unclear how long he would have expected it to take to reach intelligibility, or how complete he would have required comprehension to be.

Aristotle may have been less alive than are contemporary ethnographers to variations in usage and deliberative behavior to be found even within a single linguistic community. Informal inferential patterns tend to be characteristic of particular (sub-)cultural attitudes; these differences are not all exotic and extreme, for we move in and out of them most days of our lives (for example, from home to work). What are accepted as reasonable applications of topoi differ from time to time and place to place. They generate patterns which people follow in practice, as they move between settings, but for the most part they do so unreflectingly (Edmondson 2000). It is not yet clear how fundamental these differences are. Exploring contrasting forms of argumentation in diverse times and places allows us to speculate on at least some of the social habits and conventions that support them and give them meaning. To the extent that we believe ourselves capable of understanding them in the end, we assume that human reasoning is in principle intercommunicable, even if it demands protracted hermeneutical processes in practice.

Difficulties in this arena come to a head where there are genuine issues at stake, such as the intercultural conflicts discussed by Parekh (2000). Parekh recommends that in important disputes we should proceed piecemeal, beginning from local custom and trying to justify in dialogue, over time, what deviations from it might be justified. This cautious method, he urges, can produce unexpected progress in practical problems—for instance in debate whether nurses from Pakistan should wear the shalwar kameez at work in the UK, or if Sikh motorcyclists should be compelled to wear helmets. In effect, Parekh's method adjures us to search for *endoxa* accepted by both sides, building from there (on analogy with Neurath's raft). To the extent that this implies universal standards of deliberation, it implies seeking common opinions rather than imposing general rules. These opinions and their uses must be understood within their respective cultures of reasoning: ethos and pathos take different shape and support logos somewhat differently in different settings. This might potentially support positions such as Benhabib's (2002) desire for an "interactive universalism." It enables us to remain alive to personal and social differences, while still assuming that human beings are in principle within the reach of reason.

These arguments generate multiple directions for further research. This chapter has broached an interpretation of reasoning which embraces more substantive aspects than could be expected from exclusively emphasizing cognition. The project of understanding and practicing (wise) reasoning about social and political affairs does not seek to exclude precision, but fundamentally it is a human project. It is one in which individuals need not feel solely responsible for jointly reached (wise) public decisions, but where evolving joint decisions can demand considerable hermeneutic and moral energy. Tracing and reconstructing the processes involved demands partly ethnographic methods; supporting them needs political ones. The shared, embedded nature of reasoning highlights an understanding of deliberation which rests less on top-down regulation than on promoting engaged forms of discernment: part of a process which could be supported interpersonally and perhaps institutionally too.

NOTES

1. I owe this point to Prof. Wolfgang Schmidl (Vienna, December 2011). For Schmidl, adjustment to the hearer is at least in part an empathetic process based on an imaginative reconstruction of the hearer's position. Schmidl's account of empathy entails self-interrogation from the speaker, who should become clear about his or her own motivation in argument. Relevant questions include, Do I want the other person to change his or her view, or do I want to get them to see that their view is not the only one possible, or do I want them to see that a certain value could be different, or that some interpretation or evaluation on my own part might be acceptable to them? Or do I want the other person to do something in particular, or to act with a different motivation? Schmidl points out that many conventional attempts at communication (including some in sermons or political speeches) fail because the speaker is not prepared to recognize that the situation really is one of uncertainty and contingency, but assumes that the message is definite and only needs to be packaged in a certain way. For an examination of some respects in which argumentation can be affected by participants' sociopolitical and emotional stances, see Edmondson and Rau 2008.

2. Cf. Amélie Rorty's masterly accounts of the person of practical wisdom (2011; 1996); she shows not only how rhetorical processes work in the life of the phronimos but also in what sense rhetorical skills are needed for "every kind of discourse" (2011: 718) and are central for civic life.

REFERENCES

Ardelt, M. 2004. "Wisdom as Expert Knowledge System: A Critical Review of a Contemporary Operationalization of an Ancient Concept." *Human Development* 47 (5): 257–85.

Aristotle. 1998. *Nicomachean Ethics.* Trans. by W. D. Ross. Oxford: Oxford University Press.

———. 1946. *Rhetorica.* Trans. by W. Rhys Roberts. Oxford: Clarendon Press.

———. 1989. *Topica.* Trans. by E. S. Forster. Cambridge: Harvard University Press: Loeb.

Austin, John L. 1956–1957. "A Plea for Excuses." *Proceedings of the Aristotelian Society* 57: 1–30.

Baltes, P., and U. Staudinger. 2000. "Wisdom: A Metaheuristic (pragmatic) to Orchestrate Mind and Virtue Towards Excellence." *American Psychologist* 55: 122–136.

Benhabib, Seyla. 2002. *The Claims of Culture: Equality and Diversity in the Global Era.* Princeton: Princeton University Press.

Burnyeat, Myles. 1994. "Enthymeme: Aristotle on the Logic of Persuasion." In *Aristotle's Rhetoric: Philosophical Essays. Proceedings of the 11th Symposium Aristotelicum*, ed. by D. J. Furley and A. Nehamas, 3–55. Princeton: Princeton University Press.

Curnow, Trevor. 1999. *Wisdom, Intuition and Ethics*. Farnham: Ashgate.

Edmondson, Ricca. 1984. *Rhetoric in Sociology*. London: Macmillan.

———. 2005. "Wisdom in Later Life: Ethnographic Approaches." *Ageing in Society* 25 (3): 339–356.

———. 2007. "Rhetorics of Social Science." In *The Handbook of Social Science Methodology*, ed. by William Outhwaite and Stephen Turner, 479–498. London: Sage.

———. 2012. "A Social Interpretation of Personal Wisdom." In *Personal Wisdom*, ed. by Michel Ferrari and Nic Weststrate. New York: Springer.

Edmondson, Ricca, and Jane Pearce. 2007. "The Practice of Health Care: Wisdom as a Model." *Medicine, Health Care and Philosophy* 10 (3): 233–244.

Edmondson, Ricca, Jane Pearce, and Markus H. Woerner. 2009. "When Wisdom is Called for in Clinical Reasoning." *Theoretical Medicine and Bioethics* 30: 231–247.

Edmondson, Ricca, and Henrike Rau, eds. 2008. *Environmental Argument and Cultural Difference: Locations, Fractures and Deliberations*. Oxford: Peter Lang.

Hempel, Carl G. 1965. *Aspects of Scientific Explanation and Other Essays in the Philosophy of Science*. New York: Free Press.

Kekes, John. 1995. *Moral Wisdom and Good Lives*. Ithaca, NY: Cornell University Press.

Lawson, A. 2004. "Reasoning and Brain Function." In *The Nature of Reasoning*, ed. by J. Leighton and R. Sternberg, 12–48. Cambridge: Cambridge University Press.

Maxwell, Nicholas. 2007. *From Knowledge to Wisdom: A Revolution for Science and the Humanities* (2nd ed.). London: Pentire Press.

Parekh, Bhikhu C. 2000. *Rethinking Multiculturalism*. Cambridge: Harvard University Press.

Perelman, Chaim, and Lucie Olbrechts-Tyteca. 1958/1969. *The New Rhetoric: A Treatise on Argumentation*. Notre Dame: University of Notre Dame Press.

Rorty, Amélie O. 1996. "Structuring Rhetoric." In *Essays on Aristotle's Rhetoric*, ed. by A. O. Rorty, 1–33. Berkeley: University of California Press.

———. 2011. "Aristotle on the Virtues of Rhetoric." *Review of Metaphysics* 64 (4): 715–733.

Schön, Donald. 1983. *The Reflective Practitioner: How Professionals Think in Action*. London: Temple Smith.

Searle, John H. 2001. *Rationality in Action*. Cambridge: MIT Press.

Sternberg, Robert J. 1998. "A Balance Theory of Wisdom." *Review of General Psychology* 2: 347–365.

Woerner, Markus H. 1982. "Enthymeme—Ein Rückgriff auf Aristoteles in systematischer Absicht." In *Rhetorische Rechtstheorie*, ed. by O. Ballweg and T.-M. Seibert, 73–98. Freiburg/Br.: Alber Verlag.

———. 1990. *Das Ethische in der Rhetorik des Aristoteles*. Freiburg/Br.: Alber.

———. 1995. "Rhetorik als Logik der Rede." In *Perspektiven einer Kommunikationswissenschaft*, ed. by D. Krallman and H. W. Schmitz, vol. 2, 423–432. Münster: Nodus.

Chapter Seven

Toulmin's Rhetorical Logic

Frank Canavan

In *Knowing and Acting* (Toulmin 1976, 60), Stephen Toulmin locates the effective beginnings of the Western tradition of philosophy in the emerging societies of classical Greece, when, as a result of the growth of literacy among other developments,

> "arguments" ceased to be merely oral disputations between rival speakers, and became independent objects of contemplation and rational criticism, namely, sequences of recorded propositions laying claim to some inner connection and coherence.

This characterization of argument had been part of the Toulmin approach especially since *The Uses of Argument* (1958), in which he made the analysis of argument his central preoccupation. A central tenet of the Toulmin project was that the tradition of argumentation which developed in accordance with the mathematical template was not the instrument best suited to serve the complex debates that took place in public, private and professional life. Furthermore, he maintained the situation had been exacerbated by the Cartesian-inspired search for certainty in all aspects of reality, in accordance with the standards which mathematics could achieve.

As a result of his conviction that, in John Dewey's words, it was necessary to abandon the "dream of certainty," Toulmin sought to design a model of argumentation that could deal with the wide range of human experiences that did not provide mathematical certainty of result. By definition, argumentation could be expected where there were some things to be said for and some against a proposition. As was understood by Aristotle, nobody argues about issues that have a self-evident or necessary outcome. The purposes of argument, therefore, include assembling support for or against a point of view, where this point of view might claim either to have factual support or to be a well-founded opinion.

As Toulmin was reacting against and consciously endeavoring to dislodge the hegemony of traditional deductive logic as the criterion by which worthwhile arguments were to be judged, he was aware that there would have to be compensation for the formal tests for validity and soundness which had been hallmarks of, for example, the Aristotelian syllogism. He was not concerned to amplify or modify the existing systems of logic; in his view the structure of formal logic was simply unfit to accommodate the kind of arguments in which people engage regularly in their personal, social and professional capacities. Such arguments would be likely to have outcomes that were true "for the most part." However, even if their results lacked mathematical certainty this did not make them invalid or unworthy of acceptance. A high level of probability is the most that can be expected for claims or conclusions of arguments about politics, aesthetics, ethics, even, on occasion, medical diagnoses. This applies also to the many important issues in which humans engage and to which they bring not just their cognitive skills but also their imagination, insight, experience and judgment.

In this context, therefore, Toulmin devised a structure for the construction of arguments with two main purposes in mind. The elements of the argument would have to be laid out as candidly and transparently as possible, and the structure would have to provide opportunity for the arguer to furnish the maximum support for the claim being made while taking into account the caveats necessary when dealing with contingent human affairs. Having rejected the foundationalist notion that deduction from certain premises to necessary outcome was the standard by which arguments should be judged, he wanted to show that, in the range of fields referred to above, *substantial* arguments, in other words arguments which do not *entail* their conclusions, are the only kind of argument available. Furthermore, he wants to insist that in such situations, trustworthy arguments are not only possible but normal, and that it is entirely *reasonable*, depending on the quality of the argumentation, to find the outcome of such a process *acceptable* (see Canavan, 2012).

Toulmin was intent on providing a structure of argument that would be as candid as possible: in other words, the separate elements of the process would be distinct as regards their function. He was also determined that the model, which was to be used in real-life situations, would reflect actual experience. As he saw it, an argument typically begins with a claim which, when challenged, is supported by some kind of relevant evidence or *data*. If the weight and relevance of the support offered is deemed adequate by a questioner then the argument is concluded; the claim has been established to the satisfaction of those engaged in the exchange. This basic form of argument, the link going from support to claim, reflects the earliest form of human resolution of disagreement, predating the invention of what came to be referred to as a syllogism. Toulmin recognized, however, that data might not be accepted and that this disagreement about "facts of the matter" would have to be resolved; either new, acceptable support would have to be produced or the engagement would be discontinued. In the event that the *data* were accepted, their relevance to the present circumstances might be questioned and justification would have to be supplied in the form of a *warrant,* an overarching, lawlike statement that legitimized the passage from the given *data* to the *claim/conclusion.* Toulmin also took into account the likelihood that in some situations even the warrant might be challenged, in which case some factual basis would be forthcoming to guarantee its general applicability. Thus, a *backing* would be brought into play, a factual source of authentication of the warrant. He was aware, also, that due, for example, to incomplete knowledge on the part of an arguer, there might be circumstances within which the warrant might not apply and, prudently, he introduced a caveat into the structure, a hedging of assertion to anticipate *rebuttals.* Finally, since this model of argumentation is to accommodate uncertainties rather than necessities, the claim/conclusion will attract a *modal qualifier*, typically ranging between "possibly" and "almost certainly."

The point of narrating the familiar Toulmin layout of argument in this manner is to emphasize the extent to which he was attempting to broaden the scope of argumentation in order to encompass the range of arguments that occur regularly. Obviously, the use of natural language would be incorporated in this structure, and the departure from the syllogistic form of argument would be very clear. The ambiguity which Toulmin claimed to identify in the major premise of the traditional syllogism would be removed and any artificial reformulation of arguments would be avoided. Of course the most significant outcome would be a departure from formal validity, in other words true premises leading necessarily to a true conclusion. Toulmin's alternative would have acceptable claims/conclusions transparently established on the basis of adequate evidence/support. Such evidence would be produced in accordance with the "experience, insight and judgment" of the arguer (Toulmin 1958, 188).

Initial reactions to the Toulmin model were unfavorable: logicians insisted that he had failed to take account of developments in logic during the previous one hundred and fifty years, while they also claimed to find confusion in the layout of arguments which Toulmin was proposing. However, the potential value of his proposal was gradually recognized, especially in the schools of communications in North America where there had been a tradition of formal debate. Acceptance was facilitated by reviews such as that provided by Brockriede and Ehninger (1960, 44), and the realization that, while the original model in *The Uses of Argument* had been justificatory, in other words the argument was originally presented as implicit or explicit scaffolding for a *claim*, once the fully fledged structure had been established, it could be used to initiate arguments leading to *conclusions*.

In the event, this aspect of the layout became significant in establishing the versatility of the Toulmin model as a vector for all sorts of arguments, including those dealing with "facts of the matter" as well as arguments leading to policy action. Indeed it eventually became clear that arguments based on a variety of language-uses other than the *assertive* could be accommodated by the model.

While in *The Uses of Argument* Toulmin had dealt with arguments establishing the facts of situations, in *Introduction to Reasoning* (1979) Toulmin et al. demonstrated the use of the model for arriving at policy decisions in a range of professional activities. Since Toulmin had consciously derived the argument-structure from the practice of jurisprudence, it is not surprising to find it employed in this discipline. However, the authors show that it can be serviceable in science, business management, ethics and elsewhere. Although *Introduction to Reasoning* presents the Toulmin model in a manner suited to pedagogical purposes, the examples of the model at work are related to real experiences, in contrast to the material typically provided in previous textbooks in this area. It is not surprising, therefore, that William Dunn, a specialist in corporate decision-making, should have chosen the Toulmin model as the template for laying out an argument presented in favor of or against a particular policy decision. In *Public Policy Analysis* (1981, 44ff.), Dunn illustrates how analyses and conclusions for action in the world of business are effectively dealt with by the use of the Toulmin six-part system with a minor modification from "data" to "Policy-Relevant Information." This reflects the level of complexity and the multiplicity of factors (*grounds*) that may have to be assembled and taken into account when seeking to arrive at optimum conclusions in circumstances with wide implications.

TOULMIN IN CONTEXT

Toulmin, of course, was not alone in seeking a more satisfactory manner of delivering arguments across a range of fields wider than that afforded by traditional deductive logic. Contemporaneous with *The Uses of Argument* (1958), although not published in English until 1969, *The New Rhetoric* was seen by its authors as a contribution to argumentation of a public kind which they regarded as of particular importance in maintaining a democratic society. Chaïm Perelman and Lucie Olbrechts-Tyteca, having made a detailed study of Aristotelian and subsequent forms of rhetoric, realized its value for their own time. They saw the role of rhetoric as that of winning adherence to a point of view and, consequently, they laid particular emphasis on the part played by the audience in the argumentative process.

The central role of argumentation in the political process was the preoccupation of Howard Kahane, who found himself at a loss in trying to justify the use of formal deductive logic in the evaluation of government policy. In *Logic and Contemporary Rhetoric: The Use of Reason in Everyday Life* (1971) he deals with the analysis and evaluation of arguments representative of real life. While the title of his book, stressing the *use* of reason, echoes that of Toulmin's iconic monograph, there are also reminders of Toulmin's advice to the effect that the successful arguer will not display control of the technicalities of reasoning only; she will also exercise qualities reflecting "experience, insight and judgment." Kahane's reference to this aspect of the would-be arguer's skill-set is the injunction, in later editions, that she should engage in "the construction of cogent world views" by learning to understand herself and human motivation generally, and will develop an understanding of the physical sciences (Kahane 1984, 25ff.). Quite clearly, in his opinion, successful and relevant reasoning is not merely a technical matter involving the "intricacies of the predicate logic quantifier rules" (Kahane 1971, vii).

Toulmin's attitude to formal deductive logic arose from his conviction that it was irrelevant in the evaluation of the most widely used arguments, substantial ones. Doubt is also cast on the efficacy of immersion in formal deductive logic as a means of developing powers of reasoning and arguing by Michael Scriven, who in *Reasoning* (1976) questioned the notion that there would be a transfer of learning from exercises in formal deductive logic to reasoning in real-life situations. In his opinion "one has to view with great skepticism the very idea that formal logic is likely to help to improve reasoning skill. What it improves is skill in doing formal logic" (Scriven 1976, xv). Formal logic, he maintains, will not be adequate to analyze and evaluate "arguments and presentations of the kind you find in everyday discourse (news media, discussions, advertisements), textbooks and lectures" (Scriven 1976, ix). Toulmin's project can be seen to be reflected also in Scriven's insistence that "the only way to improve reasoning skills is by staying very close to real examples" (Scriven 1976, xv).

Real examples presented in natural language became the common currency of informal logic/argumentation in the course of the second half of the twentieth century. This was accompanied by an enhanced understanding of the great variety of uses to which language might be applied. Wittgenstein, a potent influence on Toulmin's attitude to language usage, had emphasized this, and philosophers such as Austin in "Performative Utterances" (1970) and Grice in "Logic and Conversation" (1975), had analyzed and extended the understanding of natural language-uses beyond the boundaries of literal assertion and/or description. Their insights were to inform the work in argumentation of such practitioners as Fogelin, who incorporated the results of their analysis in *Understanding Arguments* (1978). Since, as illustrated by Austin, we use language to achieve many objectives other than stating facts and/or descriptions (for example giving orders, or making promises or declarations), it is appropriate to explore the scope available to *inference* from, for instance, *performatives*. When the appropriate official, in the required circumstances, declares "I pronounce you man and wife," it is reasonable to infer that recognized advantages have been conferred and identifiable obligations have been imposed.

The concept of *implicature,* developed by Grice and brought into the mainstream of reasoning by writers such as Fogelin, identifies justifiable assumptions and obligations that are part of our sentence-making. One such obligation is the observance of the "Co-operative Principle" which assumes a commitment by those engaged in conversation to "tell the truth," to "give as much information as appropriate" and so on. Here we see the genesis of the elaborate system of protocols for the conduct of critical discussion/argumentation developed by van Eemeren, Grootendorst and collaborators as the Pragma-Dialectic system of argumentation (van Eemeren et al. 2004). This system takes the purpose of argumentation to be the finding of solutions to differences of opinion through a dialectical process which, using a detailed list of rules of procedure, controls the argumentative moves of those involved.

These brief references to a selection of the proponents of natural language argumentation are intended merely to situate Toulmin's *The Uses of Argument* in the developments within informal logic/argumentation that have been under way in the course of recent decades. Much theoretical work has been done in the effort to define "argumentation," "informal logic," "natural logic," and in identifying criteria for successful argumentation. The gradual replacement of "truth" by "acceptability" as the outcome of argumentation has been given detailed attention, as have protocols for dialogic argumentation, fallacious argumentation, argumentation-schemes and the role of rhetoric in the achievement of consensus. Sophisticated prescriptions for the conduct of critical discussions in idealized conditions have emphasized the extent to which theory has outpaced practical application, or indeed, has been seen as its own justification.

TOULMIN AND THE *USE* OF ARGUMENT

This impressive development of argumentation theory would seem to have little in common with the Toulmin project, which, in the opinion of some, is deficient in terms of detailed theory. There had been from the beginning, for example, complaints about the exact nature of, and perceived confusion between, elements of the Toulmin structure. However, it must be borne in mind that while the designers of the pragma-dialectical system, for example, recognize that the procedure they specify would be unlikely to find application in real-life argument, Toulmin's objective is to formulate argument in *use* and useful over a wide range of situations pertaining to personal, social, political and professional life. Furthermore, the Toulmin arrangement is not limited to employment in dialectical encounters: it can convey arguments in what might be seen as a *logical* format, while its chief strength can be shown to lie in the transmission of argumentation in the *rhetorical* mode. The versatility of the Toulmin model results from the fact that it was designed for use. This does not mean that theory is abandoned; *The Uses of Argument* posits and analyzes the relevant background of epistemological theories. But Toulmin is convinced "that a radical re-ordering of logical theory is needed in order to bring it into line with critical practice" (Toulmin 1958, 252). It is worth noting that the theory of argumentation advocated in *The Uses of Argument* followed his extensive analysis of reasoning in ethics and science. In the case of the former he had based his conclusions on considering the *function* rather than a *definition* of ethics. His philosophy of science concentrates on the practical manner in which scientists carry out their work and shows how well-trained operatives infer conclusions in accordance with principles accepted at a particular time.

The use of the Toulmin model, therefore, either for the construction or analysis of arguments, presupposes the possibility of its assimilation into the cognitive apparatus of the arguer so that it can be deployed as circumstances demand. This is quite distinct from the traditional account of deduction in terms of *analytic*-type arguments which produce tautology. Toulmin wants to concentrate on *substantial* arguments from which new knowledge may emerge. In his determination to design a method of argumentation which is fit for purpose in handling substantial arguments, the kind of arguments which are most common, he wants to emphasize his conviction that

> Substantial arguments in natural science, ethics and elsewhere have been severely handled by philosophers, solely on the grounds of not being (what they were never intended to be) analytic, and their genuine merits have been accounted negligible as compared with that initial and inevitable sin (Toulmin 1958, 252).

This insistence on the centrality of substantial arguments, in other words arguments of the type most commonly used in human affairs, was at the heart of the growing discipline of informal logic in the latter half of the twentieth century. Toulmin's contribution on this level placed him in the mainstream of developments. On the micro-level, however, there were specific elements of argumentation that were viewed as crucial to the project. Some consisted of reviving aspects of argumentation that had been relevant since Aristotle, such as the process of definition, fallacies, or *topoi* as sources or guarantees of arguments. Others, such as the replacement of "truth" by "acceptability" as the criterion for positing premises and inferring conclusions, as well as the prescription of detailed rules of argument which owed something to the Aristotelian dialectic, took on a new force with the pragma-dialecticians. It is worthwhile to consider whether Toulmin's work encompassed or reflected such developments.

In the tradition of formal deductive logic, *definition,* the ascription of limits in order to arrive at the essence of an entity or concept, was seen to be a concomitant of the activity of reasoning. In the course of departing from mathematically based logic to reasoning in natural language it would be necessary to achieve the greatest degree of clarity and rigor possible in the use of language. Toulmin acknowledged the importance of clarity when, introducing *The Uses of Argument* (1958), he adopted Aristotle's advice to the effect that "First we must state the subject of the enquiry and what it is about," in other words define relevant terms (1958, 1). For Walton (2006), definition is still causing difficulty. Finding universally accepted definitions of such commonly used terms as "democracy," "liberal," "abortion," has proved almost impossible (Walton 2006, xii).

This feature of argumentation was the subject of *Communication and Argumentation* by Arne Naess (1966). This study was intended to help to avoid misunderstanding in the course of critical discussion by presenting a system of *precization,* which involves peeling back layers of possible meaning in order to arrive at a shared understanding. Of course an excess of zeal in pursuing this process could delay the beginning of argument or, perhaps, render it impossible. Naess is aware of the possibility that introducing the *impractical* in this manner is just as likely to frustrate progress in argumentation as prescribing unmanageable rules for the conduct of an argument, or providing a multiplicity of qualifiers at each stage of the Toulmin model, as suggested by Trent (1968). Even defining "argument" has caused divisions among practitioners, which have arisen from differing views about the *purpose* of argument; this has meant that a lexical definition has been inadequate, and stipulative definition has resulted in individual prescriptions. For Toulmin, definition is arrived at through usage and example; it is made clear in *Introduction to Reasoning* that "meaning has to be discovered from the ways a term is used within the entire communication environment" (Toulmin et al. 1979, 146). This does not mean that Toulmin has avoided negative criticism in the matter of definition; it has been pointed out that he offers a variety of accounts of the *warrant,* the central element in his model of argumentation. It can be said in response that Toulmin is working on a dynamic system to which limits may not be put. Scope must be provided for possible future development and he is setting the direction that this is likely to take. His intentions are clarified by his explanations, painstaking analysis and everyday examples. Where, however, Toulmin is investing terms in common use with a novel connotation, such as *substantial* and *analytic* arguments, he stipulates definition in order to distinguish clearly between his usage and that of those who have preceded him.

FALLACIES AND INFORMAL LOGIC: THE TOULMIN PERSPECTIVE

Attention to fallacies as an aspect of argumentation intensified after the publication of Hamblin's *Fallacies* (1971), in which he expressed dissatisfaction with what he referred to as the "standard treatment." Even Aristotle's definition of "fallacy" was deemed no longer adequate by commentators, and renewed analysis attempted to integrate the concept of fallacy into particular views of argumentation. To the pragma-dialecticians a fallacy was considered a breach of the regulations laid down for the conduct of good argument. The list of thirteen fallacies specified by Aristotle was enlarged by others with the traditional categories retained, while for Biro and Siegel "arguments are essentially epistemic objects" (1992, 92); an argument that does not provide good warrant for its conclusion is fallacious. They allow for naming individual fallacies and extending existing lists. This reflects the remarks by Toulmin et al. in *Introduction to Reasoning,* to the effect they will not be able "to identify any intrinsically fallacious forms of argument" (1979, 157). Argument-schemes successful in one context may be faulty in another (for instance, the argument from authority); they believe that there will always be new ways in which arguments will be found to be fallacious, since they are a product of human experience.

ACCEPTABILITY AS THE CRITERION FOR EVALUATING PREMISE AND CONCLUSION

In the opinion of Ralph H. Johnson the *illative core* of an argument, the element providing support for a claim, is to be evaluated on the basis of "acceptance, truth, relevance and sufficiency" (2000, 191). For David Hitch-cock, on the other hand, it is clear that "the predicates of truth and falsity simply do not apply to many theses for which people argue" (2002, 288). Christopher Tindale has no doubt "that in the realm of argumentation, if we are to progress towards our goals we must concentrate on the question of ac-ceptability" (2004, 175).

Toulmin was aware from the beginning that a departure from the strict formality of true premises leading to a necessarily true conclusion as the outcome of argument would mean that support and conclusions would have to be *acceptable* by virtue of the relevance and weight of support offered in accordance with the standards of the field in question. He was also aware of Aristotle's injunction that it might be inadvisable or impossible, in some cir-cumstances, to engage in argument at all. If, for example, an arguer's opening factual statement in support of a claim does not find agreement, the arguer may have to engage in a *lemma* in order to justify this support. But this may in turn lead to further disagreement, ending in infinite regress. If argument is to proceed to fruitful outcome there must be acceptance of some statements on a fiduciary basis, unless the material offered is self-evident, arises from common observation and experience, or is derived from a common trusted source. Of course the best support offered by the arguer will consist of con-cessions that she knows are likely to be forthcoming from the questioner. On occasion, the trustworthiness (ethos) of the arguer and/or testator will be a crucial factor in the progress of argument on the basis of "acceptability" (see Edmondson in this volume).

Patrick Bondy proposes "to discuss the role that truth plays in the evalu-ation of arguments when the purpose of arguments is understood as truth-directed in some important way" (2010, 144). He recognizes that "most theorists have dropped either the validity requirement or the truth require-ment or both" (2010, 143). There are, he maintains, some who still see the purpose of argument as having some truth-content, but this is not to say that the purpose of argument is "to establish the truth of their conclusions beyond all doubt"; the purpose is, rather, to reach a conclusion "that is most rational, from the point of view of the participants in the argument to take to be true" (2010, 144). Here George Boger (2005) had raised the obvious objection to the displacement of the search for truth as the objective of argumentation, claiming that

> While argumentationists maintain that formal logic's adherence to soundness and embracing a Platonist absolutism renders it irrelevant, their critics maintain that informal logic's adherence to acceptability results in a pernicious relativism that renders it duplicit. (2005, 229)

The use of "relativism" or "relativistic" as terms of denigration has been well established, just as the term "rhetorical," reduced to the notion of empty verbal style, is employed pejoratively, and "sophistry" has become synonymous with duplicity. However, once a critical discussion is undertaken, in other words a verbal dispute that cannot be decided with mathematical certainty, the outcome must depend, at least in part, on well-established opinion, the relative reliability of the evidence, the relative trust placed in the arguer, and the relative extent to which the opposition or audience can be brought to empathize with the case being made or refuted. This is far from "relativism" in the sense implying that no reasonable standards can possibly be reached for assessing arguments.

To demand "truth" as the criterion of premise or conclusion is clearly futile in situations which are not merely matters of fact, and even in disputes about so-called "states of affairs" the demand to prove every assertion to the standard of demonstrable truth would frustrate the possibility of critical discussion over a wide range of areas where such interchange is a necessary feature of human experience. This is not to say that "truth" will be deliberately discarded, or that known untruths or even carelessness as regards facts will be welcome in fora where significant argumentation takes place. The "principle of cooperation" would demand, and entitle participants to assume, that in the course of argumentation each speaker/writer would be committed to the reliability of their assertions. This is as foundational to the conduct of political, social and professional life as the assumption that promises will be kept.

In this context, and with this kind of assumption, it is rational to consider "acceptability" as a criterion for good argument in situations outside the narrow range of formal deductive logic. Toulmin had adopted as exemplar the practice of the law, where decisions are arrived at on the basis of convincing testimony. This might take the form of data reportedly heard and/or seen by testators or the opinions of acknowledged experts in relevant fields. The outcomes of such exercises would have far-reaching consequences for those involved and would be decided on the basis of the testimony being "acceptable" "on the balance of probabilities" or "beyond a reasonable doubt." Such concepts have been refined and continue to be subject to constant monitoring. They are human constructs and open to being provisionally "acceptable." The *relative* nature of their application is emphasized by reference to earlier standards of legal decision-making, such as trial by combat or trial by ordeal.

Objections to "acceptability" as a criterion in the evaluation of argumentation due to the fear of introducing pernicious relativism, can, therefore, be seen to be misplaced. Given the areas of experience to which the current theories of informal logic/argumentation are applied, outcomes are bound to be relative to relevance and to weight of support offered in good faith. Toulmin had, of course, anticipated the central role of "acceptability" in argumentation. In *The Uses of Argument* he had asserted that

> logic is concerned not with the *manner* of our inferring, or with questions of technique; its primary business is a retrospective justificatory one—with the arguments we can put forward afterwards to make good our claim that the conclusions arrived at are *acceptable*, because justifiable, conclusions. (Toulmin 1958, 6; emphasis added)

Standards of acceptability would be determined, as he goes on to point out, by best practice within the relevant discipline. These standards will undergo refinement and modification and consideration of the *context* in which they are applied will also help to determine acceptability.

Toulmin et al. return to these matters in *Introduction to Reasoning*. They make it clear that standards of acceptability will not be set in terms of timeless absolutes. Rather, they maintain,

> at any given moment . . . some established repertoire of argumentation procedure . . . scientific, legal or whatever . . . possesses rational authority for the time being and so carries weight within the corresponding enterprise. (Toulmin et al. 1979, 135)

TOULMIN AND ARGUMENTATION SCHEMES

As interest in *fallacies* has increased during the development of informal logic since the middle of the twentieth century, it is not surprising that there has been a proportionate interest in *argumentation schemes*, since the former is frequently the outcome of the misuse of the latter and they both trace their origins to the work of Aristotle. Walton et al. provide the following definition of argumentation schemes:

> Argumentation schemes are forms of argument (structures of inference) that represent structures of common types of argument used in every-day discourse as well as in special contexts like those of legal argumentation and scientific argumentation. (Walton et al. 2008, 1)

Argument schemes typically take the form of arguments using such bases as *sign*, *analogy*, and *co-relation*, and the twenty-eight *topoi* registered by Aristotle find their counterparts in modern taxonomies such as those of Hastings (1963), Kienpointner (1986) and Walton et al. (2008), which provides the most comprehensive list. For Aristotle the *topoi* typically take the form of well-established opinions that have attained the status of aphorisms and are used to legitimate inferences in the affairs of the day; one might conclude that "filial loyalty is to be preferred to obedience" on the basis of a *topos* such as "that which is more lasting or secure is more desirable than that which is less so" (see also Edmondson in this volume). Aristotle's *topoi* represent a distillation of his existential experiences, of listening to public speakers and drawing on the literary tradition available to him. Perelman and Olbrechts-Tyteca, who had made a detailed study of Aristotle's *topoi*, "analyzed a range of discourse from politics, law, ethics and daily deliberations" to develop their account of arguments in use (Warnick 2000, 112).

Toulmin, however, devised his model of argumentation without full awareness of what had been done previously although he did subsequently undertake a close analysis of relevant Aristotelian texts. The traditional taxonomy of argument schemes does not feature in *The Uses of Argument* (1958) but Toulmin et al. deal with the classification of arguments in *Introduction to Reasoning* (1979), which was prepared with students in mind and would be expected to provide some background information for them. This account of argumentation schemes is, as one would expect, descriptive rather than prescriptive. The authors refer to a number of the familiar argumentation schemes, including arguments from analogy, generalization, sign, cause, authority, opposites, and degree. However, they advise that the list is not exhaustive; arguments must always be examined with an eye to the context and field in which they occur and they insist that there are no fixed rules by which to judge the most efficacious argumentation schemes (Toulmin et al. 1979, 147–48). This is not surprising since the Toulmin model of argumentation was devised with a view to accommodating arguments of every kind that people working in different fields might advance. It must, therefore, be open to new forms of argument. Toulmin et al. placed no limit on the list of fallacies: as mentioned already, new ways of being fallacious will continue to appear. The corollary of this is that new methods of argument may be developed in the service of seeking new knowledge.

Toulmin had been quite explicit on this point in *The Uses of Argument*. Insisting that logic will have to become more empirical, he goes on to assert that "great logical innovations are part and parcel of great scientific, moral, political or legal innovations," and cites the names of great innovators in the sciences who have not only changed what we believe about the universe "but also our ways of arguing and our standards of relevance and proof" (Toulmin 1958, 257). Most significant in this connection is the fact that the layout of the Toulmin model can accommodate argumentation schemes as *warrants* and is thus open to unlimited development. Hastings (1963) preferred the Toulmin model to the traditional syllogism for the layout of his schemes. Kienpointner (1986) chooses to illustrate his approach to argumentation and argumentation schemes by the use of Toulminian terminology and structure.

Walton et al. (2008), having produced a compendium of sixty types of argumenation schemes with sub-types, developed, as did Hastings, a system of *critical questions* about the efficacy of the warrant, designed to render the particular argument as rigorous as possible. These arguments, also, can be laid out in accordance with the Toulmin model; indeed the Toulmin *rebuttal* provides the catalyst for the formulation of critical questions.

The purpose of this study is to indicate the manner and the extent to which the Toulmin model of argumentation remains relevant to the ongoing development of informal logic and is serviceable in the conduct of argumentation, whether in trying to establish facts or find agreed opinions or consensus on decision-making for action. We have placed particular emphasis on the *use* of arguments, as this was Toulmin's own motivation, shown clearly in his *Reason in Ethics* and *Philosophy of Science,* both of which predated *The Uses of Argument.* His commitment to the *practice* of argument led him to discard traditional formal logic as irrelevant to arguments in a wide range of fields, and to build a theory and provide examples of arguments as they are normally couched in natural language.

The growth of interest in informal logic during the latter part of the twentieth century involved a renewal of focus in traditional fallacies and argument schemes, and we have outlined the manner in which these features of argument related to the Toulmin model. Particular attention has been given to the debate among practitioners of informal logic about the notion of *acceptability* as replacing *truth* as the dominant criterion of premise/data and conclusion since Toulmin's position, inevitable as a consequence of his abandonment of the "quest for certainty," was clear on this matter from the beginning. In *The Uses of Argument* he had declared that the criterion of good argument would be *acceptability* on the basis of justification, and justification would be in accordance with the relevant *context* and *field.*

Throughout his work Toulmin laid emphasis on the *practical,* on attitudes and actions that result from immersion in the affairs of the world. Reflection on his own experience as well as the post-Cartesian history of Europe convinced him that recapturing the outlook of a Renaissance figure such as Montaigne, with a knowledgeable interest in the whole spectrum of human affairs, was a necessary antidote to the futile demand for mathematical certainty in all aspects of living. This did not mean that scholarship either in the humanities or the sciences would be disregarded (Toulmin was a polyglot in terms of his interests), or that homespun reflections would replace serious philosophical analysis. There would have to be, however, a rebalancing of *rationality* and *reasonableness* and the application of good judgment, especially in areas other than those to which the methods of physics would apply, such as the social sciences. There must be an acknowledgment that certainty and stability are not guaranteed and that, therefore, our attempts to make sense of things through critical discussion, dialogical encounter, persuasive address, in other words through some kind of argumentation, must be capable of encompassing the contingent and adapting to the circumstances in question.

Concluding *Return to Reason,* Toulmin is of the opinion that

> The future belongs not so much to the pure thinkers who are content—at best—with optimistic or pessimistic slogans; it is a province, rather, for reflective practitioners who are ready to act on their ideals. Warm hearts allied with cool heads seek a middle way between the extremes of abstract theory and personal impulse. (Toulmin 2001, 214)

This is entirely consistent with his emphasis on function rather than definition when locating the place of reason in ethics, his elucidation of the manner in which scientists work in his examination of inference in science, his detailed analysis of the *uses* of argument, or his analysis of casuistry as a comparison of events with paradigm cases in the working out of moral dilemmas. Consistently, he sought to achieve and share understanding of reality through a combination of the informed intellect, the human imagination and a well-cultivated desire to know.

REFERENCES

Austin, John L. 1970. "Performative Utterances." In *Philosophical Papers*, 2nd ed. Ed. by J. O. Urmson and G. J. Warnock, 233–52. Oxford: Clarendon Press.

Biro, J., and H. Siegel. 1992. "Normativity, Argumentation and an Epistemic Theory of the Fallacies." In *Argumentation Illuminated,* ed. by F. H. van Eemeren, R. Grootendorst, J. A. Blair and C. A. Willard, 85–103. Amsterdam: International Society for the Study of Argumentation, Sic Sat 1.

Boger, George. 2005. "Subordinating Truth: Is *Acceptability* Acceptable?" *Argumentation* 19: 187–238.

Bondy, Patrick. 2010. "Truth and Argument Evaluation." *Informal Logic* 3 (2): 142–158.

Brockriede, W., and D. Ehninger. 1960. "Toulmin on Argument: An Interpretation and Application." *Quarterly Journal of Speech* 46 (1): 44–53.

Canavan, T. F. 2012. *Between Logic and Rhetoric: Toulmin's Theory of Argumentation.* PhD thesis, National University of Ireland, Galway.

Dunn, William. 1981. *Public Policy Analysis.* Englewood Cliffs, N.J.: Prentice Hall.

Fogelin, Robert J. 1978. *Understanding Arguments: An Introduction to Informal Logic.* New York: Harcourt Brace Jovanovich.

Grice, H. P. 1975. "Logic and Conversation." In *The Logic of Grammar,* ed. by Donald Davidson and Gilbert Harman, 64–153. Encino, CA: Dickinson Publishing.

Hamblin, Charles. 1970. *Fallacies*. London: Methuen.

Hastings, A. C. 1963. "A Reformulation of the Modes of Reasoning in Argumentation." PhD diss., Northwestern University Illinois (unpublished).

Hitchcock, D. 2002. "The Practice of Argumentative Discussion." *Argumentation* 16: 287–298.

Johnson, R. H. 2000. *Manifest Reality: A Pragmatic Theory of Argument*. Hillsdale, NJ: Lawrence Erlbaum Associates.

Kahane, Howard, ed. 1971. *Logic and Contemporary Rhetoric: The Use of Reason in Everyday Life*. Belmont, CA: Wadsworth.

———, ed. 1984. *Logic and Contemporary Rhetoric: The Use of Reason in Everyday Life*. Belmont, CA: Wadsworth.

Kienpointner, M. 1986. "Towards a Typology of Argument Schemes." In *Across the Lines of Discipline,* ed. by F. H. van Eemeren, R. Grootendorst, J. A. Blair and C. A. Willard. 275–287. Dordrecht: Foris Publications.

Naess, Arne. 1966. *Communication and Argument: Elements of Applied Semantics*. Oslo: Universitetforlage of 1947. London: Allen and Unwin.

Perelman, Chaïm, and Lucie Olbrechts-Tyteca. 1958. *The New Rhetoric: A Treatise on Argumentation*. Notre Dame: University of Notre Dame Press. (Engl. trans. 1969.)

Scriven, Michael. 1976. *Reasoning*. New York: McGraw-Hill.

Tindale, Christopher. 2004. *Rhetorical Argumentation: Principles of Theory and Practice*. Thousand Oaks, CA: Sage Publications.

Toulmin, Stephen E. 1950. *Reason in Ethics*. Cambridge: Cambridge University Press.

———. 1953. *The Philosophy of Science*. New York: Harper.

———. 1958. *The Uses of Argument*. Cambridge: Cambridge University Press.

———. 1976. *Knowing and Acting: An Invitation to Philosophy*. New York: Macmillan.

———. 2001. *Return to Reason*. Cambridge, Mass: Harvard University Press.

Toulmin, Stephen E., and A. R. Jonsen. 1988. *The Abuse of Casuistry*. Berkeley: University of California Press.

Toulmin, Stephen E., R. Rieke, and A. Janik. 1979. *Introduction to Reasoning*. New York: Macmillan.

Trent, J. 1968. "Toulmin's Model of an Argument: An Examination and Extension." *Quarterly Journal of Speech* 54 (October): 252–259.

Van Eemeren, Frans H., and Robert Grootendorst. 2004. *A Systematic Theory of Argumentation: The Pragma-Dialectic Approach*. Cambridge: Cambridge University Press.

Walton, Douglas N. 2006. *Fundamentals of Critical Argumentation*. Cambridge: Cambridge University Press.

———, C. Reed, and F. Magnano. 2008. *Argumentation Schemes*. Cambridge: Cambridge University Press.

Warnick, Barbara, 2000. "Two Systems of Invention." In *Re-Reading Aristotle's Rhetoric*, ed. by A. G. Gross and A. E. Walzer, 107–129. Carbondale: Southern Illinois University Press.

Chapter Eight

Reason, Production, and Rival Visions of Working Life

Keith Breen

This chapter explores rival understandings of what it means to be a rational subject in the world of productive work.[1] When reflecting upon this theme one might easily assume there is but one idea of productive work, as well as of productive reasoning, that is operative in all contexts. This would be a mistaken assumption. Our notions of what it means to be a rational subject in an arena of life are always socially embedded ideas tied to broader, often antagonistic, political projects. These projects, in turn, reflect particular value-commitments that, whether acknowledged or not, necessarily rule out other value-commitments and have a profound impact upon our relations to one another, the institutions we create and inhabit, and the goals we set for ourselves. This, of course, is the implicit message of the concluding passage of Max Weber's *The Protestant Ethic and the Spirit of Capitalism*, where "the tremendous cosmos of the modern economic order . . . and the economic conditions of machine production" are said now to determine the lives of modern men and women "with irresistible force." What Weber famously decries in that passage is the contingent triumph of an instrumentalist mode of rationality and vision of the rational subject that inexorably exclude alternative modes and visions, thereby condemning individuals to "mechanized petrification," to a meaningless, dehumanizing "iron cage" (Weber [1930] 1992, 123–24). While this "iron cage" increasingly threatens to absorb all spheres of life, it is in the realms of sociopolitical organization and economic production that it has reached its fullest development.

My goal is to cast partial doubt upon this dark diagnosis of contemporary life and contemporary economic production in particular. I do so by contrasting two constructions of the productive work-process, which reflect very different understandings of reason in work and of workers themselves. At stake here is the question of the intrinsic character and content of productive work:

147

how we conceive of the work process, what we do when we work, and how what we do in work alters us as human beings. The first construction of productive reasoning and work processes is the "technicist" model, classically set out in Taylor's influential *The Principles of Scientific Management* ([1911] 1947). This model of productive reasoning aims, through using scientific experimentation and precise analysis of work tasks, to replace individuals' particular knowledge and experience with systematized, general, and lawlike techniques that can be applied to ensure ever greater productivity levels. So understood, it represents an archetype of what Weber meant by "formal rationalization," presuming the expropriation of individual labor and expertise, increasing functional differentiation, and ever more exact calculations of means to given ends.[2] Drawing on the Aristotelian idea of *phronēsis* (practical wisdom), the second construction of productive reason is the "phronetic" model. In contrast to technicist conceptions, this model conceives production as a process resting upon workers' experience and holistic knowledge. It therefore presumes a division of labor and view of work-organization fundamentally at odds with Taylor's precepts. The dominant image in this conception is not of science, but of craftsmanship, of workers using their practical judgment to produce goods in a manner that not only results in excellent products but also enhances their inherent capacities and powers.

Here I wish to defend the phronetic model of productive reason on both moral and pragmatic grounds. I begin with a description of Taylor's efforts to develop a scientific theory of workplace management and the principles he arrived at in doing so. These principles inspired the twentieth-century Fordist organization of production processes, continuing to inform managerial and work-design approaches in many industries and sectors today. Taylorism (and neo-Taylorism) is thereafter criticized on three counts: first, that far from being an authentic science it represents a specific managerial agenda which is biased toward sectional interests; second, that it is suspect normatively for a number of important reasons; and, third, that despite Taylorism's aspiration to discover a uniquely best "method," it is only one among a variety of ways of organizing work-processes, and one which rests upon a serious misconception. Following these criticisms, the phronetic understanding of production is set out using Alasdair MacIntyre's idea of "practices" as a guide. This idea provides a view of productive work in which technical reason, instrumental reasoning as to means, is subsumed under a broader practical reason incorporating individual experience and judgment. Having set out the notion of phronetic production, I attempt to counter the charge that it embodies a nostalgic craft romanticism having little relevance to present industrial realities. Against this charge, there are recognizable instances of phronetic production in present-day industries, one of the most suggestive being Volvo's advances in humanistic production systems at Uddevalla and other car assembly plants.

TECHNICISM AND WORK

Taylor's theory of scientific management is one instance of a broader historical trend in workplace organization that sought to remove every element of uncertainty and waste from the work process.[3] His target (1947, 30–36) was the "ordinary" type of management that rested on a policy of "initiative and incentive." Under this type of management, the "problem of doing . . . work in the best and most economical way" was left to workers, the purpose of management being chiefly to employ special incentives—such as higher-than-average pay, better conditions, threats, et cetera—to spur and harness workers' initiative and creativity. The problem of this old-style management was that it failed to query the "inefficient 'rule-of-thumb' methods" employed by workers in their work, remaining vulnerable to "natural" and "systematic soldiering," that is, individuals' "natural laziness" and workers' collective interest "'in taking it easy'" (Taylor 1947, 19–20). To tackle these vices, Taylor offered four prescriptions. The first was that management should develop a "science for each element of a man's work," ending reliance on rule-of-thumb methods. Key here was determining "one best method and best implement" in the work process through establishing "rules, laws, and formulae which replace the judgment of the individual workman." The second demanded that managers take on the task of selecting and training workers in accordance with the one best method. The third prescription enjoined managers to "cooperate with the men," ensuring that all work is "done in accordance with the principles of . . . science." The fourth was that there should be an "almost equal division of the work and the responsibility between the management and the workmen," managers taking over tasks "for which they are better fitted" (Taylor 1947, 25, 36).

Taylor believed that proper application of these prescriptions would lead to a marked increase in productivity and a positive transformation of the workplace. Toward these ends, in his roles as shop foreman, plant manager, and consultant engineer at a number of firms, he sought to ensure optimum worker output by exactly determining the component parts of each work process and task. This was famously exemplified in his rationalization of pig-iron handling at the Bethlehem Steel Company (Taylor 1947, 41–48, 57–64). Taylor began by noting each handler was loading only 12½ tons of pig iron per day; by his calculations, each should have been loading 47½ tons without any impairment to health. These calculations were based upon a supposed law of "heavy labouring," derived by breaking the task into separate elements—lifting a load, walking under the load, releasing the load—and correctly timing each. The next step was carefully selecting a workman well suited for the job of handling pig iron and offering him a wage premium. The suitable employee secured—the "mentally sluggish" Schmidt—was then taught the "scientific" way of handling pig iron, expressly instructed when to lift, walk, release, and rest. The result, maintained Taylor, was that 47½ tons were consistently loaded per day. The work process here is simple, but Taylor applied the same procedure to more complex work activities, from product-quality inspection to the highly skilled machinist's trade. Indeed, he was convinced his principles "applied absolutely to all classes of work, from the most elementary to the most intricate" (1947, 8, 40), within factories, homes, farms, churches, universities, or governmental agencies.

The conception of productive reasoning underlying Taylor's redesign of work processes has two basic aspects. First, and most clearly, it is governed by an instrumental concern for productivity and efficiency, values left largely unquestioned. Although he devoted himself to analyzing work processes, their contents and intrinsic features as experienced by workers were not Taylor's prime concern. What counts are their extrinsic features—increased production and profitability for managers and owners, increased wages for workers. The second aspect is a pervasive wish to eliminate all elements of individual judgment, with a concomitant fetishization of scientific "laws" and replicable techniques. The goal is always to ascertain a one best method that can be applied to work processes reconceived in terms of temporal machines, and to workers who are understood exclusively as instruments to be used in these machines. This technicist model of productive reason inspired Taylor to envisage a system of workplace organization which would become definitive for much twentieth-century industry.

As suggested by Braverman (1974, 77–83), that system is based on three principles or presuppositions. The first is the disconnection of work from workers' skills and knowledge and, accordingly, the increasing superfluity of worker expertise. This is necessitated by Taylor's (1947, 36) injunction that managers "assume . . . the burden of gathering together all of the traditional knowledge which in the past has been possessed by the workmen" and reducing it to transparent rules and formulae. The second principle is the separation of conception from execution, that is, of planning work from the process of carrying it out, of managers from workers. This is because the "practical use of scientific data" requires that "all of the planning which under the old system was done by the workman, as a result of his personal experience, must of necessity under the new system be done by the management" (Taylor 1947, 38). The third organizational principle enjoins managerial control over every aspect of a standardized working process. Management must determine the nature and arrangement of all work, each worker receiving directions "describing in detail the task which he is to accomplish, as well as the means to be used," and discipline ensured through mechanisms such as instruction cards, monitoring by foremen, increasing productivity quotas, and incentive payment schemes (Taylor 1947, 39). Allied to this is the view that individual workers, as well as supervisors and planners, should be limited to one basic task in the overall work process. Seen from the perspective of those acting within this system, the consequences are a dynamic of worker deskilling, the loss of an overview of the work process on account of its fragmentation, and a "detailed division of labor" where work is shrunk to the repetition of simple tasks.

The Taylorist system of work organization was not to be confined to factories and shop floors; proselytizers gradually generalized it to service occupations, retail trades, and public and private bureaucracies.[4] Its paragon remains, of course, Henry Ford's mass-production assembly line. Dispensing with the need for supervisory foremen and instruction cards, the assembly line represents a radicalization of Taylor's principles. Work is mechanically disciplined by the line in accordance with predetermined sequences that severely restrict the scope for individual discretion; its pace is radically intensified, shrunk to the performance of tasks whose cycle time is at most one or two minutes long—often far less—and which therefore require minimal training.

Some have argued that the image of Ford's assembly line and thus Taylorism as a mode of work organization is now outdated. They contend that we have entered a post-Fordist phase characterized by reskilling, "flexible specialization," teamwork, and enhanced worker discretion (Piore and Sabel 1984). In the areas of industrial manufacture and assembly this argument is frequently expressed by advocates of Japanese "lean production" systems, viewed as departing decisively from traditional mass-production assumptions (Womack et al. 2007; Kenney and Florida 1993). Yet while it is true that Taylorism never completely eliminated other modes of production and that there have been significant developments since Fordism's 1950s heyday, it is mistaken to think it anachronistic. Many developments viewed as "post-Taylorist" are actually better termed "neo-Taylorist." Lean-production systems, for instance, are celebrated for their team-based approach, multiskilling, and engaging workers in creative *kaizen* (gradual improvement of the production process). However, studies show that work in these systems conforms in most respects with the three presuppositions of Taylorist work organization.[5] Indeed, lean production represents their further radicalization: teams are coordinated and harnessed by managers employing the rhetoric of individual empowerment to extract greater productivity from workers, who find themselves alternating between a number of simple tasks (multitasking rather than multiskilling) over which they retain strictly limited control. Outside industrial manufacture, there is the noticeable endurance of jobs structured in accordance with the detailed division of labor and requiring a low or minimal skill base, particularly in service, retail, and food-production occupations.[6] Neo-Taylorist ideas have expanded not only into traditional trades but also the professions and white-collar work in general. An example is the massive growth in managerial control, time-management drives, auditing regimes, and workload intensification in the educational professions.[7] Given these trends, to dismiss the technicist model of productive reason would seem more than premature.

DEFORMATIONS OF WORKING LIFE

Though Taylor's conception of the work process came to fruition in the early twentieth century, it reflects prejudices traceable to classical economists such as Adam Smith and, much earlier, to Greek antiquity (Murphy 1993, 19–28). One such is that work is an activity governed solely by means-end calculation and thus subject to a technical rather than a moral-practical mode of rationality, as Aristotle argues (NE VI 4/5, 1140a1–b30) when he separates "making" (fabrication, *poiēsis*) from "doing" (action, *praxis*). Another is the Platonic belief that it is fitting that some should conceive or rule and others follow, that "one type of man is needed to plan ahead and an entirely different type to execute the work" (Taylor 1947, 38). A third prejudice, also Platonic but given enduring expression by Smith (1979 [1776], 1. 1. 15) in his account of the detailed division of labor in a pin factory, is that efficiency demands individuals be limited to a single task—one man drawing out the wire for the pin, another straightening it, a third cutting it. (Smith, however, who is sometimes credited for inspiring Marx's views on alienation, did not ignore the human impacts of this process.) The long lineage of these assumptions is striking, but, even more remarkably, they are often presupposed by those who otherwise vehemently oppose technicism and its sociopolitical correlate, technocracy. Jürgen Habermas, for example, has consistently sought to counter the reduction of sociopolitical life to a technocratic consciousness that suppresses individual freedom and reduces interpersonal solidarity to instrumental, means-end relations. However, his attempt to counter technicism bifurcates "lifeworld" realms—the family and civil society—governed by "communicative action" and moral reason from "system" realms—the modern economy and bureaucratic state—governed by "instrumental action" and technical criteria of efficiency and success (Habermas 1987, 154, 309).

Regrettably, this division preserves the integrity of lifeworld domains at the cost of bolstering the assumption that economic life and the workplace comprise a complex of "norm-free sociality" where ethical-moral considerations do not figure.[8] Thus, despite emancipatory intent, Habermas and many like him neglect the intrinsic dimension of productive work and necessarily fail to question the technicist organizational assumptions underpinning contemporary production processes, with their profound impacts on individuals in their work relationships.

This failure is unfortunate for a number of reasons. One is that technicism's status as a sectional ideology remains hidden. Taylor believed he had come to an objective science of work that avoided the old-style management's vagaries and promised to reveal the one best method in all instances. On inspection, this claim to scientific standing is wholly suspect.[9] This is so because Taylor conducted his studies within an institutional context in which the three principles of technicist workplace organization—the superfluity of worker expertise, the separation of conception from execution, and the managerial prerogative to control—were taken as given as both philosophical assumptions and practical ends. Consequently, "scientific management" represents less an objective science than a meticulous strategy for organizing work in line with the detailed division of labor, with a specific vision of the respective places of management and workers. Although Taylor (1947, 10, 28) understood himself as attempting to overcome workplace conflicts by ensuring "friendly cooperation between management and the men," in actual fact the institutionalization of the technicist conception of productive reason depended upon an usurpation of worker knowledge that privileged and entrenched a rising managerial and engineering social stratum. A key consequence of this usurpation was that workers, because of deskilled work requiring minimal training, became interchangeable units progressively more vulnerable to corporate demands. This vulnerability made possible, in turn, the destabilization of worker solidarity—through, for example, heightening surveillance and creating interpersonal competition by linking pay to individual productivity—and a sharp intensification of the work-process in line with profit imperatives. The reality that technicist conceptions of work can indeed be practically efficacious is thus not due to scientific truth, but to ruthless implementation by actors with particular group interests.

Consideration of the sociopolitical aspects of technicist work organization leads naturally to reflection upon its moral implications. While the technicist model espouses the values of productivity and material abundance entrenched within our consumerist culture, it stands in deep tension with the basic principles of a democratic society—freedom and equality. It offends against the principle of freedom in two ways. First, by denying individuals control over both the contents and the overarching ends of their work activity, this form of work organization conflicts with freedom understood in the Kantian sense of "self-determination" (Schwartz 1982). In it workers are not required to deliberate over tasks, to decide between alternative ways of achieving particular ends, or to rationally establish the course of their own actions; rather, their purpose is merely to behave, to move in accordance with plans established by others. The technicist model, in short, offends against workers' status as decision-making beings. Doing so, it also offends against freedom in the Aristotelian sense of exercising and enhancing our capacities, "self-realization."[10] Because the detailed division of labor reduces work to itemized tasks in which workers have no overall view of the work process, the capacities and skills required are rudimentary at best. There is little possibility of individuals employing any of their talents, let alone the full scope of their potentialities. More than this, in such work individuals are denied the chance to develop even the minimal capacities that are in fact required, since improvements to the work process are at managers' or engineers' discretion. As regards the principle of equality, particularly strong inegalitarian relationships lie at the heart of technicist conceptions of work and productive reasoning. This is because the separation of conception from execution grants one group of actors the opportunity to assume decision-making roles and advance their capacities, whilst withholding it from others. The ensuing hierarchical division is quite different from other inegalitarian relations, such as that between teachers and pupils, whose purpose is the empowerment of weaker parties and where disparities in status and knowledge are temporary. Instead, the division is enduring and self-perpetuating; it structurally presumes a difference in kind between the tasks of managers and workers, justifying work arrangements in which this categorical difference is continually reinforced.[11]

It could be argued that these criticisms overemphasize the significance of work for ordinary men and women. There are many other areas of life—including familial networks, local neighborhoods, leisure pursuits, voluntary associations—in which people have sufficient opportunity for self-determination and self-realization, and the existence of work hierarchies should not be seen as undermining their equal status as citizens (Arneson 1987, 530). Work experiences, on this view, have no necessary causal impact on the quality of our wider lives to justify altering the character of work or its arrangement. However, while perhaps initially credible, this view does not survive scrutiny. Against it, the evidence suggests that individuals whose working hours are spent performing tedious, repetitive tasks become less able to act autonomously and develop their capacities outside the workplace. For example, in a well-known longitudinal study of a large group of U.S. employees, Kohn and Schooler found that the level of "substantive complexity" of an occupation, the degree to which it necessitated reflection and allowed for "self-direction," directly influenced workers' overall cognitive and psychological functioning, complex work leading to increases in their intellectual abilities and work lacking complexity significantly decreasing them. Decisively, the effects of jobs' "structural imperatives," in particular "those conditions that facilitate or restrict the exercise of self-direction in work," were not confined to work itself but affected "workers" values, orientations to self and society, and cognitive functioning primarily through a direct process of learning from the job and generalizing what has been learned to other realms of life.[12]

This truth that experiences of work are routinely generalized to individuals' wider lives, with palpable harmful consequences for their psychological well-being and social relationships has, in fact, been understood for a very long time.[13] It also has been clear that these effects have similarly damaging consequences for their equal status as citizens. Precisely because work is a principal area in which self-esteem and a sense of personal efficacy are generated, it conditions to a substantial degree individuals' perceptions of themselves as citizens, their estimation of their own worth, and the extent to which they avail of their political rights.[14]

There is a further ground for questioning the technicist model of production, one demonstrated in worker responses to strains induced by the detailed division of labor. Efficiency is the prime impetus of this division, yet it is subject to structural inefficiencies in terms of both output and managerial control. These arise, for instance, on account of the poor morale and frequently high levels of absenteeism and staff turnover engendered by the unappealing nature of work in technicist workplaces. They also stem from worker resistance. Such resistance takes many forms, the most direct being sabotage, go-slows, and strikes. For our purposes the more significant are those where individuals actively seek to reclaim control of a work process despite, or directly because of, its alienating content. This can be manifested in ways, including introducing elements of play, informally modifying work schedules and production goals, or flaunting work constraints.[15] Reclamations of this sort are highly suggestive for two reasons. They show, first, that the separation of conception and execution is always incomplete, that complete managerial control is impossible given the irrepressibility of human ingenuity. Just as important, they also reveal a basic misconception underlying the technicist model, intimating that the ways in which we organize work are underdetermined, open to revision and alteration. As suggested by Murphy, the detailed division of labor deemed inevitable by Smith and Taylor erroneously assumes a one-to-one correspondence between the "technical division of labor," the analysis and breakdown of work activities in terms of their constituent tasks, and the "social division of labor," the apportionment of individuals to particular tasks. While efficiency does require work to be technically "analyzed into its fundamental elements," it does not demand that workers must be socially "restricted to the performance of a few such elements." Once a work process has been technically dissected, it can thereafter "be synthesized efficiently in a variety of ways—from restricting each worker to a single task to enabling each worker to perform several tasks in sequence" (Murphy 1993, 23). There exists, in short, no "one best method" we must adopt by necessity; we are free, as successful acts of reclamation bear out, to structure our working lives in compliance with values other than, and in addition to, productivity.

PHRONETIC PRODUCTION

The technicist model is therefore morally impoverished and vulnerable to alternative views of productive work. One promising alternative finds expression in Alasdair MacIntyre's idea of "practices."[16] This idea is fruitful not so much in providing a detailed account of what specific forms of productive work should look like, but in yielding a general conception of nonalienated or meaningful work according to which we can interpret and judge existing work arrangements. For MacIntyre the range of activities classifiable as "practices" is very broad, including arts, sciences, games, familial life, and politics, as well as productive occupations such as farming, fishing, architecture, manufacture, and construction. However, not all activities can be so classified—watching television, inputting data, gathering rubbish, for example—since they lack the determinate structure definitive of practices, properly speaking. A practice is:

> any coherent and complex form of socially established cooperative activity through which goods internal to that form of activity are realised in the course of trying to achieve those standards of excellence which are appropriate to, and partially definitive of, that form of activity, with the result that human powers to achieve excellence, and human conceptions of the ends and goods involved, are systematically extended. (MacIntyre 1985, 187)

The important terms here are "cooperative activity," "goods internal," and "standards of excellence."

First, a practice is a communal undertaking presupposing not merely individuals' participation, but also their embeddedness within a distinct "tradition" or history inspiring and guiding their actions. Every practice, whether physics or carpentry, is therefore informed by principles, ideals, and systems of knowledge transmitted from the past. Second, a key distinction is made between "internal" and "external" goods. An external good, such as money or power, is one that can be achieved through any activity—mindless toil or chicanery as much as concerted effort in a profession—whereas internal goods are specific to individual practices, that is, can be attained only through sustained engagement in a practice itself. The "aim internal to productive crafts" is thus "never only to catch fish, or to produce beef, or to build houses" in order to make money or gain power. Rather, it is to work "in a manner consonant with the excellence of the craft," so that "not only is there a good product, but the craftsperson is perfected through and in her or his activity" (MacIntyre 1994, 284). The internal goods of quality products and the perfection of practitioners depend, in turn, on commitment to intersubjective standards of excellence that determine the goal of a practice, its end, and shape its internal functioning. To enter a practice one must at the outset accept the authority of impersonal norms giving expression to the highest level of achievement realized in that practice thus far. Entering a practice requires not simply deference to established standards, but also dispositions of character or virtues—honesty in judging one's limitations, justice in giving others what they deserve, courage in facing failure—without which it is impossible to advance within that practice.

This overview already suggests ways in which productive work, understood as a practice, diverges from the technicist conception. The first concerns the division of labor and the ideal of efficiency. Both conceptions presuppose specialization. Engagement in any activity or set of activities necessarily precludes equal effort being expended in other activities on account of human finitude and the truth that different endeavors are often "contingently incompatible" (MacIntyre 1985, 197). Yet the form of specialization suggested by the activity basic to practices differs radically from the detailed division of labor germane to technicist work organization. Here one's labor is spent not in executing a limited number of tasks, but in performing a "complex" set of interrelated tasks in a "coherent" fashion. "Complexity," the necessity to combine discrete operations, and "coherence," combining them in an effective manner, entail that successful performance depends upon an overarching view of the whole work process—what it means to construct a building or nurture crops to harvest—and an ability to both plan and execute, which demands possession of significant skill and know-how. Also, though all productive activity involves "cooperation," the type operative in practices is very different from that underpinning technicist work processes. In the latter, cooperation is based upon a disjuncture between managers who plan and workers who follow, their roles and interests being essentially opposed. The ideal of efficiency assumed is therefore inherently manipulative—quality control and productivity are attained by constraining workers' habits and movements and ceaselessly monitoring their performance. In productive practices, by contrast, there is no categorical division between those who lead and those who follow. Master practitioners and apprentices do differ, but the difference here is of degree rather than kind since both seek the same ends, holding to and acting in line with the same standards. The notion of efficiency characterizing practices therefore presumes mutual respect for shared principles and trust in fellow practitioners, the belief that they, once a satisfactory level of competence has been reached, are best placed to coordinate the work process.

A second distinctive feature of MacIntyre's notion of production as a practice is its adherence to an Aristotelian view of human nature and development. This view rests upon a distinction between "humans-as-they-happen-to-be" and "humans-as-they-could-be-if-they-realized-their-essential-nature," the conviction that there is a *telos* or end immanent to authentically human activities (MacIntyre 1985, 52–53). From this standpoint, the function of practical reflection and cooperative activity is not to reinforce who we presently are, but to facilitate human flourishing (*eudaimonia*), the better persons we could become in the right circumstances. In contrast to the technicist model, which assumes a static understanding of human beings as motivated simply by maximizing preferences for external goods, the idea of practices stresses the educative and transformative aspects of meaningful working life. In order to take hold, work as a practice demands a transformation in the practitioner's character, her or his desires and will. Thus, if all goes well, apprentices will in time realize that what they had initially sought (wealth, prestige) when entering the practice of tool-making or chemistry is not what they, *qua* toolmakers or chemists, should truly aim at; this is, instead, being the best toolmakers or chemists possible (MacIntyre 1998a, 225). Related to this is the truth that engagement in a practice "systematically" advances and enhances our basic human capacities and powers. The goal of learning and teaching is not only to pass on knowledge, but to enable novices to become master practitioners. Such mastery involves having the skills, experience, and sensitivities necessary to perform complex tasks in situations of uncertainty and change. Meaningful work is therefore work that contributes to the development of individual maturity in the interconnected senses of self-determination and self-realization.

The height of maturity is reached when practitioners can question in a knowledgeable manner what had formerly been accepted as best or most excellent within their practice. This ability arises from long-standing dedication to a profession, suggesting a further transformative feature of production as a practice. In becoming skilled in a practice individuals not only alter their personalities and attain greater maturity, but also "discover within the pursuit of excellence . . . the good of a certain kind of life" unattainable in other activities (MacIntyre 1985, 190). In farming, farmers realize a way of being in the world specific to the role of the farmer, just as do miners, construction workers, or mechanics when they carry out their work. The significance of this goes beyond work itself inasmuch as the goods specific to working life add to the goods internal to other roles characteristically occupied by individuals, whether those of citizens, parents, or members of communal associations. In engendering goods unique to their practice, in terms both of the execution of their work (proficiency, discernment, creativity) and the products (tools, buildings, quality produce) flowing from it, practitioners augment the multiple possibilities of human life and experience, contributing something of "universal worth" to our condition (MacIntyre 1998a, 225).

These reflections indicate a final way in which the idea of practices is at odds with technicist assumptions. Taylor agreed, we saw, with the traditional prejudice that productive work is only of instrumental significance. That presupposes the truth of Aristotle's claim that *poiēsis* (production) is engaged in simply for ends other than itself—durable products or consumer goods—whereas *praxis* (action), to the contrary, is performed as an end in itself—as in being just, or a good citizen. It also presumes his view that whereas action is governed by *phronēsis*, moral-practical reason and deliberation about the ends we should seek, production is governed solely by *technē*, technical reasoning about the most efficacious means to our ends, whatever these ends may be. Hence Aristotle's demotion of production to a status inferior to other modes of human activity, to being a mere condition, not a constitutive part, of human flourishing. However, as seen by MacIntyre, this conclusion issues more from Aristotle's aristocratic bias against the labouring classes than from any universal fact about productive work. For what the idea of productive practice reveals is that production and action, as well as moral-practical and technical reason, are inextricably intertwined. Oblivious "to the peculiar excellences of the exercise of craft skills and manual labor," Aristotle overlooked that in altering our character and dispositions, forming the persons we are and become, *poiēsis* is in truth always a formative mode of *praxis*.[17]

Appreciating this demands profoundly revising our conception of what it means to be a rational subject in the world of work. Productive reasoning involves, of course, instrumental reasoning as to means. However, so does any form of world-focused, practical reason, whether in everyday personal interactions or in the realm of political endeavor. Likewise, and importantly, as with other manifestations of practical reason, when deliberating upon and performing productive work we reflect not only upon the technical means we employ but also upon relations between these means and the "moral" goals or ends we wish to realize, in the internal sense of the excellence of our performance and the quality of the products issuing from it, and in terms of the overall social purposes served by our work. In productive practices, consequently, *phronēsis* and *technē*, far from being separate, stand interlinked, so much so that we can speak here of a "phronetic *technē*." Production is at one and the same time instrumental and moral-practical. Moreover, acquiring productive knowledge and effectively acting upon it are not appreciably dissimilar to the ways we acquire knowledge and effectively act upon it in other spheres of life. As with individuals proficient in moral-political affairs, capable productive workers are those who have been immersed into a historically rooted, intersubjective network of activities and have therefore developed, as argued by Dunne (1993, 355), a "responsiveness" to fluid situations which is never "fully specifiable in advance and which is experiential, charged with perceptiveness, and rooted in the sensory and emotional life."

CURRENT INDUSTRIAL REALITIES

Centered upon worker experience and judgment, the phronetic model of production represents the direct opposite of the technicist perspective. Evoking the notion of "craft" underlying traditional trades, it provides a vision of meaningful working life in which work simultaneously augments our innate powers and advances cooperative vocations and endeavors. Yet the question now is whether this ideal has relevance for men and women in present-day industries. One reason for disputing its relevance is proposed by MacIntyre himself. Although accepting that phronetic production had once been the basis of economic life, his view is that it is now unrealizable within the larger part of the modern economy. Most work in this economy, he contends, has become "separated from everything but the service of biological survival and the reproduction of the labor force, on the one hand, and that of institutionalized acquisitiveness, on the other." Such is unavoidable given the chief institutions of late modernity, which gradually developed in the "service of impersonal capital" and corporate profit. Hence productive practices have irrevocably retreated to the "margins of social and cultural life," the "vast majority" of citizens having been reduced to passive "consumers."[18] Thus, if we wish to find and cultivate authentic examples of nonalienated work, we need to focus on communities and associations standing outside the dominant economic order and rejecting its corrupting demands.[19]

Given, as discussed above, the reality of the endurance and extension of neo-Taylorist modes of work organization, this skeptical view would appear to have justification. If it is true, the claim that phronetic production represents a feasible alternative would therefore seem disingenuous, concealing rather than revealing the truly alienated nature of modern productive work. It would also stand guilty, as MacIntyre himself does, of nostalgia, of idealizing past economic orders and encouraging retreat to obsolete modes of production currently enjoyed by small minorities either peripheral to the dominant order or privileged within it. But whether these charges are in fact true is, in the last instance, an empirical question answerable not by theory but by close attention to real-world cases.

Attention to such real-world cases provides ground for tentative optimism. Indeed, consideration of the automotive industry, the definitive form of modern production and one where technicist views have historically held considerable sway, reveals illuminating examples of successfully institutionalizing practice-like work. Between the late 1980s and the early 1990s, the car firm Volvo, in its Uddevalla plant in western Sweden, made final-assembly innovations under the influence of the Scandinavian "sociotechnical" school of industrial job design. The goal was a "reflective production" system fundamentally at odds with Taylorist, as well as lean-production, suppositions (Ellegård 1995). The impetus here stemmed from multiple factors (Berggren 1992, 71–89), not least Volvo's wish to expand production capacity in a labor market defined by low unemployment levels, high educational attainment, and comprehensive social-security provision. Retaining reliable workers was a serious problem, necessitating far-reaching changes to the unattractive work conditions characteristic of Volvo's Taylorist assembly plants—for instance, the Torslanda car plant in Gothenburg. Unions were also comparatively powerful, with high membership rates, a history of employer-union codetermination of corporate and employment policies, and the Swedish Metal Workers' Union's commitment to institutionalizing forms of "good work." Key figures within the Volvo Corporation, including the chairman, Pehr Gyllenhammar, were also supportive of the goal of humanizing work and willing to cooperate with researchers and workers in establishing new production systems. The social context and institutional environment were thus favorable to the view that "human capabilities and needs, as well as market demands, should be the starting point" for designing both the technical and social dimensions of Uddevalla's work process (Engström and Medbo 1995, 67).

Utilizing innovations in earlier plants (the Kalmar car plant, in particular), and through protracted trial and error, the planning group settled upon a production system in which Fordist assembly principles were "completely abolished" (Sandberg 1995, 3). The moving serial line, where many hundreds of workers perform limited numbers of repetitive tasks with short cycle times, was replaced by stationary "dock assembly," where groups containing some seven to ten workers assembled whole cars. This allowed for long cycle times (up to two hours or more) in which the work was paced by the assemblers themselves and characterized by a low "horizontal" division of labor, that is, by a concentration of skills in the individual assembler as opposed to dispersing disaggregated skills across numerous assemblers. Corresponding to these technical advances in job design were noteworthy changes in the social organization of work. Breaking with the dense hierarchy typical of Taylorist factories, the plant's organizational structure was flattened to only three levels (plant manager, product shop leader, assembly team). Hence the role of management changed from continually regulating and controlling workers' performance to coordinating and sustaining a work process now the responsibility of "autonomous" assembly teams. These teams selected their own leaders on a rotating basis, team leaders carrying out much work formerly done by managerial supervisors and engineers. Team members were jointly responsible for planning the entirety of the assembly process, determining its sequence and distributing tasks. They also took on functions and roles beyond assembly itself, including instructing new assemblers, personnel issues (recruitment, leave and shift rotas), quality control, maintenance, and production engineering tasks. This decentralized organizational system was upheld by a training regime linking pay to individuals' levels of expertise in both assembly and non assembly work.

For the purposes of my argument the significance of the Uddevalla plant consists in its fundamental departure from the technicist view of productive reason and the three assumptions of technicist work organization. Far from a clear-cut determination of instrumental means to given ends, the development of the production system involved a four-year-long dialectical interplay between establishing theoretical goals, determining practical means to them, and repeatedly revising both in accordance with the hands-on experience and particular judgments of assemblers and researchers in an experimental training workshop (Ellegård 1995, 42; Engström et al. 1998, 293). And central to this developmental process was a moral conflict between traditionalists committed to retaining line assembly and those seeking to think beyond it, insisting that the goals flexibility, productivity, and product quality could be married with those of fulfilling, meaningful work.

The phronetic *technē* at play in generating the production system was also to become a key aspect of the eventual work process. In stark contrast to fragmented work systems, the fact that workers were assembling entire cars and planning the sequence of assembly required them to have a "transcendent" view of the whole production process (Berggren 1992, 238). Designers facilitated this by replacing a mechanistic nomenclature (sequential part numbers) with an "organic" vocabulary (proper names such as "brake cylinder" or "brake pedal") permitting workers to grasp relations between the different elements of their product (Nilsson 1995). Thus, the separation of conception and execution essential to Taylorism ceased to be an underlying principle, workers combining both in their core activities. Crucial here was a marked increase in worker knowledge and skill. Based on extensive on-the-job training (up to 16 months), the minimum expectation was that each individual would be able to assemble one quarter of a car, a competence that "equals the competence of at least 60 workers taken together in a plant with an assembly line" (Ellegård 1995, 54). The ultimate objective was that workers could assemble entire cars, and by the time of the plant's closure 25 assemblers had taken a general competence exam, completing a whole car in 20 hours with no more than four minor defects. Workers thus attained a proficiency "roughly comparable to a skilled car mechanic," a striking achievement in the context of existing automotive-assembly standards.[20] This reversal of Taylor's usurpation of worker expertise was accompanied by a rolling back of managers' prerogative of control. Contrary to teamwork in lean-production plants, where teams are controlled by supervisors and have little influence over the pace of work (Rhinehart et al. 1997, 86–87), the Uddevalla assembly teams enjoyed real self-direction. They had responsibility for deciding the sequence and tempo of work, but were also free to organize the work process in various ways, with two or three highly skilled team members sometimes forming mini-groups to construct cars themselves. This was in conjunction with assemblers' assumption of roles traditionally occupied by managers and engineers. The effect was a destabilization of the categorical division between white- and blue-collar work.

As regards productivity, product quality, and flexibility, the Uddevalla plant matched and in some regards outstripped Taylorist competitors in Volvo's car division, confirming that comprehensive innovation is compatible with efficiency and profitability (Berggren 1993). It also showed substantial increases in worker satisfaction and clear reductions in employee turnover, absences, and repetitive strain injuries (Engström et al. 1995). More than this, of course, the important lesson taught by Uddevalla is that it is possible to establish viable alternatives to alienated forms of work, both within the automotive industry and across working life as a whole. Although their jobs were undoubtedly demanding, the Uddevalla assemblers were not reduced to pursuing biological survival or mercilessly instrumentalized in the name of institutionalized acquisitiveness. Instead, their work permitted them to become practitioners to a real extent. Unlike most assembly workers, for whom external goods are the sole compensation of their labor, these workers enjoyed the internal good of self-realization, developing their know-how and powers, and a supervening pride in being responsible for producing a complex product in its entirety. Rather than suppressing their capacities, the very structure of their work necessitated exercising judgment and reflection. The assemblers' dealings with one another and others were not manipulative but genuinely cooperative, upheld by shared standards and directed toward a common good, the construction of a quality product under decent conditions. And in meaningfully participating in a productive organization and augmenting their competences, they acquired a "professional identity," discovering the good of a way of life beyond the reach of assemblers in the past (Nilsson 1995, 83). Work was no longer merely an instrumental condition of, or, worse, an obstacle to, their wider lives, but transformed into an essential part of who they were and could become.

CONCLUDING REFLECTIONS

The above shows the error of thinking that contemporary industries must inevitably assume a technicist guise. Contrary to pessimistic accounts of the present, we can identify successful production processes in which men and women employ the full range of their powers, acting as rational subjects in the true sense of the term. The work we do often fails to correspond with our potentialities, but there is greater scope for ensuring that it does than is commonly supposed. Of course, optimism should not give way to naiveté, and the impediments to realizing phronetic forms of production should be acknowledged. The Uddevalla example is again edifying. Although Uddevalla destabilized the division between white- and blue-collar work, it did not abolish it. Despite massively increased discretion available to workers, engineers retained control over product design and managers a decisive say over production goals and strategy at both the plant and corporate level (Berggren 1992, 161). Structural limitations on professional development thus endured and workers were still vulnerable to managerial agendas, especially when the wider economic context and institutional environment of the Uddevalla project altered. Since the 1990s, the increased unemployment and reduced social-security provision occasioned by Sweden's transition to a more deregulated market economy lessened management's need for humanistic work systems, as did Volvo's growing dependence on plants outside Sweden. This change in the wider economic context was accompanied by major shifts in the institutional environment, including a temporary (and unsuccessful) partnership with Renault, the gradual ousting of key figures committed to "good work," the rise of new management factions schooled in neo-Taylorism, and competition over jobs between worker unions at different plants (Wallace 2007, 197–205). It is not surprising, therefore, that when market conditions deteriorated Uddevalla was shut in favor of Volvo's larger, traditional assembly facilities.

Nevertheless, the case of Uddevalla encourages sober hope, not despair. Its occurrence is itself reassuring, demonstrating the limits of technicism's hegemony.[21] Just as we can degrade work activities previously defined by reflection and judgment, so too can we reclaim debased spheres of working life. In a globalized economy distinguished by increasingly complex networks of interaction and exchange and the interpenetration of local, national, and transnational institutions, there appears little likelihood of defending nonalienated productive associations from the depredations of the prevailing economic order without disputing the central tenets of that order from within. Whether this is successful depends upon contingencies that no one can predict in advance. Yet the current lines of contest are clear. If we want to increase opportunities for phronetic production, we must pay attention to the socioeconomic conditions of its coming into being. As the history of the Uddevalla project reveals, one vital condition is institutionalizing professional development programs that reverse engineers' and managers' monopoly on productive knowledge and eliminate divisions between white- and blue-collar work, a point highlighted by Braverman (1974, 307) a long time ago. Another is the fostering of strong trade unions and determined resistance to mounting attempts to erode universal social-security provision. A third condition is to fundamentally reorient our thinking about what is possible in the realm of work, the assumptions and ideologies we live by, and, at base, the forms of practical reasoning we consider most human. Together, these represent challenging, even utopian, demands. But they are hardly more utopian than the demands of scientific management at its inception, and it is assuredly true that it is out of reaching for the impossible that the possible has always been born.

NOTES

1. My interest in this topic arose through discussions I had many years ago as a Master's student with Prof. Markus Woerner over Hannah Arendt's concepts of "action" and "work." For this and for many other things, I owe Markus Woerner a debt of heartfelt gratitude. Some of the arguments here are developed further in an article that appeared in *New Political Economy*. My thanks to Taylor and Francis.

2. Weber (1978, 1156) himself considered "scientific management" the logical conclusion of formal economic rationalization, where "the optimum profitability of the individual worker is calculated like that of any material means of production."

3. On Taylorism's historical context, see Nelson 1980. Note that Taylorism was celebrated both in the liberal West and the communist East, that it is a model of productive rationality and control not historically confined to capitalist workplace organization.

4. See Braverman 1974, 179–87, 203–58, and Merkle 1980, 67–75.

5. See, for example, Berggren 1992, Parker and Slaughter 1988, Rhinehart et al. 1997, and Wergin 2003.

6. See, among others, Bryman 2004, Pruijt 1997, Ritzer 1993, and Sennett 1998.

7. See Dunne (1993, 1–8) on technicist revisions to educational practice inspired by the "behavioural objectives model." State-driven research assessment exercises and management's setting of research goals in UK universities clearly entail a neo-Taylorist revaluation of academics' roles. Relevant here are recent uses of lean-production mechanisms in a number of these universities, including the introduction of classificatory procedures reminiscent of Toyota's traffic-light *andon* system to ascertain departments' success in terms of KPIs (key performance indicators).

8. Habermas (1987, 171). For criticisms of Habermas's understanding of productive work, see Giddens 1982, Honneth 1995.

9. See Friedmann 1955. On the dubiousness of many of Taylor's "experiments," especially his account of pig-iron handling rationalization, see Merkle 1980.

10. Note that self-determination and self-realization are mutually implicated ideas. A person cannot be self-determining without exercising her capacity for autonomous judgment, just as she cannot realize her various capacities without deliberating upon her ends and determining means to them.

11. These justifications take the form of merit claims, that workers fit and thus deserve the work they do, or preference claims, that workers are happy with the work they do. Both underpin Ford's belief that "'to the majority of minds, repetitive operations hold no terrors. In fact, to some types of mind . . . the ideal job is one where the creative instinct need not be expressed'" (quoted in Berggren 1992, 203).

12. Kohn and Schooler 1983, 297, but see also Miller et al. 1985, and Hauser and Roan 2007. For discussions of these and other studies, see Schwartz 1982, 637–9, and Walsh 1999, 328–31.

13. For example, Smith 1979, 5. 1. 782, despite endorsing the detailed division of labor, bemoaned its impact on human personality, concluding that an individual whose "whole life is spent performing a few simple operations . . . generally becomes as stupid and ignorant as it is possible for a human creature to become."

14. On the effect of work on individual political efficacy, see Cohen 1989, Elden 1981, and Pateman 1970. On the role of work in generating self-esteem, see Lane 1991, 196–99, 254–55, 259.

15. Hamper 1986, for instance, relates how assembly-line workers in a Michigan GM automotive plant would routinely "double-up" jobs, lessening the monotony of their work and freeing-up time for relaxation and other pursuits.

16. This discussion of MacIntyre's theory is necessarily compressed; for fuller accounts, see Breen 2005, Keat 2000, and Knight 2007.

17. MacIntyre 1985, 159. See also MacIntyre 1988, 104–5; 1994, 301; 1999, 6–7. For the argument that Aristotle erred in thinking *poiēsis* and *praxis*, *technē* and *phronēsis*, mutually exclusive, also that the logic of his theory points to their proximity, see Murphy 1993, 88–110.

18. MacIntyre 1985, 227–28. See also MacIntyre 1988, 111–12; 1994, 286; 1998b, 249.

19. MacIntyre's (1999, 143) examples include, among others, agricultural cooperatives in Donegal, New England fishing villages, and Welsh mining communities.

20. Hancké and Rubinstein 1995, 184. Some defenders of the Uddevalla project are hesitant to describe it as a form of "neo-craftsmanship," given their belief that "craftsmanship" fails to properly express the technologically dynamic features of the system. However, regardless of the terminology used, work in Uddevalla clearly approached, even if it did not fully equal, the complexity and level of proficiency typical of established trades.

21. Also heartening is the plant's reopening, under the name Autonova, in 1995 as a joint venture between Volvo and Tom Walkinshaw Racing (Ellegård 1996; Engström et al. 1998). There are other examples of innovative work practices, including, within the automotive industry, General Motors' Saturn plant during the 1990s and early 2000s (Hancké and Rubinstein 1995). Outside the automotive industry, one could point to the diverse and successful cooperative Mondragon Corporation and, since 2001, to the achievements of the worker-led "recuperated factories" (*fabricas recuperadas*) in Argentina (Fields 2008; Ranis 2005).

REFERENCES

Aristotle. 1980. *Nicomachean Ethics*. Trans. by David Ross. Oxford: Oxford University Press.

Arneson, R. 1987. "Meaningful Work and Market Socialism." *Ethics* 97: 517–45.

Berggren, C. 1992. *The Volvo Experience: Alternatives to Lean Production in the Swedish Auto Industry*. New York: ILR Press.

———. 1993. "Volvo Uddevalla: A Dead Horse or a Car Dealer's Dream? An Evaluation of the Economic Performance of Volvo's Unique Assembly Plant 1989–1992." *Actes du GERPISA, Volvo-Uddevalla: Questions ouvertes par une usine fermée* 9: 129–43.

Braverman, H. 1974. *Labor and Monopoly Capital: The Degradation of Work in the Twentieth Century*. New York: Monthly Review Press. (2nd ed. 1998.)

Breen, K. 2005. "The State, Compartmentalization and the Turn to Local Community: A Critique of the Political Thought of Alasdair MacIntyre." *European Legacy* 10 (5): 485–501.

Bryman, A. 2004. *The Disneyisation of Society*. London: Sage.

Cohen, J. 1989. "The Economic Basis of Deliberative Democracy." *Social Philosophy and Policy* 6 (2): 25–50.

Dunne, J. 1993. *Back to the Rough Ground: Practical Judgment and the Lure of Technique*. Notre Dame, IN: Notre Dame University Press.

Elden, J. 1981. "Political Efficacy at Work: The Connection between More Autonomous Forms of Workplace Organization and a More Participatory Politics." *American Political Science Review* 75 (1): 43–58.

Ellegård, K. 1995. "The Creation of a New Production System at the Volvo Automobile Assembly Plant in Uddevalla, Sweden." In *Enriching Production: Perspectives on Volvo's Uddevalla Plant as an Alternative to Lean Production*, ed. by A. Sandberg, 37–59. Aldershot: Ashgate.

————. 1996. "Volvo—A Force for Fordist Retrenchment or Innovation in the Auto-
mobile Industry?" *Asia Pacific Business Review* 2 (4): 117–35.
Engström, T., and L. Medbo. 1995. "Production System Design—a Brief Summary of
Some Swedish Design Efforts." In *Enriching Production: Perspectives on Volvo's
Uddevalla Plant as an Alternative to Lean Production,* ed. by A. Sandberg, 61–73.
Aldershot: Ashgate.
Engström, T., J. Johansson, D. Jonsson, and L. Medbo. 1995. "Empirical Evaluation
of the Reformed Assembly Work at the Volvo Uddevalla Plant: Psychosocial Ef-
fects and Performance Aspects." *International Journal of Industrial Ergonomics*
16: 293–308.
Engström, T., D. Jonsson and L. Medbo. 1998. "The Volvo Uddevalla Plant and
Interpretations of Industrial Design Processes." *Integrated Manufacturing Systems*
9 (5): 279–95.
Fields, Z. 2008. "Efficiency and Equity: The *Empresas Recuperadas* of Argentina."
Latin American Perspectives 35 (6): 83–92.
Friedmann, G. 1955. *Industrial Society*. New York: Free Press.
Giddens, A. 1982. "Labor and Interaction." In *Habermas: Critical Debates,* ed. by
J. B. Thompson and D. Held, 149–61. London: Macmillan.
Habermas, J. 1987. *The Theory of Communicative Action,* Volume II. Cambridge:
Polity Press.
Hamper, B. 1986. *Rivethead: Tales from the Assembly Line*. New York and Boston:
Warner Books.
Hancké, B., and S. Rubinstein. 1995. "Limits to Innovation in Work Organization?"
In *Enriching Production: Perspectives on Volvo's Uddevalla Plant as an Alterna-
tive to Lean Production,* ed. by A. Sandberg, 179–98. Aldershot: Ashgate.
Hauser, R. M., and C. L. Roan. 2007. "Work Complexity and Cognitive Function-
ing at Midlife: Cross-Validating the Kohn-Schooler Hypothesis in an American
Cohort." *CDE Working Paper No. 2007–08*. Available at http://www.ssc.wisc.edu/
cde/cdewp/2007-08.pdf (accessed 2010 December 10).
Honneth, A. 1995. "Work and Instrumental Action: On the Normative Basis of Criti-
cal Theory." In *The Fragmented World of the Social: Essays in Social and Political
Philosophy,* by A. Honneth, 15–49. New York: SUNY Press.
Keat, R. 2000. *Cultural Goods and the Limits of the Market*. Basingstoke: Macmillan.
Kenney, M., and R. Florida. 1993. *Beyond Mass Production: The Japanese System
and Its Transfer to the US*. Oxford: Oxford University Press.
Knight, K. 2007. *Aristotelian Philosophy: Ethics and Politics from Aristotle to Mac-
Intyre*. Cambridge: Polity Press.
Kohn, M., and C. Schooler. 1983. *Work and Personality*. Norwood, NJ: Ablex Pub-
lishing.
Lane, R. E. 1991. *The Market Experience*. Cambridge: Cambridge University Press.
MacIntyre, A. 1985. *After Virtue: A Study in Moral Theory*. London: Duckworth.
(2nd ed.)
————. 1988. *Whose Justice? Which Rationality?* London: Duckworth.
————. 1994. "A Partial Response to My Critics." In *After MacIntyre: Critical Perspectives on the Work of Alasdair MacIntyre,* ed. by J. Horton and S. Mendus,
283–304. Cambridge: Polity Press.

———. 1998a. "The *Theses on Feuerbach*: A Road Not Taken." In *The MacIntyre Reader,* ed. by K. Knight, 223–34. Cambridge: Polity Press.

———. 1998b. "Politics, Philosophy, and the Common Good." In *The MacIntyre Reader,* ed. by K. Knight, 235–52. Cambridge: Polity Press.

———. 1999. *Dependent Rational Animals: Why Human Beings Need the Virtues.* London: Duckworth.

Merkle, J. A. 1980. *Management and Ideology: The Legacy of the International Scientific Management Movement.* Berkeley: University of California Press.

Miller, J., M. M. Slomczynski, and M. L. Kohn. 1985. "Continuity of Learning-Generalization: The Effect of Job on Men's Intellective Process in the United States and Poland." *American Journal of Sociology* 19 (3): 593–615.

Murphy, J. B. 1993. *The Moral Economy of Labor: Aristotelian Themes in Economic Theory.* New Haven: Yale University Press.

Nelson, D. 1980. *Frederick W. Taylor and the Rise of Scientific Management.* Madison: University of Wisconsin Press.

Nilsson, L. 1995. "The Uddevalla Plant: Why Did It Succeed with a Holistic Approach and Why Did It Come to an End?" In *Enriching Production: Perspectives on Volvo's Uddevalla Plant as an Alternative to Lean Production,* ed. by A. Sandberg, 75–86. Aldershot: Ashgate.

Parker, M., and J. Slaughter. 1988. *Choosing Sides: Unions and the Team Concept.* Boston: South End Press.

Pateman, C. 1970. *Participation and Democratic Theory.* Cambridge: Cambridge University Press.

Piore, M., and C. Sabel. 1984. *The Second Industrial Divide: Possibilities for Prosperity.* New York: Basic Books.

Pruijt, H. D. 1997. *Job Design and Technology: Taylorism vs. Anti-Taylorism.* London: Routledge.

Ranis, P. 2005. "Argentina's Worker-Occupied Factories and Enterprises." *Socialism and Democracy* 19 (3): 1–23.

Rhinehart, J., C. Huxley, and D. Robertson. 1997. *Just Another Car Factory? Lean Production and Its Discontents.* Ithaca, NY: Cornell University Press.

Ritzer, G. 1993. *The McDonaldization of Society: An Investigation into the Changing Character of Contemporary Social Life.* Thousand Oaks, CA: Pine Forge Press.

Sandberg, A. 1995. "The Uddevalla Experience in Perspective." In *Enriching Production: Perspectives on Volvo's Uddevalla Plant as an Alternative to Lean Production,* ed. by A. Sandberg, 1–33. Aldershot: Ashgate.

Schwartz, A. 1982. "Meaningful Work." *Ethics* 4: 634–46.

Sennett, R. 1998. *The Corrosion of Character: The Personal Consequences of Work in the New Capitalism.* New York: W. W. Norton.

Smith, A. 1979. *The Wealth of Nations* (of 1776). Oxford: Oxford University Press.

Taylor, F. W. 1947. "The Principles of Scientific Management" (of 1911). In *Scientific Management,* by F. W. Taylor, 1–144. New York and London: Harper & Row.

Wallace, T. 2007. "Is That Something We Used to Do in the 1970s?: The Demise of 'Good Work' in the Volvo Corporation." In *Dimensions of Dignity at Work,* ed. by S. Bolton, 191–207. Amsterdam: Elsevier.

Walsh, A. 1999. "Factory Work, Burdens, and Compensation." *Journal of Social Philosophy* 30 (3): 325–46.

Weber, M. 1978. *Economy and Society: An Outline of Interpretive Sociology*. Berkeley: University of California Press.

———. 1992 [1930]. *The Protestant Ethic and the Spirit of Capitalism*. London: Routledge. (Orig. in German: *Die protestantische Ethik und der Geist des Kapitalismus*, of 1904–1905).

Wergin, N.-E. 2003. "Teamwork in the Automobile Industry—An Anglo-German Comparison." *European Political Economy Review* 1 (2): 152–90.

Womack, J. P., D. T. Jones, and D. Roos. 2007. *The Machine That Changed the World*. London: Simon & Schuster. (2nd ed.)

Chapter Nine

Reasoning About Disability in the Light of Advances in Technology

Richard Hull

This chapter will look at changing conceptualizations of disability issues and the ways they are associated with reasoning. The traditional medical model of disability has faced challenges in recent years, which reflect shifting underlying assumptions about the nature of the issue of disability and how to think about it. Reasoning about disability issues has, as a result, shifted quite radically and continues to evolve. The traditional medical model of disability, and the ways of discussing human beings and their capacities which it generates, has come to be seen as excessive and one-sided. The social model of disability presents a challenge to the traditional model and, while it amounts to an important critique of the conventional view, it can be seen as a deficient account of the experience of disability in society. Recent work on ethical issues concerning disability tends to take a more nuanced approach, drawing on both the medical and social aspects of disability; this more "hybrid" version permits us to discuss issues pertaining to disability in more subtle and appropriate ways which avoid what might, in a roughly Aristotelian sense, be termed (in turn) excessive and deficient responses. I shall argue too that this is a more accurate approach with respect to the experience of disability. Moreover, it enables us to resist some of the very harsh attitudes toward choosing to have disabled children that have emerged in the light of developing technological advances. At the same time, it permits us to resist approaches to disability that may endorse the creation of life that is severely compromised from the beginning. Examining these issues casts some light on how participants in this debate treat reasoning itself; their implicit and explicit standards for what reasoning should involve feed back into that very debate.

REASONING ABOUT DISABILITY: SPHERES OF RELEVANCE

For years, reasoning about disability issues revolved around the medical model of disability, which informed both medical and social policy. Some would argue that, in the main, it still does. With the medical model, the sole focus of attention is physical impairment since, by definition, all disability or handicap is thought of as resulting from physical impairment. Take, for example, the World Health Organization definitions of impairment, disability and handicap, which used to be widely accepted:

Impairment: any loss or abnormality of psychological, physiological or anatomical structure or function.

Disability: any restriction or lack of ability (resulting from an impairment) to perform an activity in the manner or within the range considered normal for a human being.

Handicap: a disadvantage for a given individual, resulting from an impairment or disability, that limits or prevents the fulfillment of a role (depending on age, sex and social and cultural factors) for that individual (Massie 1994, 5).

Clearly, this definition places the problem firmly with the person who has an impairment of one kind or another. In this approach disability "results" in a fairly factual way from impairment and amounts to a restriction or lack of ability to perform an activity that is considered to be normal for a human being. However, both of these claims can be seen to be problematic. That is, much of the experience of disability does not necessarily result from impairment. Moreover, there can be a social influence on what we consider to be normal and what we are expected to do as normal people. Both of these issues complicate our analysis of and reasoning about disability in ways that render the medical model, at the very least, incomplete. It imposes limitations on what it considers relevant to understanding disability that circumscribe both the meaning of the term and our appreciation of real causal influences on human capacities.

Disability tends to concern us given the impact that it can have on our capacity to flourish as human beings. As Jonathan Glover argues:

Disability requires failure of functioning. But failure of functioning creates disability only if (on its own or via social discrimination) it impairs capacities for human flourishing. It would not be a disability if there were a failure of a system whose only function was to keep toenails growing. With arrested toenail growth, we flourish no less (Glover 2008, 5).

Thus, it is the impact that an impairment has on our capacity to flourish that is critical to our evaluation of how severe a particular disability is. In turn, our evaluation of the severity of a disability tends to correlate with an assessment of how far a particular condition deviates from the norm, hence the "normal range" caveat of the medical model. Making judgments about what should count as an acceptable or desirable form or aspect of human life can be very contentious. The idea that there is a social influence on what we consider to be normal only serves to reinforce that point.

As Glover notes, the boundary between normality and disability is often a blurred one, "a continuum of severity." He adds, "We only count functional limitations as disabilities when there is a contrast with normal human functioning" (Glover 2008, 7). Some idea of normal or species-typical functioning is always at work, as evidenced by the medical model of disability where it is departures from the normal range that denote what we consider to be disabling. Underlying accounts of disability and functioning, therefore, there is always an extensive submerged network of underlying reasoning, however unconscious of it the participants in debate may be. Moreover, as Glover also notes, what we consider to be normal is entrenched within a social context that may not remain static. So, for example, "if a widespread mutation (or widespread use of genetic engineering) gave most people wings, those of us unable to fly might start to count as disabled" (Glover 2008, 8). The fact that most people without wings do not currently feel disabled because of their lack of wings illustrates the social context of what we consider to be normal. This can be further illustrated by considering what could happen in a society where some could fly and others could not. So, for example, if our feathered peers started to build public buildings without stairs, lifts or ramps to any floors and started to build houses and social venues in the tops of sturdy trees, those without wings would start to face considerable disadvantages. Yet, clearly, those disadvantages would have much more to do with social structures, attitudes and arrangements than they would with the newly defined imposition of being unable to fly. By implication, to claim that those who cannot fly are in this scenario, by definition, disabled, is rather harsh—especially if it leads to life-and-death choices being made on the basis of that assessment. Instead, we would do well to remain aware of the social context of what we consider to be normal and, potentially, the social influence upon that very definition. This is especially the case in the light of advances in genetic technology, where we may have the opportunity to change our biological and social futures.

Another point worth making here is that, even if a particular condition deviates radically from what we consider to be normal, it need not be inevitable that our flourishing be adversely affected. The example of conjoined twins is illuminating in this regard given that, if anything is a good candidate for being outside the range of what we consider to be normal, conjunction is. This, along with the perception that conjunction is severely disabling, is likely the reason as to why it is often assumed that conjoined twins should be surgically separated where at all possible. However, some accounts of conjunction suggest that such an assumption is a little bit hasty.

Alice Dreger writes, for example, that "the evidence tells us that conjoined twins who have remained conjoined do in fact become individuals in the psychological sense, if not in the physical sense; each speaks of him—or herself as an individual, and they develop personalities and tastes distinct from those of their siblings. . . ." "Conjoinment does not automatically negate individual development and expression, any more than other forms of profound human relations do" (Dreger 2004, 40, 44). She argues, in addition, that "the notion that a conjoined twin must individuate to the same degree singletons do takes singleton development, unjustifiably, as the standard for everyone" (Dreger 2004, 44).

Dreger's contention is that conjunction does not significantly reduce human flourishing, no matter what we might assume. She cites as evidence the "practically universal" desire among communicating conjoined twins to remain together:

> People who are conjoined and able to communicate seem to be almost as disinclined to be surgically separated as singletons are to be surgically joined. The Bijanis' remains the only case in which conjoined twins old enough to express preferences have consented to separation. Moreover, conscious conjoined people whose twins have died have invariably chosen to remain attached, knowing that this means that they will soon also die, and that in the interim they will be attached to their dead sibling. (Dreger 2004, 46)

Dreger also provides an account of the more positive aspects of being conjoined. She writes of conjoined twins being "never lonely," "models of cooperative behaviour," possessing a "double strength and a double will" and describing their lives as "like being born with your soul mate" (Dreger 2004, 34, 40, 44). Such considerations, according to Dreger, should "lead the thoughtful, sympathetic singleton to consider the degree to which any of us truly are or wish to be independent of others, and to ask why individuality—or any other aspect of humanity—need be thought of as limited to one particular kind of anatomy" (Dreger 2004, 50). Indeed, she asks whether "we might not all benefit from more twin-type behaviour in this world—that is, whether we might not all benefit from a little less 'individuation'" (Dreger 2004, 44).

While there is plenty of analysis to suggest that conjunction is profoundly disabling (for example, Hull and Wilkinson 2006), accounts such as Dreger's persuasively suggest that conjoined twins can lead flourishing lives. This in turn suggests that an analysis of how far particular conditions deviate from what we consider to be a normal range should not be the end of the story when we are reasoning about disability issues, while reinforcing the point that our conceptualizations about what is normal need not be inevitable or fixed. And while our ideas of what is normal can provide a very useful point of comparison[1] when thinking about disability, too strong an unquestioned emphasis on a particular conception of normality can be clearly off the mark, both now and in many possible futures. Such a clinical account of disability as is the medical model seems to miss these more subtle considerations, which is critical given that life-and-death decisions can be made on the basis of such a model. As mentioned earlier, the medical model also advances the dubious claim that disability *results* from impairment. It is this claim that convincingly shows to many that it is an incoherent approach.

The problem with the purely medical model of disability is that too strong an emphasis is placed on impairment, and "impairment" is interpreted too unquestioningly. Disability is said to *result* from impairment in a way that suggests a direct and inevitable connection, but this is simply false in many cases. For example, inadequate welfare measures, education, health and so-cial support services, housing, transport and built environments do not simply *result* from impairment, nor does institutional or personal discrimination. Yet these are the sorts of issues that tend to comprise much of the experience of disability for people with impairments. Rather obviously, they need not just follow or result from the fact of impairment; they depend on how a society responds, or fails to respond, to the needs of some of the people within that society. Thus, many disabilities would be much less disabling if society were differently organized. For example, if ramps and lifts were just as common as stairs, people who rely on wheelchairs to get around the built environment would be a lot less disabled than they currently are.

Functional limitation or impairment necessitates disability only if the ac-tivity in question requires the use of the functionally limited part or system. Taking the example above, if I cannot walk and rely on wheels to get around, I will clearly be unable to *walk* or *run* to the shops. If, however, I cannot get into the shops because they all have steps leading up to them, that is an entirely different matter—and here the disability is dependent on social struc-tures and arrangements, like unsympathetic architectural design. Similarly, if I am color-blind, it is unlikely that I will get a job as a hair colorist in any but the most adventurous of salons, but if I cannot get a variety of other jobs (that do not require being able to distinguish color accurately) because of the selec-tors' discriminatory attitudes toward people with impairments, that again is an entirely different matter. In both cases, my experience of disability entails joblessness but, in the latter case, my joblessness is all about a response to my impairment that is far from inevitable or fair. Of course, things are rarely this simple in reality. Disability more often than not involves a highly complex interplay of impairment and social factors. Nonetheless, what is crucial to establish here is that disability can result primarily from a socially inadequate or discriminatory response to impairment. Therefore, disability does not simply result from impairment and so the medical model of disability is, simply, false.

The perception that society can compound or create disability led to the evolution of the social model of disability. Disabled People's International articulated the social model as follows:

Impairment: the functional limitation within the individual caused by physical, mental or sensory impairment.

Disability: the loss or limitation of opportunities to take part in the normal life of the community on an equal level with others due to physical or social barriers (Barnes 1991, 6).

These definitions pick up on the main failing of the medical model, denying that disability necessarily results from impairment. They "allow for people to have an impairment without having a disability. If society was arranged in such a way that the functional loss had no impact there would be no handicap or disability" (Massie 1994, 6). However, while the social model was clearly an important step in the progression of reasoning about disability issues—and is still widely accepted by disability organizations and activists—it can be said to be as incomplete an account of disability as the medical model. That is to say, while the medical model ignores the social aspect of disability, the social model ignores disability resulting from impairment. If "physical barriers" referred to impairment, the social model might not do this; but that is not at all clear and neither would it be in keeping with the political agenda associated with the social model of disability. As such, the social model can be termed deficient in that it neglects the physical realities of impairment, which can and do cause disability.

Going back to the example of conjunction, it was said that there is plenty of analysis to suggest that conjunction is profoundly disabling. In a similar way to the color-blind hair colorist example, it is likely that the condition of conjunction will directly entail disability with respect to activities requiring the use of a functionally limited part or system. So, for example, it is likely that the site of conjunction will be both functionally limited and functionally limiting, with the degree of restriction depending on the location and scale of the join. The most common form of conjunction is *parapagus*, which entails that twins are "intimately joined at the pelvic region and sometimes also much farther up the body, toward the head." The site of conjunction is extensive and can include the joining of limbs; "it generally looks as if there are two persons at the upper end of the body and one at the lower end" (Dreger 2004, 29). In contrast, *omphalopagus* twins (joined at the umbilical region) can have a less extensive site of conjunction, leaving all limbs free. Functional limitation will generally be less substantial in the latter case than in the former.

Given these considerations, there are at least two ways in which conjunction can be said to result in disability. One is the inability to be in a private space—or lack of privacy. The ability to be in a private space is something that we tend to take for granted, whether or not it is conditional to our flourishing. Yet, inasmuch as we value privacy and the modes of life and life choices associated with it, the inability to be in a private space will constitute an impediment to our capacity to flourish.

The second way in which conjunction can be said to be disabling is closely related. It is the inability to go anywhere or do very much at all without the cooperation of a third party. There will be a need for compromise over major lifestyle issues: for example, both twins may not be able to pursue their preferred careers. Thus, conjunction is disabling insofar as independent choice and action are valuable, which often they are. Also, depending on the location and extent of the site of conjunction, there may be mobility disabilities related to, for example, loss of limb function. How serious these disabilities are will, again, depend on which activities are precluded by these functional limitations and the importance and value placed on these activities.

Leaving aside disabilities that can result from other serious physiological concerns often associated with conjunction, it is clear that conjoined twins are disabled by their impairments in the ways described above. Inasmuch as the social model denies that we can be disabled by impairment or functional limitation at all, it is a deficient account of the experience of disability. Moreover, this need not entail that we have to deny the earlier claim that conjoined twins can lead flourishing lives. It is just that we do not need to show, nor should we, that conjunction is *not* disabling in order to support that claim. This is a crucial step in the argument. It urges us to avoid the claim, which seems implicit in much "social model" reasoning: that we cannot accept that someone can flourish as a human being without denying that that person has a disability. It may be the contentious nature of the debate with the powerful "medical" model that has backed the "social" model into this corner, but it is one from which we need to extricate ourselves.

So far, it has been shown that, contrary to the implications of the medical model, the experience of disability can very much depend on social structures and arrangements. As such, disability does not simply result from impairment. It has also been shown that some disability *does* result from impairment, a claim somewhat ignored by the social model. Moreover, we have seen that our concept of normality need not be inevitable or remain static and, while considerations about normal human functioning can provide a useful point of comparison when thinking about disability, we should be mindful of the potential social influence on such considerations. In addition, even when a particular condition departs considerably from our thoughts about what is normal, there need be no automatic inference that the living of a flourishing life is precluded, as was seen with the example of conjoined twins. All of these points together suggest that our reasoning about disability and about ethical issues concerning disability should take a more nuanced approach. With that in mind, a hybrid approach to disability will be explored here, along with the implications of such an approach for disability issues in the light of developing technological advances.

THE "HYBRID" APPROACH AND
UNDERSTANDING FLOURISHING

A hybrid approach to disability acknowledges *both* the social and the medical aspects of the experience of disability. As Jonathan Glover succinctly puts it, it is the impact that a particular functional limitation (or impairment) has "either on its own or—more usually—in combination with social disadvantage," that concerns us (Glover 2008, 6). As noted earlier, disability more often than not involves a highly complex interplay of impairment and social factors. That said, it is useful to distinguish disabilities that result primarily from impairment from those that result primarily from a socially inadequate or discriminatory response to impairment, when we are thinking about disability issues in the light of advances in genetic technologies. For example, my back injury "on its own" will prevent me from playing cricket or running down hills with gay abandon. In addition, I may find myself unable to get a job given inaccurate appraisals of my work potential, misconceived projections about the amount of time off I may need because of my injury or, simply, rank discrimination. I may also find that, given that I have to spend most of my money on physiotherapists and osteopaths, I struggle to meet all my costs and have no money left over to enjoy life; and here we can see the impact that my impairment might have "in combination with social disadvantage." Clearly, I need not meet discriminatory attitudes when I apply for work or seek promotion and I need not be assessed based on prejudice or ignorance. Likewise, more adequate health, welfare and social support services would entail that I need not endure a quality of life that is significantly lower than others in a similar position to me but without the costs associated with a back injury. However, if we take away the combination with social disadvantage, I will still have my back injury, as the hybrid approach rightly acknowledges. Both aspects of the experience of disability then, either on their own or in combination, are likely to have an impact on our capacity to flourish given current social and medical realities.

Moreover, in the context of present and future reproductive choices, current technology presents the possibility of eradicating disability where we can through pre-implantation genetic diagnosis and IVF treatment, or through termination of pregnancy when functional limitation is identified during that pregnancy. However, given the arguments above, rushing in to that sort of thing without further thought could be said to be a little hasty. That is, it would be less fatal to life and potential life if we changed social structures and arrangements so that they were much more sympathetic to functional loss. Indeed, removing social disadvantage and implementing the right kinds of changes to social structures and arrangements could render many functional limitations relatively unproblematic, whereupon the functional loss would have much less of an impact on our capacity to flourish. The social aspect of much disability, then, encourages that we seriously question the justice of our present social structures and arrangements. This does not mean that all social barriers or failures bound up with the experience of disability are *necessarily* unjust (see, for example, the "bottomless pit" problem in Brock [2009]), but merely that the fact that they are social (and in principle remediable) enables us to question whether we want such conditions to continue. And a variety of theorists converge on the idea, albeit in different ways, that a more inclusive society where disadvantages were reduced and people's capabilities or freedoms were increased would reflect both a defensible and a desirable notion of social justice (see, for example, De-Shalit and Wolff 2007; Hull 2007; Terzi 2009).

If we add to this the earlier point that even if a particular condition deviates radically from what we consider to be normal, it need not be inevitable that our flourishing be adversely affected, then adopting something like a blanket policy of screening with a view to termination in cases of projected disability could be said to be excessive, as could any corresponding attitude. At the same time, we might think seriously about the impact that more permissive approaches to disability could have on the lives of future children, given that impairment can and does cause severe disablement. I have argued elsewhere that the more the severity of a projected disability errs toward what could be considered to be wrongful life, the more we can claim that it is irresponsible (while permissible) to bring that life about.[2] That is to say, one way of articulating our worry about such a choice is to describe it as lacking sufficient concern for the gravity of the impairment that the potential child will face. We clearly need to take great care here if the opposite choice necessitates termination of pregnancy, given the deep beliefs about that issue that some people may hold.

However, the more medically serious the projected impairment is likely to be and, in turn, the more it ties in with our considerations about what constitutes wrongful life, the more seriously we might be concerned about the choice to bring that life about, especially if refraining from bringing that life about does not require termination of pregnancy. David Wasserman, for example, discusses the view that parents show deficient concern, "a carelessness, disrespect, or insensitivity," by causing or allowing children to come into existence with severe hardships (Wasserman 2005, 132).[3] And, while we may resist the implication that the parent thereby harms or wrongs the child in such cases, it is perhaps enough to observe that parents can potentially exhibit a lack of concern for their future child and that that insensitivity can be regarded as a moral fault. We can legitimately worry about and not encourage, then, some kinds of attitudes and their correlative behaviors. Having said that, whether cases of concern should entail any forms of prohibition is a separate and very contentious issue.

Acknowledging that disability can come about through both impairment and social discrimination enables us to identify potentially excessive and deficient attitudes toward disability in the light of developing genetic technologies. The social aspect of much disability encourages that we think twice about overenthusiastic "screening out"—and, on the other hand, the medical realities of functional limitation warn against deficient care or concern about bringing avoidable suffering in to the world. Of course, between these two extreme ends of the scale is a huge gray area where "only a monster of self-confidence would come up with an easy judgment—or a judgment at all" (Glover 2008, 58)[4] about potential parents' reproductive choices. Moreover, it is interesting to note that within that gray area are many conditions that we all have a chance of experiencing. Indeed, a raft of different functional losses or limitations can have an impact on our capacity to flourish at one time or another. As Nancy Ann Davis points out, "in statistical terms, illness, injury, accident or infirmity beset most of us. And the longer we live, the greater are the odds that we will live some portion of our lives as disabled persons" (Ann Davis 2005, 153). Moreover, "the odds that we will all be related or closely connected to someone who is disabled are overwhelming" (Ann Davis 2005, 153). While this is no reason in itself to create challenges for people at the start of life, it could be helpful to shift the emphasis of our thinking about disability issues away from rigid categorizations, stereotypes and separatist political agendas. An emphasis on the similarities between people rather than the differences, on what we share rather than what sets us apart, might encourage that we become a lot more sympathetic to the experience of functional loss—to current and future people with disabilities.

Recognizing that frailty and vulnerability unite us all should also encourage us to change our social structures and arrangements to be more inclusive with respect to people with disabilities. As Davis argues,

> In continuing to advocate—or even tolerate—our society's subscription to a human paradigm that marginalizes disabled persons, and a dominant ideology that pathologizes them, we not only harm those whom we now marginalize but also do something that threatens to make our own lives go less well by our own lights. (Ann Davis 2005, 153)

In addition to that, given the earlier observation about the social influence on what we consider to be normal, in an era of developing genetic technologies we risk defining ourselves *out* of the normal range. A more nuanced approach to reasoning about disability as sketched above might enable us to resist some of the implications that doing that could have. It would be nuanced in at least three connected senses. First, it would avoid imposing schematic criteria on reasoning that blocked out relevant considerations about what disability is and how it arises; thus it could recognize the sociality of human capacities without totalizing them. Second, taking account of the full range of reasons for which disability matters, not just to individuals immediately affected but also to society at large, both demands that we think more about what human flourishing means and allows us to do so. Third, taking human flourishing seriously in this way would highlight its radical implications in terms of our views of each other, but it would also allow us to defend ourselves against some unwelcome implications of technological developments.

It has been shown here how reasoning about disability issues has shifted quite radically in recent years and how these debates have widened from attempts to envisage disability in a limited and technical sense to encompass our understanding of what it is to be human. The traditional medical model of disability was seen to be one-sided. At the same time, I argued that the social model of disability, while an important critique of the conventional view, offers a deficient account of the experience of disability in society. The example of conjoined twins further challenged our assumptions and sensibilities about human flourishing, especially outside what we consider to be the normal range. I stressed, therefore, that recent work on ethical issues concerning disability tends to take a more nuanced approach, drawing on both the medical and social aspects of disability. Further reflection about our assumptions with respect to normality and human flourishing is also encouraged by such an approach. It was argued that that is a more accurate approach with respect to the experience of disability in society. Moreover, it enables us to resist some of the very harsh attitudes toward choosing to have disabled children that have emerged in the light of developing technological advances. At the same time we can resist approaches to disability that may endorse the creation of life that is severely compromised from the very start.

NOTES

1. Jonathan Glover writes, for example, that "accepting that the boundaries of normal functioning may to some extent be context-dependent and may have an element of social construction is consistent with seeing normal human functioning as providing the background contrast to the limitations that count as contributing to disabilities" (Glover 2008, 8).

2. Hull 2009, 379. A wrongful life claim amounts to the claim that it is preferable not to exist than to exist with the kind of life that is subject to the claim. This is considered to apply to particularly severe medical conditions, those that are judged to be worse than death.

3. Wasserman argues that we should not do "things as momentous as bringing a child into the world—unless we do them for appropriate reasons." The implications of this suggestion are potentially enormous if they are taken to have application beyond questions relating to disability.

4. Glover uses this phrase in a slightly different context. I use it here because it brilliantly captures the worry about judging most reproductive decisions too quickly or too harshly.

REFERENCES

Ann Davis, Nancy. 2005. "Invisible Disability." *Ethics* 116: 153–213.

Barnes, Colin. 1991. *Disabled People in Britain and Discrimination: A Case for Anti-Discrimination Legislation*. London: Hurst.

Brock, Dan W. 2009. "Cost-Effectiveness and Disability Discrimination." *Economics and Philosophy* 25 (1): 27–47.

De-Shalit, A., and J. Wolff. 2007. *Disadvantage*. Oxford: Oxford University Press.

Dreger, Alice D. 2004. *One of Us: Conjoined Twins and the Future of Normal*. Cambridge, MA: Harvard University Press.

Hull, Richard, and Stephen Wilkinson. 2006. "Separating Conjoined Twins: Disability, Ontology and Moral Status." In *Cutting to the Core: Exploring the Ethics of Contested Surgeries*, ed. by David Benatar, 113–126. Lanham, MD: Rowman & Littlefield.

Hull, Richard. 2007. *Deprivation and Freedom*. New York: Routledge.

———. 2009. "Projected Disability and Parental Responsibilities." In *Disability and Disadvantage,* ed. by Kimberley Brownlee and Adam Cureton, 367–384. Oxford: Oxford University Press.

Glover, Jonathan C. B. 2008. *Choosing Children: The Ethical Dilemmas of Genetic Intervention.* Oxford: Oxford University Press.

Massie, Bert. 1994. *Disabled People and Social Justice.* London: Institute for Public Policy Research.

Terzi, L. 2009. "Human Diversity, Disability and Justice: A Capability Perspective." In *Disability and Disadvantage*, ed. by Kimberley Brownlee and Adam Cureton, 86–111. Oxford: Oxford University Press.

Wasserman, David. 2005. "The Nonidentity Problem, Disability, and the Role Morality of Prospective Parents." *Ethics* 116: 132–152.

Chapter Ten

Principles in Practice

Reasoning with Principles in Biomedical Ethics

Heike Felzmann

This chapter explores the role of principles in Beauchamp and Childress's *Principles of Biomedical Ethics* (PBE), which first appeared in 1978 and proved to be a lasting success. This textbook not only had a continuing significant impact on how biomedical ethics was perceived by health-care practitioners, it also formed a focal point in a sustained and constructive debate about the nature of biomedical ethics among philosophers. In its revisions over the last three decades, it has kept pace with the rapid developments in the field and at the same time driven further reflections; each new edition, including the most recent, sixth edition in 2009, has included significant changes, in terms both of issues covered and more general theoretical reflection about the nature of their approach.

Of particular interest here are the ways Beauchamp and Childress deal with concerns that come into play when bringing (biomedical) principles to bear on practice. These include reflection on specification, balancing, casuistry, wide reflective equilibrium, and common morality. While this chapter engages with the details of one particular approach only, these reflections are of general relevance for clarifying what is involved in moral reasoning that draws on principles. In addition to being of philosophical interest, this is also significant for the practical implementation of ethical practice in the professions, where formal expressions of professional ethics frequently contain reference to ethical principles. Here it can sometimes seem that hard-pressed health-care professionals would prefer an ethical approach in which ethical "experts" identified principles which could be applied relatively straightforwardly to problems in professional practice, a need that Beauchamp and Childress's approach initially seemed designed to meet. This chapter takes seriously these authors' ongoing efforts to clarify the theoretical and practical implications of their approach, which have increasingly opened it up to complexities and ambiguities similar to those affecting other ethical positions too. In the end, the principlist method is less distinct from casuistry, virtue ethics and approaches to practical wisdom than its authors, and readers, had originally expected.

THE FOUR PRINCIPLES IN BEAUCHAMP AND CHILDRESS'S *PRINCIPLES OF BIOMEDICAL ETHICS*

The most enduring misrepresentation of PBE's approach is probably its simplification to being in essence a checklist of four general ethical principles with an added wealth of clinically relevant examples, a view that is sometimes referred to (both mockingly and affectionately) as the "Georgetown Mantra of Bioethics." It tends to go hand-in-hand with the assumption that what Beauchamp and Childress propose is a top-down, deductive view of the role of principles that takes principles as universal starting-points for any ethical argument, suggesting that they should straightforwardly be applied to cases, without requiring engagement with wider theoretical concerns. While there is enough truth in this picture to allow such a view to endure, the discussion of the role of principles in PBE, especially in the most recent editions, significantly qualifies this view and paints a much more complex picture of the role of the principles. However, a presentation of the four principles remains the obvious starting-point for an introduction to Beauchamp and Childress's approach.

As the title of the book indicates, the core ethical elements of PBE are four principles:

1. Respect for autonomy: This principle addresses issues around self-rule, meaningful choice and the freedom from interference. It is particularly relevant in the context of facilitating patients' choices about treatment through a process of informed consent and addressing potential impediments to meaningful choice. These include both situational factors and impairments of the capacity for meaningful choice, such as immaturity, mental illness, dementia, coma or PVS. In this context the book also addresses issues around the extension of autonomy into states of incapacity, for example, through advance directives and proxy decision-making.

2. Nonmaleficence: This principle addresses the general demand not to do harm, as for example traditionally contained in the maxim "*primum non nocere*" in the medical profession. It is relevant for determining the scope of legitimate choices regarding different kinds and risks of harm in treatment, from side effects and risky interventions to the issue of risk in

research. Beauchamp and Childress focus in particular on issues around death. This includes the moral significance of the distinction between killing and letting die, intending and foreseeing harm, withholding and withdrawing treatment, and the issue of intentional death, in other words, physician-assisted suicide and euthanasia.

3. Beneficence: This principle addresses the demand that institutions and individuals should contribute to other persons' well-being. It is relevant especially for determining obligations of beneficence in the face of competing obligations. In particular it is concerned with questions around the obligation to rescue, the balance between benefits, risks and costs, decision-making on the basis of quality-of-life assessments and the problem of paternalism, in other words the conflict between beneficence and autonomy that occurs for example in nonvoluntary hospitalization for suicidal patients.

4. Justice: This principle addresses the demand that equals should be treated equally, and resources distributed fairly, based on adequate assessments of entitlement. It addresses different potential sources of entitlements, based on different theories of justice. It is concerned in particular with opportunity, discrimination, and disadvantage, as well as vulnerability, exploitation, the right to health care and resource allocation.

According to Beauchamp and Childress, these principles are general norms that are central to biomedical ethics. They caution against ranking these principles; none of them is of higher importance than any other. In exploring the principles, they dedicate one extended chapter to each, beginning with clarifications of the core concept and then exploring the subordinate concepts and issues most closely related to the principle that are of particular significance for biomedical ethics. Each of the chapters is replete with examples that clarify the practical use and significance of the concepts and issues that the authors discuss.

However, the authors do not restrict their discussion to principles alone. The most recent edition, which is the basis for the present discussion, is comprised of three parts. While the larger part is dedicated to the discussion of the principles in the second part of the book, over forty percent of its volume consists in a discussion of methodology, the nature of morality and moral justification. In the first part, the authors discuss their understanding of norms and requirements for the application of moral norms, including specification and balancing, and their view of universal "common morality" versus particular moralities, for instance, the ethics of particular professions, or moralities of specific cultures. They also address the importance of character and moral ideals for moral practice, and finally, they discuss moral status and the question of the scope of moral concern. In the third part, the authors discuss a range of moral theories and their own view regarding the role of moral theory in their own approach. They finish with a discussion of method and moral justification, contrasting impartial rule theory and casuistry with their own approach, and presenting their own combination of reflective equilibrium and what they call "common morality theory." The relation of these elements to principles will be discussed in more detail in what follows.

DEALING WITH CONTEXTS AND CONFLICTS: THE SPECIFICATION AND BALANCING OF PRINCIPLES

Beauchamp and Childress acknowledge explicitly and at an early stage in PBE that the use of principles in practice is not unproblematic and requires significant additional normative input. Here they give particular attention to the notions of specification and balancing. Their view on specification has been strongly influenced by Richardson's "Specifying Norms as a Way to Resolve Concrete Ethical Problems" (1990), mediated by DeGrazia's "Moving Forward in Bioethical Theory: Theories, Cases and Specified Principlism" (1992), in which Richardson's proposal was first applied to Beauchamp and Childress's approach. Richardson proposed the notion of specification to provide a better methodological understanding of "what it would be to bring norms to bear on a case so as to indicate clearly what ought to be done" (1990, 280). His goal was to replace the notions of deductive application and intuitive balancing of norms.

Richardson describes specification as "qualitatively tailoring our norms to cases" (1990, 283), based on the rationale that "the complexity of the moral phenomena always outruns our ability to capture them in general norms" (294). One reason Richardson favors specification over the application-cum-balancing approach is the flexibility of specification that acknowledges that norms are subject to revision over time (290), while simultaneously ensuring stability of norms and thereby doing justice to "the seriousness of our commitment to our initial norms" (297). Richardson rejects the pragmatist alternative where any element of the whole might be revised, including the general norms, and considers it important that in the process of making norms practical for particular cases these norms can be relied on to remain the same (291–92). Specification is a process of *"extensional narrowing"* (2000, 289) of norms, in the sense that the specified norm will apply to a subset of the norms that fall under the original, nonspecified norm. It is nondeductive in the sense that it proceeds by adding content through "setting out substantive qualifications that add information about the scope of applicability of the norm or the nature of the act or end enjoined or proscribed" (1990, 296). He refers to this in a later publication also as "*glossing the determinables*" (2000, 289). It includes

> adding clauses indicating what, where, when, why, how, by what means, by whom, or to whom the action is to be, is not to be, or may be done or the action is to be described, or the end is to be pursued or conceived. (1990, 295–96)

At the same time specification is a process that Richardson considers to be subject to significant rational constraints, in the sense that he requires specified norms to be argumentatively connected with the overall framework of norms; not only compatible with them in the sense of noncontradiction, but fully integrated with them: "A specification is rationally defensible then so long as it enhances the mutual support among the set of norms found acceptable on reflection" (1990, 302). For Richardson, one of the most important selling points of specification is its attitude to conflicts, in the sense that they are treated not as threats to the norms themselves or as something to be adjudicated on the basis of intuitions which are not clarified further, but as opportunities to learn and develop "a more concrete and definite understanding of the relevant norms" (308).

To illustrate his position, Richardson gives the example of the case of a "severely malformed newborn" whose parents have requested to withhold nutrition and hydration, so as to let it die (1990, 303). Instead of a conflict between three principles, "(1) a prohibition on directly killing innocent persons . . . , (2) a duty to respect the reasonable choices of parents regarding their children . . . , and (3) a duty to benefit the persons over whom one has responsibility, . . . the patients" (303), Richardson proposes a specification of principle 1 and 3 to "it is generally wrong directly to kill innocent human beings who have attained self-consciousness, and generally wrong directly to kill human beings with the (genetic?) potential to develop self-consciousness who would not be better off dead, but it is not generally wrong directly to kill human beings who meet neither of these criteria" (304) and principle 2 to "that one respects the reasonable choices of parents regarding their children so long as they respect the children's rights" (305).

In their own account of specification, Beauchamp and Childress rely strongly and explicitly on Richardson. They describe specification as essential for rendering their principles useful for practical guidance, and as "a process of reducing the indeterminate character of abstract norms and generating more specific, action guiding content" (PBE, 17). Specification is presented as an iterative process; the degree of specification required for moral decision-making in practice is variable and depends on the particular subject area as well as the particular outlook and approach of the person who is interpreting and specifying the rules. Especially when early-stage specifications stating quite general rules of behavior conflict to some extent, further specification may be required to dissolve the conflict by clarifying the specific circumstances in which one or the other rule takes priority. A conflict is resolved once "norms have been made sufficiently determinate in content that, when cases fall under them, we know what ought to be done" (PBE, 19). One of Beauchamp and Childress's examples of a norm specification might illustrate what a norm with a sufficient level of determinacy might look like: "Always obtain oral or written informed consent for medical interventions with competent patients, *except* in emergencies, in forensic examinations, in low-risk situations, or when patients have waived their right to adequate information" (PBE, 19).

However, disagreements may arise between different moral agents or between cultures, due to the fact that the interpretation of norms is to some extent dependent on the interpreter's background experience, knowledge and individual attitudes. Beauchamp and Childress's discussion is devoid of any reference to hermeneutics in their brief reflection on interpretation, but they do acknowledge that in problematic cases, "competing specifications are likely to be offered by reasonable and fair-minded parties," insofar as "different persons and groups will offer conflicting specifications" (PBE, 18–19). This is due to the varying interpretations of the exact scope and meaning of concepts used in rules and specifications; what may be a conflict of rules under one interpretation might seem unproblematic and consistent under another. However, they state that there are significant constraints on what constitutes an appropriate specification. Beauchamp and Childress argue, as Richardson (1990) does, that specifications need to be assessed with regard to the strength of the arguments underlying them as well as their wider compatibility with other norms, and they claim that frequently a superior specification can be identified through such process of assessment which in Beauchamp and Childress's model relies on wide reflective equilibrium, as discussed further below (PBE, 19).

Beauchamp and Childress then address the balancing of norms, and present this as different from specification, considering each as "a separate dimension of moral norms" (PBE, 19). They define balancing as "the process of finding reasons to support beliefs about which moral norms should prevail" and as being "concerned with the relative weights and strengths of different moral norms" (PBE, 20). De Marco and Ford (2006) introduce balancing as

a metaphor for the attempt to determine the relative importance of conflicting values in particular cases or classes of cases in order to come to a conclusion . . . about moral obligations. (2006, 490)

This process involves deliberation and judgment. Beauchamp and Childress state that this process is not just a matter of "intuition or feeling," but that it can be supported by good reasons:

> We do not suggest that balancing is a matter of on-the-fly, unreflective intuition without reasons. Instead we propose a model of moral judgement that focuses on how balancing and judgement occur through practical astuteness, discriminating intelligence and sympathetic responsiveness (PBE, 22).

Similarly, De Marco and Ford (2006) highlight the rational features of what they call "deliberative balancing."

Beauchamp and Childress disagree with Richardson's (2000) criticism of the notion of balancing as lacking in transparency and justifiability, and reject the suggestion that balancing could ultimately be reduced to or merged with specification. They claim that while attractive in some respects, such a view is "too streamlined to handle all situations of balancing" (PBE, 20). They also question the practicability of conceptualizing moral judgment as solely dependent on specification: "a scheme of comprehensive specification would constitute a package of potentially hundreds, thousands or millions of rules, each suited to a narrow range of conduct," a practical impossibility (PBE, 22), a point echoed by De Marco and Ford (2006, 486). Their main concern regarding the merging of balancing with specification seems to be that specification of rules still leaves a degree of generality that requires additional processes to be employed in the case of application to the complexity of a particular situation:

> [I]t often seems that the responses of caring agents, such as physicians and nurses, are specific to the needs of *this* patient or *this* family in *this* circumstance. Numerous considerations must be weighed and balanced and any generalizations that could be formed might not hold even in related cases. . . . Balancing allows for a due consideration of all norms bearing on a complex very particular circumstance. (PBE, 20–21)

Using a case example of demands in deciding how to interact with a distressed patient faced with a HIV diagnosis, they attempt to illustrate how decisions on a particular course of action cannot be understood as purely based on generalization:

> any such generalisation will . . . not be subtle enough to provide practical guidance for this patient, and certainly not for all desperately upset patients. . . . Behavior that in the context of one desperate patient is a caring response will intrude on privacy or irritate the next desperate patient. (PBE, 21)

Beauchamp and Childress address the question of whether there are any firm constraints on balancing that could counteract the potential arbitrariness and obscurity of the intuitive aspects of balancing norms. They propose a number of conditions to constrain the scope of intuitive balancing, including for example the requirement to have good reasons for justifying infringements of norms, realistic prospects of achieving stated objectives, no availability of preferable alternatives, impartiality regarding stakeholders and so on (PBE, 23). De Marco and Ford similarly distinguish between "intuitive" and "deliberative" balancing, with the latter involving "an articulation of the possibly competing values" and providing "reasons for believing that one value has greater importance than another" (2006, 491). Such conditions would bring balancing much more in line with Richardson's requirement that decisions regarding norms need to be publicly justifiable (2000, 298), while, however, not subsuming them under specification, as Richardson proposes.

Despite highlighting the importance of objectively justifiable aspects in specification and balancing, Beauchamp and Childress emphasize that there will always be cases where reasonable disagreement will exist between different "conscientious and reasonable" moral agents. They identify different sources of disagreement, some of which depend on the information available to the moral agent, while others depend on more fundamental differences in judgment regarding the applicability of norms, their relative weights or the specific interpretation of their meaning and scope (PBE, 24–25).

However, Beauchamp and Childress consider disagreement a normal fact of moral life and state that "the phenomenon of moral disagreement provides no basis for skepticism about morality or about moral thinking" (PBE, 25). They go even further in claiming that disagreement "offers a reason for taking morality seriously and using the best tools we have to carry our moral projects as far as we can" (PBE, 25), apparently in the sense of considering disagreement a positive challenge that can incentivize the moral agent to achieve clarification and affirm their commitment to morality.

PRINCIPLES AND METHODOLOGICAL CASE RESOLUTION

The goal of ethical reflection in professional contexts is practical; practitioners turn to ethical reasoning in order to find ethically acceptable solutions to particular cases. Accordingly, the goal of biomedical ethics could be conceived of as "methodological case resolution" (Iltis 2000), in order to provide practitioners with relevant normative and methodological guidance that will enable them to discover ethical solutions to cases they might encounter in their practice. In the previous section, balancing and specification were presented as Beauchamp and Childress's first line of argument regarding the question how principles can be made practical. Both of these processes were presented as applying to the assessment of certain types of situations as well as particular cases. The specific characteristics and requirements of reasoning about particular cases beyond the general account of specification and balancing will now be the focus of this section, with particular emphasis on casuistry.

Much of the debate around specification and balancing refers also to casuistry, a case-based approach to moral reasoning. At first sight, casuistry seems to advocate an approach that is quite the opposite to a principle-based approach. Casuistry is generally conceived of as relying on a "bottom-up" approach to justification, where careful attention to the individual case details constitutes a significant part of the normative work, whereas much of the argumentative work in principle-based approaches would be seen to move from the "top-down." The focus of attention in casuistic reasoning is always a particular case, rather than general norms. Reasoning in casuistry proceeds largely by comparing individual cases in terms of their similarities and differences. The method generally involves relating novel cases, with yet-to-be-determined ethical assessments, to "paradigm cases," where ethical assessment is widely consensual. These cases are well established and representative of a given society's values. The method then proceeds by comparing the individual features and constellations of factors in these cases and assessing the similarities between the novel case and the paradigm cases. Strong describes this comparison as being "made in terms of certain morally relevant factors, which I refer to as 'casuistic factors' . . . and which can vary from case to case. . . . The strength of the conclusions depends on the plausibility of the comparisons with the paradigm cases" (Strong 2000, 331).

To demonstrate casuistic reasoning, Strong discusses the case of a newborn child with a severe genetic defect, Trisomy 18, where a decision needs to be taken whether the treatment team should accede to the parents' requests not to attempt a surgical correction of one of several significant physical impairments and to withhold nutrition and hydration (2000, 327–28). Strong compares this with similar cases where the child is suffering from different underlying conditions, but where there would be clearer agreement regarding appropriate actions. In the comparison cases the child is diagnosed with Klinefelter syndrome, a comparatively mild syndrome, on the one hand and anencephaly, the absence of a cortex, on the other hand. His case comparison then leads him to conclude that the Trisomy 18 case is closer to the anencephaly case and that therefore the parents' request should be honored (2000, 331).

Rather than reflect on specific problems with Strong's or other casuists' accounts, or deal with casuists' specific criticism of the principlist account, I shall instead primarily consider similarities and differences between the casuistic and principlist positions, especially in relation to what they have to say about the role of principles themselves.

On the standard account of casuistry, which describes casuistry as a bottom-up account of justification, principles are considered secondary to cases, insofar as they are derived from case analysis and can only hold "rule of thumb" status rather than provide what is sometimes claimed to be genuine normative guidance. However, several casuists have come out in favor of giving principles a more prominent role in casuistic reasoning. Strong is one of those who argues against understanding casuistry as necessarily a bottom-up account of justification:

> [A]lthough casuistry often is interpreted as holding that judgments about cases are more fundamental and important than principles and rules, it need not hold this view. In the version I have defended, judgments about cases are among the ethical components to be considered, along with principles, rules, etc. There is no need to assign an epistemic priority either to judgments about cases or to principles. This shows that casuistry as a case-based decision procedure can be separated from the meta-ethical view that intuitions about cases provide the grounds for rules and principles, the so-called "bottom-up" view. Casuists need not hold this bottom-up view. (2000, 337)

Jonsen, one of the authors of *The Abuse of Casuistry*, the book that re-established casuistry as a promising method for contemporary ethics, has also come to increasingly emphasize the complementarity of principles and casuistry, as for instance in his "Casuistry: An Alternative or Complement to Principles" (1995). Here he argues,

> When maxims, such as "Do no harm" or "Informed consent is obligatory," are invoked [in casuistic reasoning], they represent, as it were, cut-down versions of the major principles relevant to the topic, such as beneficence and autonomy cut down to fit the nature of the topic and the kinds of circumstances that pertain to it (1995, 244).

Again,

> Principles . . . are invoked necessarily and spontaneously in any serious moral discourse. . . . Moral terms and arguments are embedded in every case, usually in the form of maxims or enthymemes. The more general principles are never far from these maxims and enthymemes and are often explicitly invoked. Thus, casuistry is not an alternative to principles, in the sense that one might be able to perform good casuistry without principles. (1995, 246–247, also quoted in PBE)

While Beauchamp and Childress seem, at first sight, to present casuistry as a separate and competing approach to their own, on closer reading, much of what they present in their own account is compatible with the casuistic approach. The process of specification requires a significant extent of casuistic reasoning in the area which is being specified, as DeGrazia points out (1992, 531). Beauchamp also accepts that paradigm cases can have a significant and legitimate influence on how normative commitments are perceived: "[They] often become enduring and authoritative sources of reflection and decision making. Past decisions about moral rights and wrongs in cases serve as a form of authority for decisions in new cases" (2003, 269).

Beauchamp and Childress's primary critique of casuistry is based on their assumption that general norms are required in order to be able to connect and compare cases:

> For the casuist to move constructively from case to case, some recognised and morally relevant norm must connect the cases. The norm is not part of the case, but rather a way of interpreting and linking cases. . . . It is not enough to know that certain features of a case are morally significant. We must know *how* they are significant. Such cross-case evaluation seems to require general principles. (PBE, 379; see also Beauchamp 2003, 269)

This view is closely linked to their concern that casuistic reasoning, despite being an important method of thought, is lacking in substantive normative guidance beyond the contingencies of the current social context: "[C]asuistry is a method that fails to provide content. It is a vital tool of thought that displays the fundamental importance of case comparison and analogy in moral thinking, but it lacks initial moral premises" (PBE, 380). DeMarco and Ford make a related point when they point out that in Strong's examples, it is not some abstract measure of similarity between cases that does the ethical work in casuistry, but the substantial consideration of the weight of different circumstances in the cases that are being compared (2006, 489).

Apart from these concerns, Beauchamp and Childress explicitly concede significant overlap between their own approach and casuist methodology, especially as proposed by Jonsen:

> Casuists and principlists should be able to agree that when they reflect on cases and policies, they rarely, if ever, have in hand principles that were formulated without reference to experience with cases, or paradigm cases that have no embedded commitment to general norms. (PBE, 381)

Rauprich considers this connection to be even stronger, arguing that "[p]aradigm cases and specified norms that are based on the same morally relevant facts can immediately be transformed into each other. In this respect, both methods share strong structural and functional similarities" (2011, 596).

However, despite these striking similarities, the question of what exactly allows norms to be employed adequately in cases has not been fully addressed.

At this point, I would like to draw attention to one potentially significant aspect in the assessment of cases that tends to attract little attention in the debate, but is addressed by Beauchamp and Childress in this context. This is the link between reasoning on cases and virtue ethics, in particular the virtue of practical wisdom.

Correct appreciation of what is ethically at stake in a particular situation has traditionally been the domain of the Aristotelian virtue of *phronesis* (practical wisdom). Beauchamp and Childress explicitly draw on virtue-ethical notions when they discuss the balancing of complex moral concerns, insofar as they suggest that the capacities involved in successful balancing are connected to "capacities of moral character"; they also mention "wise moral agents" as models for such successful balancing and more generally for the ability to perceive and process moral concerns accurately (PBE, 22). They also state, regarding the notion of the virtues, that "these categories complement the analysis [of principles and rules] without undermining principles, rules, obligations, and rights" (PBE, 30), and that "[a] morally good person with the right configuration of desires and motives is more likely to understand what should be done, more likely to perform attentively the acts required, and even more likely to form and act on moral ideals" (PBE, 32–33).

They highlight the similarities in terms of practical requirements between realizing a virtue in action and the requirements of applying principles to particular situations:

> [It] will not be clear-cut, and it will render virtue ethics very similar to the theory of moral norms that we proposed. . . . At the same time, this theory does not prove some sort of triumph of virtues over principles and rules of obligation. Rather it shows their close connection. (PBE, 47)

Beauchamp and Childress seem to ask the principlist to learn a lesson from the attitude of the virtue ethicist regarding the process of practical decision-making:

> Proponents of virtue ethics do not lament that their approach lacks a complete decision procedure for such conflicts. Rather, they rightly note the limitations of principles, rules, and so on as well as of the virtues, in resolving moral dilemmas. (PBE, 47)

In a similar vein, Jonsen quotes the well-known passage from the beginning of Aristotle's *Nicomachean Ethics* regarding appropriate expectations for what moral theory can deliver:

> [W]e must be content in speaking about ethics . . . to reach conclusions that are only for the most part true . . . for it is the mark of an educated person to look

for precision in each class of things just so far as the nature of the subject admits: it is evidently equally foolish to accept probable reasoning from a mathematician and to demand from a rhetorician scientific proof. (NE I 1, 1094b19–27; in Jonsen 1995, 245)

The virtue-ethical aspect in Beauchamp and Childress's views on bringing to bear principles to cases may be the most underappreciated part of their theory so far. Its further exploration might be relevant for elucidating the still somewhat elusive notion of balancing, as well as the question what covers the remaining gap between specification and making a judgment on particular cases. At the same time, it also provides a bridge to the notion of the "morally committed person," which is significant for understanding Beauchamp and Childress's views on what they call the "common morality," a topic that will be briefly addressed in the following section.

MORAL JUSTIFICATION AND
THE PLACE OF PRINCIPLES

Beauchamp and Childress develop their own model of justification after engaging with top-down and bottom-up models of moral reasoning, where they prominently discuss casuistry. They present it as an integrated model which attempts to combine features of top-down with bottom-up approaches, with the main difference that the unidirectional nature of each of the models is replaced by a coherentist approach to justification, based on the model of reflective equilibrium which was originally proposed by John Rawls, and further elaborated by Norman Daniels as "wide reflective equilibrium."

In that model "[t]here is no fixed order of inference or dependence from general to particular or from particular to general"; justification is "a reflective testing of our moral beliefs, moral principles, theoretical postulates, and the like to make them as coherent as possible" (PBE, 382). A core element of this approach are the "considered judgments," which are those "moral convictions in which we have the highest confidence and believe to have the least bias" (PBE, 382), or as Rawls himself describes them, "judgments in which our moral capacities are most likely to be displayed without distortion" (quoted in PBE, 392); that is, judgments that are formed in conditions where distortions are least likely. Importantly, considered judgments can be judgments at any level of generality, thus they can concern particular situations as well as principles or even more abstract theoretical notions. When different features conflict, the conflicting assumptions will need to be reconsidered in order to allow for optimal coherence within the theory. Considered judgments are usually the cornerstones of such theories and therefore much less likely to be revised. However, according to Rawls, considered judgments are not in principle immune from revision; but the threshold for their modification is significantly higher than for judgments that are not considered judgments.

> The goal of reflective equilibrium is to match, prune and adjust considered judgments and their specifications to render them coherent with the premises of our most general moral commitments. We start with considered judgments of moral rightness and wrongness, and then construct both a more general and specific account that is consistent with these judgments, rendering the whole as coherent as possible. We then test the resultant guides to action to see if they yield incoherent results. If so, we must go back and readjust the guides further. We can never assume a completely stable equilibrium in our moral beliefs. The pruning and adjusting of beliefs occur continually in light of the goal of reflective equilibrium. (PBE, 382)

Beauchamp and Childress highlight that reflective equilibrium comes into play in particular during the process of specification, when competing specifications will be selected or tailored based on their coherence with the wider picture:

> All general moral beliefs are indeterminate for some range of cases and require that we eliminate contingent conflicts among the beliefs. Any specification aimed at eliminating a conflict is justified only if there is a maximal coherence of the overall set of relevant beliefs. (PBE, 383)

Based on the assumption of continuous specification in a changing world, the reflective equilibrium model considers our views on morality to be "continuous works in progress rather than finished products" (PBE, 383). These authors also point out that the plurality of what they call "particular moralities," that is, specific moral outlooks in different cultures, religious traditions and so on, can be understood as based on different specifications of general moral norms (PBE, 384).

Reflective equilibrium approaches, as outlined above, are usually thoroughly coherentist and anti-foundationalist; all their elements are potentially subject to revision, including even the considered judgments (albeit their modification is much more unlikely). However, Beauchamp and Childress's position is explicitly not a coherentist approach, but a hybrid that uses reflective equilibrium as the method of justification, while exempting certain judgments from revisability, namely those that belong to what they call the "common morality," in particular their own central four principles. They "accept reflective equilibrium as a basic methodology" but they conjoin it "with the common morality approach to considered judgments." For them it appears to follow that "coherence serves as a basic constraint on the specification and balancing of the norms . . . and it escapes categorization by labels such as foundational-ism and coherentism" (PBE, 385). This stipulation is rather puzzling, meth-odologically speaking, and has accordingly been criticized as problematic and unnecessary, for example by Rauprich (2008) and Arras (2009). It is outside the scope of this chapter to engage more deeply with the problems associated with this claim; instead I will outline Beauchamp and Childress's understand-ing of the common morality and the role of the principles in it.

What characterizes theories that rely on common morality is the assump-tion that there is a number of moral norms that are shared by all moral agents (or in some versions, including Beauchamp and Childress's, all moral agents that share ethically significant features), and that a theoretical justification of those norms within a wider theoretical framework is not necessary. Beau-champ and Childress claim that the common morality is the universal core of morality and is valid across cultures: "The common morality is applicable to all persons in all places and we rightly judge all human conduct by its stan-dards" (PBE, 3). They add one significant qualification to the claim of the universality of the common morality by claiming that it comprises only the beliefs of "all persons who are *committed* to morality" (PBE, 4) or "morally committed" (PBE, 5, 6). This apparently replaces the term "morally serious" that was used in the previous edition. In relation to the common morality, morally committed persons "adhere to the standards that we are calling the common morality," whereas those who "do not care about or identify with moral demands" are excluded (PBE, 4). By virtue of this (unfortunately still rather underdetermined) qualification, aberrant opinions of those who are not committed moral agents can be neglected and will not require consideration within the reflective equilibrium.

Beauchamp and Childress present the elements of the common morality "as worthy of belief independent of whether they can be supported by argu-ment" (PBE, 386) and as "hav[ing] a rich history of moral experience that undergirds confidence that they are credible and trustworthy"; they "therefore cannot be simply matters of individual intuition" (PBE, 385). They are con-cerned about the danger of drawing on parochial and inherently conservative judgments and therefore advocate the inclusion of a wide range of concerns and perspectives and try to identify points of convergence between them (PBE, 386). In order to allow wide convergence, the norms in question need to transcend the limits of particular moralities and be quite "abstract, uni-versal and content thin" (PBE, 5). Beauchamp and Childress claim that their principles are a crucial part of the common morality: "We believe that the general public and the mainstream of moral philosophy have found a 'locus of certitude' in universal moral principles"; "[P]rinciples . . . form the cement of the common morality . . . [and] enjoy a high level of certitude" (PBE, 381).

CONCLUSION

This chapter has explored Beauchamp and Childress' approach to biomedical ethics as presented in the sixth edition of their *Principles of Biomedical Ethics*. Its primary aim was to provide an exposition of the concerns that Beauchamp and Childress raise in relation to the role of principles for practical reasoning. Five points were identified as particularly important:

1. Principles require specification to contexts in order to become practical; specification is a nondeductive process in which norms are tailored to contexts in a complex reasoning process.
2. Complex cases require balancing of different principles and norms, in the sense of assessing their comparative relevance. This process seems different from specification.
3. In assessing cases with the help of principles, the appropriateness of the top-down model of case deliberation and resolution has come into question. Instead, the intertwining of case-based and principle-based reasoning has become increasingly acknowledged.
4. It appears that virtues of perception and reasoning may well play a significant role in dealing with the complexity of judgment on cases.
5. Moral justification is a complex process in which a wide range of norms and facts are balanced against each other in the multidirectional justificatory process of wide-reflective equilibrium. While general principles are conceived of as anchor points with special status in this process, any use of principles for specific problems needs to meet the reflective equilibrium requirements.

Whether or not one agrees with the details of Beauchamp and Childress's approach, what this exploration should have made clear is the sheer complexity of concerns implicit in the use of principles in practical reasoning. Even in an approach that is as explicitly focused on principles as theirs, the significance of those principles cannot override all the ambiguity, uncertainty and scope for interpretation characteristic of alternative accounts of ethical reasoning that are otherwise quite different.

REFERENCES

Arras, J. 2009. "The Hedgehog and the Borg: Common Morality in Bioethics." *Theoretical Medicine and Bioethics* 30: 11–30.

Beauchamp, T. 2003. "Methods and Principles in Biomedical Ethics." *Journal of Medical Ethics* 29: 269–274.

Beauchamp, T., and J. Childress. 2009. *Principles of Biomedical Ethics*. 6th edition. New York: Oxford University Press.

DeGrazia, D. 1992. "Moving Forward in Bioethical Theory: Theories, Cases, and Specified Principlism." *Journal of Medicine and Philosophy* 17: 511–539.

DeMarco, J., and P. Ford. 2006. "Balancing in Ethical Deliberation: Superior to Specification and Casuistry." *Journal of Medicine and Philosophy* 31: 483–497.

Iltis, A. 2000. "Bioethics as Methodological Case Resolution: Specification, Specified Principlism and Casuistry." *Journal of Medicine and Philosophy* 25 (3): 271–284.

Jonsen, A. 1995. "Casuistry: An Alternative or Complement to Principles." *Kennedy Institute of Ethics Journal* 5 (3): 237–251.

Jonsen, A. , and S. Toulmin. 1988. *The Abuse of Casuistry: A History of Moral Reasoning*. Berkeley: University of California Press.

Rauprich, O. 2008. "Common Morality: Comment on Beauchamp and Childress." *Theoretical Medicine and Bioethics* 29: 43–71.

———. 2011. "Specification and Other Methods for Determining Morally Relevant facts." *Journal of Medical Ethics* 37: 592–596.

Richardson, H. 1990. "Specifying Norms as a Way to Resolve Concrete Ethical Problems." *Philosophy and Public Affairs* 19 (4): 279–310.

———. 2000. "Specifying, Balancing, and Interpreting Bioethical Principles." *Journal of Medicine and Philosophy* 25 (3): 285–307.

Strong, C. 2000. "Specified Principlism: What Is It, and Does It Really Resolve Cases Better Than Casuistry?" *Journal of Medicine and Philosophy* 25 (3): 323–341.

Part Three

ENGAGEMENT FOR THE PRACTICAL UNITY OF LIFE

Chapter Eleven

The Theory of
Double Truth Revisited

Karsten Harries

On May 13, 2009, I had a conversation over lunch with a colleague, Professor Drew McDermott of Yale's computer science department. What we then talked about has continued to occupy me. Professor McDermott told of how he had recently returned to the thought of Martin Heidegger, which he had encountered in college quite some time ago, but to which for many years he had given little thought. But now he had come to see that what Heidegger had to say did justice to our first-person awareness of being in the world. In that sense much of what he had to say could be called true. From the third-person perspective of the scientist, however, it had to be judged false.

The comment made me think of Søren Kierkegaard's distinction between subjective and objective truth. Kierkegaard knew of course very well that first of all "the question about truth is asked objectively, truth is reflected upon objectively as an object to which the knower relates himself." Why then should we oppose to it a subjective truth and how are we to understand such a truth? Kierkegaard defines it as "An objective uncertainty, held fast through appropriation with the most passionate inwardness"—Kierkegaard was thinking of love and faith. This subjective truth he calls "the highest truth there is for an *existing* person." In such attainment the individual is said to perfect him- or herself. We may well wonder whether we should speak in such cases of knowledge at all. But what is at issue is clear enough: the value of objective truth:

> The way of objective reflection makes the subject accidental, and thereby transforms existence into something indifferent, something vanishing. Away from the subject the objective way of reflection leads to the objective truth, and while the subject and his subjectivity become indifferent, the truth also becomes

indifferent, and this indifference is precisely its objective validity; for all interest, like all decisiveness, is rooted in subjectivity. (Kierkegaard 1974, 178, 182)

Kierkegaard speaks of an objective uncertainty, not of an objective falsehood.
That avoids the paradoxical claim advanced by McDermott that what we are
convinced is absolutely true, for example the claim that there are absolute
values, must yet be judged, without overturning such conviction, objectively
false.

McDermott followed this conversation up by sending me the draft of a
paper on which he was still working with the thought-provoking title: "How
Moral Absolutism Can Be True and False at the Same Time; Or: Non-Phenomenological Existentialism." Here the paper's abstract:

We examine ethics from the point of view of cognitive science. Science commits one to a view in which ethics is just an arbitrary aspect of culture, and the
study of cultures is value-free, so that relativism seems axiomatically true. But
intelligent agents cannot take the view of pure science, because certain built-in
beliefs contradict it. These inescapable framework illusions (IFI's) include a
belief in free will, the persistence of the self through time, and, among humans,
the universalizability of moral statements.

McDermott takes us moderns to be confronted with something like an antinomy: as intelligent agents we are compelled to believe certain things, most
importantly that our will is free, that we are selves that persist through time,
that there are moral truths that can be universalized, beliefs which as individuals committed to science we yet know to be false. A somewhat weaker
version of this claim, closer to what Kierkegaard was going to maintain, is
familiar from the work of philosophers such as Kant and Fichte,[1] who insist
that as free, responsible actors we have to take as true what theoretical reason
is unable to establish, indeed cannot even make sense of. But they would
have refused to assert that what practical reason forces us to accept as true is
from an objective, third-person point of view false. Thus they would not have
wanted to say that "moral absolutism can be true and false at the same time."

The title of McDermott's paper brought to mind that theory of double truth
condemned by the theologians at the university of Paris in 1277. Should I
understand McDermott in the image of Siger of Brabant, the Aristotelian philosopher of nature, who was perhaps the leading target of that condemnation?
Aristotelian science also left no room for certain key beliefs and especially
for the kind of freedom demanded by Christianity. Given Aristotle's understanding of nature, such claims had to be judged false. How then could a good
Christian be a follower of Aristotle? Could Aristotelian science and Christian theology, while they contradicted each other, both lay claim to truth?

Must such a theory of double truth not be rejected by every right-thinking person?—and there is indeed reason to wonder whether Siger ever really endorsed it. And similarly we must ask today, how can moral absolutism be true and false at the same time, except by relativizing the truth in question? Does the very essence of truth not rule out the theory of double truth? But what is truth?

The question brought to my mind the young Friedrich Nietzsche, who wrestled with it in "On Truth and Lie in an Extra-Moral Sense."[2] In that never-completed fragment I found another version of the theory of double truth, although Nietzsche not only does not use that expression but would probably have rejected it as suggesting that he wanted to hold on to something that he sought to jettison, namely to the truth. Still, despite all that distinguishes the medieval Aristotelian philosopher of nature, the cognitive scientist very much of today, and the nineteenth century critic of objectifying reason and its truth, all three wrestle with what has remained fundamentally the same problem: rigorous reflection on the essence of truth leads us into an antinomy to which the title of McDermott's paper gives expression. Reason, however, refuses to accept such an antinomy; it is forced to go beyond it. But reason has nowhere to go. Thus, I will argue, it is forced to recognize its own limits. As Nicolaus Cusanus might have put it, the antinomy of truth lets us become learned about our ignorance.

This essay divides into three parts, corresponding to the three versions of the theory of double truth I have named. What is important, however, remains the same: the antinomy of truth. The conclusion will address that antinomy.

THE THEORY OF DOUBLE TRUTH

Whether Siger was sincere or whether he invoked a theory of double truth only to placate the Church authorities who would deny him the freedom of thought that is a presupposition of scientific inquiry does not matter here. That there is tension between the truths that science, as he then understood it, proclaimed and Christian faith is obvious. Siger was convinced of the truth of Aristotle's philosophy, as explicated by the Commentator, Ibn Rushd, known in the West as Averroes. Natural science for him, as for many others at the time, had come to mean Aristotle's philosophy of nature. But that philosophy was in obvious ways incompatible with Church doctrine. To mention just three of the most important: According to Aristotle the world has no beginning in time; this denies the Biblical creation account. According to Aristotle the order of nature is such that neither man nor God can change it; this denies divine as well as human freedom, denies miracles as well as sin. And

Aristotle denies that there is an individual soul; this denies the possibility of a personal afterlife and with it heaven and hell. The Condemnation of 1277 was the culmination of the Church's attempt to stem what it understood as the subversive Aristotelian tide.

The city of Toledo in Spain deserves mention in this connection. Until 1085, when it was taken by Alfonso VI of Castile, it had been under the rule of the Caliphate of Cordoba. Until the expulsion of Muslims and Jews from Spain in 1492, it was known for its tolerance. Here Muslims, Christians, and Jews lived in harmony for centuries. It was Francis Raymond de Sauvetât, archbishop from 1125 to 1152, who here promoted the translation of many of Aristotle's works, which had been unavailable to Christian Europe, and of the works of the great Arab philosophers, including especially Averroes, who claimed there is nothing that philosophy does not know better than faith, that theology is indeed the worst kind of speculation, since it is neither faith nor philosophy, but a corruption of both.[3] Anticipating Galileo, he insisted that Scripture and philosophy cannot be in contradiction; where they appear to be, Scripture needs to be interpreted allegorically (Averroes in Hyman and Walsh 1973, 302). This makes philosophy, or human reason relying on its own resources, the proper custodian of the truth. The Church could not accept this.

In *De doctrina Christiana* Augustine had presented this understanding of "Christian Wisdom," which would place all profane knowledge in the service of sacred science, "that is, theology, or the scientific study of divine revelation accepted on faith. This is why the schools of liberal arts were viewed as preparatory schools, providing a general formation that was indispensable for those entering the advanced fields of study, theology, law, or medicine" (Van Steenberghen 1980, 75). The supremacy of theology went unchallenged.

Acquaintance with Aristotle's science of nature was to change all this. At the center of this development was the Arts Faculty of the University of Paris (ibid., 76). Ever since its founding in 1215 the impact of Aristotle would appear to have been significant. Indeed, even earlier, in 1210, the archbishop of Sens thought it important to put the teaching of Aristotle's writings on natural philosophy and of their commentaries under penalty of excommunication (Gilson 1955, 244). And in the statutes of the university, only the study of Aristotle's logic was authorized, while his metaphysics, along with all his books dealing with natural philosophy, were forbidden, along with the writings of a number of Aristotelians suspected of heresy.[4] But the progress of Aristotle's influence could not be stopped, although another attempt was made in 1231 by Pope Gregory X, who forbade the teachings of Aristotle's *Physics*, at least until censors had purged the text of its errors. All such attempts to stem the

Aristotelian tide were ineffective. In 1255 study of all the known works of Aristotle was made obligatory in the arts faculty of the University of Paris.[5] By then to be a philosopher had come to mean to immerse oneself in the works of Aristotle and those of his Arab commentators. Churchmen like St. Bonaventure, who from 1252 to 1257 was a colleague of St. Thomas on the theology faculty, must have seen in this a sad sign of decline and decay and they could only have been dismayed by the way Gothic naturalism had found its philosopher in the pagan and very worldly Aristotle, especially as interpreted by the Arab Averroes.

At the university of Paris Aristotle at the time was brilliantly represented by Thomas Aquinas (1225–1274) and Siger of Brabant (ca. 1240–1284).[6] Conservatives, to be sure, many of them Franciscans led by St. Bonaventure, continued to invoke the authority of Augustine, while Thomas Aquinas sought to appropriate Aristotle for a distinctly Christian worldview, striving for a genuine, but finally impossible synthesis. Many students, however, would seem to have found Siger's insistence on the autonomy and independence of philosophy, on freedom of thought, so opposed to the Augustinian understanding of Christian Wisdom, more attractive.

The Church's Condemnation of 1277 represented a victory of mostly Franciscan neo-Augustinians over often Dominican Aristotelians. On January 16 of that year Pope John XXI, worried about the effect which speculation that would free philosophy from the tutelage of theology might have, had asked Étienne Tempier, the bishop of Paris, to address the matter. The bishop responded with the condemnation on March 7. Siger was especially targeted.

The tenor of Siger's philosophizing makes it easy to understand the Church's objections to what he taught. Consider his answer to the question: "whether the human species had a beginning in time." Appealing to Aristotle, Siger denies such a beginning:

> Now, from the explanation it is clear in what way the human species is considered by philosophers eternal and caused. For, it is not to be thought of as eternal and caused as if it existed abstracted from individuals. Nor is it eternally caused in the sense that it exists in an eternally caused individual, as the species of heaven or an intelligence; but rather because in the individuals of the human species one is generated before the other eternally, and the species has to be and be caused through an individual's existing and being caused. Hence it is that the human species always exists and that it did not begin to be after previous non-existence. For to say that it began to be after it had not existed before is to say that there began to be a certain individual before whom no other individual of that species had existed. (Siger of Brabant 1973, 454)

What was one then to think of Adam and Eve? Of original sin?

And, Siger continued: just as "man does not begin to be when he had in no way existed before," "neither does time." The impossibility of the Christian creation account is said to be evident to reason.

> And the given reason is similar to the reasoning by which Aristotle speculates in IV *Physicorum* whether past time is finite. All past time whether near or remote is a certain "*then*," and the certain "*then*" has a measured distance to the present now; therefore all past time is finite. And each of the aforementioned propositions is clear from the meaning of that "*then*" which Aristotle speaks of in IV *Physicorum*. The solution of this reasoning, according to Aristotle, is that although every second is finite, nevertheless since in time there is a "*then*" before the "*then*" to infinity, therefore not all past time is finite. For what is composed of things finite in quantity yet infinite in number has to be infinite. So also, although there is no individual man but that he has begun to exist when he had not existed before, yet there is an individual before the individual so that man does not begin to be when he had in no wise existed before, and neither does time. And the case is similar—just as past time has to be thought through a certain then, so also species have to be through the existence of any one of its individuals. (ibid., 455)

Of special interest in this connection is this proposition, one of 219 condemned in 1277:

> 89. That it is impossible to refute the arguments of the Philosopher concerning the eternity of the world, unless we can say that the will of the first being embraces incompatibles. ("Condemnation of 219 Propositions," in Hyman and Walsh 1973, 546)

This claims that, to disagree with Aristotle on the eternity of the world, one would have to accept the theory of double truth. This does indeed appear to be the position of Siger, who now could 1) embrace incompatibles, 2) follow Averroes and insist that the truth of philosophy trumps theology, or 3) admit that the truth of philosophy is only a precariously established human truth and that God dwells beyond the principle of noncontradiction. As we will see, in a very different, secular key to be sure, McDermott faces a similar choice.

The Church found especially unacceptable the way Aristotelian science could not be reconciled with the Biblical account of creation, more especially of the creation of man. According to Siger the fact that the prime mover is always moving and acting rules out both:

> No species of being proceeds to actuality, but . . . it has proceeded before, so that the same species which were, return in a cycle; and so also opinions and laws and religions, and all other things so that the lower circle around from the cir-

cling of the higher, although because of the antiquity there is no memory of the cycle of these. We say these things as the opinion of the Philosopher, although not asserting them as true. (Siger of Brabant 1973, 460)

That such a cyclical view of nature is incompatible with the Christian understanding of history which insists on uniquely significant times and events is evident. Think of the creation of Adam and Eve, of the birth and death of Christ. Siger was of course all too aware of that. It is therefore not surprising to discover that he immediately weakens his claim by seeming to grant that the truth claimed by philosophy may not be identified with "*the*" truth. Did the Averroist Siger really believe this?

Nominally the truth of philosophy here remains subordinated to the revealed truth of religion. But there is also the suggestion that the latter must be considered unreasonable, where, to be sure, there is the obvious theological rejoinder that the philosopher must not forget that human reason and divine reason are finally incommensurable. But those who want to use their own God-given minds are invited by Siger to forget theology. We find ourselves on the threshold of a theory of double truth that would cut the bond that had tied philosophy to theology. But it is difficult to remain on this threshold. Should we not follow Averroes and cross it, leaving theology behind?

Did Siger propose his guardedly stated version of the theory of double truth only to pull the wool over the eyes of a suspicious establishment? If so, he failed. Here at any rate is how the "Condemnation" responded to it:

So as not to appear to be asserting what they [teachers of philosophy such as Siger] thus insinuate, they conceal their answers in such a way that, while wishing to avoid Scylla, they fall into Charybdis. For they say that these things are true according to philosophy, but not according to the Catholic faith, as if there were two contrary truths and as if the truth of Sacred Scripture were contradicted by the truth in the sayings of the accursed pagans, of whom it is written: *I will destroy the Wisdom of the Wise* [I Cor. 1, 19; cf. Isa. 29, 14], inasmuch as true wisdom destroys false wisdom. ("Condemnation of 219 Propositions," in Hyman and Walsh 1973, 542)

The theologians who issued the Condemnation were particularly concerned to hold on to a robust understanding of both divine and human freedom, which would allow both for miracles and for sin. Readily apparent is the threat the claim to truth made by the science of nature, which has to appeal to natural laws, poses to divine omnipotence. Or to put in the reverse way: readily apparent is the threat the freedom of an omnipotent deity poses to rational, scientific inquiry.

The authors of the Condemnation wanted to make sure that the faithful not limit God's freedom by subjecting it to supposed laws of nature. Consider the following condemned proposition:

> 22. That God cannot be the cause of a newly-made thing and cannot produce anything new. (ibid., 544)

Both the creation account and miracles are here ruled out. According to the condemned proposition, God, too, is bound by the laws of nature. To challenge this is to shake the foundation of Aristotle's physics. But a Christian thinker has to reject such a proposition. And this rejection inevitably leads to another thought: the world cannot be as Aristotle describes it. God's freedom may not be imprisoned in Aristotle's philosophy.

Nor may human freedom. Consider, for instance,

> 151. That the soul wills nothing unless it is moved by another. Hence the following proposition is false: the soul wills by itself.—This is erroneous if what is meant is that the soul is moved by another, namely by something desirable or an object in such a way that the desirable thing or object is the whole reason for the movement of the will itself. (ibid., 548)

The condemned proposition would deny human freedom and thus responsibility. The Condemnation insists that the individual bears responsibility for his misdeeds and cannot excuse himself by insisting that he could not help but do what he did. He cannot even shift responsibility for his misdeeds to God who chose to create him and the world as he did, as the condemnation of proposition 153 warns. Here we are touching on the tension between Divine omnipotence and omniscience and human freedom.

The authors of the Condemnation take the infinity of God's power and wisdom for granted. And they take for granted the authority of Scripture. But the works of Aristotle, they are convinced, should not be granted a comparable authority: they are after all but products of finite and fallible human reason. Aristotle offers us one, perhaps even plausible, account of nature, but such an account may not be invested with the authority of absolute truth, certainly not where such truth conflicts with Christian Wisdom.

It is tempting to understand the Condemnation of 1277 as just another example of the Church's unwillingness to accept intellectual progress, represented at the time by the rediscovery of Aristotle's science of nature, another sad chapter in the suppression of free thought, a precursor perhaps of the later trials of Bruno and Galileo. And yet, precisely by challenging the too-readily-taken-for-granted authority of Aristotle, the claim that as far as fundamentals were concerned, he was in possession of the truth, the conservative theologians helped prepare the way for a revolution in the understanding of nature that was to issue in the science to which McDermott is committed, which could not have developed as it did without this undermining of the authority of Aristotle. Paradoxically, it was Christian conservatives who opened up the way for what was truly progressive. Aristotelian physics, which depends on a geocentric cosmology, and the Copernican revolution cannot be reconciled. A very Christian reaction to Aristotelian ideas thus helped open up the intellectual space that made our modern science and that makes also our modern technology and thus our modern world possible. What is especially troubling and thought provoking is that, like its Aristotelian predecessor, our science once again would seem to leave no room for freedom, even though, as McDermott points out, as actors we cannot help but proclaim ourselves free.

SCIENCE AND FREEDOM

Let me return to McDermott's draft. Is it really possible for us to hold something, take for example Moral Absolutism, to be true and false, as he insists we must do? As we have seen, in the thirteenth century there were indeed philosophers who in public at least came close to defending some such view: then it was Aristotle's newly imported philosophy of nature which clashed with Christian common sense, watched over by the theologians. McDermott is free of such theological commitments. He speaks instead of certain "built-in" "inescapable framework illusions," where the very words "built in" and "framework illusions" suggest that in the end he, too, may not hold a robust theory of double truth, but ends up making science the privileged custodian of truth.

There is much I agree with in his paper. First of all, I agree with the claim that science as we know it is ideally value-free. McDermott invokes what, referring to *An Enquiry Concerning the Principles of Morals*, he terms Hume's principle: "No statement about the way things ought to be can be derived from any set of statements about the way things are" (McDermott 2009, 2). I would not want to endorse this principle without asking: how should we understand: "the way things are"? Does science hold the key?

Regardless of whether this question must be answered in the affirmative, we can conclude with McDermott: "Because science is entirely about the way things are, nothing in science bears on whether one moral system is superior to another, or whether there is some supersystem that encompasses all the little ones. . . . Science is crushingly indifferent to our affairs. . . . From the purely scientific point of view, the self doesn't exist at all; all that is observable are agents that *believe* they are selves." (ibid., 3 and 10)

I agree with McDermott that science knows nothing of values, persons, or freedom, although I hesitate to conclude from this that for science relativism seems axiomatically true. If science knows nothing of values it cannot say with confidence that they are either time-bound or timeless, either relative or absolute. What it can say is that, as a matter of fact, there has been a great deal of disagreement about what human beings have taken to matter most profoundly or to value. In that sense value judgments have been relative. But that does not show that values are in fact relative. The fact that there has been disagreement about the possibility of squaring the circle does not mean that there is not a truth of the matter. Questions of truth and validity, it would seem, cannot be settled by appeals to what people happen to think. McDermott would seem to overplay his hand when he writes, "relativism is not just true, it is almost axiomatically true, given my premises" (ibid., 5). He seems to me more nearly correct when he writes, "IFI's are illusions in the sense that they are false or meaningless" (ibid., 8). I think "meaningless" here is the better term. Given the scientific understanding of truth, McDermott's IFI's are meaningless.

But what is the scientific understanding of truth? I shall have to return to that question.

If I pretty much agree with McDermott about what he calls Hume's Principle, at least if restricted to the scientific understanding of nature, I have questions about his second fundamental principle. McDermott calls it Neurath's Principle—the reference is to Otto Neurath's *Foundations of the Unity of Science: Toward an International Encyclopedia of Unified Science* (1971): "The world discovered (and yet to be discovered) by science *is* the world" (ibid. 2). Science here means fundamentally physics:

> The world revealed by physics is bizarre and alien to us. But it's the only world there is. All the other sciences are reducible to it, in what is by now a well known sense. Nothing happens in chemistry that can't be explained in terms of physics; nothing happens in biology that can't be explained in terms of physics and chemistry; and so forth. (ibid., 3)

This would mean that we really need only one concept of nature and that physics provides the key to that concept.

I find this principle questionable. I, too, want to say that "The world discovered (and yet to be discovered) by science *is* the world." But with Heidegger I would want to raise the question of the being of the world thus discovered. Heidegger's question of Being is the question of our mode of access to beings. What justifies the equation of the world or of nature with the world or nature discovered or to be discovered by science? What about the way an artist discovers the world; or a religious person? Are they obviously in error?

What can be said in support of the equation of the world with "The world discovered (and yet to be discovered) by science"? A first answer: it would seem to be entailed by our familiar everyday understanding of truth as the correspondence of our thoughts or propositions with the things—but with the things as they really are, not as they appear to be to an observer limited by his subjective perspective. This entails a privileging of the aperspectival and objective.[7] Isn't such objectivity a presupposition of really understanding what is?

But what does it mean to "really understand" something? What conception of reality is here being presupposed? Is our human reason able to fathom reality? Kant presents us with considerations that render the commensurability of human reason and reality, a presupposition of Neurath's principle, not just questionable, but untenable. What renders it untenable is what I want to call, with reference to Kant's antinomies, the antinomy of Being. But more on that later. Here I only want to state where I disagree with McDermott.

And yet, there is a great deal we agree on. I agree that we find it impossible to let go of what McDermott calls "inescapable framework illusions" and I, too, would include among these the belief in free will and the belief that we are selves that exist until we die. McDermott's "inescapable framework illusions" look a great deal like what Kant would have called ideas of reason. But although not supported by science, are such ideas therefore false?

According to McDermott "we are compelled to live by key foundational beliefs that are false" (McDermott 2009, 30). Belief in the freedom of the will is said to be one such error:

> The odd thing about the free-will error is that it is impossible for us to correct it, at least when it comes to contemplating our own decisions. That's because our brains are "wired" in such a way as to treat a decision in the process of being made as exempt from causal laws. As explained in McDermott (2001), it would be completely pointless for a brain to use causal reasoning, i.e., simulation or some other modeling technique, to predict what it was going to do, because what it is going to do depends on the computation it is in the middle of. . . . Evolution has made sure that any such attempt is blocked by the hard-wired belief that the decisions currently under review is exempt from causal modeling. It is this hard-wired belief that we introspectively perceive as freedom. (ibid., 6–7)

McDermott includes in these IFI's the belief in an absolute ethical truth. And so he concludes the paper with a plea for religious tolerance. He even takes it to be an absolute ethical principle:

> This principle was mostly unnecessary until the debut of multiple evangelizing monotheisms on the world stage, and it took a few centuries for Europeans to realize that without it too many people would perish in this life without really

settling the question of who would control the next one. European culture then spread throughout most of the world, but there are still places where the idea of tolerance hasn't yet gotten through. I fervently hope that we can get it through without too may people getting killed in the process. Because, if you ask me, the principle of tolerance is an absolute ethical truth. (ibid., 32)

But that absolute truth, he also insists, while I cannot renounce it, is really a falsehood. He explicitly agrees with J. L. Mackie (*Ethics, Inventing Right and Wrong*, 1977), "that moral thinking is inevitably permeated by fundamental errors" (ibid., 5). The beliefs in freedom, in a stable self, in absolute values are said to be such errors.

McDermott is a materialist, and he holds that science holds the key to all that can reasonably be said to be. He is well aware of the unbelievability of such a materialism. Our first-person experience of the world argues against it. But from the point of the scientist's sober third-person awareness such first-person awareness supports us with a web of lies. For science to develop as it did, reason had to free itself from the grip of these lies. McDermott could have agreed with Nietzsche, when the latter celebrates Copernicus and Boscovich as "the greatest and most victorious opponents of what appears to the eye."[8] This victory relies on a pattern I want to call Copernican reflection: "Appearance to the eye" ("*Augenschein*") is devalued by being shown to be no more than perspectival appearance. The world opened up by the scientist is opposed to the comparatively superficial world that continues to be our life-world. But as Nietzsche also knows, this victory brings with it "the self-diminution of man, his will to self-diminution," which since Copernicus is said to be "in an unstoppable progress." "Since Copernicus the human being seems to have stumbled onto an inclined plane—he rolls ever faster away from the center—where? Into nothing? Into the penetrating awareness of his own 'nothing'?"[9] The other side of the Copernican victory is nihilism. Modern science is inescapably shadowed by nihilism. As we can read in Wittgenstein's *Tractatus*:

6. 4 All propositions are of equal value.
6. 41 The sense of the world must lie outside the world. In the world everything is at it is and happens as it does happen. In it there is no value—and if there were, it would be of no value. (Trans. C. K. Ogden)

McDermott could not have disagreed. But his theory of double truth suggests that the specter of nihilism is in fact banished, as soon as a first-person point of view is adopted. I wonder. Can I really say: "I know x is false, but I nevertheless believe x, indeed believe it to be an absolute truth"? I am unable to do so. I consider this the expression of a true antinomy, and, as Kant suggests, the solution of such antinomies lies in recognizing that the reason that lets us call McDermott's IFI's false does not circumscribe reality. That is to say, what McDermott calls Neurath's principle must be rejected.

McDermott suggests another way out: "But if materialism provides an explanation of its own unbelievability, an explanation I have sketched above, then this inferential step loses whatever plausibility it might have had" (McDermott 2009, 13). In *Being and Time* Heidegger, according to McDermott, offers us a convincing account of our inescapable framework intuitions and in this sense can claim them to be true, but true only relative to our first-person awareness. McDermott thus claims "that first-person awareness is a belief system that brains inhabit, a web of IFIs that ensure it can never accept the whole truth as revealed by science" (ibid., 9). I agree that science has to look at consciousness in that way. According to McDermott the progress of science has compressed the sphere of IFI's, but he insists that it won't be able to eliminate it altogether, even though as a scientist he is forced to admit that these IFI's are false.

This invites another look at the "theory of double truth."

TRUTH AS LIE

According to McDermott, what we, caught up in our first-person understanding, call truths are, seen from the superior third-person understanding of the scientist, lies. With this claim McDermott would seem to be close to the position the young Nietzsche developed in "On Truth and Lie in an Extramoral Sense." Nietzsche, too, considers our first-person awareness of our life-world a web of lies.

> To be truthful means to employ the usual metaphors. Thus, to express it morally, this is the duty to lie according to a fixed convention, to lie with the herd and in a manner binding upon everyone. (Nietzsche 1979, 84)

Presupposed is a doubling of the meaning of both "truth" and "lie," for within the lie that is said to rule our everyday we must distinguish once more between being "truthful" and "lying":

> The liar is a person who uses the valid designations, the words, in order to make something which is unreal appear to be real. He says for example, "I am rich," when the proper designation for his condition would be "poor." He misuses fixed conventions by means of arbitrary substitutions or even reversals of names. (ibid., 81)

This presupposes that there is a proper use of a linguistic convention. That proper use links what is real to valid and binding designations in a way we can check. This again presupposes that the reality in question is available to those who participate in such a language game, if in a way that cuts them off from *the* truth and in this sense is a lie. But, given our life-world, we have generally no difficulty distinguishing between truth and lie.

How then does Nietzsche understand his higher truth, which lets him call such everyday truths lies? An answer is suggested by the following passage:

> And, besides, what about these linguistic conventions themselves? Are they perhaps products of knowledge, that is of the sense of truth? Are designations congruent with things? Is language the adequate expression of all realities? (ibid.)

To be true, Nietzsche insists, designations must be congruent with things. Language must be the adequate expression of reality. But we have no access to things unmediated by language. If truth is taken to demand the congruence of our designations with things in themselves there is no truth. Nor is this something that would seem to matter very much:

> The various languages placed side by side show that with words it is never a question of truth, never a question of adequate expression; otherwise, there would not be so many languages. The "thing in itself" (which is precisely what the pure truth, apart from any of its consequences, would be) is likewise something quite incomprehensible to the creator of language and some thing not in the least worth striving for. (ibid., 82)

Nietzsche's understanding of truth as, not just a correspondence, but a congruence of designations and things allows him to say that pure truth would be the thing in itself. This formulation is in accord with tradition. Consider Thomas Aquinas's definition of truth as "the adequation of the thing and the understanding": "*Veritas est adaequatio rei et intellectus.*"[10] Quite in keeping with our everyday understanding, the definition claims that there can be no truth where there is no understanding. But can there be understanding without human beings? Does truth then depend on human beings? Aquinas rejects such a suggestion: the truth of our thoughts or propositions has its measure in the truth of things, and that truth must be understood as the adequacy of the thing and the divine intellect. Nietzsche's understanding of pure truth thus looks back to the theocentric understanding of truth that once gave human discourse its measure in God's creative word, which is nothing other than the thing in itself understood as a *noumenon*, as a term that relates it to the divine *nous*. "*Omne ens est verum.*" Given such an understanding of "the pure truth," it is indeed denied to us finite knowers, as Kant knew and as Thomas Aquinas may have insisted, challenging Siger.

To pure truth so understood Nietzsche opposes an anthropocentric understanding of truth.

> This creator [of language] only designates the relations of things to men, and for expressing these relations he lays hold of the boldest metaphors. To begin with, a nerve stimulus is transferred into an image: first metaphor. The image, in turn, is imitated in a sound: second metaphor. And each time there is a complete overleaping of one sphere right into the middle of an entirely new and different one. (Nietzsche 1979, 82)

But that anthropocentric understanding is itself unstable in that language is discussed as a human creation, which presupposes a reality that transcends language. But to think that creation we have to rely on language, and are thus caught in the web of metaphors. There is thus a sense in which reality can be said to transcend language, even though, if it is to be for us at all, reality has to be mediated by language, which in this sense can be said to transcend reality.

Nietzsche's first metaphor refers to a natural process in which language does not figure, while his second metaphor speaks of the origin of language. What matters to me here, however, is not Nietzsche's metaphorical use of the term "metaphor," but something else: Nietzsche speaks of a nerve stimulus that is translated in a way that remains obscure to us into an image; equally obscure is the way the image is said to be imitated by a sound. To just this obscurity Nietzsche wants to call our attention:

> One can imagine a man who is totally deaf and has never had a sensation of sound and music. Perhaps such a person will gaze with astonishment at Chladni's sound figures; perhaps he will discover their causes in the vibrations of the string and will swear that he must know what men mean by "sound." It is this way with all of us concerning language; we believe that we know something about the things themselves, when we speak of trees, colors, snow, and flowers; and yet we possess nothing but metaphors for things—metaphors which correspond in no way to the original entities. In the same way that the sound appears as sand figure, so the mysterious X of the thing in itself first appear as a nerve stimulus, then as an image, and finally as a sound. (ibid., 82–83)

But science can explain the appearance of the sand figure. And if the appearance of the thing in itself, first as a nerve stimulus, then as an image, and finally as a sound should be thought "in the same way," does this not suggest that we should replace the mysterious X of the thing itself with some object in "the world discovered (and yet to be discovered) by science"?

Nietzsche invites that move even as he resists it. The world of science, too, is said by Nietzsche to be dependent on our reason's mode of operation, that is to say, it too is ruled by an "inescapable framework illusion."

All that conformity to law, which impresses us so much in the movement of the stars and in chemical processes, coincides at bottom with those properties which we bring to things. Thus it is we who impress ourselves in this way. In conjunction with this it of course follows that the artistic process of metaphor formation with which every sensation begins in us already presupposes these forms and thus occurs within them. The only way in which the possibility of subsequently constructing a new conceptual edifice from metaphors themselves can be explained is by the firm persistence of these original forms. That is to say, this conceptual edifice is an imitation of temporal, spatial, and numerical relationships in the domain of metaphor. (ibid., 88)

Nietzsche here accepts something very much like the Kantian a priori, which is said to be presupposed by all metaphor formation. Science, too, is thus said to be concerned with appearances that are essentially for us, never with the things in themselves. Thus science cannot claim truth understood as the identity of thought and thing in itself. The truth it pursues

is a thoroughly anthropomorphic truth which contains not a single point which would be "true in itself" or really and universally valid apart from man. . . . Similar to the way in which astrologers considered the stars to be in man's service and connected with this happiness and sorrow, such an investigator considers the entire universe as the infinitely fractured echo of one original sound—man; the entire universe as the infinitely multiplied copy of one original picture—man. His method is to treat man as the measure of all things. (ibid., 86)

Nietzsche is well aware that such an idealism conflicts with our faith in science, faith that we daily affirm in our everyday behavior.

Every person who is familiar with such considerations has no doubt felt a deep mistrust of all idealism of this sort just as often as he has quite clearly convinced himself of the eternal consistency, omnipresence, and infallibility of the laws of nature. He has concluded that so far as we can penetrate here—from the telescopic heights to the microscopic depths—everything is secure, complete, infinite, regular, and without any gaps. Science will be able to dig successfully in this shaft forever, and all the things that are discovered will harmonize with and not contradict each other. How little does this resemble a product of the imagination. (ibid., 87)

To be sure Nietzsche immediately counters this remark, which would seem to give science all that it might possibly ask for, with an observation that seems to call what has just been asserted into question:

Against this, the following must be said: if each of us had a different kind of sense perception—if we could only perceive things now as a bird, now as a worm, now as a plant, or if one of us saw a stimulus as red, another as blue, while a third even read the same stimulus as a sound—then no one would speak of such a regularity of nature, rather nature would be grasped only as a creation which is subjective in the highest degree. (ibid.)

But if each of us were locked in his or her own subjective world, there would be no language and thus even this thought experiment would be impossible. That thought experiment once again presupposes an objective nature that different subjects are here imagined to perceive in such different ways that thoughts of such a nature could not even arise. It is therefore not surprising that Nietzsche should return to a position that seems very much in accord with what Kant has to say:

> But everything marvelous about the laws of nature, everything that quite aston-ishes us therein and seems to demand our explanation, everything that might lead us to distrust idealism: all this is completely and solely contained within the mathematical strictness and inviolability of our representations of time and space. But we produce these representations in and from ourselves with the same necessity with which the spider spins. If we are forced to comprehend all things only under these forms, then it ceases to be amazing that in all things we comprehend nothing but these forms. For they must all bear within themselves the laws of number, and it is precisely number which is most astonishing in things. (ibid., 87–88)

To repeat, we cannot but presuppose a world of objects spread out in space and time and understand whatever we experience as an appearance of that world. We can thus relate the way things appear to us first of all and most of the time, mediated by our senses and by our language, and that is to say also by history, to what science has discovered or will discover to be true about nature. Truth now comes to mean "the adequation of the objects discovered or still to be discovered by science and our understanding." Given such an understanding of truth, there is a sense in which our first-person awareness of our life-world can be considered a web of lies, even if, from the perspec-tive of our life-world, the world of science is, as McDermott puts it, "bizarre and alien."

But why does Nietzsche call the description of the world on which science is laboring a lie—a higher order lie, perhaps, but still a lie? Why appeal to things in themselves and invoke an understanding of truth that, while it could make sense to a Thomas Aquinas, lost its foundation with the death of God? Nietzsche's description of science gives us a hint:

> We have seen how it is originally *language* which works on the construction of concepts, a labor taken over in later ages by *science*. Just as the bee simultaneously

constructs cells and fills them with honey, so science works unceasingly on this
great columbarium of concepts, the graveyard of perceptions. (ibid., 88)

The analogy that compares cells filled with honey with a columbarium
demands consideration: science replaces honey with ashes. The metaphor
speaks to the nihilism that shadows science. To banish the specter of nihilism we have to return from the third-person perspective of the scientist to
the first-person perspective of the actor who knows about his responsibility
to others. The pursuit of truth, the desire to grasp things as they really are,
turns its back on life. From a first-person point of view that pursuit may not
be allowed to circumscribe our understanding of reality, a point that McDermott is prepared to grant. But that means, to preserve a sense that our life has
significance we have to lie, have to insist on the absolute truth of inescapable
framework illusions that our science forces us to judge false.

THE ANTINOMY OF BEING

Nietzsche calls that judgment into question by challenging what McDermott
calls Neurath's principle. That principle, Nietzsche might have insisted, rests
itself on an IFI of a higher order. The transcendental idealism of Kant and
Schopenhauer is credited by Nietzsche with having demonstrated this (Nietzsche 1967, 112).

Kant offered his antinomies as proof. But since McDermott refers us to *Being and Time*, let me offer instead what I call the antinomy of Being, as it sur-
faces in that text in Heidegger's attempt to think the ontological difference, the
difference between beings and Being, the latter referring, in a way that recalls
Berkeley's "*esse est percipi*," to the way beings present themselves to human
beings. So understood, Being is constitutive of and therefore transcends beings.
Beings can present themselves only to beings such as we are, conscious, embodied and dwelling in language, open to a world in which beings have to take
their place and present themselves if they are "to be" at all. That world could
not be without human beings. That holds also, indeed especially of the world
constructed by science. The bizarre and alien world revealed to us by physics is
a human construct, supported by reason and experience. Read in this way *Being
and Time* belongs with the tradition of transcendental idealism.

But Heidegger qualifies this when he speaks in § 43 of *Being and Time* of
the dependence of Being, *but not of beings*, of reality, *but not of the real*, on
care, in other words, on the always understanding and caring being of human
beings.[11] There is therefore a sense in which beings and the real can be said
to transcend that Being which is said to be relative to human being. To be

sure, these beings could not "be" in the above sense without human beings. Only human consciousness provides the open space that allows things to be perceived, understood, and cared for. That space is a presupposition of the accessibility of things, of their Being. But this is not to say that we in any sense create these beings. Our experience of the reality of the real is thus an experience of beings as transcending Being. The battle between idealism and realism has no resolution. It is itself an expression of the antinomy of Being. Two senses of Being here clash: the first transcendental sense makes Being dependent on human beings, while the second transcendent understands Being as the ground of our historical being and thus also of Being understood transcendentally. But any attempt to conceptually lay hold of that ground, as materialism attempts to do, must inevitably fail in that it loses sight of the transcendence of reality and substitutes for it a humanly constructed reality. Whenever it attempts to do so, for instance by attempting to prove Neurath's principle, our thinking bumps against the limits of language and logic. And yet we experience this transcendent reality which eludes the reach of our concepts whenever we experience the reality of the real, for instance when we recognize another person as a person. Those critics of Siger who insisted that human science may not claim to have seized *the* truth about nature were right. Reason and reality are not commensurable. A theory of double truth suggests itself only when we insist on their commensurability and then have to confront the way our conscience protests.

NOTES

1. See, especially, J. G. Fichte's *The Vocation of Man* (1800/1956).
2. Friedrich Nietzsche, "On Truth and Lie in a Nonmoral Sense" (1873). In *Philosophy and Truth. Selections from Nietzsche's Notebooks of the early 1870's*, trans. and ed. by Daniel Breazeale, 79–91. Atlantic Highlands: Humanities Press, 1979.
3. See Gilson's *History of Christian Philosophy in the Middle Ages* (1955), 219.
4. Such as David of Dinant, Amaury of Bene, and a certain Mauritius of Spain, of whom we know next to nothing: Gilson 1955, 244.
5. Including some mistakenly thought to be by him, such as the *De causis, De plantis, De differentia spiritus et animae*. See Heer 1953, 162.
6. See Hyman and Walsh 1973, 450ff. (on Siger of Brabant) and 463ff. (on Thomas Aquinas).
7. Cf. Harries, *Infinity and Perspective*, Cambridge, Mass.: MIT, 2001, 309–317; *Art Matters: A Critical Commentary on Heidegger's "The Origin of the Work of Art"* (New York, Heidelberg: Springer, 2009), 125–138.
8. F. Nietzsche, *Beyond Good and Evil* (1886). See *Jenseits von Gut und Böse*, I, 12. *Sämtliche Werke: Kritische Studienausgabe*, ed. by G. Colli und M. Montinari.

(Munich/Berlin/New York: Deutscher Taschenbuch Verlag/de Gruyter 1980). Vol. 5, 117.

9. F. Nietzsche, *Genealogy of Morals* (1887), III, 25. See *Kritische Studienausgabe*, vol. 5, 404.

10. Thomas Aquinas, *Quaestiones disputatae de veritate*, qu. 1 art. 1. See Martin Heidegger, "Einführung in die phänomenologische Forschung," (WS 1923/24), G17: 162–194.

11. Martin Heidegger, *Being and Time*, trans. by John Macquarrie and Edward Robinson (New York: Harper and Row 1962), 255 (G2: 281/212).

REFERENCES

Aquinas, Thomas. 1964. *Quaestiones disputatae de veritate*. Rome: Marietti.

Averroes. 1973. "The Decisive Treatise Determining the Nature of the Connection Between Religon and Philosophy." In *Philosophy in the Middle Ages*, ed. by Arthur Hyman and James J. Walsh, 287–306. Indianapolis: Hackett.

"Condemnation of 219 Propositions" (of 1277). 1973. In *Philosophy in the Middle Ages*, ed. by Arthur Hyman and James J. Walsh, 542–549. Indianapolis: Hackett.

Fichte, Johann Gottlieb. 1800. *Die Bestimmung des Menschen*. Berlin. Repr. in *Werke*, vol. I/6, 189–309. Stuttgart: Frommann-Holzboog, 1981. Eng. ed.: *The Vocation of Man*, ed. and intro. by Roderick M. Chisholm. New York: Liberal Arts Press, 1956.

Gilson, Etienne. 1955. *History of Christian Philosophy in the Middle Ages*. New York: Random House.

Harries, Karsten. 2001. *Infinity and Perspective*. Cambridge, Mass.: MIT.

————. 2009. *Art Matters: A Critical Commentary on Heidegger's "The Origin of the Work of Art."* New York, Heidelberg: Springer.

Heer, Friedrich. 1953. *Europäische Geistesgeschichte*. Stuttgart: Kohlhammer.

Heidegger, Martin. 1962. *Being and Time*, trans. by John Macquarrie and Edward Robinson. New York: Harper and Row. (Orig. in German: *Sein und Zeit*, of 1927: *Gesamtausgabe*, vol. 2, Frankfurt: Klostermann 1977).

————. 1994. "Einführung in die phänomenologische Forschung," (WS 1923/24). In Heidegger, Martin. *Gesamtausgabe*, vol. 17, 162–194. Frankfurt: Klostermann.

Hyman, Arthur, and James J. Walsh, eds. 1973. *Philosophy in the Middle Ages*. Indianapolis: Hackett.

Kierkegaard, Søren. 1974. *Concluding Unscientific Postscript*. Trans. by David F. Swenson and Walter Lowrie. Princeton: Princeton University Press.

Mackie, John L. 1977. *Ethics, Inventing Right and Wrong*. Harmondsworth: Penguin Books.

McDermott, Drew. 2009. "How Moral Absolutism Can Be True and False at the Same Time; Or: Non-Phenomenological Existentialism." Draft.

Nietzsche, Friedrich. 1967. *"The Birth of Tragedy" and "The Case of Wagner."* Trans. by Walter Kaufmann. New York: Vintage.

————. 1979. "On Truth and Lie in a Nonmoral Sense" (1873). In *Philosophy and Truth. Selections from Nietzsche's Notebooks of the Early 1870's,* trans. and ed. by Daniel Breazeale, 79–91. Atlantic Highlands: Humanities Press.

Siger of Brabant. 1973. "Question on the Eternity of the World." In *Philosophy in the Middle Ages*, edited by Arthur Hyman and James J. Walsh, 453–462. Indianapolis: Hackett.

Van Steenberghen, Fernand. 1980. *Thomas Aquinas and Radical Aristotelianism.* Washington: Catholic University of America Press.

Chapter Twelve

Philosophia sine qua non

John Rawls's Transcendental-Political Reflections

Sebastian Lalla

Among John Rawls's achievements, albeit an unintended one, is the fact that he lived long enough to virtually write his own secondary literature. With his book *Justice as Fairness* he takes up a discussion that had continued for nearly three decades and throughout various disciplines, reexamining the basic ideas of his *A Theory of Justice*. He responds here to various criticisms of his political and philosophical positions by offering a *restatement*. Surprisingly, despite the diversity of objections they produce, Rawls's critics show a remarkable consensus with regard to one central aspect of his views. Rawls's theory is standardly situated within the liberal tradition of theories of the state, a tradition that determines the rights and duties of those in power and those subject to them as if they were based on *contract*. Located on an imaginary line of progress from Hobbes via Rousseau to Kant and the liberal economists and politicians of the twentieth century, Rawls's attempt is viewed as a form of social theory in which it is taken to be the foremost task of the state, almost its raison d'être, to disappear into the rationally legitimated functional structure of its own institutions. This consensus is surprising because Rawls himself refers to his work as a separate development, abstracted from contractual theory: "My aim is to present a conception of justice which generalizes and carries to a higher level of abstraction the familiar theory of the social contract" (Rawls 1971, 19).

Nonetheless, this form of abstraction has so far attracted little interest in a discussion of Rawls's theses. Moreover, any specification of what he might have meant by a further development seems to be entirely absent in this debate. Taking his claim to a "higher level of abstraction" seriously does not automatically imply that central aspects of contractarianism should also be retained. In order to understand Rawls's main views on the particular relevance of his own theory vis-à-vis traditional contractual theories, we therefore need to clarify

227

what is involved in the transformational process of achieving a higher level of abstraction. At the core here is a sketch of a contract that—on Rawls's own account—cannot be taken literally, but is merely analogous to a state contract.

Rawls' own view of the contract, in which the liberty of the State is understood in terms of freedom from the State, appears to be motivated primarily by individualist idealism—in contrast both to utilitarian considerations based on economic actuality and to communitarian conditions of political reality. In the following, I should like to concentrate on three aspects of his work leading to the claim that Rawls's *A Theory of Justice* is not primarily a practical guidebook for the formation of a polity but a transcendental-political instantiation of idealist metaphysics. First, we need to discuss the argumentative role of the "Original Position" in Rawls's theory—the hypothetical state of affairs that contractarian theory envisages as "before" the contract between people and government is made. Subsequently, we shall explore the issue in what sense Rawls's conception should be called transcendental-political. Finally, we shall make an attempt based on this interpretation to find an answer to the question in how far Rawls's theory of "justice *a priori*" implies a dissolution between history and politics.

WHY THE ORIGINAL POSITION IS NOT A CLASSICAL CONTRACTUALIST MODEL

The major problem with interpreting political theory in terms of practical application lies in the proneness to error that this type of interpretation has, and its own inability to eliminate this source of confusion. This becomes apparent when we compare the original claim in Rawls's theory with its implementation. It is fairly clear that barely any noteworthy changes in the real-world political landscape have actually occurred as a result of any impact of *A Theory of Justice* on the reorganization or redrafting of actual political structures; it is hard to claim that the world has become more just in substantial terms (rather than in limited areas only) over the past twenty years.

This observation appears to contradict Rawls's own claim that his theory can provide an account of principles by which a polity can make itself just. It would follow from this claim that every political community ought to be anxious for access to such highly general principles, to use them to compensate for political deficits in relation to justice. If it is accepted that Rawls's claims can be taken to be generally valid and to have no alternative, then a fortiori it is by no means clear why putting these same principles into practice keeps failing so continuously. Conversely: if his system is convincing and appropriate, why does no one adhere to it in practice?

There is an obvious possible answer here; however, it is ultimately unconvincing simply to argue that selfishness and extreme deformations of power structures to the benefit of small numbers of individuals are responsible for obstructing or undermining the practical implementation of the kind of polity Rawls intends. This is because one of Rawls's crucial methods, perhaps his most decisive method, is to base his position on a rational legitimation of his principles—which should not be understood as intellectualism, since this would imply that only especially intelligent persons were capable of understanding political justice; instead it needs to be interpreted anthropologically. On Rawls's view, since human existence is intrinsically social, it is connected with a kind of rationality such that understanding it *itself* obliges us to promote a transformation of real conditions of living in the direction of greater justice.

This principle might appear Platonist, insofar as it seems to suggest that knowledge of the Good should by itself be productive of the good. However, a closer examination of the status of the Original Position will reveal that the basis of the Good itself is not constituted by the pragmatics of persons acting ethically, but by the unconditional status of rational rightness. According to Rawls, knowledge of the relation between the Right and the Good is not a mutual implication (as it is with Plato) but recognition of the transcendental identity of each. This will become clearer below.

Rawls's quest for the basic principles of justice entails a rejection of positions that regard "justice" itself as so fundamental that it does not permit further justification. For Rawls it is crucial that raising the problem of the epistemological and legitimizing structures of its capacity for practical attainment does not mean that justice itself is being put into question from a metaphysical standpoint. No interpretation of his work that disregards this conviction can be accurate, and without it his views on the identity of the Right and the Good cannot be understood adequately either.

Such a position emphasizes two features: first, the principles fundamental to justice must be general to the extent that everybody can understand them and choose to opt for them. Second, precisely due to their generality they must be so intensely value-laden that their acceptance could only be put into question by virtue of additional and strongly justificatory argumentative efforts. Quintessentially, this does not portray human nature as evil but as basically good—to the extent that it is rationally informed. The Rawlesian coincidence of the Good and the Rational is not a fortunate and exceptional case of Hegelian optimism, rather it takes a position on unspoiled human nature that is chiefly inspired by Kant (although Kant himself spoke of fundamental deficiency or "hole" in human nature). The Original Position also—contrary to most interpretations of Rawls—refers to an original state of humanity;

though not, of course, in a temporal sense in which present-day civilization is seen as having evolved from an original pre-historical state. Rather, this is an *essential* original state in which the coincidence of the Good and the Rational can count as given.

The failure of Rawls's conception of justice under real practical conditions cannot be explicated as the perversion of an illusion which is incapable of being put into practice, even though it is both based on the intrinsically noble character of human beings and also takes individual cases of evil into account. Historical reality is in fact an insufficient indicator of the validity of Rawls's theory of justice, because the commensurability of historical reality and the Real can only be claimed for the area of practice, not for that of theory—with which Rawls is actually dealing. In other words, the truth of theory cannot be falsified by practice—even though real conditions might suggest that they can. The reason why this is the case in respect of Rawls (and why it is not a universalizable phenomenon) becomes clearer if we look more closely at the structure and content of the Original Position.

Rawls's description of the Original Position is couched in terms of a hypothesis, but it is essential for his entire theory. It is debatable whether or not other authors of theories of sociopolitical development considered their positions to refer to the empirical world: whether Hobbes, for instance, intended a war of all against all to be regarded as a historical or pre-historical fact. This is clearly not the case with Rawls. His conception of the Original Position is decidedly a-historical and hypothetical. Not only is it the case that it never occurred in reality; it is conceptually impossible that the Original Position could ever exist. How, then, should the Original Position be understood, since it is intended as more than a mere thought experiment? The obligatory character of its contents means that it cannot share the same hypothetical status with the theory in its entirety. Nonetheless, it is still possible for it to be less than a factual description of a real historical process.

The point of designating the Original Position is the attempt to discover principles of justice that are independent of the contingent, actually existing order of societal facts. However, why should facticity be an insufficient foundation for detecting such principles? One might try, for instance, to proceed via the natural sciences by describing an evolutionary-biological scheme of morality in which unchanging features of nature also provide constants for the formation of society and its moral restrictions; these might include, for instance, an evaluative criterion of justice. Rawls rejects such a determination of justice by means of premises mirroring the structure of the given, since no debate can coherently be held about a principle which is beyond the consensus of those who must judge the validity of its determination. Since nobody is in a position to check the correctness of the assumption in question, the argumentative status of referring to a natural component of justice cannot be treated differently from, say, a religious justification referring to the authority of divine natural law. A natural component would thus serve the purpose of finding principles of justice rather poorly. Without accepting a wider framework of beliefs to make plausible any claim of unconditionality, the authenticity of whatever is posited as having the authority of the law could only have a decisionist status; it would be incapable of being *demonstrated* at all.

For Rawls, the essential function of the Original Position is to mediate between general principles and individuals, thinking and acting morally, who must adopt these principles for themselves. The notion of the free individual, capable of making his or her own decisions in respect of the conditions of a just society, is effectively axiomatic and cannot be justified further. This does not conflict with Rawls's view that there are no moral facts that are unchangeably true, but that there do exist a set of principles which individuals are free to choose. This does not mean at all that there are no true moral conditions; however, human beings lack full knowledge of them. Yet a supernatural legitimation of certain positions is incompatible with the formal condition of keeping the whole procedure fair and free. Anything that causes predispositions in decision-making undermines the conditions needed for impartial choice. Hence Rawls emphasizes the so-called Veil of Ignorance that acts like a reduction filter, deleting from the context all individually relevant determinants of the decision process. Hence, reasonable, autonomous persons attempting to determine principles of justice (Rawls differentiates between this and rational, perfected autonomy; see below) are for the most part ignorant as to the practical incorporation of these principles in an existent, spatio-temporal but not equally determinable world.

This relates in particular to knowledge of personal abilities (bodily strength, intelligence, emotionality), as well as social status dependent on wealth and societal hierarchy. Without abstracting from the facticity of reasonableness entirely—which must exist if the act of choice is to be performed meaningfully—Rawls constructs it in such an abstract, formal way that every individualized aspect is conceptually excluded. A priori, as it were, anyone who puts him- or herself in the Original Position must be committed to minimal conditions in terms of which divergent conceptions of justice can be set out and adjusted to each other. According to Rawls, it is always possible to put oneself in the Original Position, precisely because it is not real but is an imaginary construct of the judicative imagination, complementary in function to the evaluation of facts.

There are, in Rawls's view, two principles to which everybody in the Original Position would consent and which would therefore be chosen as a common basis for ideas of justice. These are the principle of equality and the principle of inequality legitimate under particular circumstances. The first principle states that everyone should enjoy the most comprehensive system of fundamental freedoms compatible with the same system for everybody else. This type of freedom can only be posited as universally valid under the condition that a freedom granted to particular groups or individuals on no account puts any other group at a disadvantage. The second principle states that cases of injustice can only be tolerated if the resulting disparity in distribution of goods ("goods" understood in a very broad sense) operates in favor of the least privileged group of society. Disparity serving the worst-off in society rather than the best-off is the only way in which deviation from the equality implied in the first principle can be permitted. This is the only exception that may be made from the system of equal freedoms: Rawls's lexical order of specifications of the principles of justice stipulates that violations of higher-order principles cannot be sanctioned by referring to the value-ladenness of lower-order ones.

At first glance, comparison with models of traditional contractualism does not seem to be very instructive. Consequently, Rawls can rightly claim to be offering an abstraction from social contract theory. On closer inspection, however, two important issues come to the fore. One is the problem of legitimating the choice of these principles—(formality rather than materiality) and the other is the question of the degree of authentication regarding the universalizability of the personal choices of principles made by individuals (political solipsism). As far as the second problem is concerned, it is worth keeping in mind that in classical social contract theory, mutually binding treaties were discussed as having been made in order to put to an end an original state which threatened human beings' security. The political conceptions of Hobbes and Rousseau, for instance, which Rawls mentions, are not necessarily descriptions of actual historical conditions. Yet they function according to a discernible pattern, of which Hobbes's argumentation provides an example. The despotic freedom of individuals and its inherent threatening potential can be channeled when the claim to individual sovereignty is abandoned, or at least restricted, in favor of a centrally-instituted protective power. State structures and the representative exercise of power replace untrammeled individual freedom; humans might in theory benefit from such freedom but, de facto, due to human frailty, they are incapable of profiting from it really comprehensively, constrained by fear for their own lives.

This constellation—surrendering power in exchange for security—can only work successfully provided that two conditions are fulfilled. First, the contracting parties must abide by the agreement. Second, devolving sovereignty to a designated decision-maker may not be prohibited by special requirements of the contract. While the latter aspect is of secondary importance for conceptualizing the Original Position, the first proviso is of focal importance. It directly concerns the structure of the contract itself, since it becomes operative in the transition from a no-longer-factual (possibly per se hypothetical) situation to a historically identifiable, determinate, political-societal civilization.

For Rawls, the question who should take part in the choice of determining principles of justice by no means opens the doors of the Original Position to a democratic ballot about normative axioms. Ultimately, the Ought implied in the validity of principles is what decisions concerning these principles are about. However, it cannot be a matter of balloting because the Right, whose priority over the Good is clear here, cannot and must not be bought at the price of relinquishing Truth. Hence, majorities cannot decide that a particular principle of justice should be valid when it may in fact be intrinsically insufficient to serve as such a principle. What looks at first sight like a relapse into a metaphysical account of the Original Position is actually its specification as conjoining the a priori-valency of the Good and the Right. Their factual non-identity within concrete societies is only relevant for Rawls insofar as their identity constitutive of the Original Position is maintained there; or, putting it more precisely, insofar as their identity is maintained on the basis of the axiomatic character of the un-justifiability of the Right as such.

From an epistemological point of view, a coincidence of the Good and the Right in the Original Position can only be claimed provided that normative aspects of possibilities of putting justice into practice can be cognized as such, not insofar as they are put into practice due to knowledge of the Right, but because the structures of our cognitive faculties themselves are such that they are informed by a parallelism of Truth as the Good in the form of the Right. Rawls's concept of rationality is of crucial importance here, but by mentioning "rationality," it seems prima facie, he is stressing only the end-oriented character of actions. In *A Theory of Justice*, Rawls generally understands rationality in a manner compatible with an economist's efficiency- and effectiveness-oriented interpretation: he takes into account only choosing the most suitable means for pursuing any goals in question. *A Theory of Justice* does not inquire how this kind of rationality should be regarded in an anthropological context or whether there exist other forms of rationality (and if so, which). However, the terms of the model of the Original Position already show that the explicitly reductionionist notion of rationality in *A Theory of Justice* remains underdetermined. Rawls himself was aware of this; his concept of understanding is relevant here. Only after *A Theory of Justice* does Rawls explicitly differentiate between understanding and reason, particularly in his essays "Kantian Constructivism in Moral Theory" and "Justice as Fairness: Political Not Metaphysical." Following Kant, this position subordinates reason (rationality) to understanding, which is in a nonempirical sense ultimately responsible for maintaining the normative character of the axioms involved in Original Position thought. In other words: the fact that the Right is understood as conjoined with the Good does not merely depend on the activity of reason, which can only find occasional, extrinsic congruences here. First and foremost, it depends on the understanding as an authority of absolute autonomy, in other words an authority with which we do not only think through the hypothetical Original Position but due to it we should also build a concrete society according to an ideal of freedom which presupposes the identity of the Rational and the Good, an identity which cannot be legitimated as such on merely empirical grounds.

Despite his respect for Kant, Rawls's model of the Original Position (*pars pro toto* for *A Theory of Justice*) can scarcely be understood without its noticeable indebtedness to Hegel. This applies to the declaredly non-metaphysical function of the principles of justice, such as providing the basis for a concept of society in which free individuals can express self-respect by respecting others. Consequently, it applies to the political dimension as such, which not only connects but also reconciles the universal with the individual. Admittedly, Rawls does not comment on this indebtedness in any detail—and the question whether his theory is more Kantian or more Hegelian is not of central concern here. It is more crucial that, within the process of decision-making involved in the choice of principles of justice, the aspect of normativity already transcends the communicative and intersubjective level of choice. This axiological character of the principles of justice does not result from consensual recognition, nor can it be inferred from the fact that the principles in question would be chosen (even though Rawls sometimes seems to suggest this). It is clearly not a position extrapolated from his theory but is rather part of its metaphysical framework that our understanding, so to speak as authority of highest rank as well as the authority to adjudicate rank, guarantees that the credit on our anthropological deficit of the Good can be repaid, and hence that his theory can take it for granted that people will not ask the question whether or not questions concerning the meaning of legitimacy are justified themselves, and will not try to define the value of value.

Since Rawls cannot adduce metaphysical implications for the validity of his theory unless he intends to jeopardize their universalizability, the structure of the theory of justice is secured in two respects, as it were, by the status of the individual that determines the principles of justice. Contrary to conventional contractualist conceptions of an original state, in which two parties form a contract in which—in theory though not in practice—every individual in the state thus constituted participates, approval of the principles of justice is an act, according to Rawls, which must be performed, even if no one else performs it. In other words, it is irrelevant for the *choice* of principles of justice whether or not they are generally accepted in reality, as long as they are understood as having their basis in a binding, optimal choice intrinsically authorized and legitimated by reason.

The only person able to say anything about the conditions and expectations connected with the Original Position and subsequent conceptions of justice is the individual who—under the restrictions imposed by the veil of ignorance—places him- or herself in the Original Position. In this position, s/he must be impartial as regards the interests of other individuals, provided that these interests are particular and not universalizable a priori. Rawls is here describing a kind of egotism that treats itself as the only really existing agent, and also as encapsulating the entire social environment. The difference to classical conceptions of contractualism made by Rawls's theory is not only that the former include varieties depending on representation based on a general will, but also that *A Theory of Justice,* contrary to utilitarian cost-benefit analysis, for example, must filter out the existence of others, given that their real competition presupposes different individuals as absolute real entities. The individual who is choosing principles of justice is not representative of others who are not making their own choices (as would be the case if someone born into a political system formed after a supposedly original contract, "acknowledged" it by virtue of his own birth), because everybody is capable of entering the Original Position at any time. The individual concerned here *is* all the others all alone, because s/he cannot assume that anybody else would reach different conclusions in a given situation (political solipsism).

The existence of other people is not irrelevant in concrete reality, since any political community depends on coexistence; yet it is irrelevant with regard to the structures of legitimation. The determination of a principle of justice which is only capable of being made as the best possible choice, raises the subjectivity of the choice itself to the universality of a permanently existing determination of the Good. This is not in the sense in which objectivity would serve as a benchmark for political structuring, but in the sense in which universality and subjectivity coincide. Hence, political solipsism is primarily based on the assumption that the representation of others is to be seen in terms of the presence of oneself. The idea of representative replacement is dissolved into the schema of a renewed determination, a restitution of the primordial (the individual) as such and, therefore, as all other individuals too. Since it is no longer imaginable under such conditions that alternative decisions might be taken with equal responsibility, the actual plurality of morally independent alternative decisions collapses into the real singularity of an (ontologically) possible determining decision that is ethically real.

At this point it becomes clear how the presumed merging of the Good itself with rational procedures does not represent an illegitimate premise but instead forms the condition of the possibility of coming to a decision at all as to which principles should be chosen. Given the under-determination of sufficient and practically relevant information according to which someone might appropriately assess his or her own self and position, and given the demand of the unconditional imperative to choose the Just in a justified way, the only way forward is to guarantee the reliability of whatever is chosen via the legitimation of its formal unchangeability. Since the components of the Good and the Rational must apply to everybody equally—and since, therefore, they are excluded from the decision-making process because they are transcendentally constitutive of human rationality—in Rawls's theory they can function as conditions for any possible choice. The actual determination of the principles of justice can abstain from normative determination *materialiter* because it has been made *formaliter*. As it were without being ethical, the conception of the Original Position represents the form of morality itself. Consequently, it also refers directly to the topic of a transcendental-political theory, its connections with the problem of its practical relevance and the a priori validity of political assumptions.

WHY PRACTICE—REALITY—IS OF NO IMPORTANCE FOR RAWLS'S THEORY OF JUSTICE

From a Kantian transcendental point of view the function of principles of justice does not appear to be to provide concrete rules of conduct from the start. Its function consists in delineating what might become an expression of deliberations within society concerning justice as a basis of any human society. However, the question arises here to what extent Rawls's conception is of practical relevance, since the determination of principles of justice refers to the universality of an unspecific kind of social order where only the possibility of its realization is envisaged for the analysis of politics. Prima facie, the major achievement of Rawls's theory seems to be in delineating the foundations for the social relations which can ground society—but this account of his work is not compatible with the fact that its actual merits lie in a very formal model that offers no explicit instructions as to how political units should behave in conflict situations. Rawls certainly develops ideas concerning problems such as the distribution of wealth, civil disobedience or the critique of utilitarianism. These areas, however, remain on a level of abstraction which is to be understood almost exclusively in terms of the principles of justice themselves: Rawls precisely does not explain how a particular situation should be assessed or solved, but how it should be perceived, in the first place, under the conditions of justice of the Original Position. It is far from obvious in *A Theory of Justice* what follows concretely if the distribution of important goods, for example, does not correspond to the idealized criterion of a rule in the Original Position but which was never effective in reality. Rawls's theory is a *theory*, not a *practice* of justice. Thus it may be objected to Rawls's approach that it is too strongly focused on an ideal of societal conditions that entirely ignores the corruption of actual life. Moreover, long-term perspectives, for instance, are ignored almost entirely—such as sustainability, international law or the problem of the legitimate implementation of revolutionary concepts in cases where the principles of justice have failed. In fact, Rawls does not consider even the bare possibility of their failure. The topics with which he deals systematically are precisely not paradigms of empirical social research.

However, the formal character of his principles of justice raises even more serious issues than these material omissions as far as the relevance of Rawls's theory for practice is concerned. They are formulated in such a way that no definite construction may be inferred from them, even though they are presented as having a regulative, evaluative function. In order to apply to all possible concrete models of society, formal determinants of the Just must be unconstrained by particular conditions and hence independent of any connection to reality. What is valid in principle cannot be restricted by further principles. Delineating the fundamental principles of justice thus forms a kind of semantically ultimate justification for the basis of a just political order. In spite of the fact that Rawls repeatedly emphasizes that he is not putting forward a metaphysical position, demands concerning the validity of nonmetaphysical political principles—here, for instituting principles of justice—cannot be justified other than metaphysically. To legitimate the intrinsic authority of justice by transcendentally relocating its authenticity is in effect to identify the structure of any possible capacity for political order with the metaphysical precondition that order itself can be connected with the contingency of human decision-making.

Whenever Rawls is able to assess some practical constellation in terms of its assessment in terms of justice—it is already apparent that the principles of the Original Position have less a constitutive than a regulative function as far as practical reality is concerned—everything that might claim to transcend theory remains vague. How any recognition that a society is not just might be gained other than by recourse to his principles can be inferred from Rawls's theory as little as can the question how such a situation might be changed. The fact that the principles of justice are compatible with many different constellations of practical, societal order cannot make clear which of these should ultimately be put into practice. The principles of justice are certainly constitutive; however, they are constitutive only for theory. In theoretical terms they not only justify the pattern of order by stipulating minimal requirements for just institutions, they also legitimate the process of justification itself. With the co-incidence of the Good and the Rational they set out a paradigm of ways in which theories of justice (theories, not practices) must be construed in order to claim consistently to represent truth. Even though he does not explicitly say so, Rawls's implicit metaphysics of rationality qua unmediated cipher of truth must claim that it is the only paradigm admissible both as a constitutive exemplar of metaphysical politics and as a political theory of society, since it is the only one that can be conceived without inherent contradiction.

The connection between the Just and the True claimed here appears to contradict Rawls's view that principles of justice are not "true" or "false" but only plausible, in the sense that they are chosen due to their force of conviction. The fact that they are preferred to others indicates, according to Rawls, that they are the right ones; consequently a society may use them to construct just institutions. He does not claim that this makes them "true" and therefore rules out alternatives. However, Rawls's reluctance to engage with a metaphysical foundation of the Just undermines his own theory: if only the best of all possible alternatives may be chosen—and everyone would accept this at any time because (under the conditions of the veil of ignorance) they acknowledge it as the most reasonable choice—then no other possibility could be imagined in which competing theories on principles of justice were conceivable. Rawls is therefore not talking about practical truth, here, in a sense relevant to a problem-oriented debate, but a transcendental truth. The fact that the aforementioned principles of justice are chosen is not a fact in an (empirical) world in which they would be chosen. For Rawls, foregoing the aspect of validity does not mean that principles of justice are not true; they are true in an a priori sense, because the conditions of the possibility of constituting a just political community are *eo ipso* conditions of the possibility of community. The term "transcendental-political" indicates that it follows from this model that the actual implementation of the Real, in other words the instantiation of particular political and societal affairs in practice, is possible because, as theoretically anticipated, it is already understood as "true." Yet this is not a judgment about actual facts but what makes such a judgement possible. Rawls's position here is idealist through and through— and his severest criticism of utilitarianism is not moral but concerns what it means to be a person. The independence and sovereignty of the individual making free choices can only be guaranteed when it is free from the arbitrary rule of others—however politically authorized; free a priori, in fact, for this is transcendentally constitutive of the concept of the individual and hence of humanity as such.

In application-oriented interpretations of *A Theory of Justice*, the relation between theory and practice turns out to be just as difficult as the concept of justice itself. While, in the process of determining principles of justice, the concept of justice itself was reduced to a methodically narrowed-down version of distributive justice in order to better portray the specifics of the Original Position, it was also justified transcendentally. Its material content, which might have allowed it to be placed in contrast to a nonmetaphysically motivated theory of the Right, was dissolved into the formal character of the process. In the end, Rawls's model specifies how principles can be considered just, but it does not discuss which specific institutions may operate on the basis of these principles in concrete cases and how they should actually proceed. In *A Theory of Justice* Rawls certainly provides repeated examples of ways in which institutions must be constructed in order that their conformity to principles of justice should be acknowledged: but these determinations are only recognizable as such from an a posteriori perspective. They do not constitute these institutions, they only indicate their level of moral authenticity. Practice is hence not the perfected end of the theory; it is merely a field of its application, for which Rawls has created a corrective instance at the most. Clearly, the real world does not appear to be just. Rawls's theory offers analytical tools for describing this more precisely, but no original insight into what should be changed in order to make the world more just. In a sense *A Theory of Justice* is an abstract version of an intuitionist approach which makes it unmistakeably clear how things should not be; it does not say how they ought to be; however, in the case of *A Theory of Justice* it is relatively undecided about what should not be the case, in comparison with how it ought to be. Yet this does not imply that this state of affairs actually should be the case nor how it could be put into practice. Rawls forgoes the connection with practice not only because of the universalizability of his theory, which is unable to take any *specific* practice into account, but also because of its entirely theoretical character, which makes it incompatible with practice as such.

Explaining this position is not easy, but a brief summary must suffice here. A transcendental approach intended to explain not only the conditions of its own possibility but also the conditions of the possibility of anything, can only conceive of itself as mode of representation by foregoing a delimitation of "possibility" as "potential actuality." "To be potentially actual" is no longer an option for characterizing the concept of "possibility." Consequently, practice, commonly understood as the real-world application of a theory, does not formally correspond to an actuality in terms of which possibility can also be called real.

This type of possibility is to be understood as the contingency of a self-contained, semantic perspective which functions as pure noncontradiction, never intended to be made actual. The situation of the Original Position is a-historical in so far as it is possible at any time, regardless of circumstance. Owing to its a-temporality it can never be actualized (in a manner of speaking, this is the categorical subjunctive). It is incorrect to ascribe to the theory of justice any particular corresponding practice, representing it as the real form into which the theory can be transformed. If such a real set of practices could be produced, the theory would still only be an anticipation of a real application, not its *Aufhebung* into a transcendental reality.

However, this interpretation does not condemn Rawls's conception to insignificance by attributing to it a purely self-referential detachment from the world, irrelevant for politics. Instead, we must revise our perception of the problem. The implementation of a theory we consider to be correct does not consist in the practice itself, but in the subsequent legitimation that can be offered for it. The capacity to indicate reality only implicitly and in anticipation is not a deficiency of the theory but its constitutive element. The way in which practice relates to reality cannot simply be read off from the theory as if it were a model of reality; the theory only describes what reality would be like *if* it were as it were ideally imagined. In this sense the idealist perspective does not recognize the empirical Real as such but regards the True as the Real; this is the transcendental character of a theory which is—like Rawls's—unconditional.

WHY THE THEORY OF JUSTICE ALSO
MEANS THE END OF HISTORY

The end of history is a *topos* which returned to debate after Francis Fukuyama's publication of this name. A mistaken account of Fukuyama's thesis was sometimes popularly received, diagnosing the end of history in terms of a (probably eschatological) repetition of events that have already taken place, to the exclusion of anything new. As in the case of Hegel's world-historical self-revelation of absolute spirit, Fukuyama in fact understood the end of history as an immanent stage characterized by the perfection of an intrinsic rationality. Such a stage does not negate historical events, although it does negate their significant development in terms of substantial content, in the sense that it is regarded as a direct or indirect instantiation of an ultimate state of freedom. Fukuyama understands western civilization, in the sense of its foundation in democratic order, as the value-oriented legitimation of a human community beyond which nothing better can be thought, because it offers the maximal development of the triad equality, liberty and justice. Ultimate justifications in political philosophy often fail due to historical developments. Fukuyama, in contrast, proposes a model that a priori excludes empirical reality as offering possible cases of falsification. The democratically authorized individuality of justice, in terms of the historical and rational self-representation of all possibilities of human personal responsibility and organizational capacity, renders absurd the quest for anything even better; it therefore cannot be replaced by any configuration not formally identical with it in the sense of essential conformation to the structure of the same optimal configuration.

Though Fukuyama's approach seems correct in this regard, it is appropriate here only to point out respects in which his approach may be read as a philosophical adaption of Rawls's own philosophy of history, using methodical parallels but differing methodological presuppositions. Conversely, the problem arises to what extent *A Theory of Justice* can claim to be a conception of an ultimately decisive (and metaphysical) philosophy of justice. The resulting question is immediately whether and in what sense Rawls also conceptualizes the end of history in the sense described here—namely as the end-point of any *constitutional* improvements in existing political systems understood as representing the quest for the perfect human society.

In this context, the clearest resemblance between these two theories is their treatment of a particular theoretical constellation (the consolidation of legitimizing justice on the one hand, the authentication of the perfection of a democratic and liberal free state on the other) as an inherently authorized prefiguration of the Real which is made necessary by an intrinsic, self-referential rationality that has no real alternative.

Both Rawls and Fukuyama are using an instrument of normative legitimacy that is independent of practical reflection and possible changes that might occur in reality. While the principles of justice mark the starting point for any possible rendering of human communality into the form of a society, Fukuyama's making absolute of liberal individuality is, so to speak, the final end of such a communal development. It would be too easy to understand these extreme positions merely as conceptual radicalizations pointing in opposite temporal directions, both regarding the authentic immanence of the Just as a criterion for a claim of exclusivity—in the first case for the past, in the second for the future.

Such a view would be seriously mistaken, because it misconceives what is more important for both philosophers than merely providing a political or moral assessment of whatever is possible by using explanatory tools for the description of society. In fact, both positions are more closely related than their systematic historical positioning might suggest. Both accord the Actual (*das Wirkliche*) priority over the Real (*das Reale*), merging in a mutually inclusive and anticipatory manner. It is not the Possible that is explored to its fundaments in Rawls's theory of justice (which is also the theory of liberal individualism that, although freed from a democratic form of justification, is nevertheless the foundation of democracy); it is the Actual that is interrogated, the totality of possibilities manifesting the immediate presence of the Transcendental. When Rawls understands his political principles as stabilizing the institutionalization of a just community, then this is true of every society at any time and irrespective of any particular historical constellation. In other words: history, which might enable, accompany or promote specific elements in a certain level of development of political ideas, is put aside even before it might be considered how to apply such a concept of securing justice in a historical context. Almost as if history had come to an end before it even begins, Rawls's identification of the Possible with the Actual (rather than the Real) is the immanent abolition of historicity under the aegis of rationality. The Original Position is hypothetical insofar as it is a theoretical concept with no historical location; insofar as it is simultaneously the condition of the possibility of a human society that legitimizes the Just, it also abrogates real history. Reconstructing the Actual as a hypothetical undertaking remains a real issue, even and specifically against the opposition of the Real. However, this understanding of the end of history does not mean (as it does not for Fukuyama) the end of historical development; it is rather its intrinsically inherent end after all options are exhausted. It is the Actual that remains.

A conception of the Right perfected due to its rational structure is a position that probably cannot be defended without having to posit its universal validity too. Rawls takes pains to point out repeatedly that his theory of justice is only one of several possible approaches. It specifically does not prescribe how a community must be arranged in reality. But this reservation can, if the premises of *A Theory of Justice* (namely that it determines mandatory principles of the Just) are taken seriously, only be understood as maintaining that several kinds of practical formation are admissible—while many are not.

The groundwork in particular, representing as it were the fundamental ontological skeleton of the Good, is predetermined in the figuration of the Just to the extent that Rawls's open continuation of what is socially mandatory cannot be understood in any other way than that it inevitably must acknowledge principles of justice. Culturally relativist or historically specific conditions of the Good, True and Just cannot be relevant here, since the transcendental justification of justice is not the basis for any particular justice but of the concept of justice itself. In Rawls's view, this concept is not negotiable in particular models of a political or moral community but is determined a priori insofar as it constitutes a formal identification of material principles for any possible (rationally justified) social system. In this regard, the reduction of the concept of justice to procedural equality is not hard to understand: Rawls cannot provide a determination that would go beyond it. If he did it, then since the equality in question is a form of self-legislation by the rational individual, this would mean that the autonomy of the morally responsible individual would also become the ultimate standard for this individual's potential denial of legitimation.

Thus *A Theory of Justice* implies the end of history in yet another perspective too, because it brings the subject of the Historical to the perfection of autonomous self-determination in its very self-constitution. To be located at the end of the Possible makes it impossible that the future could be organized in a fundamentally new and different way: the actuality of the Just (the Good) is explicated as inherently present in the structure of the cognition and will of the self qua subject of determination of the principles of justice, the self which acts as the condition of the possibility of real justice in society. However, the person individually present obtains the freedom to understand him- or herself as an authentic and legitimate source of justice. Here it becomes apparent why *A Theory of Justice* is a *philosophia sine qua non* in its constitution as a fundamental theory in philosophy: to forgo it would mean to lose the opportunity to determine individual freedom a priori. We might forgo it; it remains questionable whether reality, not to mention actuality, would thereby be improved.

ACKNOWLEDGMENT

The author wishes to thank Markus Woerner and Ricca Edmondson for translating this article.

REFERENCES

Fukuyama, Francis. 1992. *The End of History and the Last Man*. New York: Free Press.
Rawls, John. 1971. *A Theory of Justice*. Cambridge, Mass.: Belknap Press.
———. 1980. "Kantian Constructivism in Moral Theory." *Journal of Philosophy* 77 (9): 515–572.
———. 1985. "Justice as Fairness: Political Not Metaphysical." *Philosophy and Public Affairs* 14 (3): 223–251.
———. 2001. *Justice as Fairness: A Restatement*. Cambridge, Mass.: Harvard University Press.

Chapter Thirteen

Skeptical Wisdom

Descartes, Pascal, and the Challenge of Pyrrhonism

Felix Ó Murchadha

Wisdom is worldly; it assumes a common, finite and implicit context of meaning and significance from which it is then possible to think and act. The worldlessness or world-alienation of modernity, the scandal of philosophy (in its Kantian and Heideggerian interpretations), by making a strict distinction between the thinking self and an external reality, removes from wisdom its very conditions. Yet, in early modernity an ancient way of wisdom was not alone rediscovered, but played a fundamental role in the development of philosophy, namely the skeptical way. The skeptical way found wisdom not in knowledge but in aporia: in the place *between* claims to know. Here, wisdom is the recognition that in the face of uncertainty the appropriate response is a life without belief. One of the ironies of modernity is that the crisis of late Medieval thought made it possible to take this skeptical way seriously again, but that in the process skeptical wisdom was transformed into a mode of reflecting on the fallen state of humanity and the possibilities of truth and goodness in that state (see Popkin 2003, 3–43). Skepticism was transformed into a way of being in relation to a world which had lost its basis as the connectedness of God, nature and human life. Differently but interconnectedly, both Descartes and Pascal responded to this situation.

Modernity emerges and maintains itself as a crisis of what "world" can be taken to be; "world," that is, in the sense of a context of understanding in which things can appear meaningful. Skepticism is a fundamental response to this crisis. To understand (modern) skepticism and its significance we must leave behind any assumption of a neutral understanding of "world."[1] The crisis of world is rather a crisis of understanding with respect to the three related constituents which with variations great and small make up "world" in ancient and Medieval thought and practice: G/god(s), human and (physical) nature.[2] In the inner relations of these domains within their respective *metaphysica specialis* "world" could be understood as the unity of relations of creatures with respect to the ground of worldly being in the Creator; "world" is the unity of those domains of humanity and nature with respect to the unifying ground or their meaning and significance. Once those inner relations are questioned, the actuality of world is displaced in relation to an absolute subjectivity which itself becomes the measure of what counts as meaning and significance. World then ceases to be understood in its actuality and becomes known only as possibility, and further as a projected and contingent context of meaning.[3] Whereas the project of modernity is to achieve the conditions for objectivity, it does so by elevating human subjectivity to be the arbiter of reasonableness and in so doing cuts itself off from accepting without "proof" the existence of the nonhuman world.

This elevation of the human mind can be traced back to the nominalist voluntarism of the Late Medieval period, which understood entities not in terms of their place in a relational whole, but as singly created by God. The theological question here is one which concerns power and possibility, specifically the distinction between *potentia Dei ordinata* and *potentia Dei absoluta*: between—as this distinction became formulated by William of Ockham— what was *actually* ordained by divine power and that which is *possible* for divine power. For Ockham only the law of noncontradiction can limit divine capacities; otherwise, the Creator can do whatever he wishes (see McGrale 1999, 279; and Gillespie 2008, 23). This opens up a domain of speculative thought concerning the first principles of things, which is prior to, and (in principle) unlimited by, the world.[4] The world can now be understood not from itself but as a contingently actual world among a multitude of possible worlds. Understood voluntaristically, if the ordered unity of things experienced as world has no necessary ontological connection to the principle of being, then the world becomes for all practical and indeed theoretical purposes a human creation—a creation indeed of signification, first of language understood as expression and then of mathematics.[5] Hypothesis replaces categorical syllogism as the mode of reasoning appropriate to things as they appear (see Gillespie 2008, 23), and as such "world" appears not as what has been, what is always already there, but rather as that which is projected by a (human) mind as a suggested context for proof.

The principal question this situation poses is not the epistemological one concerning knowledge and truth, but—if reality is simply founded in a thinking self—the ethical one of how to live a good life in such a "world." Among the principal figures of the period (stretching from early Renaissance Italy to seventeenth-century France), key personalities such as Petrarch, Luther, Erasmus, Montaigne, Jansen, Descartes and Pascal invoked St. Augustine to respond to this ethical question. The crisis of world thus brought with it a renewal of Augustine's debate with Pelagius, albeit in a new key.[6] Philosophically the Augustine-Pelagian debate—in its original occurrence as well as the manner in which it was renewed in modernity under different guises—is significant because it addresses what became a fundamental set of philosophical questions in modernity, namely those of the autonomy of reason, the nature of the will and the project of mastery of nature.[7] Furthermore, the working-through of this debate, in early modernity and later, was informed by Stoic and Skeptical motifs, such that one can speak of a self-denying Augustinian skepticism and a self-mastering Pelagian stoicism.

Both Descartes and Pascal responded in different ways to this situation. For both, philosophy concerned how to live a happy life, which was impossible without knowledge of truth and goodness. For both, the skeptical is a fundamental, but relative, *moment*: it is symptomatic of loss, but by the same token points beyond itself to an origin which can be reached only by passing through it, an origin written into the human soul. The skeptical moment indicates a fallenness which is constitutive of human existence, but nonetheless contingent, to be overcome only through a transformation of existential conditions. Neither the diagnosis of this origin nor its overcoming can be achieved by reason alone. In seeking for grounds, reason can conceive loss only as privation, as absence relative to a self-sufficient presence. Only if within the self another mode of being toward itself and the world is present, which can both guide reason and help it to see its own limits, can the skeptical moment be traversed and an original unity be recovered. For Descartes this is to be found in the will, for Pascal in the heart.

RESPONSES TO THE FALL:
CARTESIAN WILL / PASCALIAN HEART

Clearly Descartes' autobiographical accounts, above all in the *Discourse*, are stylized, yet precisely for that reason they can be read as his attempt to account for the manner in which a self constitutes itself as most human, in other words as wise. The crucial stage in this self-constitution is the *spontaneous* skeptical, reflexive movement of reason against those propositions, which he has been taught by his teachers.[8]

Method is fundamental in overcoming this skeptical crisis. The place of method, however, reflects the ambiguity of the fallen situation in which he finds himself. For all the rigor of the method that he sets out first in the *Rules*, he denies that it functions prescriptively. Rather, his method is simply describing how the intellect *already* operates: "Nothing can be added to the clear light of reason which does not in some way dim it" (Descartes 1985/

Rules, 16). Hence, in effect, the method he is proposing is a reflection of the intellect on itself: the intellect by virtue of its own operations attempting to set the limits of these very operations.[9] Yet, if the clear light of reason functioned simply naturally, there would be no need for a method, or that method would be known intuitively by all. Again, Descartes begins the *Discourse* by saying that all people have good sense, yet the very project of the *Discourse* would be meaningless if that good sense was exercised by those who possessed it. He is assuming here a logic of fallenness: the human has the calling both to truth and goodness and yet for reasons which are constitutive of its present self, fails to reach either. The symptom of this, which shows it to be more than simply a contingent failure, is the classically Augustinian one of disunity and disobedience within the self, between will and desire, a conflict which for Descartes is rooted in the relation of body and soul. As the reality and origin of this conflict are not recognized by persons who possess good sense but do not use it properly, it is experienced as a conflict of the passions, through which the will can only employ representations to excite opposing passions.[10] This is the fallen state of the human being, one in which no clear distinction of body and soul is achieved and as such one in which the human is forever subject to a conflict of the passions. What is lacking here is a purity of judgment (Descartes 1985/*Discourse*, 117), judgment which is purified of bodily influence. The fallen nature of the human being, then, is one in which the soul is clouded by the body. Descartes' response to this situation is, however, radically anti-Augustinian: not the appeal to divine grace, but the employment of method.

The initial spontaneous skeptical movement arises in the self-recognition of its subjection to a twin governance of teachers and appetites, of society and nature.[11] Their complicity makes necessary a metaphysical meditation, a move away from both nature and society, a movement within.[12]

This inward movement arises from Descartes' diagnosis of human fallenness as a fallenness into corporeality. Corporeality can be understood metaphorically in terms of "relating to" nature, but it also has specific meaning in Descartes' work as subjection to the externality of time as habit. The time of habit is the time of the past in the present, molding the present in terms of the past; the inward movement is thought of as a liberation from that time. The inward movement is from the external relations of time in the causal connections of past and present toward the bracketing of those forces. This temporal indifference, this foreclosing of past and future, makes possible the will's indifference, which is operative in systematic doubt. This temporal foreclosure, the inward movement resistant to the body's externality, attempts to undo fallenness in the body and by that token fallenness as such.[13]

Descartes understands "will" as the action of thought to affirm or deny, pursue or avoid: the will affirms truth and pursues the good (Descartes 1984, 41). But the will is dependent on that which is given to it by the senses or the intellect. The will in itself is empty, powerless even to want the benefit of the embodied soul. The passions ideally function to bring the soul to the proper disposition, namely of "wanting the things which nature deems useful for us" (Descartes 1985/*Passions*, 372). In transforming his spontaneous skeptical thoughts into a systematic skeptical meditation, Descartes seeks to reduce the content of the will—that which I in fact will—to nothing, to allow the will to begin again in nothingness. Thus, he intends to open up a space in which the self can build itself as if sui generis. The strongest souls are those in which the will most easily conquers the passions (ibid., 347–48). In conquering the passions the will curbs the bodily consequences of particular passions, for instance fleeing in fear, then controls the passion itself (ibid., 342). This latter task is only possible through firm and determinate judgment concerning truth and goodness (ibid., 347). While the intellect is an instrument in this task, the will is that which governs: the will for Descartes needs to both control the passions and guide the intellect, indeed these tasks operate in tandem.

In agreement with Descartes, Pascal's diagnosis of the human predicament also concludes that neither society nor nature can resolve it. Much more explicitly than Descartes, Pascal places this discussion within the discourse of the fall, but seeks to show that fallenness can be understood initially *without* reference to *Genesis*.[14] The trace of this fallenness is to be found in the fundamental contradictions of being human. "We have in ourselves the capacity for knowing truth and for enjoying happiness, but we have neither a truth which is constant nor one which satisfies" (Pascal 1963/1999, 119/151).[15] If this were simply a contingent state, such that we have not *yet* found that truth, there would be no contradiction here. The contradiction lies rather in the fact that the capacity we have for truth and happiness is one which is incapable of realizing itself. A capacity is a natural power, a power to fulfill something, implying a natural relation of capacity to the object of that capacity and as such to the fixed nature of that capable being. The fallenness of the human being is indicated for Pascal precisely in that lack of fixed nature. Human nature is rather defined negatively for Pascal, as neither that of a beast nor of an angel (ibid., 121/154). The human being is caught between the baseness of his actions and the grandeur which he can perceive as his end, discovering in himself a mass of contradictions: he is to himself an "unfathomable monster" (ibid., 130/163).

At play here for Pascal is the "paradox of the fallen state":

> If man had never been corrupted, he would enjoy in his innocent state both truth and happiness with confidence. And if man had never been other than corrupted, he would have no notion of either truth or beatitude. (ibid., 131/164)

In the face of this condition of paradox and contradiction, Pascal rejects both a movement without and a movement within. The former he associates with a mere attempt to find happiness in diversions; the latter does not break out of the state of contradiction, but simply returns the self to its own incapacity. The (Stoic, but implicitly also Cartesian) promise of peace in the self is thus an illusion. The way within is a way beyond the passions, it is a way which, in the Stoic guise at least, involves a therapy of the passions and with Descartes a ruling by reason of the passions. This again assumes that reason has a capacity for truth which is constant and satisfying. What such an ambition ignores is the manner in which reason itself is undermined: "Reason and the senses mutually mislead one another" (ibid., 45/78). The senses mislead reason with false appearances, but reason through the passions of the soul gives the senses false impressions in turn. Reason for Pascal cannot be disassociated from the passions of the soul; reason arouses these passions, which mislead the senses. What is at stake here is the relation of body and soul. Pascal, like Descartes, understands fallenness in terms of their relation, but understands this relation as indicative of an incapacity in the human soul to negotiate its own ontological fixity (ibid., 410/29).[16]

Reason alone does not recognize this contradictory state, nor do the senses. To see the contradiction as such is to perceive that which offends, indeed humiliates, reason, and yet in turn gives reason its due place. Such sight requires a faculty, a capacity, to see beyond both the objects of the intellect and those of sense. For Descartes, the will assents (or not) to that which is presented to it by intellect and sense. What this account neglects, for Pascal, is that the will lies at the origin of belief at a more fundamental level: things appear to us aspectively, and the aspect which appears to us is that which is most pleasing and most attracts us (ibid., 539/458). The will is orientated toward that which attracts us and as such it directs the mind to one aspect over another, in terms of preference. The will does not await the intellect nor is it in any straightforward sense in a posterior relation to sense: the will directs the intellect and the senses toward the object, but does so in a manner which is pre-structured by desire. This faculty of desiring will is what Pascal terms the heart.

Pascal's account of the heart recaptures key elements of Augustine. As James Peters puts it: "As Augustine conceives of the mind as both cognitive and passionate, so Pascal conceives of the heart as a unity of cognition and will" (Peters 2009, 172). In the heart Pascal seeks to capture both that which is constitutive of the nature of the human being and that which simultaneously reveals the limits of its capacity and its receptivity for that which is beyond its nature. This is reflected in the manner in which Pascal understands the heart to stand outside Descartes' conceptual distinction of mind and body. The heart is not, as for Descartes, simply an organ of the body; love is not simply a confused thought, which the mind experiences as a result of something happening in the body, an emotion caused by the movement of the spirits impelling the soul to join itself willingly to objects that appear agreeable to it (Descartes 1985/*Passions*, 387). For Pascal, one of the failures of Cartesian philosophy is not to have succeeded in understanding the mixed nature—corporeal and spiritual—of the human.[17] This failure has the corollary of misunderstanding love. The love of God, of which Pascal speaks, is ambiguous in its effects. It is through this love that the human recognizes the difficulty of his predicament and yet, when this love is faced up to, it opens up the only possibility of happiness. The heart is the organ of love: it is both of the soul and of the body, it is the organ of feeling and of understanding. The heart mediates between will and instinct, between that faculty which threatens to escape altogether into a transcendent nature and the earthly feeling shared with animals.

What is known by the heart, is known through feeling rather that by reasoning.[18] What is felt in this way is a reality, which is recognized as prior to reason and to causes. The first principles are felt not proved, as is the case with love, which does not seek proof. The heart is the organ of trust, which as such grounds the human being's natural belief in the truth of first principles and his love of God. Common to both is a relation of trust which is pre-cognitive, affective and yet is foundational to the endeavors of reason. To understand this requires a recognition of finitude, situatedness and the relation to that which transcends such finitude. It is precisely here that the question of skepticism arose as a mode of response to the fallenness of human nature and a recognition of the gulf between the finite human intellect and the transcendence of God.

THE SKEPTICAL MOMENT IN DESCARTES AND PASCAL

For both Descartes and Pascal the skeptical is a moment which is both inevitable and relative; inevitable for the human condition of embodied intellect, but by the same token relative to a certain way of being embodied, which by means of will and heart respectively could be overcome.

For Descartes, the first metaphysical task is to give systematic expression to his spontaneous skepticism, to transform it into a methodical and universal skeptical investigation, so as to find a way through skepticism by gaining clear insight into the fallen state and finding a way of overcoming it. In the first *Meditation* he begins with, so to speak, a completed skepticism, with a skeptical aporia, and then attempts to show the reducibility of this aporia.[19] The aporia with which he begins is that between his received opinions and beliefs and those beliefs which arise from his critical self-reflection. From the beginning, however, Descartes resists the force of the aporia: he speaks of finding received beliefs false, but this is an empirical or nonmetaphysical falsity. At this early stage in the *Meditations* he cannot, from the metaphysical point of view which he is taking, legitimately claim certain beliefs to be false. In effect, in terms of what he can claim, he is beginning from opposing beliefs where he has no criterion for deciding between them. He then takes the opposite course of the Pyrrhonian skeptic: instead of pursuing a dialectical strategy of putting forward contrary positions and then demonstrating the failure of all criteria to arbitrate between them, he claims that the lack of such criteria itself indicates falsity. There are no conflicting positions, because the possibility of conflict, namely two opposing claims to truth, is disallowed: while between claims to truth there can be conflict, between two falsities there can be none.

What allows Descartes to do this is not only that he has translated the Pyrrhonist strategy of suspension of belief into one of doubt, but also that he has from the beginning stipulated a criterion of truth in terms which escape any possible aporia, namely a truth sui generis. The Pyrrhonian skeptic is radically dependent on others: she invents nothing herself, but feeds off the words others give her. Such a self is a responsive self. Descartes, by seeking to "demolish everything and . . . start again from the foundations" (Descartes 1984, 12), has in Pyrrhonist terms destroyed the conditions for such a self. His truth sui generis is a truth to be found—if at all—not in dogmatism or skepticism, but rather at that extreme point where the very conditions of the dialectic of dogmatism and skepticism have been taken away.

The issue from the beginning of the first *Meditation* is not simply whether Descartes is mistaken in his beliefs, but that he is "unwilling to be deceived" (Descartes 1984, 19). The senses deceive (*falleret*), in sleep he is deluded (*delussum*), he deludes himself (*me decipio*) and finally the deceiving demon deceives him (*falleret*) (ibid., 12–15). It is then not surprising that in contrast to the calmness of mind (*ataraxia*) to which the *epoché* leads the ancient skeptic, at the end of the first *Meditation* he is left "in dread" and "amid inextricable darkness" (ibid., 15). At the beginning of the second *Meditation* he speaks of being in a "whirlpool . . . so that I can neither stand on the bottom nor swim to the top" (ibid., 16). Far from tranquility, skepticism has brought him close to despair.

That Descartes overcomes despair in the discovery of the *cogito* and then the proof of God's existence, is well known. Central to both arguments is the question of origin or authorship (authority): the *cogito* as the author of its thoughts and God as the author of his existence (ibid., 16, 33). Despair is overcome only through a restoration of trust in that authority. That final restoration in the figure of the good, creator God is responded to by Descartes with an outpouring of reverence (ibid., 36). This reverence responds to God's grace (the grace of the "craftsman" God (ibid., 35), the grace which is at the center of Pelagius's concerns), a grace which has been affirmed as rational and comprehensible. His trust in this grace is at once a trust in the self, a trust in the testimonies of that self, and a trust in the source of all truth and goodness. Descartes refers to this trust in terms of faith (*fidam*) in the natural light (in the third *Meditation*) and lack of faith in the natural impulses (in the sixth *Meditation*).[20] The restoration of trust is one which at the same time offers a cure to the fallen state itself: once trust is placed in the natural light then it needs to be kept free from all corruption. The movement is from deception to trust (faith), a movement mediated by reason. But reason alone does not achieve this transformation; it is at its basis a movement of will.

When Descartes comes (in the fourth *Meditation*) to ask what the source of his errors is (and as such what the source of his vulnerability to deception is), he finds this source in the lack of correlation between his will and his understanding. Indeed, he argues that the will and the understanding have two different natures in the human being: the one is finite and the other infinite. It is quite consistent that while he talks of the understanding as *created* by God, Descartes refers to the will as *given* to him by God.[21] The human will is not created by God, because anything created lacks in perfection. The will, because it is indivisible, can only be given in its perfection. We have seen that in the Stoic understanding will is indifferent, but not in the Augustinian account. Descartes charts a course between these two which corresponds to his movement from skepticism to trust. Although he argues that the indifference of the will is its lowest freedom, it is in fact constitutive for the will as such. In the "Fifth Replies" (written to criticisms made of his *Meditations* by Pierre Gassendi, a contemporary of Descartes who developed a skeptical philosophy), he states that indifference arises when the person does not see clearly enough to allow for no doubt (ibid. 259f.). But in that case the skeptical will is indifferent in its operations, such indifference reflecting the limits of the self's power in the exercise of doubt. The nonindifferent will, the truly free will turning toward the good and the true, is only possible as a sincere, philosophically justified, exercise of the will due to its having passed through the skeptical stage of indifference and restricting itself to indifference beyond what it knows of the true and good (ibid., 40f.).

The point for Descartes is to "convert," to turn around, to that which the intellect perceives clearly. This turning is not for him (as it would be for

Augustine) a result of being attracted by one aspect or other of the object, but rather involves the will disciplining itself to remain within the limits of clear and distinct perceptions. Precisely because she has been given only the divine will and not his understanding, the human is prone to error. Here Descartes alludes to the fallen condition: with a trace of the infinite prelapsarian condition, the human being cannot exercise it because of its clouded understanding. Hence, the "limiting" of the will is in fact its true expression, its unity with the understanding in which it is free. Such a condition requires a discipline which limits the will to assent only to that which the intellect can perceive clearly and distinctly. The skeptical is not simply traversed but can be systematically suspended—so long as the human being retains a harmonious relation of will and intellect (and as we will see of desire and power). If the will does not depart from the clear and distinct perceptions, human judgment cannot fall into error.

For Pascal, however, the claim to find a way of thought immune from error (or sin) is the greatest presumption: far from allowing the human being to escape its fallen nature, it simply accentuates one symptom of that fallenness and indeed one cause of it, namely pride and arrogance. Similarly to Descartes, Pascal relates the skeptical to the fallenness of human reason and to its embodied state. The skeptical is true and will remain true because of human fallenness. While for Descartes the skeptical can be overcome through a metaphysical method, for Pascal the fall cannot be undone by human effort alone and as such the skeptical is a legitimate, but partial, philosophical response to it. As he says (Pascal 1963/1999 "Discussion," 189), while Stoics "observe some traces of its [humanity's] primordial grandeur and ignore its corruption," Pyrhonians "experience its present misery and ignore its primordial dignity." If, following Pascal, we read the movement of the *Meditations* from doubt to judgment as a movement from Pyrrhonism to Stoicism, then Descartes can be said to be imprisoned in this very abyss. For Pascal the point is not so much to overcome this abyss but to live in it, not to knock down and rebuild the buildings, but to find a proper mode of dwelling within them, not to reduce contradictions, but to accept the "paradox of the fallen state" in the hope of divine grace.

While both Pyrrhonism and Stoicism are limited perspectives on human fallenness, Pascal remains closer to the Pyrrhonian. This is so because the Pyrrhonian has the virtue of humility.[22] As such the Pyrrhonian poses the objection to the Stoic (and for Pascal to all "dogmatic" philosophies, above all the Cartesian), which he cannot answer: "from the uncertainty as to our origins derives uncertainty as to our nature" (Pascal 1963/1999, 131/164). Fallen nature is uncertain because it has no natural knowledge of its former grandeur. Lacking such knowledge means being radically alienated from its origins. The Pyrrhonist has seen this alienation most clearly and the skeptical moment is a moment of its realization. The skeptical gives expression to a fundamental truth of human experience. It does so, however, as a corrective. Pyrrhonism is true only because there are non-Pyrrhonians (ibid., 33/67); philosophers make outrageous claims not to be by nature steeped in inevitable weakness, and this provokes Pyrrhonian arguments. The clear implication is that Descartes' claims to find certain truth do not overcome the skeptical, but rather provoke it. This is the case because both Descartes and the skeptic share the one principle, which Pascal wishes to contest, namely that fundamental principles are to be discovered by reason or not at all. Pascal sees in the skeptical movement of thought that which it shares with dogmatism, namely the understanding of truth as certainty. The Pyrrhonist denies that certainty is possible and suspends judgment; the dogmatist claims that he has found certainty. In both cases the measure is certainty. Pascal's argument against both is that the very claim to certainty as a measure fails to account for the peculiar, indeed contradictory, place of the human being, which causes deep unhappiness. The key to overcoming the skeptical then is not to seek certainty, because this remains unachievable, but rather to probe deeper into the source of unhappiness. Unhappiness for Pascal is something felt; felt not as a discrete state, but rather as a fundamental condition. Within this feeling of unhappiness is discovered a truth which reason can only find if it listens to that feeling itself. But in doing that, reason discovers its own limitations.

Unhappiness indicates the between state of being human: human beings sense in themselves both grandeur and wretchedness (*misère*). These relate to each other in an "unending circle," which Pascal states as follows: "So it is wretched to know one is wretched, but there is grandeur in the knowledge of one's wretchedness" (ibid., 114/146). To know oneself as wretched is to recognize a higher state within oneself which has been lost: not to know one's true place, but to know that one has fallen from it and to have no *capacity* to return (ibid., 400/19). This is both the source and the limitation of the skeptical moment. The human finds itself in a nonplace, "suspended between two gulfs of the infinite and the void" (ibid., 199/230), or between angels and beasts. This nonplace is one in which no repose is possible and as such the Pyrrhonist promise of tranquility is a vain one (cf. ibid., 109/141; 76/111). It is so because the suspension of judgment simply reflects the state of unhappiness. The a-topos of human being is an aporia considered in terms of reason alone, because it embodies a contradiction, at the level not of logic but of practical reason: the contradiction between desire and capacity. Faced with this contradiction, to suspend judgment is in effect to limit desire to capacity. But the capacity in question is that of reason, and desire teaches reason not simply of its incapacity but of the presence of a higher capacity, the capacity of reception rather than action, that namely of the heart, which seeks both truth and goodness.

PRACTICE, ETHICS, AND THE GOOD

Truth and goodness are intertwined for both Descartes and Pascal: the skeptical moment concerns both. But while Descartes protects morals from skeptical doubt, Pascal makes no distinction between the theoretical and practical significance of the skeptical moment.

The skeptical thoughts which trouble Descartes in principle affect his account of the good as much as of the true: in respect to both, neither the authority of his teachers nor the inclinations of his nature are certain. He consistently pursues an investigation of the basis of each. Yet, with respect to his *practice* of the good and the true, he finds that he cannot suspend belief. Although he speaks of a provisional *moral* code (Descartes 1985/*Discourse*, 122–25), in effect it is a provisional *practical* code, a code about how to act while investigating the justification of the opinions on whose basis he acts.[23] There are two concerns here, regarding the place of thinking and the happiness of life. The provisional moral code supplies for him nothing other than the goal of his scientific endeavor, but in a provisional manner. The rational basis is not yet in place, but the code expresses the main elements of the way of life to which he is seeking to give rational foundation.[24]

The provisional moral code prestructures the way of life of someone who has, through an indubitable method, reached a clear understanding of the true and the good. This has been put in place through two distinct processes, those of tearing down and of building up the house of his beliefs. While tearing down, he in practice needed to accept some guidance as to how to act. Faced with this situation he accepts the authority of the customs of the society into which he was born (maxim 1) (ibid., 122–3). This acceptance is provisional on a number of levels. In the first place Descartes recognizes the arbitrariness of custom: what is customary is not necessarily either true or just, but is rather the mode of life of a particular place. Second, within any society there are more moderate and more extreme opinions and modes of action. In the face of this he looks toward the opinions of others, specifically those he judges to be the most sensible of those amongst whom he lives. But even then, he attends not to what they say, but what they do. Third, and most important, the very basis of his commitment to such customs and opinions is provisional: he counts promising as excessive, for example (ibid., 123). This declaration undercuts the apparent conservatism of the first maxim. Descartes understands the present acceptance of custom as entailing no obligation into the future.

What this means is that his very membership of the community is provisional. It is important to read the provisional moral code as itself dynamic, as containing within itself the outlines of a path to a more definitive morality, a dynamism of increased perfection of his judgments.

As his judgments become more perfect they will become more resolute. But in practice he cannot wait for this development. Hence, he needs to imitate the final definitive morality already in his judgments (maxim 2) (ibid., 123). In practice he needs to judge without sufficient justification. His judgment cannot reflect this lack of justification, because he cannot wait for the time when his judgment will be justified. Having to act now, he must do so with a decisiveness which he can only justify pragmatically. What occurs here is the inverse of the denial of the aporia which Descartes practices in his systematic doubt: what is doubtful is treated as if certain. This is justified only by the practical consideration of having to act. If we follow this course of action, we will not be subject to regret or remorse (ibid.). What is being practiced here is constancy of resolution. The self is developing the habit of judgment, which is necessary to a good life of one who has reached certainty.

This constancy is one which comes from the self, and requires a mastery of that self (maxim 3) (ibid., 123–4). As in the fourth *Meditation* the will limits itself to the intellect, so too in morality desire is limited to the possible: in morals as much as in theoretical life, error and sin derive from overreaching the power of the self. The point is not to change the world, but to limit desire to that which is within my power (ibid., 123). Only my thoughts are fully within my power. Again, though, while at first sight this maxim seems to imply a deep conservatism, an inner dynamic is evident: limiting desire to what is within my power means limiting desire to what I can fruitfully pursue. Within my power are the thoughts through which I rebuild the buildings of my knowledge. The results of that building will make us "the lords and masters of nature" (ibid., 142f.). The key to this whole quest lies in the limiting of desire in the sense of honing it toward the goal of knowledge of nature.[25] The human being as such is capable of goodness and truth and requires a method to help him reach this potential. The very project of science set out here is premised on Stoic and Pelagian principles regarding the human capacity for self-betterment and the reward for such fulfilled efforts by a good and just God.

"[N]either divine grace nor natural knowledge ever diminishes freedom" (Descartes 1985/*Passions*, 353–6). Against the extreme "Augustinianism" of Luther, Calvin and the Jansenists, Descartes understands divine sovereignty and natural necessity as working in harmony with human freedom. To be able to fully affirm this, he needs to show how the body, long associated with human fallenness, can be understood not as a prison, but rather as an instrument of freedom. The key to this is the place of desire. The passions are the operations of the body on the soul, for Descartes, actions which dispose the soul to want certain things. Wonder is the first of the passions, because it is through wonder that something in the world commands our attention (ibid.). Attention is not directly related to the object itself, but to its benefit or harm for the body. Desire is a passion directed toward a future good (ibid., 358–9). The whole of Descartes' project arises from the passion of desire and indeed does so in a most radical sense: both the destruction and the building up of his world are motivated by a desire for an as yet absent good.

The seeking after certainty is a passionate seeking; it is a seeking which aims not at pure knowledge, but at contentment. Such contentment is not achieved by the soul alone, but rather by the soul in relation to its body and the material world around it. Cartesian method is lived method, doubt is a lived doubt. The self which emerges from Descartes' œuvre does not serenely accept his lack of justification regarding truth and goodness, but is driven forward to find justifications precisely through its desire for certainty. It is for this reason that in the first and second *Meditations* Descartes describes himself as oscillating between anxiety or despair and hope or confidence. These passions arise precisely when desire seems to go beyond his powers. The results of the *Meditations* calm these passions to the extent that they demonstrate that knowledge of truth and goodness is within the finite intellect's powers. Read backward from the *Passions*, the *Meditations* are an attempt to overcome these passions through uncovering the true power and capacity of the self. Understood in this way, the whole project is one of finding tranquility, not through skeptical aporia, but rather through establishing the conditions for resolute judgment and happiness. For Descartes these conditions are met, however, only when the power of cognition is adequate to the object of desire. This is not present at the beginning, but only at the end of the process. In other words, the dynamic structure of the moral code corresponds to his project only to the extent to which the third maxim is understood in such a way that change occurs neither in the world nor in his desires, but in the *capacity of the self* to fulfill its desires.

"Generosity" is the passion which discloses to the soul its own true exercise of free will and consists in knowledge and feeling (Descartes 1985/ *Passions*, 384): knowledge that nothing belongs to him but the free exercise of his will and the feeling of a firm resolution to use it well. The passion of generosity in effect combines the second and third maxim of the provisional moral code. The generous self recognizes the limits of its own capability not by acknowledging its dependence on anything beyond it, but in striving to extend the boundaries of its capabilities indefinitely.

The generous self has self-esteem, loves itself and is humble only in the sense of recognizing that this capacity for self-esteem is shared with all others. For Pascal, on the contrary, the self is hateful and unjust (Pascal 1963/1999, 597/494). The fallenness which skepticism sees is for Pascal radical; the self which would attempt to bring itself out of such fallenness even by means of its self-limitation is destined simply to reinforce that state. In agreement with Descartes, Pascal states that we should understand custom as custom, but while for Descartes this is simply a recognition of the relativity of cultures, for Pascal it arises out of a rejection of the claim of custom to justice. Laws are customary and result from past usurpations.[26] Their claim to justice attempts to disguise their inherent injustice. If justice were known then it would not need to be laid down that one should follow one's own customs (ibid., 60/94). We do not know justice because of the weakness of our reason, but we are then locked in a lie: if people did not believe their laws to be just they would not follow them. Hence, to follow custom is not the starting point to the development of true moral principles, but rather affirms an injustice: namely the claiming of a place in the sun (ibid., 65/99). The point then is not to deepen this usurpation, but to seek redemption from it. The continual expansion of the Cartesian self is opposed in Pascal by the "thinking reed": starting from a Cartesian opposition between thought and space (extension), Pascal understands thought as a turning not toward mastery of nature—"a drop of water is enough to kill him"—but toward that through which thought can be "lifted up." Thinking brings about no such effects, but rather welcomes that which can redeem the self, even in—particularly in—its mortality.

The search for happiness is doomed, if it remains on the level of human capacity alone: "we search for happiness and find only wretchedness and death" (ibid., 401/20). The Cartesian attempt at a provisional moral code is, for Pascal, self-defeating because it is rooted in the illusion that there is time for philosophy. "To have no time for philosophy is truly to philosophize" (ibid., 610/679). What is it to *have time* for philosophy? It is Descartes as he portrays himself in Part 2 of the *Discourse* (cf. Descartes 1985, 116–7) in a heated room separate from the world of his obligations both to himself and to others, a state of abstraction from situatedness that allows for a purely rational reflection. Such a philosophy of the mind, however, is impossible for someone who has no such secluded time, whose time remains the time of the heart, the time of the lover, who is uncertain that he will be there in one hour (Pascal 1963/1999, 428–9/681–2). While for Descartes the cogito is not certain of the future, it does not require this certainty because it has in the moment a sort of eternal insight, an adurational glimpse into the foundations of being, for Pascal the uncertainty of the future involves nothing less than the possibility of death without wisdom and a destiny of eternal damnation. The beginning of philosophy, for Pascal, takes place in the shadow of death, the shadow of the uncertainty of a next hour. The delay which Descartes speaks of, the waiting for an appropriate time to reflect, is premised on the assumption that each moment can be viewed *per species aeternitatis*, that is, for him the moment of intuition is one which binds the thinker directly to the creative act of God, who preserves the world in being from moment to moment.

This radical dependence on God is one which has to do with the will of creation, one which affects the thinker not so much in his personal being as in his participation in the being of all that is. But Pascal's thinker is faced not with the dependence of things on the creative will of God, but rather with his own death and the question of his mortality. In the face of the contradictions of human existence, for Pascal the first, and in a sense the only, philosophical question concerns the immortality of the soul. This question is inescapable, because it opens up the possibility of redemption in the face of fallenness.[27] Philosophers who neglect this question are undermining the very project of philosophizing itself. Pascal does not mention Descartes directly in this regard, but Descartes, despite the centrality of the immortality of the soul in the title of the first edition of the *Meditations*, admits in his *Replies to Arnauld* that he had failed to prove it and drops all mention of it from the title of later editions of that work (Descartes 1984, 108–9).

The question of immortality is not ultimate for Descartes, because philosophy is not concerned with death, but rather with survival: being masters of nature for him could lead also to being masters of our own bodily nature— death as failure of the organism could, he thought, be overcome by advances in medicine. For Pascal the only way to be happy is to become immortal (Pascal 1963/1999, 134/166), which is beyond human capacity. Pascal offers no argument for the immortality of the soul. If philosophy begins and ends with this question, it does so because the question is both unavoidable and unanswerable either by reason or by the heart in their natural states. The human being is faced with mortality and with the question of his destiny. The unhappiness of the present state of being in the world indicates something beyond the world, beyond, that is, the mortal existence which the human being knows. Reason cannot respond to this unhappiness, because it is rooted in contradiction. Reason seeks to take one side or other of the contradiction, but in doing so argues in circles. The heart recognizes the contradiction as being insurpassable and thus if reason is to follow from the intuitions of the heart it cannot begin from itself. It has rather to begin from that which humbles it, namely its failure to find a fundamental unity, a starting point of pure presence. The starting point which the heart reveals is one of disunity and of loss. This does not mean that philosophy has been rendered impossible, but rather that it begins in a situation which calls not for reconstruction but for eluci-dating the prephilosophical condition. The prephilosophical is not to be set aside; rather the goal of philosophy is to think back to that beginning which always comes before it and which, as fallen, is hidden from it. This thinking back is one which is for Pascal fundamentally a seeking for God, a thinking the paradox of the fall in its reasonableness (ibid., 164/196).

CONCLUSION

The scientific revolution of the seventeenth century was an aspect of a wider existential crisis to which Descartes and Pascal responded in different ways. Descartes' response was in fundamental ways Pelagian: it limited the self to its own capacity in order to increase and optimize that capacity. Pascal's Augustinian hope in grace warns against the presumption of any such con-fidence in the self. The skeptical moment of both courses is a moment of deep uncertainty, where, in Montaigne's terms (Montaigne 1957, 455), "we have no communication with being." This is a modern, not a Pyrrhonist, as-sumption, one which disengages the practical, moral life, on the one hand, and the theoretical pursuit of knowledge, on the other, from any fundamental ontological anchorage—from any grounding in an account of world as prior to and normative for human thought in respect both of being and of goodness. Such a disengagement leads either to a self understood in terms of mastery (both of self/other and of nature) or to an ultimately ascetic self, concerned only with its own immortality. In both cases, the worldly conditions for wis-dom, which sustain communities and recognize the requirements of reason as neither certain nor humiliated, are undone.

The worldly conditions of wisdom demand nothing less than the attempt to find a way through and beyond Descartes and Pascal to a communica-tion with being, and in doing so transcending those conditions of autonomy, technological mastery and alienation which the late Medieval crisis of world instituted. To achieve this, it is necessary to think again the skeptical aporia as a mode of living in the world without certainty and to find there, if not tranquility, at least a way of being which thinks nature and divinity in a mood which can again but in a new way hear that which resonates between hu-man, divine and nature. The loss of this was famously expressed by Pascal: "The eternal silence of these infinite spaces terrifies me" (Pascal 1963/1999, 164/196). To hear in this infinity not the silence of threat but the gift of being is not simply to think again the possibility of wisdom, but fundamentally to rethink—beyond Pelagianism and Augustinianism—the relation of the self to the infinite, the relation of existence to its ultimate, if hidden, ground.

NOTES

1. As Hans Blumenberg writes regarding the rise of modernity, "world is not a constant" (1983, 8).

2. The story here is quite complex as we find once we try to translate "*physis*" from the Greek. Undoubtedly the difference between polytheism and monotheism, the tragic and the biblical accounts of the human, the understanding of nature in Greek cosmology and the Judeo-Christian account of nature as created, all involved fundamental changes in the account of world. Nevertheless, a relation of unity and ultimate harmony of the three relata God, human and nature remains in Christian thought; when that unity begins to dissolve in late medieval philosophy the crisis of world which defines modernity begins. See Dupré 1993, 15–22. The present account is indebted to Gillespie 2008.

3. "World" is being understood here in the sense developed by the German phenomenological thinkers Husserl and Heidegger; "world" does not refer then to the earth as that which can be photographed from the moon, but rather more in the sense in which we talk of the "world of soccer," the "academic world" or "It's a man's world." Cf. Christensen 2011.

4. This consequence was anticipated by the 1277 condemnations of Aristotelian doctrines on the basis of a claim to the omnipotency of God. See Grant 1982.

5. Implicit here is the fruitful analysis of Toulmin of two beginnings of Modernity: one humanistic and literate, one rationalist and scientific (Toulmin 1990, 19). On this issue, cf. Dupré 1993.

6. The classic debate of the period between Erasmus and Luther exemplifies this, with Luther playing the role of Augustine and Erasmus that of Pelagius. This example also brings out the complexities of this debate, as Erasmus saw himself writing within an Augustinian framework. Cf. Rupp 1969. Pelagius (ca. AD 354–420), born in Britain or possibly Ireland, died in Palestine. He denied the need for direct divine aid in the form of "infused" grace (grace as something more than what is given to human beings in their natural created state) in performing good works, which was directly related to his denial of the doctrine of original sin as developed by Augustine of Hippo. Partly as a result of Augustine's polemics against him, Pelagius was declared a heretic by the Council of Carthage in AD 418. Pelagian doctrines continued to influence Christian thinking, however, and can be understood as a conduit for Stoic thought into Christianity. Fundamentally at issue is the autonomous capacity of human beings to decide for, and to achieve, moral goodness.

7. On this theme, see Hanby 2003, 134–143.

8. "I found myself beset by so many doubts and errors that I came to think I have gained nothing from my attempts to become educated but increasing recognition of my ignorance" (Descartes 1985/*Discourse*, 113); "Some years ago I was struck by the large number of falsehoods that I had accepted as true in my childhood, and by the highly doubtful nature of the whole edifice that I had subsequently based upon them" (Descartes 1984, 12).

9. Cf. Descartes 1984, 30: "We discover by means of the Rules that nothing can be known prior to the intellect, since knowledge of everything else depends on the intellect"; while presumably this discovery is itself an act of knowing.

10. Descartes 1985/*Passions*, 345. In this Descartes might be responding directly to Montaigne, for whom to dissuade someone from entering a foolish course of action it is more productive to incite in them the opposite appetite than to give them good reasons against their chosen course. Cf. Montaigne 1957/*Essays*, 634. Only God touching the heart of man can give him the courage to listen to his reason, in which case the appetite is not diminished, but reason becomes stronger. Against Montaigne, Descartes seeks to uncover the human capacity for reason, independent of grace.

11. Descartes 1984, 117: "We are all children before being men and had to be governed for some time by our appetites and our teachers."

12. On the Augustinian parallels in this inward movement, cf. Menn 1998, 53–54.

13. As we will see, however, this cannot be dismissed as an angelic view of the human (as Maritain amongst others would have it), but rather is a breaking from the body as fallen in order to retrieve it following its methodological "cleansing."

14. For an account of the fall in Pascal in the historical context of his work, cf. Kolakowski 1995.

15. Pascal's *Pensées* were compiled after his death from his papers. It is unclear in which order Pascal intended these fragmentary thoughts to be presented, and since the first edition a number of different principles of organization have been used, varying greatly from each other. For this reason for each reference to the *Pensées* I give the reference to one of the standard French editions in the *Œuvres Complètes*, ed. by L. Lafuma, 1963 (Paris: Seuil). This number is given first followed by the fragment number in the English translation: *Pensées and Other Writings*, trans. by H. Levi, ed. by Anthony Levi, 1999 (Oxford: Oxford University Press). Originally the *Pensées* appeared in 1669, the *Discussion with Monsieur de Sacy* in 1728.

16. For an account of Pascal's critique of Descartes in relation to the fall, cf. Melzer 1986, 97–100.

17. Pascal 1963/1999, 199–72/230: "They [human beings] cannot understand what the body is, far less the spirit and least of all how the body can be combined with the spirit."

18. Ibid.: "The principles are felt, and the propositions are proved, both conclusively, although by different ways."

19. Pyrrhonian skepticism is primarily associated in this period with the writings of Sextus Empiricus which had been "re-discovered" and translated into Latin in the sixteenth century. For Sextus Empiricus, skeptical reasoning led through the employment of a suspension of judgment and belief—*epoché*—to an *aporia* where one could find no compelling reason to accept one claim to truth over another. However, in translating his work, where Sextus uses the term *aporia*, or the verb *aporein* or derivative terms, the translators used *dubitare, dubitatio*—to "doubt"—and its derivatives. Descartes then begins at the end—with "aporia"—and employs "doubt," which for Sextus was not a skeptical method, but rather one characteristic of the Academicians (the middle and later Academy in Athens), whom he opposed. To quote Hegel (2006, 307): "Skepticism is not a doubt, for doubt is the very opposite of the tranquility that ought to be skepticism's result." At the beginning of the *Outlines of Pyrrhonism* Sextus divides philosophers into three groups: Dogmatists who think they have the truth, Academics who doubt everything, and Pyrrhonists, who continue to seek the

truth (Sextus Empiricus 1996, 89). Significantly, Pico Della Mirandola, who we know possessed Greek manuscripts of Sextus, writing in the fifteenth century, divides all thinkers into Dogmatists, who affirm, Academics, who deny, and Pyrrhonists, who doubt. Cf. Popkin 2003, 29. On this topic, see Benson Mates's "Introduction" to the work of Sextus Empiricus (1996, 30–32).

20. Cf. the original Latin text of the *Meditations*: "quia nulla alia facultas esse potest, cui aeque fidam ac lumini isti, quaeque illa non vera esse possit docere . . . nec video cur iisdem in ullâ aliâ re magis *fidam*." (Descartes 1983, 38–9; my emphasis); and "Cùm enim viderer ad multa impelli a naturâ, quae ratio dissuadebat, non multùm *fidendum* esse putabam iis quae a naturâ docentur" (Descartes 1983, 77; my emphasis).

21. On two occasions in the *Meditations* Descartes talks of man receiving the will from God (cf. Descartes 1984, 39 and 41).

22. This is true, however, only of the "Christianized" Pyrrhonian. The Pyrrhonist tranquil aporia is for Pascal the arrogant presumption of living without God. On the "Christianisation of Pyrrhonism," see Neto 1995.

23. On Descartes' provisional moral code, cf. Rodis-Lewis 1998, Marshall 1998 and Steiner 2004.

24. The mistake is to think that this provisional moral code simply expresses a code of life which has no relation to the content or goal of the scientific process itself. On the contrary, the goal of that process is to live in dwellings of truth and goodness which are certain, where we can make decisive judgments regarding the true and the good and where we can live happily. While it is certainly true that Descartes never worked out a fully fledged morality, the moral code itself concerns the way of life implicit in the totality of his philosophical work.

25. Descartes 1984, 19: "I could not have limited my desires, or been happy, had I not been following a path by which I thought I was sure to acquire all the knowledge of which I was capable, and in this way all the true goods within my reach."

26. Cf. Pascal 1963/1999, 60/94: "Such is the caprice of man that there is not a single [universal law]."

27. Pascal 1963/1999, 164/196: "It matters to the whole of life to know whether the soul is mortal or immortal."

REFERENCES

Adams, M. 1999. "Ockham on Will, Nature and Morality." In *The Cambridge Companion to Ockham,* ed. by Paul Vincent Spade, 245–272. Cambridge: Cambridge University Press.

Annas, Julia, and Jonathan Barnes. 1985. *The Modes of Skepticism: Ancient Texts and Modern Interpretations*. Cambridge: Cambridge University Press.

Blumenberg, Hans. 1983. *The Legitimacy of the Modern Age*. Trans. by Robert M. Wallace. Cambridge, Mass.: MIT Press.

Christensen, C. 2011. "The World." In *The Routledge Companion to Phenomenology*, ed. by Sebastian Luft and Søren Overgaard, 211–221. London: Routledge.

Descartes, René. 1983. *Œuvres de Descartes,* vol. 7. Ed. by C. Adam and P. Tannery. Paris: de Vrin.

———. 1984. *The Philosophical Writings of Descartes,* vol. 2. Ed. by John Cottingham, Robert Stoothoff and Dugald Murdoch. Cambridge: Cambridge University Press. (Containing inter alia "The Meditations Concerning First Philosophy.")

———. 1985. *The Philosophical Writings of Descartes,* vol. 1. Ed. by John Cottingham, Robert Stoothoff and Dugald Murdoch. Cambridge: Cambridge University Press. (Containing inter alia "The Rules for the Direction of the Mind," "The Discourse on Method" and "The Passions of the Soul.")

Dupré, Louis. 1993. *Passage to Modernity: An Essay in the Hermeneutics of Nature and Culture.* New Haven: Yale University Press.

Gillespie, Michael Allen. 2008. *The Theological Origins of Modernity.* Chicago: University of Chicago Press.

Grant, E. 1982. "The Effect of the Condemnation of 1277." In *The Cambridge History of Late Medieval Philosophy,* ed. by Norman Kretzmann, Anthony Kenny, Jan Pinborg and Eleonore Stump, 537–539. Cambridge: Cambridge University Press.

Hanby, Michael. 2003. *Augustine and Modernity.* London: Routledge.

Heidegger, Martin. 1991. *Being and Time: A Translation of "Sein und Zeit."* Trans. by Joan Stambaugh. Albany: State University of New York Press.

Hegel, G. W. F. 2006. *Lectures in the Philosophy of History.* Vol. II: Greek Philosophy. Ed. and trans. by Robert Brown. Oxford: Oxford University Press.

Kolakowski, Leszek. 1995. *God Owes Us Nothing: A Brief Remark on Pascal's Religion and on the Spirit of Jansenism.* Chicago: University of Chicago Press.

Marshall, John. 1998. *Descartes' Moral Theory.* Ithaca: Cornell University Press.

McGrale, A. 1999. "Natural Law and Moral Omnipotence." In *The Cambridge Companion to Ockham,* ed. by Paul Vincent Spade, 273–301. Cambridge: Cambridge University Press.

Melzer, Sara E. 1986. *Discourses of the Fall: A Study of Pascal's "Pensées."* Berkeley: University of California Press.

Menn, Stephen. 1998. *Descartes and Augustine.* Cambridge: Cambridge University Press.

Montaigne, Michel E. de. 1957. *The Complete Works of Montaigne,* trans. by D. Frame. Stanford: Stanford University Press.

Neto, José R. Maia. 1995. *The Christianization of Pyrrhonism.* Dordrecht: Kluwer.

Pascal, Blaise. 1963. *Œuvres Complétes,* ed. by Henri Gouhier. Paris: de Seuil.

———. 1999. *Pensées and Other Writings.* Trans. by H. Levi; ed. by Anthony Levi. Oxford: Oxford University Press. (Containing inter alia "Discussion with Monsieur de Sacy" and "Pensées.")

Peters, James R. 2009. *The Logic of the Heart.* Grand Rapids, MI: Baker Academic.

Popkin, Richard H. 2003. *The History of Skepticism: From Savonarola to Bayle.* Oxford: Oxford University Press. (Revised and expanded ed.)

Rodis-Lewis, Geneviève. 1998. *La morale de Descartes.* Paris: Quadridge/Presses Universitaires de France. (3rd ed. 1970.)

Rupp, E. Gordon, and Philip S. Watson, eds. 1969. *Luther and Erasmus: Free Will and Salvation*. Philadelphia: Westminster Press.

Sextus Empiricus. 1840. *Sexti Empirici Opera Graece et Latine*, vol. 1. Leipzig: Kühnian.

———. 1996. *The Skeptic Way. Sextus Empiricus's "Outlines of Pyrrhonism."* Trans., with intro. and comm., by Benson Mates. New York, Oxford: Oxford University Press.

———. 2005. *Against the Logicians*. Trans. and ed. by Richard Bett. Cambridge: Cambridge University Press.

Steiner, G. 2004. *Descartes as Moral Thinker*. New York: Humanity Books.

Toulmin, Stephen E. 1990. *Cosmopolis: The Hidden Agenda of Modernity*. New York: Free Press.

Wood, R. 1999. "Ockham's Repudiation of Pelagianism." In *The Cambridge Companion to Ockham*, ed. by Paul Vincent Spade, 350–374. Cambridge: Cambridge University Press.

Chapter Fourteen

Art as "Organizer" of Life

The Case of Jackson Pollock

Elizabeth Langhorne

Immanuel Kant distinguishes between science, understood as organized knowledge, and practical wisdom, which organizes life using as its principle the understanding of the highest good that theoretical wisdom provides.[1] What need is there for such an organization of life? At one level, nature has already organized our lives for us, with the genes we inherit or the natural environment we find ourselves in. We might equally well say that society organizes life for us: we are socialized in a certain way. But we need more than this. Granted the organizing forces of nature and society, the questions remain: how ought we to live our lives? What ought we to make of our selves, how ought we meet our need for love, cope with the fact of death? In the past, religion offered guidance here, but now perhaps less often functions in this way, while science is unable to offer what we need in these respects. Kant thought that our reason could become practical and lead us toward true wisdom, in other words, guide us in organizing our lives. But reason as such, by itself, has failed to provide the necessary guidance, as was made very clear by the horrors of the twentieth century. Given all this, it is now hard to take comfort in the Enlightenment's faith in what it saw as reason as the answer to the question "What organizes life?" If we are not to turn to the old religion or to the Enlightenment, is there an alternative answer?

One suggestion put forward at the end of World War II was that the organization of life was the task of the individual. But with existentialism, the basic problem of what can validly circumscribe individual freedom remained. Reason alone proved unequal to the task. Could it be that, as Schiller had already hinted, the acquisition of practical wisdom requires art? (See Schiller 2004.) This chapter explores this question with a case study, the work of the American painter Jackson Pollock. It considers the practice of art—here, painting—as a boundary case of practical reasoning, the struggle with how to live: not in the sense of answering particular moral questions as much as how to live in a way that instantiates a fundamentally human attitude. First, looking from his own point of view, what did it mean for this particular artist to use art as a means for discovering how to live? Second, I shall suggest that the effort of grappling with Pollock's art, and the light it casts on the human condition, can offer a certain sort of wisdom or insight to the viewer—through a unique form of reasoning in practice.

Throughout his life, Pollock understood the making of art as a vehicle for discovering how to live, at first through visual thinking with symbolic images, then later through the very process of painting his mature, abstract, poured canvases. Meeting personal and public crises, he discovered how, in the face of death, to aspire toward an erotic opening, whether to woman, to nature, or simply to paint. The specificity of the forms and rhythms in his mature work make them powerful conveyors of moods. Responding to these moods, the viewer encounters Pollock's struggle between an existential desire for unbound freedom and a longing for totalization and homecoming.

ART "FOR ART'S SAKE," OR A SEARCH FOR WISDOM?

If our age does not usually look to art for wisdom, at first Jackson Pollock seems a particularly unlikely candidate. He had a meteoric career—he had his first one-man show in 1943 in New York; by 1949 *Life* Magazine ran a spread asking if he was "America's greatest living painter." But by 1956 Pollock died drunk in a car accident, his mistress at his side. What wisdom are we to find here? And not only was his end a sad one. At the beginning of his life Pollock was already at sea, tossed by an almost megalomaniac ambition and debilitating self-doubt. To make some sense of his life he seriously considered religion, toying at age eighteen with thoughts of following Krishnamurti to his camps in India and Holland (Naifeh and Smith 1989, 142–43). But he decided to study art with the muralist Thomas Hart Benton in New York City. As he explained to his father,

> And when I say artist I don't mean it in the narrow sense of the word—but the man who is building things—creating molding the earth—whether it be plains of the west—or the iron ore of Penn. Its [*sic*] all a big game of construction—some with a brush—some with a shovel—some choose a pen. . . . There are to be some mural jobs for the new radio city which is under construction—that's the new artist's job to construct with the carpenter—the mason. (Pollock 1978, IV 212: letter from Jackson to his father, Feb. 1932 = *CR*, Doc. 12)

For him, the task of art is to build, not so much a house to shelter the body, but to shelter the soul.

Such vaulting ambition was shadowed by deep-rooted personal problems. Ever since Pollock had joined a surveying crew on the Grand Canyon as a fifteen-year-old, a drinking problem plagued him. This problem was compounded by his difficulties in relating to girls and his deep-rooted ambivalence to his family. He was the youngest of five boys; his mother offered him a smothering love. Searching for the best for her boys, she was the driving force behind the family's nine moves westward, finally ending up in the outskirts of Los Angeles, all before Pollock's sixteenth birthday. His father was a weaker presence who took to drink and left his family for good when Jackson was only nine. The latter's feelings about his family, shown in a photograph from 1917 when Jackson was five (see *CR,* IV, 204, fig. 5), are revealed in the painting *Woman* (c. 1930–1933; fig. 14.1). More than a nurturer, the mother becomes a force of death, making skeletons of all the men in her life, including his father. To address his many personal problems, Pollock saw a Freudian analyst, Dr. Wall, in 1938, then two Jungian analysts, Dr. Joseph Henderson in 1939–1940, Dr. Violet de Laszlo in 1940–1943.

Doubt about Pollock as a candidate for a discussion of art, practical reasoning and wisdom is further underscored by a first glance at his mature art, for instance a masterwork from 1950, *Autumn Rhythm* (fig. 14.2), a 17-feet-3-inches mural-scaled painting, an all-over web of abstract poured colored lines. In their very abstraction, these poured works invite appreciation as "art for art's sake." Clearly, the mimetic illusion of a three-dimensional Renaissance space is a thing of the past here. This abstraction and the formal achievement of a re-created flatness are two grounds on which the critic Clement Greenberg, who helped propel him into the limelight, celebrated Pollock's art.[2] But must art created only for art's sake not renounce any claim to wisdom? Would the search for meaning and insight not demand an art for the sake of truth?

But we can see that Greenberg's aesthetic, formal approach does not do Pollock's art justice when we look at a copper plaque, CR 1046, in a circular design that Pollock hammered out, as part of his therapy with Dr. Wall. Here he clearly uses art as a vehicle to organize life. The theme, Pollock told his doctor, was "the cycle of man." A child is at the center of the design, held by a nude couple; to the right an adolescent figure with arm outstretched moves away from the family. On the rim of the plaque he completed the cycle, "moving away from infancy and parents," with four scenes, depicting, as Dr. Wall describes it, "mating, the chaos of life and death at top, man helping another to the left, and death at the base. I can hear him talking now as

Figure 14.1.   Jackson Pollock, *Woman*, c. 1930–1933

he pondered this out" ("Remarks," CR 1046, in *CR*, IV, 124). In a spiraling design Pollock depicted the universal flow of life—with which he himself was experiencing difficulty. If wisdom seeks to organize life, art here seems genuinely to form part of a search for wisdom. This search, I shall argue, animates the entirety of Pollock's oeuvre.

Figure 14.2.   Jackson Pollock, ***Autumn Rhythm: Number 32, 1950***

Birth and "Visual Thinking"

The need to organize life was never more obvious than in the late 1930s. The globe was in crisis and Pollock was a personal mess. It was Picasso who gave expression to the world's crisis in *Guernica*. This mural painting (1937) responded to the German bombing of the Basque village of Guernica in 1937, protesting the brutal destruction of war and fascist aggression. To help raise money for Spanish refugees from fascism, this painting, along with all the related study drawings, was exhibited in New York in 1939. When Pollock saw it, Picasso immediately became for him a foil and a rival. *Guernica* demonstrated that an artist could engage the great modern tradition of abstraction and serve the cause of humanity. For Pollock, Picasso became a hero. Even in late 1945, or later, he was heard to yell "God damn it, that guy missed nothing!"[3] In Picasso he also found a father figure with whom he had to do battle in an oedipal conflict. Picasso's approach to creativity and to women was one of mastery. This expressed itself in Picasso's alter ego, the bestial minotaur who rapes the beautiful woman. European history itself showed how problematic such an attitude of macho mastery toward woman and nature proved to be, and in his own art Picasso ended by slaying this beast, resurrecting the image of the bull to preside over the scene of destruction in *Guernica*. In this image of world crisis Pollock found a mirror of his own personal crisis. But he dreamed of finding an alternative to such destructive mastery. Couldn't there be another way of "organizing" life, an American way?

Pollock's answer appears in one of his first modernist canvases, *Birth* (c. 1941; fig. 14.3). Three-quarters of the way up the canvas, amid amorphous forms, a spiraling masklike motif, containing a striking red disc and a larger circular red area, both encapsulated in a yet larger white crescent shape tinged with gray, arrests the eye. The origin of this motif can be identified; it is the American Indian plumed serpent associated with Quetzalcoatl, the great god of Pre-Columbian art and culture. This identification is supported by CR 521r, c. 1939–1940, one of the drawings that Pollock gave to Dr. Henderson, his first analyst, during the course of his therapy.[4] The motif in the upper left of the sheet within a rectangular framed sketch shows coils of a snake plumed with feathers which reappear in *Birth*: the circle at the center of the coil in the drawing becomes the small but striking dotted red disc in the canvas. Occupying the right side of the round medallion in the drawing's upper center we find a more easily identified plumed serpent, which suggests a source for Pollock's interest in this fantastic animal: Orozco's serpent with feathers, symbol of the Aztec god Quetzalcoatl, depicted at the bottom of the *Aztec Warriors* panel at Dartmouth, 1932–1934.

Pollock had driven with friends up to Dartmouth to see these murals in 1936, and had been greatly impressed, not only producing his own glosses on Orozco's powerful imagery, but internalizing Orozco's challenge.[5] In telling *The Epic of Latin-American Civilization* Orozco dramatizes the presence of Quetzalcoatl as the god of Pre-Columbian art and culture, and his departure with a promise to return. Given Orozco's damning assessment of contemporary Anglo culture in *Gods of the Modern World,* the promise of return appears crucial and, given the following panel, *Modern Migration of the Spirit,* possible. Orozco himself in a 1932 press release spoke of the significance of the renewal of this American Indian symbol:

> The American continental races are now becoming aware of their own personality, as it emerges from the two cultural currents—the indigenous and the European. The great American myth of Quetzalcoatl is a living one embracing both elements and pointing clearly, by its prophetic nature, to the responsibility shared equally by the two Americas of creating here an authentic New World civilization.[6]

In *Birth*, Pollock appears to celebrate such an American renewal. Art not for art's sake, but for the sake of a new myth.

As important as identifying the American cultural symbol of the plumed serpent, is recognizing how Pollock came to it through a struggle with Picasso's *Guernica* as he sought out alternative imagery; this was a struggle that helped him to grow personally. His responses to *Guernica* are concentrated in the drawings that he gave Dr. Henderson. Particularly striking are his responses to *Guernica*'s central image, the stricken horse impaled on a spear and the fallen warrior to the side. In CR 548 he reiterates Picasso's theme of destruction: a horse's head and a man's head with hand appended, suspended, as if destroyed by the violent knifing of a wooden limb. Violence dominates

Figure 14.3.   Jackson Pollock, *Birth*, c. 1941

the scene and partially eclipses the big orange-red disc in the background. But more important for the future of his art than this straightforward response to images of pain and death are the doodles in which he explores different scenarios and meanings for the man and his horse.

To Fritz Bultman, who became a friend in early 1942, Pollock described how impressed he was with Picasso's active development of the images related to the masterpiece—a practice of which he, too, was to become a master.[7] Rudolf Arnheim has described this process as "visual thinking." Such thinking first of all uses visual imagery to sort out one's thoughts and feelings. One condition of such visual thinking is that

> every perceived property or object be taken to be symbolic. . . . When objects are related to each other by location, shape, or color, that relationship is never merely optical or physical, but is always to be understood as an existential tie in the deeper sense. (Arnheim 1962, 10–11)

Thus Picasso was experimenting with "variations of meaning" when he tried out different attitudes for the horse as victim: "with its head and neck bent down it was entirely a victim among victims. . . . With its head turned upward, it performed the outcry of despair, appeal, and accusation" (ibid., 82). An instance of Pollock's interest in the *Guernica* images and of his own visual thinking occurs in the lower right-hand corner of CR 521. There he depicts a collapsing horse that is very close to one of Picasso's studies for *Guernica*; but in his version of the horse the body of a man is flung over its back and the horse's attitude more protesting than stricken.

On the reverse of the sheet Pollock pursues the theme of a human figure attempting to mount and ride a horse. In the upper right-hand corner a figure is shown approaching the whinnying horse; just below we see a figure balanced astride the horse; dominating the lower right hand corner a skeletal figure rides a galloping horse just below a sun disc and crescent moon, between them a serpent. By allowing the human figure to ride the horse, Pollock appears to negate the theme of destruction. By making the rider a skeleton he calls this negation into question. The presence and variations of yin-yang symbols throughout the rest of the drawing speak of his desire for a harmony he found difficult to reconcile with reality.

That Pollock did not find the Picassoid imagery of man and horse satisfactory becomes clear in flipping back to the doodles on the recto of CR 521, and in particular to those in the upper left-hand quadrant. Here we see the small man with his horse hailing a looming serpent, its head and eye above, its tail coiled in the motif that he will later use to project the rebirth of the plumed serpent in *Birth*. Just how deeply this motif spoke to his personal turmoil is evident in another of the Henderson drawings. In CR 531 a central triangular being, flanked by wooden horses, strikes down with its arrow toward a humanoid figure lying below, engulfed by a coiling serpent. Years later Dr. Henderson described this drawing as an example of extreme introversion (Henderson, quoted in Wysuph 1970, 15). He points to the strong vertical axis to be found in a number of Pollock's drawings, and to the symbolism associated with height and depth: spirit and sex. His comment, "In one of these, the symbol for spirit appeared as unreal or death-dealing, whereas sex appeared as a devouring monster," could well be a description of CR 531 (Henderson 1967, 108–111). Pollock more explicitly drew in CR 620 (c. 1941–1942) his own frightened face wrapped around by the coils of a serpent, showing real and horrific emotion. The fact that he was then able to imagine the serpent rising upward, plumed, and expressing more spiritual aspirations signals a positive emotional release.[8] Through visual thinking, Pollock is attempting to work his way from overpowering feelings of death and constriction to empowering feelings of self-renewal. The symbol of the plumed serpent is not just a potent cultural symbol but carries the promise of "organized" life.

More than with particular content, insight or wisdom here has to do with the creation of a mood of release and aspiration. This mood is generated by the way the release of the serpent rising manifests itself in a play of forms. In *Birth* the shift, from bottom to top, from the ambiguous forms of the amorphous masks to the more defined features of the plumed serpent being born, is orchestrated with interlocking arcing and spiraling rhythms, which play across the entire canvas, as curves in the releasing hand and bent leg start off the rhythm that then mounts up in looping lines. Linear rhythms suggest a jagged and bubbling release in a process of birth. Already we have here an intimation of the long linear rhythmic gestures with which he will ultimately create the allover energy field of *Autumn Rhythm*.

Male and Female: The Dream of Relationship

Riven by polarities, Pollock dreamed of integration and harmony. The next major life problem, hinted at in *Birth*, is the challenge of eros, the ability to relate to another and give birth. In *Male and Female* (c. 194; fig.14.4) Pollock addresses this challenge.

There is tension in this attempt. On one hand the artist hopes to find a wholeness for himself in embracing the other, on the other to give birth to a new entity, beyond himself, a child. This hope becomes complicated by Pollock's tendency to equate and confuse art and life. Is the other a real woman or a canvas, is what is to be born a real child or a work of art? This confusion stemmed from his lifelong conviction that, as he had written to his mother in 1932, "Painting is life itself" (*CR*, IV, 213, Doc. 13).

Figure 14.4. Jackson Pollock, *Male and Female*, c. 1942

Following the invitation of Pollock's title, the viewer immediately looks for a male and a female. Amidst an architecture of flat rectangular white and black planes, arrayed like stage-flats left and right of center, against what might be read as a flat blue ground, a pink female torso from stage right is impossible to overlook. But where is the male? To the left of center another female torso in red, topped by a black head with starry yellow eyes, appears to wait "off-stage," constrained by the vertical of an implicit panel; however, to the left of this red female torso, a white panel, columnar and phallic, spews forth startling passages of automatist paint handling—a suggestively male force. Further passages of painterly automatism are located in the upper right of the canvas, tumbling downward from the back of the white orb that functions as a moonlike head, its sharp yellow triangle marked by nostrils and white starry eye, for the pink female torso. The torso of this "moon woman" (Pollock titled another canvas of that year *Moon Woman*) is appended to a blackboard-like rectangle, which in this context would seem more male than female. While androgyny characterizes the two main personages in this canvas, the presence of scumbled passages of paint just below the yellow pubic triangle of this torso suggests a distinctly female sexual excitement.

Does *Male and Female* simply refer to Pollock's new relationship with Lee Krasner, whom he was to eventually marry in 1945? Do the striking white diamond shapes on the central white panel suggest the diamonds traditionally associated with engagement, the promise of a permanent union? But the strange ambiguities of figuration and symbolism suggest a complexity beyond such literal interpretation.

Playing with symbols and their shapes and colors, Pollock finds in *Male and Female* a stage for his continued visual thinking, exploring what he thinks and feels. The central white rectangular panel with, not only the pink torso, but its three hieratic diamond shapes draws our attention. The juxtaposition in one of Pollock's drawings of this period, CR 584r, of a Buddha head with a diamond shape, the latter positioned along a central vertical axis above a caduceus-like serpent and below a sun disc-moon crescent motif, attests to Pollock's interest in "Eastern wisdom."

Sometime in 1939–1940 his Jungian analyst had shown Pollock a book of Chinese mystical alchemy and Taoist yoga, *The Secret of the Golden Flower: A Chinese Book of Life*, with its introductory commentary by Jung.[9] The "diamond-body" is an important symbol for the harmony of opposites sought in this Chinese book of life, signifying not just the goal, spiritualized matter, but a way to the union of opposites: a circulatory, transformative process, whereby consciousness or spirit continuously descends into the chaos of unconscious matter, in order to awaken it and to give birth to a harmonious union and balancing of opposites in an ongoing flux (Wilhelm 1975, 24, 28,

31, 33). Having to do with matter and its transformation, this goal and process can be seen as a discourse on artistic creativity. Certainly Pollock was fascinated at this level. But given his equation of art and life, he was also attracted to this proffered wisdom as a guide to life and increased spiritual awareness.

The Secret of the Golden Flower holds out the promise of spiritual rebirth, figured by a union of male and female which issues in something new, a seed, a fetus, a new man.[10] Thus the centrally placed diamonds in *Male and Female* invite interpretation as an ambiguous symbol, not just of sexual union with its promise of a real child, but of such a fetus, a spiritual embryo, a new self. Trying to organize his life, Pollock teetered between two conceptions of life: other-directed, self-directed. Jung encouraged the immanentization of the other, insisting on the need to address the *anima*, the woman within, as a cultural challenge too, given the Western overemphasis on rationality as the center of personality (Jung in Wilhelm 1975, 110, 115).

If one looks ahead to Pollock's future development as an artist, what is of greatest interest in *Male and Female* is how Pollock handles paint. In discussions of his artistic development, the spiritual dimension which is present even in Pollock's most abstract canvases is barely considered. In *Male and Female* that significance is difficult to overlook. Consider once more the painterly automatist passages communicating sexual excitement. Striking is the intimation of a transformative circulatory rhythm, as in response to the male's desire, scumbled and spattered paint issues from the ambiguously gendered lunar head and cascades down the far right-hand panel, helping to generate a circulatory rhythm of erotic excitement. The diamonds symbolize the painterly goal of an animated matter. For the moment the central white panel, on which the diamonds are placed, is characterized by the flat thick paint of late Synthetic Cubism, "the thickness of white," as Pollock wrote on CR 697, a drawing of c. 1943. This panel, which reads as a painting within a painting, is but a material field unshaped and unstructured, except for its edges, symbolic diamonds, and female torso. Pollock's pictorial logic allows us to understand the thick materiality of the pictorial field itself as representing the most fundamental "female" realm that the artist proposes to transform by discovering within it a circulatory play of opposites. The architectonic structure of this putative canvas, with its vertical and horizontal axes, its in-out axis, the last latent in the thickness of the painted field, remains to be more thoroughly differentiated, transformed, and finally unified by a more spontaneous pictorial action. For the time being these energies swirl around the edges of the central "canvas," figuring a still only hoped-for art. The materiality of paint here looks forward, not to a base materialism, but to an alchemical, in other words pictorial, spiritualization of matter. This is Pollock's dream, a way to abstraction radically different from that taken by Cubism.

Male and Female can be understood as a challenge to Picasso. In *Painter and Model* (1928) Picasso, too, probes the nature of creativity in terms of male and female figures. Here, too, the figures are placed to either side of a central white "canvas." The comparison allows us to distinguish between Picasso's and Pollock's understanding of pictorial creativity. Picasso's art remains rooted in the split between subject and object that marks the Renaissance optical paradigm of painting as a "window looking out on the world." But the depicted artist and the three-eyed model are both represented in an angular Cubist style, while on his canvas the artist transforms the model's face into a naturalistic classical profile. The canvas here is the arena where the artist exerts aesthetic mastery in a creative act of artistic metamorphosis, where the natural beauty of the model on the canvas contrasts with the artificial reality represented, calling into question the meaning of artifice and reality.

Pollock's formulation of art in *Male and Female* is of a different order. The central "canvas" is presented, not as a surface on which the male artist works his transformations of the female model, but as a field to be animated. Such animation is the work of an erotically charged imagination. That Pollock's understanding of art was indeed very different from that of Picasso is indicated in two accounts of encounters with Hans Hofmann in the early 1940s. When Lee Krasner first introduced Hofmann to Pollock in 1942, Hofmann is said to have reacted at once to the paintings, "You do not work from nature." "I am nature," Pollock replied, implying that the images in his 1942 paintings were not derived from nature, but products of himself as part of nature (Landau 1989, 159, 259n. 2). In a similar vein, Fritz Bultman recalls an intense and ongoing dialogue between Hofmann and Pollock the summer of 1944 in Provincetown. One evening Pollock was

> trying to get across to Hans Hofmann his concept of the image: that you could paint from nature, which Hans was doing, but that if you painted out of yourself you created an image larger than a landscape. Hans disagreed with him in principle, and finally in talking about the origin of the image, Jackson said, "I *am* nature." (Bultman, quoted in Potter 1985, 77)

Exactly when Pollock made this statement is not crucial. He had been supported by this conviction ever since around 1941. That conviction is easily misunderstood: "People think he means he's God." To counter this misconception, Krasner explained: "He means he's total. He's undivided. He's one *with* nature, instead of 'That's nature over there, and I'm here'" (Krasner, quoted in Wallach 1981).

In *Painter and Model* Picasso depicts the male artist reacting to the female model, exterior to himself, to "nature that is out there," imaginatively transforming her in his act of creation. Pollock's statement "I am nature," on the other hand, reflects a belief in "a oneness" between inner and outer worlds. The split between subject and object no longer exists. This, to be sure, raises the question: once unmoored from the tension between subject and object around which the Renaissance paradigm of art is built, does the artist simply get caught in the subjective? Does not the belief in "oneness" between inner and outer worlds simply lead the individual to lose him or herself in the inner world? The immanentization of the other applies to nature as much as to woman. Meaning in life is discovered in interactions with the world around us, with others. Attempts to discover "the other" in the self may block such discovery.

Shimmering Substance: Spontaneity and Self-Integration

That Pollock does after some four years of visual thinking and formal play finally arrive at the painterly goal put forward in *Male and Female* is evident in *Shimmering Substance* (1946). Comparing the two canvases, we are struck by the novel formal aspects of *Shimmering Substance*: the nonfigurative abstraction, the animated materiality of the entire surface, the spontaneity with which this has been achieved. All that was promised in the symbolic figuration of *Male and Female* is delivered. The movement of spontaneous paint handling, restricted to the outside perimeter of the thick paint of the central white rectangle of *Male and Female*, now penetrates and animates thick paint throughout the entire surface of *Shimmering Substance*. Over the years as an artist-alchemist Pollock had worked at casting linear impulse down into colored paint, finally producing in 1945–1946 colored lines of paint sometimes extruded directly from the tube. In *Shimmering Substance* he began to experiment with their all-over application, creating these colored lines in fluid looping rhythms, generating relationships and elisions between opposites: black-white, yellow-red-blue, up and down, left-right, in-out, thick-thin. The architectonic structure implicit in the central white panel in *Male and Female* with its vertical and horizontal axes, its in-out axis, the last latent in the static thickness of the painted field, is realized now throughout the animated field of *Shimmering Substance*. The mud-pie painterliness of the canvas is not chaotic, but is a structured spontaneity.

The suggestion of a single glowing yellowish circle in *Shimmering Substance* provides a new emphatic unitary structure in Pollock's art, which can simultaneously be differentiated in endless looping rhythms. The viewer is either drawn to the circle as a figure that structures and unifies an all-over field, or lets go of it, becoming absorbed in the activity of the field. In the mystical alchemical terms of his search for wisdom, Pollock has found the golden flower or the diamond-body, found it not just as the primordial spirit which finds expression in endless process, but as the One, the origin of all opposites (Wilhelm 1975, 12, 27).

Did such an achievement of the diamond-body in art reflect a new level of self-integration in his life? Discovering the fully differentiated but integrated field of spirit-matter in *Shimmering Substance* Pollock probably did feel he had achieved self-integration, and not just an integration of his spiritual consciousness with his anima, the woman within. In November 1945 Pollock had married Lee Krasner and moved from New York City to the small village of Springs, on the tip of Long Island. Does the new unitary structure in *Shimmering Substance* reflect the wholeness that he discovered in embracing the other, a real woman? Might not it even embody his hopes to give birth to a new entity, beyond himself, a child?

Only after they were married, probably in the spring, certainly by the summer of 1946, did Lee tell Jackson that she would not have children with him, "because he couldn't be counted on for the long haul."[11] Lee's "no" emphatically broke any confusion between his art and reality for Pollock. His art was to be his child.

Now that art was no longer confused with the possibility of having a child, Pollock's feelings for the female were in part transferred to the female as nature, Mother Nature, if you will. *Shimmering Substance* is the final painting of a series of paintings he titled *Sounds in the Grass* (Landau 1989, 163, 166). He started this series after he had in June left his house studio for a new studio in the barn, moved to a site between the house and a beautiful inlet of Accabonac Harbor. Jeffrey Potter, a neighbor, remarked,

> Land meant a great deal to Jackson, and not only because of his love for the Bonac landscape. Land to him also meant Gardiner's Bay, the Atlantic, the sky, the weather. They were parts of a whole in which he felt as right as he could. (Potter 1985, 175)

The titles in the *Sounds in the Grass* series are evocative: *The Blue Unconscious*, *Something of the Past*, *The Dancers*, *Croaking Movement*, *Earthworms*, *Eyes in the Heat*, and *Shimmering Substance*. They suggest Pollock's desire to have his painting be more like nature, to have the process of painting itself be more natural, less in the service of making symbolic hieroglyphs.

Having come to understand erotic union as a dynamic interplay of opposites in *Shimmering Substance*, Pollock was able to let go of his imagery, to go abstract. The imagery had done its job. He could then release his creative energies directly into a dialogue with paint, playing on his own androgynous intuitions and sensitivity to the life inherent in paint. The dream of "I am nature," of being one with the other, with Mother Nature, of overcoming the split between subject and object, seemed to become reality. The one qualification to be made about *Shimmering Substance* was that it remained but a figure for what Pollock wished to translate into the immediacy of lived experience: a figure of future happiness.

POURED PAINTINGS: ENACTING FEELINGS

The step that Pollock next took was revolutionary. Given his conviction that art and life were one, he forced a move from art toward life. He embarked on the extraordinary new technique of pouring paint onto a canvas placed on the ground. To discuss this technique I will use a photograph taken by Hans Namuth of Pollock in the process of painting *Autumn Rhythm*, the culmination of his poured style, in the summer of 1950 (fig. 14.5).

Viewing *Autumn Rhythm* one immediately senses the directness of Pollock's application of paint, not by the traditional brush, but through pouring, and in this instance probably directly from the can (Coddington 1999, 102). In making the poured paintings, Pollock works with an almost unprecedented spontaneity. The matter that once resisted him so horribly is now responsive. Intention and execution are not at odds. Indeed beyond the size of the canvas and the choice of colors, black, white, and bronze/russet, there seems to be no clear intention. As Pollock himself put it:

> When I am *in* my painting, I'm not aware of what I'm doing. It is only after a sort of "get acquainted" period that I see what I have been about. I have no fears about making changes, destroying the image, etc., because the painting has a life of its own. I try to let it come through. It is only when I lose contact with the painting that the result is a mess. Otherwise there is pure harmony, an easy give and take, and the painting comes out well.[12]

He throws out a painterly mark, and responds, makes another mark, and responds to that in a situation of increasing complexity. "The painting has a life of its own. I try to let it come through." Pollock here is no longer the self-confident artist in charge of his materials, molding them to his will. Creativity is tied to responsiveness.

"Technic is the result of a need—new needs demand new technics" (*CR*, IV, 253, Doc. 90; Jackson Pollock handwritten statement, c. 1950). These notes, made by Pollock probably in 1950, invite the question: "What need?" At a fundamental level, it is the need to enact his feelings. "The modern artist," he explained, "is working with space and time, and expressing his feelings rather than illustrating" (*CR*, IV, 250, Doc. 87: Jackson Pollock, Interview with William Wright, The Springs, Long Island, New York, late 1950). As early as 1943 Pollock had experimented with the technique of pouring

Figure 14.5. Jackson Pollock, painting *Autumn Rhythm,* 1950

paint; in 1946 and 1947 this technique expands to become the chief pictorial means to express his new feelings of oneness with nature, of being part of a larger totality, a larger energy field. To his neighbor Jeffrey Potter some time after 1948, speaking of the ocean, he confided: "That ground swell is the universe breathing, over and over, short and long. On a good day, my work feels like that—alive, strong, all me."[13] In the more straightlaced format of an interview for radio in 1950, he stated: "The modern artist, it seems to me, is working and expressing an inner world—in other words—expressing the energy, the motion, and other inner forces." Such energies merge with other energies. In the same interview: "It seems to me that the modern painter cannot express this age, the airplane, the atom bomb, the radio, in the old forms of the Renaissance or any other past culture. Each age finds its own technique"

(*CR*, IV 249, 250: Doc. 87). To capture the flow of these energies he needed a line longer than the looping configurations in *Shimmering Substance*. He had first explored the release of linear rhythms in *Birth*. Now that he understood the circulation of energies throughout a pictorial field, he turned to a longer, fluidly poured line. With this he captured the flow of energy: mimesis, not as pictorial representation, but as reenactment.

In 1951, Pollock could assert: "My paintings do not have a center, but depend on the same amount of interest throughout."[14] But Pepe Karmel, with the help of photo-composite images created by overlapping Namuth's still photos, has uncovered the strong presence of a circle on the central axis of *Autumn Rhythm*, appearing during the early stages of making the painting, only to submerge as a hidden lodestone into the fabric of a finally all-over composition, in which Pollock rightly claims that the final paintings "depend on the same amount of interest throughout."[15] But look more closely for the distinctive features of this canvas: a sense of rhythm and journey moving on the horizontal axis through the all-over web.

The formal unities that Pollock was able to generate in the large paintings of 1950 led Greenberg to declare them instances of aesthetic "perfection"—in a sense "art for art's sake."[16] But Greenberg's aesthetic approach does not do Pollock's art justice. Certain details of *Autumn Rhythm* speak particularly to Pollock's continuing search for wisdom in the making of art. The central circle that Karmel observed in the photo-composite images of Pollock's creative progress he sees not only as functioning compositionally but as suggesting a full-length vaguely female figure (Karmel 1998, 119–20). The female thus maintains her essential role in Pollock's art. In reconstituting Pollock's process, Karmel observes that Pollock, after creating this central figure, then moved on to the left portion of the canvas where he threw a long "pole" stick figure, tilting up and out. Karmel notes the way Pollock amplified the original composition, reinforcing existing forms with additional black lines or "splats." Such reinforcement is particularly evident in the upper part of the left-hand figure where the major lines have become thicker and more insistent; in the central section where the effect of the original concentric order is obscured with a succession of horizontal bars in the lower center; in the upper right where among other marks a "lozenge" (I would be tempted to call this a diamond shape) is reinforced.[17] Even in these most abstract, poured paintings, Pollock still, at least sometimes, relies on the suggestion of his old images, his visual thinking, to trigger his gestural marks. Karmel is right to assert that the energy animating the poured paintings "seems in large part to have resulted from the interaction between Pollock's figurative imagery and his all-over, all-absorbing web" (Karmel 1998, 129). The energies that animate the poured webs remain the complexities of human emotions: in

Pollock's words "memories arrested in space,/ human needs and motives—/ acceptance—" (*CR*, IV 253 Doc. 90).

PAINTING AS ACTION AND REDEMPTION

A friend, Alphonso Ossorio, was behind a project, which Pollock embraced, of a Roman Catholic Church to be built on Long Island and which was to house six of Pollock's large poured paintings. The project hung fire from the summer of 1950–August 1952, when it was finally rejected by a group of prominent Catholics. One has to wonder how Pollock's poured paintings would relate to the meaning of a Catholic church and to its very specific program. The project, they said, was too abstract. But the fact that they and Pollock entertained the commission speaks to Pollock's attraction to religion, where his understanding of religion blurred with his understanding of Jung. Jung himself devoted the penultimate chapter of *The Integration of the Personality* (1939), entitled "The Idea of Redemption in Alchemy," to the analogy between his thinking and Catholicism. Catholic liturgy and alchemy share, he said, the transformative process of death and rebirth. While Pollock had finished his Jungian therapy in 1943, Jungian thinking was once again a topic of conversation in Pollock's circle in the summer of 1950 (Naifeh and Smith 1989, 610). Tony Smith, the architect for the Catholic church, and Pollock's very close friend, was both Catholic and a font of Jungian wisdom.[18] Pollock embraced the universal cosmic dimensions of the Jungian archetype of death and rebirth, and translated its symbolic representation into the abstract interplay of canvas and poured paint. Such abstraction, however, did not meet the demands of Catholic liturgy.

It was this cosmic dimension of Pollock's art, new in the summer of 1950, which led Harold Rosenberg, who had earlier been like a brother to Pollock, to attack his old friend (Solomon 1987, 166). At the end of World War II, as an answer to the evident failures of both Enlightenment reason and the old religions, Rosenberg became the spokesperson for those in the art world who embraced existentialism. In his now-famous article of December 1952, "The American Action Painters," Rosenberg agreed with Pollock's conviction that art is life.

> At a certain moment the canvas began to appear to one American painter after another as an arena in which to act—rather than a space in which to reproduce, re-design, analyze or "express" an object, actual or imagined. What was to go on the canvas was not a picture but an event. . . . The act-painting is of the same metaphysical substance as the artist's existence. The new painting has broken down every distinction between art and life. (Rosenberg 1952, 22, 23)

Action is central to both life and the art. The key question for Rosenberg is what constitutes an act, or as Rosenberg puts it, "the dialectical tension of a genuine act" (1952, 49).

Rosenberg, an acquaintance of Sartre, stood for action on the part of the individual in the face of the Void. For him it was fundamental to assert, as he did in 1949: "There is no use looking for silos or madonnas. They have all melted into the void."[19] As the 1952 article puts it:

> Art as action rests on the enormous assumption that the artist accepts as real only that which he is in the process of creating . . . the artist works in a condition of open possibility. . . . To maintain the force to refrain from settling anything, he must exercise in himself a constant No.

The existential actor must always exercise a "no" to any absolute.

Pollock, however, felt himself part of something larger. The fact that Pollock had given himself over to the "weak mysticism" of a "cosmic I" in 1950, Rosenberg found unforgivable. Earlier, in work of 1948 and 1949, Pollock had appeared to exercise the constant No demanded by Rosenberg, pushing from one possibility to the next, always possibilities "lacking in reality," as the new image of man turned into a mirage, always beckoning to a future. But hadn't something qualitatively different happened in Pollock's art in 1950? For Rosenberg, the grand summation of the dynamism of death and rebirth smacked of the Absolute, of God. Seeming to aim his judgment against the huge canvases of 1950, he wrote, "When a tube of paint is squeezed by the Absolute, the result can only be a Success. . . . The result is an apocalyptic wallpaper" (Rosenberg 1952, 48). Much later in 1967, years after Pollock's death in 1955, Rosenberg is even more blunt: "For Pollock, the aim of painting was to achieve not a balance of antagonistic factors, as in de Kooning, but a state of grace."[20] An artist whose aim was "a state of grace" was no action painter!

The larger and unstated issue behind his condemnation of his old friend is the distinction between a totalizing wisdom and the existential stance. Here we realize that artists were indeed grappling with fundamental questions of how to organize life. As an existentialist, must one, free from all binding values, create oneself? Or as someone who believes that a human being is part of something larger than him- or herself, must one discover oneself in relationship to what transcends the individual? Jungian thinking held out the promise of a homecoming to the collective, the universal. But, once achieved or "got," this "it" threatened closure and certitude. Rosenberg's existentialism responds to this threat. Had World War II not just been fought to defeat such totalizing certitude, as embodied in Nazism? To people like him, Jungian thinking seemed not so very distant from fascism; as Lee Krasner commented later, one did not dare talk of Jung following World War II.[21]

Pollock did pursue his art to an ending, an "it," and achieved an aesthetic perfection in his art, as Greenberg recognized. But for an artist convinced that art and life are one, to have made a perfect painting, to have achieved "it," is life-threatening. The dream that had long supported Pollock's art finally had become reality. But now he had to ask himself, what was it he had really done? Had he done more than create just another well-wrought aesthetic object divorced from life, beautiful but impotent? All the creative tensions had harmoniously ordered themselves in the plenitude of the aesthetic. Removed from life, this art is self-sufficient and pleasing. Such success invited repetition. But it was just this invitation to recycle what he had achieved that Pollock had to reject: he had never accepted art for art's sake alone.

Pollock's dream that art and life are one now turns destructive. Following his conviction of the oneness of art and life, the expectation is that the plenitude in art be accompanied by a plenitude in life. The tension between fantasy and reality that has haunted Pollock's art since 1942 meets a final test. The fact that his life was in increasing disarray forces from Pollock the growing realization: art is *not* life. Profound doubts about himself as a man and as an artist begin to set in.

There is the famous story of the shooting of the film documenting his creative practice and on which he and Namuth collaborated, brought to conclusion on Thanksgiving Day 1950. Celebrating, Lee had invited ten friends to the Thanksgiving feast. Pollock poured himself a shot of whiskey, having been completely off the bottle since fall 1948. Proceeding to get drunk, he began to taunt Namuth, "You're a phony. I'm not a phony. You're a phony" (Pollock, quoted in Naifeh and Smith 1989, 652). He ended by upending the Thanksgiving table laden with all the food. This debacle signaled his descent into drink, his retreat from the making of abstract poured paintings, the gradual return of his old imagery. His art, however, continued to testify to his struggle for meaning in his life and in his art—another whole story. Suffice it to say Pollock never did recover the flow of energy that animates such a canvas as *Autumn Rhythm*. His marriage disintegrated, he took a lover; his life ended when his car swerved off the road.

CONCLUSION

Even if the artist fails in life, can the viewer, whose point of view is different from the artist's, find wisdom in the art? By its style more than by its content, his artwork testifies to the ups and downs of Pollock's search for a way of existing in harmony with himself and with others. This search continues beyond that abrupt collapse in November 1950. In the end, for him it is still eros that holds the key to the meaning of life. But eros appears in two forms in Pollock's life and art: one seeking to overcome the lack that is part of the human condition by actually seizing the dreamed-of whole, the other by recognizing that full self-affirmation demands remaining open to the other. The last line of Goethe's *Faust*, "the eternal feminine draws us higher," thus also provides this chapter with a fitting end. Pollock's art is not so much a communication of specific insights; rather, it makes the person who struggles with his art more wise, by revealing to us something about the meaning of the human condition in an age that has experienced the death of God.

NOTES

1. As to I. Kant's concept of science, see, for example, his *Metaphysische Anfangsgründe der Naturwissenschaft*, A III (Riga: Hartknoch, 1786); as to practical wisdom, for example, his *Critik der praktischen Vernunft*, A 235 (Riga: Hartknoch, 1788).

2. See Clement Greenberg, "'American-Type' Painting," *Art and Culture: Critical Essays* (Boston: Beacon Press, 1961), 218–19.

3. *CR*, IV, 263, Doc. 102b; Lee Krasner, interview with B. H. Friedman, in Lieberman, W. S. 1969. *Jackson Pollock: Black and White*. New York: Marlborough-Gerson Gallery.

4. See Langhorne 1989, 68. For illustrations of CR 521r and related works discussed in this chapter, Orozco's *Aztec Warriors* panel at Dartmouth; Picasso, *Horse*, 1 May 1937; CR 521verso, CR 531, see figures 41, 43, 46, 47, 45 respectively.

5. Sanford McCoy, interview with James T. Valliere, August 1973, Archives of American Art, Microfilm Roll 3047, frame 660. Also see Naifeh and Smith 1989, 290, 298, 843.

6. Orozco, written for a Dartmouth College news release, May 25, 1932, cited by Jacquelynn Baas, "Dartmouth College and *The Epic of American Civilization*," in *Orozco at Dartmouth: The Epic of American Civilization* (The Trustees of Dartmouth College, 2007), 6.

7. Fritz Bultman, Interview with author, March 25, 1973.

8. Pollock continued his meditation on the integration of opposing forces, the snake and the bird, in canvases titled *Bird*, and then *Naked Man*, in which he presents himself as a bird-man. See Langhorne 1989, 70–82.

9. Wilhelm 1975, 138, and plate 4. Henderson remembers showing Pollock a mandala illustrated in Wilhelm 1975, pointing out particularly the image of the tail-biting snake, and explaining its significance as "a simple form of mandala which represents integration" (Henderson, quoted in Naifeh and Smith 1989, 333).

10. See Wilhelm 1975, 19, 34, and plate 8 with a human fetus central to the mandala.

11. May Tabak, quoted in Potter 1985, 190. Also see Naifeh and Smith 1989, 531.

12. Jackson Pollock, "My Painting," *Possibilities* (Winter 1947–1948), in *Jackson Pollock: Interviews, Articles, and Reviews*, ed. by Pepe Karmel (New York: Museum of Modern Art, 1999), 18.

13. Quoted in "Jackson Pollock: Fragments of Conversations and Statements, Selected, Extracted and Categorized, from His Own Notes by Jeffrey Potter 1949–56," in Harrison 2000, 86.

14. Robert Goodnough, "Pollock Paints a Picture," *Art News* (May 1951): 60.

15. For analysis of *Autumn Rhythm* from photo-composite, see Karmel 1998, 119–124.

16. Clement Greenberg, "'American-Type' Painting," *Partisan Review* (Spring 1955), in *The Collected Essays and Criticism*, Vol. 3, *Affirmations and Refusals, 1950–1956*, ed. by John O'Brian (Chicago: University of Chicago Press, 1986), 226.

17. On central circular configuration, reinforcement of left figure, and on lozenge, see Karmel 1998, 121, 124.

18. Naifeh and Smith (1989, 688) place Pollock's quizzing of Tony Smith on Oriental philosophies and reliving his earlier flirtations with Krishnamurti and Jung in summer 1952.

19. Harold Rosenberg, in *The Intrasubjectives*, exh. cat. (New York: Samuel M. Kootz Gallery, Sept. 14–Oct. 3, 1949), in *Reading Abstract Expressionism: Context and Critique*, ed. by Ellen G. Landau (New Haven: Yale University Press, 2005), 156.

20. Harold Rosenberg, "Mythic Act" (1967), in Harrison 2000, 130.

21. Lee Krasner, interview with author, May 2, 1975.

REFERENCES

Arnheim, Rudolf. 1962. *The Genesis of a Painting: Picasso's Guernica.* Berkeley: University of California.

Coddington, James. 1999. "No Chaos Damn It." In *Jackson Pollock: New Approaches*, ed. by Kirk Varnedoe and Pepe Karmel, 101–115. New York: Harry N. Abrams.

CR: see Pollock 1978.

Harrison, Helen A., ed. 2000. *Such Desperate Joy: Imagining Jackson Pollock.* New York: Thunder's Mouth Press.

Henderson, Joseph L. 1967. *Thresholds of Initiation.* Middleton, Conn: Wesleyan University Press.

Karmel, Pepe. 1998. "Pollock at Work: The Films and Photographs of Hans Namuth." In *Jackson Pollock: exhibition catalogue.* New York: Museum of Modern Art. 87–137.

Landau, Ellen G. 1989. *Jackson Pollock.* New York: Abrams.

Langhorne, Elizabeth. 1989. "Pollock, Picasso and the Primitive." *Art History* 12 (1): 66–92.

Naifeh, Steven, and Smith, Gregory White. 1989. *Jackson Pollock: An American Saga.* New York: Clarkson N. Potter.

Pollock, Jackson. 1978. *A Catalogue Raisonné of Paintings, Drawings, and Other Works.* 4 vols. Ed. by Francis Valentine O'Connor and Eugene Victor Thaw. New Haven, London: Yale University Press. [Abbreviated as *CR*; CR followed by a number refers to the number assigned to each artwork in *CR*].

Potter, Jeffrey. 1985. *To a Violent Grave: An Oral Biography of Jackson Pollock.* New York: G. P. Putnam's Sons.

Rosenberg, Harold. 1952. "The American Action Painters." *Art News* 51 (8): 22.

Schiller, Friedrich. 2004. *On the Aesthetic Education of Man.* Trans. by Reginald Snell. Mineola, New York: Dover Publications.

Solomon, Deborah. 1987. *Jackson Pollock: A Biography.* New York: Simon and Schuster.

Wilhelm, Richard, ed. and trans. 1975. *The Secret of the Golden Flower: A Chinese Book of Life.* With a "commentary" by Carl Gustav Jung. New York: Causeway Books. (Repr. of the 1st ed. London: 1931).

Wallach, Amei. 1981. "Out of Jackson Pollock's Shadow." *Newsday,* Sept. 23.

Wysuph, C. L. 1970. *Jackson Pollock: Psychoanalytic Drawings.* New York: Horizon Press.

PICTURE CREDITS

Fig. 1: Jackson Pollock, *Woman,* c. 1930–33. Oil on fiberboard, 35.8 × 26.6 cm. (14⅛ × 10½ in.). Nagashima Museum, Kagoshima City. Photo Credit: Jackson Pollock Catalogue Raisonné Archives, Pollock-Krasner Study Center. © 2012 The Pollock-Krasner Foundation/Artists Rights Society (ARS), New York.

Fig. 2: Jackson Pollock, *Autumn Rhythm: Number 32, 1950,* 1950. Oil on canvas, 266.7 × 525.8 cm (8 ft. 9 in. × 17 ft. 3 in.). The Metropolitan Museum of Art, New York. George A. Hearn Fund, 1957. Photo Credit: Jackson Pollock Catalogue Raisonné Archives, Pollock-Krasner Study Center. © 2012 The Pollock-Krasner Foundation/Artists Rights Society (ARS), New York.

Fig. 3: Jackson Pollock, *Birth,* c. 1941. Oil on canvas, 116.4 × 55.1 cm (45¹³⁄₁₆ × 21¹¹⁄₁₆ in.). Tate Gallery, London. Purchased 1985. Photo Credit: Jackson Pollock Catalogue Raisonné Archives, Pollock-Krasner Study Center. © 2012 The Pollock-Krasner Foundation/Artists Rights Society (ARS), New York.

Fig. 4: Jackson Pollock, *Male and Female,* c. 1942. Oil on canvas, 184.4 × 124.5 cm (6 ft. 1 in. × 49 in.). Philadelphia Museum of Art. Gift of Mr. and Mrs. H. Gates Lloyd, 1974. Photo Credit: Jackson Pollock Catalogue Raisonné Archives, Pollock-Krasner Study Center. © 2012 The Pollock-Krasner Foundation/Artists Rights Society (ARS), New York.

Fig. 5: Pollock painting *Autumn Rhythm,* 1950. Photograph © Hans Namuth Ltd., courtesy Pollock-Krasner House and Study Center, East Hampton, NY.

Afterword

Signs, Bodies, Artworks

Terry Eagleton

An alternative to Enlightenment rationality was born at the heart of the Enlightenment. It was known as aesthetics, and as the etymology of the word suggests, it had to do in the first place not with art but with perception and sensation. Aesthetics began life, in short, as a discourse of the body. It was a response to the scandal that the established form of rationality of the age seemed unable to cope with the textures of sensory experience, and thus to have disarmed themselves in a number of vital ways.

The aesthetic, to be sure, first arose less as a rival to Enlightenment reason than as a humble supplement to it. For Alexander Baumgarten's treatise *Aesthetica* (1750), it represents a kind of handmaiden to reason, extending its sovereignty into areas which were previously closed to its power. It signifies a kind of logic of the senses, one illustrated above all by art; and as such it behaves as an inferior but essential form of reason, discerning as it does a certain rational design in both art and everyday experience. Claude Lévi-Strauss would later find such concrete logic in the secret operations of myths, which are not in his view inimical to reason but which are rather a kind of reasoning otherwise, a sensuous or incarnate form of rationality. The various tangible bits of the natural world which go to constitute a body of myth are "good to think with," instances of thought in action, as exemplary in their own everyday fashion of the higher operations of the mind as science or philosophy.

As Jacques Derrida has taught us, however, it is in the manner of supplements to end up subverting what they seek to extend; and this is certainly the case with aesthetics, which only a handful of decades after Baumgarten, as Idealism and Romanticism come into their own, is to be found boldly proposing itself as a model of rationality all of its own. This new venture takes a number of forms, not least the idea that the creative imagination is a mode of cognition in itself. Or as George Eliot's Adam Bede more pithily puts it,

"Feeling's a sort of knowledge." Art is that peculiar mode of communication
in which affective, intuitive and imaginative forms of access to reality are
not only central, but for the most part predominate over the strictly cognitive.
Realist fiction may tell us much that is factually true, but it does so as part
of a more encompassing rhetoric and moral vision, not for its own sake. Yet
there is more to the matter than this. For art also advances a new model of totality, one radically different from that of the universal reason of a Leibniz or
Diderot. If the work of art becomes so insistent a philosophical preoccupation
at the time, it is not because art itself is cherished by middle-class society (far
from it), but among other things because it seems to offer the utopian promise
of a form of generality or universality which is intimately wedded to the sensuously specific. The work of art is governed by an overall law, structure and
design, yet this law is accessible only in its concrete instantiation. Indeed, it
is no more than the complex interrelation of the artwork's sensory particulars,
and has no existence over and above this palpable presence. It inscribes itself
on the body of the work, which accordingly steers a middle course between
the anarchic (a mob of unruly particulars) and the monolithic (the subjugation
of each feature of the work to a dominant principle or idea).

This, plainly enough, is as much a political notion as an artistic one. If it
were only an aesthetic affair, it is doubtful it would have gained the force and
authority it did as the modern age unfolded. In fact, one might see aesthetics
as a bridge or transition between a theological age and a political one. Most
aesthetic concepts (creation, inspiration, unity, autonomy, self-foundedness,
spiritual communion, symbolic or epiphanic revelation and the like) are
fragments of displaced theology; but the work of art is now also becoming a
paradigm of the good society, a cooperative commonwealth in miniature in
which the various parts work together to enrich and enhance one other. Each
of these features is self-determining, but finds the basis of its autonomy in the
context created for it by the others. Politically speaking, this subtle interplay
of freedom and relatedness resembles nothing quite as much as a republican
or democratic form of government, in which (to borrow a celebrated phrase
from *The Communist Manifesto*), the free self-development of each is the
condition for the free self-development of all. Friedrich Schlegel anticipates
Marx and Engels's comment, remarking that "Poetry is republican speech: a
speech which is its own law and end unto itself, one in which all the parts are
free citizens and have the right to vote."

Marxist aesthetics in the wake of the *maître* himself also regards the sensuous specificity of the artwork as an implicit critique of the abstraction of
the commodity, while in the *Grundrisse* Marx outlines a relation between
the abstract and the concrete rather different from that of either rationalism
or empiricism. The abstract or general concept ("money," for example) is

not to be rejected in some access of myopic particularism. Marx knew well enough the emancipatory as well as oppressive powers of the abstract and universal. Even so, the abstract is to be seen as more simple and anaemic than the concrete, which is the irreducibly rich product of many such general determinations. Marx accordingly speaks of "rising" from the abstract to the concrete, which is not how the relation between those two realms is commonly imagined.

The work of art as a whole, faithful to no heteronomous law but true only to its own stubbornly specific being, is thus a model of freedom grasped as radical self-determination. It is a theory of art that was to survive at least as late as Yeats. Art represents a form of politics in which overall sovereignty works through and in terms of self-governing individuals. If this can furnish the basis for an assault on the autocracy of the *anciens régimes*, however, it can just as easily be seen in the light of an emergent bourgeois hegemony, in which the law or sovereign power installs itself so deeply on the interior of the sensory bodies over which it has command that for these individuals to put it in question would be to undermine their own identities. Besides, if the law presents itself as nothing but the interrelation of sensory particulars, then it seems to disappear into them, becoming far less easy to objectify, thus harder to challenge. It is this distinctively modern form of political hegemony, based on a certain understanding of the aesthetic, that informs Schiller's meditations on aesthetic education; and it is not until Freud arrives on the scene that this miraculous coincidence of law and desire will be exposed as the impossible fantasy that it is. What is at stake is the production of a citizen who has so internalized the law, so assimilated it to his passions and desires, that his very self-determination will signify a kind of spontaneous conformity.

Such a human subject will work all by itself, constituting a law unto itself (one thinks of the etymological root of "autonomous"), without need of the centralized autocracy or constant surveillance which is in any case being gradually dismantled with the growth of market relations and civil society. Aesthetics is an allegory of the political from start to finish. From Plato to postmodernism, it is not really possible to reflect on the relations between the august universality of reason and the immediacy of the senses without casting an anxious sideways glance at a much less comfortably academicist problem, namely the desirable relations between the high-minded rulers and the impassioned masses. As with so many issues, it is Nietzsche who will deal this whole lineage a blow from which it scarcely recovers.

The work of art can be seen as a form of practical reason, though of a peculiarly impractical, purposively purposeless kind. Its function for a certain current of Romanticism is precisely to be functionless, and thus to provide a tacit critique of all vulgarly utilitarian conceptions of functionality. Like virtue, it is a form of praxis or knowledge-in-action whose goods are internal to it, and its truth is inseparable from its concrete self-performance. As with a sacrament, sign and reality are at one, the substance of the work inseparable from its act of signification. Like virtue, too, the work of art can effect its most powerful interventions in reality precisely by remaining true to its inherent principles. It is not by stepping outside itself, but by remaining faithful to the unique law of its own being, that it is at its most ethically relevant.

There is a sense in which this whole aesthetic conception, in the sense of "aesthetic" as sensation and perception, is born again over one and a half centuries later, though its name is now phenomenology. I am thinking less of Husserl than of Heidegger and Merleau-Ponty, and less of the eidetic or transcendental than of a certain phenomenological understanding of the body. The human body is itself a form of practice, a point from which a world of meaning is organized, a source of significations in which it is itself caught up. As with the work of art, its self-organizing or self-determining power does not mean that it is miraculously free of determinations. In the case of both art and the body, it means rather that the world becomes the material for its active self-making, so that the autonomy of both body and artifact exists only in relation to a deeper dependency. It is the peculiarly transformative relationship to their determinants that makes art and the body akin in this respect.

One might claim that those activities in which the body engages as ends in themselves, as opposed to more instrumental ones like extracting wisdom teeth or clearing ice from a windscreen, are the forms of practice we count as most precious. It is when the body is incarnate in some piece of praxis like dance, festive celebration or sexual love that it is at its most insistently, materially present. In an older aesthetic idiom, doing and being are here at one. What allows the body to be at its most materially expressive, luminously meaningful and eloquently self-productive is not a suspension of practice as such, but of particular impoverished or crassly instrumental forms of practice. The point of these more valuable activities lies not in achieving ends outside themselves (though they may involve this as well), but in constituting forms of self-realization. Kicking a ball into a net involves fitting means to ends, but to say that this is done as part of a game is to claim that it is done for its own sake. Even Rio Ferdinand presumably plays football for more than just the money.

Art has traditionally been one name for this self-grounding, self-validating, self-determining activity, as virtue has been another. Art and the body are both strategic practices which organize themselves for the accomplishment of certain ends. When these ends are internal to such performances, as they are by definition in the case of art and can be from time to time in the case of the body, human flourishing is at its most valuable and vigorous. It is this above all we should understand by the apparently frivolous, overbred aestheticist injunction that to live well is to turn oneself into a work of art. The finer forms of aestheticism are not about replacing life with art, but about aestheticizing life itself. This is also a political affair. If Marx and Oscar Wilde both believed in socialism, however incongruous a couple in most other respects, it was because they both held that self-realizing energies should become an end and delight in themselves; that this, as with all far-reaching ethical projects, was in Aristotelian fashion inseparable from the question of political institutions; and that securing this ethico-political goal for as many men and women as possible meant an end to the commodifying, instrumentalist reason of industrial capitalism. Marx writes in his *Economic and Philosophical Manuscripts* of how capitalism plunders the body itself of its sensory wealth, reducing it to a mere instrument of labor or profit. If we are to experience our corporeal existence to the full, he believes, political change is indispensable.

What also links art to human bodiliness is the fact that both involve a peculiar interweaving of meaning and materiality. It belongs to the idea of the poetic that the more "corporeal" language becomes—the denser, more thickly textured its material presence—the more richly allusive it becomes, which is to say the more it opens itself as a medium to a world beyond itself. In this sense, the poetic sign is autonomous and allusive at the same time. Indeed, the more it flaunts and foregrounds its materiality, the more profusely referential it becomes. Something similar might be claimed of the human body, the materiality of which, being the stuff of a set of practices, is not separable from its active relations to a world. Practice is the life of the body in the sense that meaning is the life of a sign. This is doubtless one reason why Thomas Aquinas refuses to speak of a dead body. For him, a corpse is the remains of a human body, a lump of material that had finally ceased to signify, a piece of the world from which meaning had hemorrhaged to leave it no more than a brute parcel of matter. The fact that the phrase "the body in the library" spontaneously brings to mind a corpse is simply part of a malign dualism which Aquinas rejected out of hand. True to this theological materialism, Aquinas also saw the body as the principle of human identity. He would by no means have believed that the disembodied soul of Michael Jackson is Michael Jackson.

The body is a sign; but it is not a sign of something beyond or outside itself. To see it as a semiotic phenomenon is to see its stuff as being as inherently expressive of significance as a word is expressive of meaning. Like a word or a poem, a body is a piece of signifying matter. The enigma of how black marks on a sheet of paper can be expressive of something as momentous as meaning is matched by the mystery of how the movement of a hand can signify a greeting—how meaning, so to speak, is as incarnate in this bit of physical motion as it is in a smile (but not in a sneeze . . .). The action of seizing another's hand in greeting is human action rather than mere physical motion, of interest to the sociologist as well as the physicist, only because it is caught up in language, and the meaning is to the action as the lining is to a sleeve. Even before it can speak, a small child stretches out his hand to grasp a toy, and this action is intrinsically meaningful, not simply meaningful to an observer equipped with language.

Human meaning is always carnal meaning, as art makes most graphically evident. Aquinas held that we think as we do because of the kind of bodies we have. Our thought is discursive because that is the nature of our sensory experience. If an angel could speak, we would not be able to understand what he said. To call the human body rational is not to suggest that it always behaves in the most impeccably reasonable of ways, but that it is suffused with sense. In the same way, there is no particle in the classical work of art (the modernist, postmodernist or avant-garde artifact is a different matter) that is nonsignifying. This, one might claim, is the artwork as redeemed or resurrected body, the word made flesh, its material as translucent a medium of sense as the spiritual or risen body of St. Paul. Aquinas considered metaphor to be the most appropriate language in which to discuss spiritual truths, since being sensory it is best suited to our corporeal natures. One might call this at a stretch a Dominican theory of meaning. Swayed by Aristotle's doctrine that the soul is not separate from the body but its animating form, the Dominican order in the thirteenth century converted this belief into a form of hermeneutics, for which the "spirit" of a piece of writing was not to be grasped kabbalistically, as some esoteric mystery secreted within the outer husk of the text, but as one accessible in common literal and historical terms.

Scriptural fundamentalism might then be seen among other things as a kind of vulgar materialism of the text. It represents the kind of obtusely literal reading in which, for example, Shakespeare's Portia engages so outrageously in *The Merchant of Venice*. As spokeswoman for the Venetian Christian ruling class, Portia manages to foil the schemes of an odious Jewish outsider by arguing that Shylock's legal right to carve flesh from Antonio's body makes no reference to the taking of blood. Any actual court would, of course, throw out such sophistry without a second thought. Portia is deliberately blind to the inferences and tacit understandings inscribed in Shylock's bond. As more than one contributor to this volume argues, it is of such implications, contextual judgments and intuitive uptakes that practical reasoning is constituted, and it is in art and bodily experience that this is most tangibly illustrated.

Index of Names

Academics, 41, 49, 263f.
Alexander of Aphrodisias, 42
Alvarez, Maria, 106
Ammonius, 41f., 51f., 61f.
Ann Davis, Nancy, 180f.
Antipater of Tarsus, 44
Aquinas, Thomas, ix, 2, 6, 69, 88f., 209, 218, 221, 295
Ardelt, M., 126
Arendt, Hannah, 25
Aristotle, ix, 2, 4f., 7f., 10, 17–36, 40–42, 45, 49, 57, 61, 66–68, 70, 73, 76, 89, 92, 103, 111–128, 131, 152, 154, 158f., 206–213, 262, 295f.
Arnheim, Rudolf, 274
von Arnim, Hans, 61
Augustine, 208f., 246f., 250, 253f., 257, 261–263
Austin, John L., ix, 2, 39, 41, 56, 61, 126, 136
Averroes (Ibn Rushd), 10, 207–211

Baltes, P. B., 126
Baumgarten, Alexander, 291
Beauchamp, Thomas, 9f., 185–200
Bengston, B. H., 36
Benhabib, Seyla, 3, 128
Berkeley, George, 222
Biro, J., 139

Blumenberg, Hans, 262
Bobzien, Susanne, 44
Bodéus, Richard, 22
Boger, George, 140
Bonaventure, 209
Bondy, Patrick, 140
Boscovich, Giuseppe Ruggero, 216
Brandom, Robert B., 107
Braverman, Harry, 150, 165
Breen, Keith, 8, 147
Brockriede, E., 134
Brown, Richard Harvey, x
Bruno, Giordano, 212f.
Bultman, Fritz, 274, 279
Burns, Robert, 90
Burnyeat, Myles, 115
Butler (Bishop), 80, 83

Calvin, Johannes, 257
Cambridge Platonists, 91
Canavan, Frank, 7, 131
Carrasco, Maria A., 91
Casey, Gerard, 6, 79
Castagnoli, Luca, 63
Cavini, Walter, 63
Childress, James, 9f., 185–200
Christensen, C., 262
Chrysippus, 42–46, 49, 55, 58, 60f., 63
Cicero, 7

Clark, Stephen R. L., 34
Cleanthes, 44
Cleary, John, xi
Confucius, 84f.
Cooper, John M., 24, 34
Copernicus, Nicolaus, 213, 216
Crawford, Robert, 90
Cudworth, Ralph, 79
Curnow, Trevor, 122f.
Cusanus, Nicolaus, 207, 216

Depew, David J., 24f.
Derrida, Jacques, 291
Descartes, René, 11, 245–264
Dewey, John, 131
Diderot, Denis, 292
Diodorus Cronus, 57
Diogenes Laertius, 40, 43, 52, 54,
　　59–62
Diogenes the Babylonian, 44
Dionysius of Halikarnassus, 62
Dreger, Alice, 174, 177
Dürrenmatt, Friedrich R., 101
Dunn, William, 134
Dunne, Joseph, 3, 160, 166
Dupré, Louis, 262

Eagleton, Terry, 10, 12f., 291
Edmondson, Ricca, xi, 7, 13, 111, 140,
　　243
van Eemeren, Frans H., 8, 136
Egli, Urs, 52, 62
Ehninger, D., 134
Eliot, George, 291
Epictetus, 58
Erasmus of Rotterdam, 246, 262

Fehling, Detlev, 61
Felzmann, Heike, 9f., 185
Fichte, Johann Gottlieb, 206
Finley, Moses I., 35
Fogelin, Robert J., 136
Ford, Henry, 151
Fowler, William Warde, 36
Fukuyama, Francis, 240–243

Gadamer, Hans-Georg, 2
Galen, 58
Galilei, Galileo, 208, 212
Gassendi, Pierre, 253
Gaut, Berys, 12
Gellius, Aulus, 44, 61
Gigon, Olof, 28
Gil, Thomas, 6f., 95
Gillespie, Michael Allen, 246, 262
Glover, Jonathan, 9, 172f., 178, 180,
　　182
Goethe, Johann Wolfgang von, 288
Grant, E., 262
Greenberg, Clement, 269, 284, 287
Grice, Herbert Paul, 136
Grootendorst, Robert, 8, 136
Gyllenhammar, Pehr, 161

Habermas, Jürgen, 2, 152f.
Hamblin, Charles, 139
Hanby, Michael, 262
Harries, Karsten, 10f., 205
Hastings, A. C., 142–144
Hegel, Georg Friedrich Wilhelm, 28,
　　229, 234, 240, 263
Heidegger, Martin, 3, 11, 13, 25, 205,
　　214, 217, 222, 245, 262, 294
Hempel, Carl G., 117, 130
Henderson, Joseph, 269, 272, 275
Heraclitus, 31
Herder, Johann Gottfried, 36
Hicks, Robert D., 43, 59
Hirzel, Rudolf, 42
Hitchcock, D., 140
Hobbes, Thomas, 30, 227, 230, 232
Höffe, Otfried, 36
Hofmann, Hans, 279
Homer, 20
Hülser, Karlheinz, xi, 5f., 13, 39
Hull, Richard, 9, 171
Hume, David, 79f., 90f., 213f., 217
Husserl, Edmund, 11, 262, 294
Hutcheson, Francis, 79, 86, 90f.

Isocrates, 112, 123

Jansen, Cornelius, 246, 257
Johnson, R. H., 139
Jung, Carl Gustav, 269, 277f., 285–287, 289

Kahane, Howard, 135
Kakkuri-Knuuttila, Marja-Liisa, x
Kant, Immanuel, 2f., 11f., 154, 206, 212, 215f., 218, 220–222, 227, 229, 234, 236, 245, 267
Karmel, Pepe, 284
Kekes, John, 122
Kenny, Anthony, 6, 106
Keyt, David, 29
Kienpintner, M., 142f.
Kierkegaard, Søren, 205f.
Kohn, Melvin, 154
Kolakowski, Leszek, 263
Korsgaard, Christine M., 107
Krasner, Lee, 277, 279, 281, 287
Krishnamurti, 268, 289
Krüger, Hans-Peter, x
Kullmann, Wolfgang, 22f., 25, 28f., 34f.

Labarriere, Jean-Louis, 27
Lalla, Sebastian, 11, 227
Langhorne, Elizabeth, 12, 267
Lawson, A., 117
Leibniz, Gottfried Wilhelm, 292
Lévi-Strauss, Claude, 291
Luther, Martin, 257, 262

MacIntyre, Alasdair, 2, 8, 35, 147, 156–160
Mackie, John L., 21
Marcovich, Miroslav, 62
Maritain, Jacques, 263
Marrone, Livia, 45, 62f.
Marshall, John, 264
Marx, Karl, 292f., 295
Mates, Benson, 264
Maxwell, Nicholas, 123
McDermott, Drew, 205–207, 210–222
McGrale, A., 246
Melzer, Sara E., 263

Menander, 63
Menn, Stephen, 263
Merleau-Ponty, Maurice, 13, 294
Miller, Fred D., 21, 30f.
Montaigne, Michel de, 144, 246, 261, 263
Mulgan, Richard G., 24
Murphy, James Bernard, 155f.

Naess, Arne, 138
Namuth, Hans, 282, 284, 287
Nasti de Vincensis, Mauro, x
Neto, José R. Maia, 264
Neurath, Otto, 128, 214f., 217, 222f.
Newman, John Henry, 83
Newman, William L., 31f.
Nicholson, Jack R., 101
Nietzsche, Friedrich, 207, 216–222
Nisters, Thomas, 5f., 65
Nuchelmans, Gabriel, 40, 46–51, 62
Nussbaum, Martha, 3

Ó Murchadha, Felix, 11, 245
O'Rourke, Fran, 5, 17, 112
Olbrechts-Tyteca, Lucie, 116, 135, 143
Origenes, 54, 62
Orozco, José Clemente, 272
Ossorio, Alphonso, 285
Otteson, James R., 90f.

Parekh, Bhikhu C., 128
Parfit, Derek, 106
Pascal, Blaise, 11, 245–264
Pearce, Jane, 126
Pelagius, 247, 253, 257, 261f.
Perelman, Chaim, 116, 135, 143
Peripatetics, 40, 42, 51
Peters, James, 250
Petrarch, 246
Picasso, Pablo, 271f., 274, 279
Pico Della Mirandola, Giovanni, 264
Plato, 12, 79, 122, 152, 229
Plutarch, 45, 52, 54f., 61–63
Pollock, Jackson, 12, 267–289
Popkin, Richard H., 245, 264

Posidonius, 42, 44, 52, 62
Protagoras, 42

Rau, Henrike, 129
Rawls, John, 11, 197f., 227–243
Raz, Joseph, 6, 99, 104
Rehbock, Theda, 4
Rodis-Lewis, Geneviève, 264
Rorty, Amélie O., 122, 129
Rosenberg, Harold, 285f.
Rousseau, Jean-Jacques, 227f., 232
Rüstow, Alexander, 63
Rupp, E. Gordon, 262

Sakellariou, Michael B., 21, 31
Sartre, Jean-Paul, 286
Schenkeveld, Dirk, 40, 42, 44, 46, 48,
    50–52, 60–63
Schiller, Friedrich, 12, 267
Schmidl, Wolfgang, 129
Schön, Donald, 125
Schooler, Carmi, 154
Schopenhauer, Arthur, 222
Scriven, Michael, 135
Searle, John H., 112
Sellars, Wilfrid, 106
Seneca, 61, 63
Sextus Empiricus, 11, 40, 43, 62, 263f.
Shakespeare, William, 296
Siegel, H., 139
Siger of Brabant, 10, 206f., 209–211,
    218, 223
Simonides, 32

Simpson, Peter L. Phillips, 32
Smith, Adam, x, 4, 6, 79–92, 152
Smith, Tony, 285
Snow, Charles P., 13
Sophocles, 20, 35
Sprat, Thomas (Bishop), 4
Staudinger, U., 126
Steiner, G., 264
Sternberg, Robert J., 126
Stoics, ix, xi, 39–63, 79
Sturges, Preston, 90

Taylor, Frederick Winslow, 148–152
Theon, Aelius, 61–63
Tindale, Christopher, 140
Toulmin, Stephen E., 7f., 131–145, 262
Trent, J., 128

Verbeke, Gerard, 22

Walton, Douglas N., 142, 144
Warnick, Barbara, 143
Weber, Max, 147, 165
Wilde, Oscar, 295
William of Ockham, 246
Wittgenstein, Ludwig, 2, 136, 216
Woerner, Markus H., ix, 13, 39, 41, 56,
    112, 115f., 243
von Wright, Georg Henrik, 6, 102

Xenocrates, 41

Zeno of Citium, 47

Index of Subjects

abstraction, 269, 271, 278, 281, 284f.
acceptability, 136, 139–145
actors, 49, 55, 58, 60f.
address, 40, 43f., 48, 50, 53, 58f.
aesthetic, aesthetics, x, 3, 12, 291–296
alchemy, 277f., 280, 285
aporia, 245, 252, 255, 257f., 261, 263f.
argument, 95–107
argumentation, 131–145
art, artwork, x, 291–296
Augustinianism, 257, 261

backing, 133
benefaction, 68–70, 72–76
benefactor, 68–70, 72f., 75f.
beneficiary, 67–70, 73, 75f.
benevolence, 69, 74, 84, 86, 89
Bethlehem Steel Company, 149
"biomedical model," disability
biomedical principles: balancing of,
    185, 187f., 190–193, 196–198, 200;
    specification of, 185, 187–193, 195,
    197f., 200; *Principles of Biomedical
    Ethics*
blame, 83, 91f.
body, 291–296
body/soul relation, 248

casuistry, 185f., 188, 193–195, 197
cause/effect, 47f., 62
certainty, 245, 254f., 257–261
citizen, 30–34
claim, 133
co-operative principle, 136, 141
cogito argument, 252f., 259
cognitive science, 206
Common morality, 185, 187f., 197–199
Commonplace, 115
complete *lekta*: list of, 40f., 44, 51–55,
    60, 62; schema for the definition of,
    40, 43, 47, 53–57; *lekton/lekta*
concord, 81
Condemnation of 1277, 208–212
conjoined twins, 174, 176f.
conscience, 82–85, 90
constitution, 32f.
counter-benevolence, 69, 74f.
cubism, 278
custom, 256, 259

data, 133
death, 259f., 267–269, 274f., 285f.
deception, 252f.
deduction, 111, 114f., 117
deductive logic, 132

deductive-nomological model, 117
desire(s), 95–107, 248, 250, 254–258,
    264
despair, 252f., 258
detailed division of labour, 151–155
dialectic, Stoic concept of, 40–42, 44,
    48, 54, 61
dialectical discourse, 45f., 48f.
disability: and human flourishing, 172,
    179, 181; and impairment, 175; and
    normality, 173; and social justice,
    179; hybrid model of, 178–182;
    medical model of, 9, 172; social
    model of, 9, 176
disposition, 68, 76
doubt, 252–254, 256f., 263

efficiency, rival ideals of, 157f.
ekthesis, 44, 52, 58, 62
emotion, 65–69, 71–73, 75f.
endoxa, 114, 128
enthymeme, 114f., 117, 119, 130
epideictic speech, 112, 123, 125
equilibrium, 81
eros, 268, 275, 278f., 281, 288
ethics, 3f., 9f., 13, 206, 215
ethnography, 112, 127–129
ethos, 111–129, 113
existentialism, 206, 267f., 285f.

faith, 205, 208, 211, 253
fallacy, 138–145
falleness/the fall, 248–255, 257, 259–
    261, 263
family, formation of, 18f.
Fordism, post-Fordism, 151f.
forensic speech, 112
freedom, 253, 257f.: divine, 206f.,
    211f.; human, 206f., 212, 214, 216
friendship, 26

generosity, 258f.
Genesis, 249
God, 245, 253, 260
good life, 19

grace, 248, 253f., 257, 261–263
grateful, 66–68, 71–76

habit, 248, 257
habits, 84
happiness, 33
heart, 249–251, 259f., 263
human nature, 25
humility, 254
hyper-grateful, 69f., 72f.
hyper-gratitude, 69f., 73
hypo-gratitude, 69

idealism, 29
illative core, 139
illocutionary speech acts, 41, 56–61
immortality, 260f.
impartial spectator, 79–83, 85, 89, 91
implicature, 136
induction, 87f., 111, 114, 117
inescapable framework illusions (IFI's),
    206, 213, 215–217, 219, 222
informal logic, 136, 138–145
ingratitude, 67, 69f., 72f.
instincts, 84

Jansenists, 246, 257
jurisprudence, 134
justice, 82, 85, 87–89, 227–243; and
    Law, 259

language, 218f., 221–223
Lean production, 151f.
lekton/lekta, 39–63; term, definition and
    division, 40, 42f.; complete *lekta*
liar antinomy, 60, 63
linguistic doing, 39–46, 50f., 55f.
Logical investigations (Chrysippus),
    45f., 49, 55, 58, 60, 63
logos, 111–129, 113
love, 251, 259

malefaction, 76
malevolence, 70, 74f.
mathematics, 62

metaphysica specialis, 245f.
method, 246f.
modal qualifier, 133
moods of the verb, 40, 42, 44f., 47, 50,
    61f.
moral quality, 71f.
myth, 291

naturalism, moderate, 95
nature, 23
nihilism, 216, 222
norms, 95, 100f.

orders, 95, 101: types of commands

pain, 67, 70, 73–75
passions, 248–250, 257f.
pathos, 111–129, 113
Pelagianism, 247, 253, 257, 261f.
performatives, 136
phenomenology, ix, 3
phronēsis, 159
phronetic production and productive
    reason, 156–160
pleasure, 67, 69, 73–75
poiēsis, 152, 159
polis, 17–20, 27, 29–34: formation of,
    18f.
political animal, 17–38
political deliberation, 112–114, 117,
    119, 121, 123, 125, 128f.
politics, 4, 10f., 13, 33
pouring technique, 282f.
"practices," idea of (MacIntyre), 156–
    160
pragma, 46–51, 55, 62
Pragma-dialectical method, 136
praise, 82f., 90
praxis, 152, 159
pre-implantation genetic diagnosis, 179
prenatal testing and disability, 179
Principles of Biomedical Ethics, 185–
    200
probability, 132
professional ethics, 185

promises, 5f., 95f., 98–101
promising, act of, 250, 255f.
proposition, concept of, 43–46, 54, 57f.,
    60
propriety, 79–82, 85, 89
proverbs, 124
provisional moral code (Descartes),
    256–259
pseudo-benefaction/-factor, 70
Pyrrhonism, 11, 245, 252, 254f., 263f.

quasi-proposition, 41, 56f., 59–61
Quetzalcoatl, 272, 274f.

reason, 79f., 82, 84–89, 91f.
reasoning, 111–129
reasons to act, 95–107
rebirth, 274, 278, 285f.
rebuttal, 133, 144
"reflective production," 161
relativism, 206f., 213f.
reputable opinion, 114
rewarding/to reward, 71, 73–76
rhetoric, ix, 3, 7f., 111–129, 136, 141
romanticism, 291, 293
rules, 80f., 85–91

Scandinavian "sociotechnical" school of
    industrial job-design, 161
scepticism, 245–264
scientific management, 149–151
Scottish Enlightenment, 2
The Secret of the Golden Flower, 277f.,
    280
self-consciousness, 26
self-determination and self-realization
    (freedom), 153
sign, 291–296
"social" and "technical" divisions of
    labor, 155f.
social behavior, 21
sophists, 123
soul, 22f.
specialization, 157
speech acts, 39–42, 46f., 51, 55, 58, 62

speech, forms of, 40, 42, 51
speech/logos/reason, 20, 24f., 27, 35
Stoicism, 5, 247, 250, 253f., 257, 262
substantial arguments, 132, 137–139
suspension of belief/judgment *(epoché)*,
    252, 254–256, 263
Sweden, 161, 164
syllogism, 40, 42, 52, 58f., 112, 114,
    132
sympathy, 79–82, 84, 86, 89f.

Taylorism, neo-Taylorism, 8, 148–152
technē, 159f.
technicism and work, 149–152
thanking/to thank, 69, 73–76
time, 248, 257, 259f., 263
topos/topoi, 115–117, 119f., 127f., 138,
    143
tranquility *(ataraxia)*, 252, 255, 258,
    261, 263
trust, 251, 253
types of: commands, 40, 44–46, 49f.,
    53f., 58, 60–62; questions, 44–46,
    48f., 52f., 55, 58, 60

Uddevalla car assembly plant, 160–165
ungrateful, 69f., 72f.
unhappiness, 255, 259f.
utilitarianism, 237f.
utopianism, 165

value, 205f., 214, 216
veil of ignorance, 231, 235, 238
vice, 65f., 69, 72f., 75
Village, formation of, 18f.
virtue, 65–69, 71–73, 75f., 294
virtuous, 66, 72
visual thinking, 268, 271, 274f., 277,
    280, 284
voluntarism, 246f.
Volvo Corporation, 160–165

warrant, 133
West of Ireland, 127
wide reflective equilibrium, 185, 190,
    197, 200
will, 247–251, 253f., 257f., 260, 264:
    indifference of, 253
wisdom, wise arguing, x, 7, 12, 111–
    129, 245
wonder, 258
work and working life: deformations
    of, 152–156; effects on cognitive
    and emotional functioning
    and identity formation, 154f.;
    normative significance of, 153–156;
    organization of, 149–165; phronetic
    conception of, 156–160; technicist
    conception of, 149–152
world, 245f.
wretchedness, 255, 259f.

About the Contributors

Dr. Keith Breen lectures in political theory in Queen's University, Belfast. His interests lie in theories of modernity, political ethics, and the philosophy of work. He has published in a number of journals on the thought of Alasdair MacIntyre and Hannah Arendt, critical theory, and the ethics and politics of work. He is the author of *Under Weber's Shadow: Modernity, Subjectivity, and Politics in Habermas, Arendt, and MacIntyre* (2012) and coeditor (with Shane O'Neill) of *After the Nation? Critical Reflections on Nationalism and Postnationalism* (2010).

Dr. Frank Canavan, M.A., M.Ed., LL.B, H.D.E, is a former headmaster at Colaiste Iognaid, a Jesuit second-level college in Galway, Ireland. He has always been, and remains, a keen student of public discourse, and has recently completed a study of the work of Stephen Toulmin and its effects.

Prof. Gerard Casey is associate professor in philosophy at University College Dublin, adjunct professor at the Maryvale Institute (Birmingham, UK) and adjunct scholar at the Ludwig von Mises Institute (Auburn, AL, USA). He has previously taught at the University of Notre Dame and the Catholic University of America in Washington. His most recent book is *Murray Rothbard* (Major Conservative and Libertarian Thinkers Series, Continuum, 2010) and his *Libertarian Anarchy: Against the State* appears in 2012.

Prof. Terry Eagleton is distinguished professor of English literature at the University of Lancaster, having served as Thomas Warton Professor of English Literature at the University of Oxford (1992–2001) and John Edward Taylor Professor of English Literature at the University of Manchester. Since 2009 he has also been Distinguished Visitor in the Department of English at the University of Notre Dame. He has written more than forty books, including *Literary Theory: An Introduction* (1983); *The Ideology of the Aesthetic* (1990), and *The Illusions of Postmodernism* (1996). He delivered the Terry Lectures at the University of Yale in 2008 and gave a Gifford lecture on "The God Debate" in 2010.

Dr. Ricca Edmondson studied philosophy at the University of Lancaster and argumentation in the social sciences at the University of Oxford before working as a translator in Berlin and carrying out research at the Max Planck Institute for Human Development. She now lectures in the School of Political Science and Sociology at the National University of Ireland, Galway, where her interests include wisdom and the life course, ethnographic methods, intercultural understanding, and the history of political thought. Her publications include *Rhetoric in Sociology* (1984), *Collective Action in Context: Power, Argumentation and Democracy* (1997), *Environmental Arguing and Cultural Difference: Locations, Fractures and Deliberations* (2007), and *Valuing Older People: Towards a Humanist Gerontology* (2009). She is currently working on further aspects of wisdom and wise communication.

Dr. Heike Felzmann lectures in philosophy at the National University of Ireland, Galway. Her academic background is in philosophy and clinical psychology, and a central theme in her work has been to make philosophical reflection meaningful for practical concerns. Her main research areas are health-care ethics, research ethics, moral theory and issues at the intersection of philosophy, psychology and psychotherapy. Her recent publications include a national review of research ethics committees in Ireland.

Prof. Thomas Gil is professor of philosophy at the Technical University of Berlin, director of the postgraduate college "Rationalism and Empiricism" of the Franco-German University and member of the "Kolleg: Technikphilosophie" of the Association of German Engineers. His research interests include the philosophy of action and the theory of rationality; his publications include *Die Rationalität des Handelns* (2003), *Argumentationen: Der kontextbezogene Gebrauch von Argumenten* (2005), *Die Praxis des Wissens* (2006), *Actions, Normativity, and History* (2010), and *On Reasons* (2011).

Prof. Karsten Harries is the Howard H. Newman Professor of Philosophy at Yale University. He is the author of over 200 articles and reviews and the following books: *The Meaning of Modern Art* (1968), *The Bavarian Rococo Church: Between Faith and Aestheticism* (1983), *The Broken Frame* (1990), *The Ethical Function of Architecture* (1997), *Infinity and Perspective* (2001),

Art Matters: A Critical Commentary on Martin Heidegger's "The Origin of the Work of Art" (2009), *Die bayerische Rokokokirche: Das Irrrationale und das Sakrale* (2009), *Between Nihilism and Faith: A Commentary on "Either/Or"* (2010), and *Wahrheit: Die Architektur der Welt* (2012).

Dr. Karlheinz Hülser has studied philosophy, theology, classics, and sociology; he has published on Wittgenstein's earlier writings, and on Plato, and prepared a new collection of fragments on Stoic dialectic. He teaches ancient philosophy at the universities of Jena and Konstanz. He is currently working with several publishing houses as a coordinator of philosophical projects, as well as studying the topic of friendship, retracing the influences of Stoic philosophy (particularly in the field of law), and exploring the influence of ancient logic in sixteenth- and seventeenth-century Europe.

Dr. Richard Hull is lecturer in the Department of Philosophy and a director of the Centre of Bioethical Research and Analysis (COBRA) at the National University of Ireland, Galway. His research interests lie primarily in the area of ethical and political theory, with particular focus on bioethics, medical ethics and various topics in applied philosophy. Selected publications have appeared in *Res Publica*, *Ethical Theory and Moral Practice*, and *Bioethics*; his book, *Deprivation and Freedom*, has recently been published in paperback.

Dr. Sebastian Lalla studied philosophy, linguistics, and theology at the universities of Passau and Berlin. After teaching philosophy at the Free University, Berlin, he completed his Habilitation in 2007 with a work on Ethics in Pre-Wittgensteinian Austrian Philosophy. He continues to teach at the Free University, Berlin, where he has held several temporary chairs in philosophy. He is now editing early works by Hans Jonas for the critical edition *Collected Works of Hans Jonas*. His areas of interest are metaphysics, medieval philosophy, philosophy of religion, and political philosophy.

Dr. Elizabeth Langhorne teaches modern art history at Central Connecticut State University. Her interests include twentieth-century and American art, environmental art, and spirituality and modernity in art; she has published widely on Jackson Pollock ("Pollock, Picasso and the Primitive," "The Magus and the Alchemist: John Graham and Jackson Pollock," "Jackson Pollock: The Sin of Images," "'The Effort of the Dance': Gravity and Levity in the Poured Paintings of Jackson Pollock," "Pollock's Dream of a Biocentric Art: The Challenge of His and Peter Blake's Ideal Museum," and "Jackson Pollock und das Sakrale: Das Kirchenprojekt"). Her book *Selbstbildnis und Traum: Jackson Pollocks Sinnsuche* will appear in 2012.

Dr. Thomas Nisters has studied and worked at the universities of Cologne and Freiburg, besides acting as visiting professor in the Department of Philosophy at the National University of Ireland, Galway in 1993. He has taught philosophy at secondary schools in Brühl and Cologne, and is currently lecturing in the University of Cologne, from which he also obtained his Habilitation. His publications include *Aristotle on Courage* as well as work on Kant's categorical imperative and Aquinas on the circumstances of human action.

Dr. Felix Ó Murchadha lectures in philosophy at the National University of Ireland, Galway. He is the author of *Zeit des Handelns und Möglichkeit der Verwandlung* (1999) and editor of *Violence, Victims, Justifications* (2006). His articles deal with the phenomenology of religion as well as with Heidegger, Merleau-Ponty, Levinas, Marion, and Gadamer. He is currently working on a study of skepticism in relation to faith and reason both in modern philosophy and contemporary phenomenology.

Prof. Fran O'Rourke is associate professor of philosophy at University College Dublin. He is primarily interested in the tradition of classical metaphysics and has published widely on Plato, Aristotle, Aquinas, and Heidegger. His book *Pseudo-Dionysius and the Metaphysics of Aquinas* was reissued by University of Notre Dame Press (2005). *Allwisest Stagyrite: Joyce's Quotations from Aristotle* was published by the National Library of Ireland in 2005. His collection of essays, *Aristotelian Interpretations*, has been published by the Athens Academy; he is completing a book on James Joyce, Aristotle, and Aquinas.

Lightning Source UK Ltd.
Milton Keynes UK
UKOW040427211112

202485UK00001B/55/P